MY WYL AND MY WRYTYNG

Medieval Institute Publications is a program of
The Medieval Institute, College of Arts and Sciences

 WESTERN MICHIGAN UNIVERSITY

MY WYL AND MY WRYTYNG
ESSAYS ON JOHN THE BLIND AUDELAY

Edited by
Susanna Fein

MEDIEVAL INSTITUTE PUBLICATIONS
Western Michigan University
Kalamazoo

© 2009 by the Board of Trustees of
Western Michigan University

Library of Congress Cataloging-in-Publication Data

My wyl and my wrytyng : essays on John the Blind Audelay / edited by Susanna Fein.
    p. cm.
 Includes bibliographical references and indexes.
 ISBN 978-1-58044-135-3 (casebound : alk. paper) -- ISBN 978-1-58044-136-0 (pbk. : alk. paper)
 1. Audelay, John, fl. 1426--Criticism and interpretation. 2. Christian poetry, English (Middle)--History and criticism. I. Fein, Susanna Greer.
 PR1818.A93Z78 2009
 821'.2--dc22

2008047792

Printed in the United States of America
1 2 3 4 5 C P 5 4 3 2 1

CONTENTS

Acknowledgments	vii
Abbreviations	ix
Table, Appendices, and Figures	xi
Note on the Presentation of Texts from the Audelay Manuscript	xiii
The Audelay Manuscript: Table of Contents	xv
John Audelay and His Book: Critical Overview and Major Issues *Susanna Fein*	3
John Audelay: Life Records and Heaven's Ladder *Michael J. Bennett*	30
The Vatic Penitent: John Audelay's Self-Representation *Robert J. Meyer-Lee*	54
John Audelay and John Mirk: Comparisons and Contrasts *Susan Powell*	86
The Make-Up of John Audelay's *Counsel of Conscience* *Oliver Pickering*	112
Audelay's *Marcolf and Solomon* and the Langlandian Tradition *Derek Pearsall*	138
Langland and Audelay *Richard Firth Green*	153

"Choose yourselves whither to go": John Audelay's
Vision of Saint Paul
    Robert Easting   170

John Audelay and the Bridgettines
    Martha W. Driver   191

Audelay's Carol Collection
    Julia Boffey   218

"Wo and werres . . . rest and pese": John Audelay's Politics of Peace
    John C. Hirsh   230

The Alliterative *Three Dead Kings* in John Audelay's MS Douce 302
    Eric Gerald Stanley   249

Death and the Colophon in the Audelay Manuscript
    Susanna Fein   294

Works Cited   307

Contributors   331

Index of Items, Sequences, and Sections in the Audelay Manuscript   333

Index of Manuscripts   339

General Index   343

Acknowledgments

The making of this volume owes a great debt of gratitude to Martha Driver and the Early Book Society for sponsoring a pair of sessions on John Audelay at the Fortieth International Congress on Medieval Studies in Kalamazoo, Michigan, in 2004. These events made apparent the latent desire among many that we revisit and re-evaluate the chaplain-poet from Haughmond Abbey. I am especially grateful to Richard Firth Green, Derek Pearsall, Eric Stanley, and Martha for offering bracing talks at these sessions that eventually became essays for this collection. I also acknowledge the other contributors to this volume—Michael Bennett, Julia Boffey, Robert Easting, John Hirsh, Robert Meyer-Lee, Oliver Pickering, and Sue Powell—for sharing their pioneering forays into material for which the editions were, at that time, outdated, and for which the sources and analogues still remain a challenge to track. Others cheered this project from the start, and their encouragement and advice have proved beneficial: John Burrow, Tony Edwards, Radd Ehrman, Ann Hutchinson, Maureen Jurkowski, Melissa Jones, Linne Mooney, Russell Peck, Helen Phillips, Ad Putter, and James Simpson. I am grateful to the staff of Duke Humfrey's Library at the Bodleian, especially to Greg Colley for his help in tracking the library of Richard Farmer. I acknowledge the support of three offices at Kent State University: the Institute for Bibliography and Editing, for nurturing work such as this; Research and Graduate Studies, for funding my research time as well as travel to Oxford; and the English Department, for permitting textual studies to flourish as a subdiscipline. Deep appreciation goes to editor Patricia Hollahan, copy editor and compositor Heather M. Padgen, designer Linda Judy, and other staff of Medieval Institute Publications for their expertise and patience during the production process. Abiding gratitude goes to my family—David, Elizabeth, Carolyn, and Jonathan—who graciously allowed the shade of a pious penitent to reside for a time in our midst.

ABBREVIATIONS

Addit.	Additional
ANTS	Anglo-Norman Text Society
ASPR	Anglo-Saxon Poetic Records
BL	British Library (London)
BnF	Bibliothèque nationale de France (Paris)
Bodl. Lib.	Bodleian Library (Oxford)
CCR	*Calendar of Close Rolls*
CIPM	*Calendar of Inquisitions Post Mortem*
CPL	*Calendar of Entries in the Papal Registers Relating to Great Britain and Ireland, Papal Letters*
CPR	*Calendar of Patent Rolls*
CUL	Cambridge University Library
EETS	Early English Text Society
IMEV	*The Index of Middle English Verse* (Brown and Robbins)
IMEV Suppl.	*Supplement to the IMEV* (Robbins and Cutler)
LALME	*A Linguistic Atlas of Late Mediaeval English* (McIntosh et al.)
MED	*Middle English Dictionary* (Kurath et al., eds.)
MWME	*A Manual of Writings in Middle English* (Severs et al., eds.)

NIMEV	*A New Index of Middle English Verse* (Boffey and Edwards)
NLS	National Library of Scotland (Edinburgh)
NLW	National Library of Wales (Aberystwyth)
OED	*Oxford English Dictionary*
PL	*Patrilogia Latina* (Migne)
STC	*Short-Title Catalogue* (Pollard et al., eds.)
STS	Scottish Text Society
TCC	Trinity College Cambridge
TNA, PRO	The National Archives, Public Record Office (Kew)

Table, Appendices, and Figures

The Audelay Manuscript: Table of Contents	xv
Length of Poems and Verse Forms in *The Counsel of Conscience*	115
Appendix. Alliterative Phrases in Audelay, Langland, and an Alliterative Corpus	163
Fig. 1. The Ladder, book 5, *The Revelations of Saint Bridget*. London, British Library MS 489.i.1 (sig. C3v)	200
Fig. 2. Drawing of the Vernicle, John Audelay Manuscript. Oxford, Bodleian Library MS Douce 302 (fol. 27v)	202
Appendix. The Eighteen Signatures and Three Endings of the Audelay Manuscript	303

Note on the Presentation of Texts from the Audelay Manuscript

Item titles. The texts of the Audelay Manuscript are cited from the companion edition: John the Blind Audeley, *Poems and Carols (Oxford, Bodleian Library MS Douce 302)*, ed. Susanna Fein (Kalamazoo: Medieval Institute Publications, 2009). The table provided on pp. xv–xix lists the contents of the manuscript, and the titles found there are used by the contributors to this volume. It should be noted that the contents-listing published in a recent article (Susanna Fein, "Good Ends in the Audelay Manuscript," *Yearbook of English Studies* 33 [2003]: 97–119) has been revised. Regarding these refinements, readers may consult the explanatory notes in the edition. When items are referenced by title in endnotes and parenthetical citations, a simple shorthand system has been adopted: "Instr." denotes "Instructions," and "Salut." denotes "Salutation."

Item numbers. For ease of comparison, the table on pp. xv–xix provides the original scribal numbering (where it survives) and the frequently cited numbering system created by Ella Keats Whiting, ed., *The Poems of John Audelay*, EETS o.s. 184 (1931; repr. Oxford: Oxford University Press, 2006). The designation of items by title rather than number, generally adopted here, is occasionally altered to accommodate specific circumstances, such as when authors cite original orthography, examine editorial punctuation, or reference textual sequences. In such cases, the Whiting system may be used, with the following form adopted: W18.14–15 = Whiting's Poem 18, lines 14–15; by the standard notation, one would cite these lines as *Epilogue* 14–15. Numerous inaccuracies—lines unnumbered and misnumbered, undetected item boundaries, and omissions—detract from the usefulness of the numbering system Whiting created.

Line numbers. Verse and prose texts are cited by line number as found in the companion edition. Where line numbers differ in Whiting's edition, the Whiting citation is also provided.

Orthography. Letter forms are altered from manuscript forms in accordance with the style of the Middle English Texts Series (TEAMS). METS editions maintain the linguistic integrity of the original work but within the parameters of modern reading conventions. While adhering to original scribal copy, texts are given modern capitalization and printed in the modern alphabet, with select archaic forms standardized. Thus, *y* or *gh* replaces yogh, *th* replaces thorn, and spellings with *u/v* and *j/i* are regularized. The second-person singular pronoun *the* is regularized to *thee*.

Abbreviations. Manuscript abbreviations are silently expanded.

Punctuation. Punctuation of texts, including stanza layouts, follows modern convention, as found in the companion edition.

Foliation. Material from the manuscript is cited by folio number, recto or verso ("r" or "v"), and, where appropriate, column ("a" or "b").

THE AUDELAY MANUSCRIPT
TABLE OF CONTENTS

The texts of the Audelay Manuscript are listed below by title, sequence, and section, as established in the companion edition to this volume: John the Blind Audelay, *Poems and Carols (Oxford, Bodleian Library MS Douce 302)*, ed. Susanna Fein (Kalamazoo: Medieval Institute Publications, 2009). The roman numerals listed on the left replicate the numbers written by a scribe at the top of columns in the manuscript. The numbers listed on the right, prefixed "W," provide a key to the itemization of contents in Ella Keats Whiting, ed., *The Poems of John Audelay*, EETS o.s. 184 (1931; repr. Oxford: Oxford University Press, 2006).

THE COUNSEL OF CONSCIENCE

[X.]	TRUE LIVING	W1
	Instructions for Reading 1	(omitted)
XI.	MARCOLF AND SOLOMON	W2
[XV.]	THE REMEDY OF NINE VIRTUES	W3
XVI.	SEVEN BLEEDINGS OF CHRIST	W4
XVII.	PRAYER ON CHRIST'S PASSION	W5
XVIII.	THE PSALTER OF THE PASSION	W6
	Instructions for Prayer 1	
	Latin Verse Prayer *Anima Christi sanctifica me*	
	Instructions for Prayer 2	
	Latin Verse Prayer *O pendens dudum*	
	Instructions for Prayer 3	

	Latin Verse Prayer *O Deus qui voluisti*	
	Latin Prose Prayer *Tu Domine per has sanctissimas penas tuas*	
XIX.	SEVEN WORDS OF CHRIST ON THE CROSS	W7
XX.	DEVOTIONS AT THE LEVATION OF CHRIST'S BODY	W8
	Instructions for Prayer 4	
	Salutation to Christ's Body	
	Instructions for Prayer 5	
	Prayer for Pardon after the Levation	
	Latin Prose Prayer *Adoramus te Christe et benedicimus*	
	Latin Verse Prayer *Laudes Deo dicam per secula*	
XXI.	VIRTUES OF THE MASS	W9
XXII.	FOR REMISSION OF SINS	W10
	Saint Gregory's Indulgence	
	Instructions for Prayer 6	
	Prayer of General Confession	
	Instructions for Prayer 7	
	Prayer for Forgiveness	
XXIII.	VISITING THE SICK AND CONSOLING THE NEEDY	W11
	BLIND AUDELAY'S ENGLISH PASSION	[W12–W14]
	Instructions for Reading 2	W12
	On the World's Folly	
XXIIII.	Pope John's Passion of Our Lord	W13
	Audelay's Prayer Explicit to *Pope John's Passion*	
	Seven Hours of the Cross	W14
XXV.	OUR LORD'S EPISTLE ON SUNDAY	W15
XXVI.	THE VISION OF SAINT PAUL	W16
XXVII.	THE LORD'S MERCY	[W17–W18]
	God's Address to Sinful Men	W17
	Audelay's Epilogue to *The Counsel of Conscience*	W18
	Latin Prose Colophon *Finito libro*	

THE AUDELAY MANUSCRIPT   xvii

SALUTATIONS

XXVIII.	DEVOTIONS TO JESUS AND MARY HIS MOTHER	W19
	Salutation to Jesus for Mary's Love	
	Prayer Rubric	
	Prayer on the Joys of the Virgin	
	Instructions for Prayer 8	
XXIX.	OTHER DEVOTIONS TO MARY	[W20–W21]
	Salutation to Mary	W20
	Gabriel's Salutation to the Virgin	W21
XXX.	SONG OF THE MAGNIFICAT	W22
XXXI.	SALUTATION TO SAINT BRIDGET	W23
XXXII.	DEVOTIONS TO SAINT WINIFRED	[W24–W25]
	Saint Winifred Carol	W24
	Salutation to Saint Winifred	W25
	Latin Verse Prayer *Virgo pia Wynfryda*	
	Latin Prose Prayer *Deus qui beatam virginem tuam Wenfrydam*	
XXXIII.	DEVOTIONS TO SAINT ANNE	W26
	Salutation to Saint Anne	
	Latin Prose Prayer *Deus qui beatam Annam*	
XXXIIII.	MEDITATION ON THE HOLY FACE	W27
	Latin Instructions *Quicumque hanc salutacionem*	
	Drawing of the Holy Face on the Vernicle	(omitted)
	Salutation to the Holy Face	
	Latin Prose Prayer *Deus qui nobis signatum vultis*	

CAROLS

XXXV.	CAROL SEQUENCE	[W28–W52]
	Instructions for Reading 3	
	Carol 1. Ten Commandments	W28
	Carol 2. Seven Deadly Sins	W29

Carol 3. Seven Works of Mercy		W30
Carol 4. Five Wits		W31
Carol 5. Seven Gifts of the Holy Ghost		W32
Carol 6. Day of the Nativity		W33
Carol 7. Day of Saint Stephen		W34
Carol 8. Day of Saint John the Evangelist		W35
Carol 9. Day of the Holy Innocents		W36
Carol 10. Saint Thomas Archbishop of Canterbury		W37
Carol 11. Day of the Lord's Circumcision		W38
Carol 12. King Henry VI		W39
Carol 13. Four Estates		W40
Carol 14. Childhood		W41
Carol 15. Day of Epiphany		W42
Carol 16. Saint Anne Mother of Mary		W43
Carol 17. Jesus Flower of Jesse's Tree		W44
Carol 18. Joys of Mary		W45
Carol 19. Mary Flower of Women		W46
Carol 20. Chastity for Mary's Love		W47
Carol 21. Virginity of Maids		W48
Carol 22. Chastity of Wives		W49
Carol 23. Love of God		W50
Carol 24. Dread of Death		W51
Carol 25. Saint Francis		W52

MEDITATIVE CLOSE

XXXVI.	DEVOTIONAL PROSE		
	Instructions for Reading 4		(omitted)
	The Sins of the Heart		(omitted)
	Over-Hippers and Skippers		(omitted)
	An Honest Bed		(omitted)
XXXVII.	PATERNOSTER		W53

XXXVIII	THREE DEAD KINGS	W54
	LATIN POEM *CUR MUNDUS MILITAT SUB VANA GLORIA*	(omitted)
	AUDELAY'S CONCLUSION	W55

My Wyl and My Wrytyng

JOHN AUDELAY AND HIS BOOK
CRITICAL OVERVIEW AND MAJOR ISSUES

Susanna Fein

Middle English scholars have been slow to find the literary niche of John the Blind Audelay (fl. 1417–26). His contemporaries are Thomas Hoccleve (ca. 1367–ca. 1426), Margery Kempe (fl. 1436–38), and John Lydgate (ca. 1371–ca. 1449), writers who sought and wrote themselves into traditional forms (orthodox, hagiographic, Chaucerian), during an age of profound contradiction and uncertainty, an age marked by political usurpation, Lancastrian propaganda, wars, and religious dissent. As these authors structured their writings by recognizable models, following strategic agendas to ensure their own survival (whether it be for Christ, sovereign, patron, or posterity), they negotiated and enacted the tensions of their time.[1] For Hoccleve and Kempe especially, personal and public conflict stirred up autobiographical moments that now invite profoundly psychological, even postmodern, interpretation.

Among the writers of this generation John Audelay truly fits. His extant oeuvre compares to theirs in its self-proclaimed displays of idiosyncratic autobiography, orthodox yet troubled allegiances, authorial proclivities and preoccupations, earnest refashioning of traditions, and dependency on scribal fidelity—all made more interesting when set against the social, political, and ecclesiastical forces of his day. Consequently, as we seek to understand early fifteenth-century sensibilities in response to the times, we ought to attend to this largely unheard literary voice: beside the Westminster clerk of the Privy Seal, the bourgeois mystic of Lynn, and the monk of Bury St. Edmunds, we should include the blind, ever-penitent chantry priest of Haughmond.

John Audelay's authorial passions are certainly of a distinctive cast. His penchant for didactic warning and personalized petition seems a bit oddball—veering from prophet of doom to preaching egotist—beside the more politically savvy fare of Hoccleve and Lydgate. Though Chaucer-like in his determination to record his name, Audelay's motive is penance and pastoral zeal, not muse-driven artistry and worldly fame. At the same time, this seemingly "apoetic" poet is an innovator in verse forms—revealing himself an aficionado of style matched to expression, and capable, in some of the sweeter carols and salutations, of earnest piety made lyrically eloquent.[2] In several poems, many of them quite lengthy, he develops a poetic idiom in thirteen-line stanzas as distinctive as iambic pentameter couplets are for Chaucer. Moreover, portions of his verse (whether borrowed or not) bear tail-end witness to high alliterative verse traditions. By 1426 the fashion had largely passed, but one senses that John Audelay came of age during the heyday of alliterative poetry in the West Midlands, though we may guess only by inference the degree of direct knowledge he had of either Langland or the *Gawain* poet.[3]

By avowing himself the maker of a book—by all signs the very book that survives, Oxford, Bodl. Lib. MS Douce 302—and by declaring the contents to exist according to his own personal plan, which he emphatically terms "my wyl and my wrytyng," Audelay seems a provincial version of the just-then budding fashion for anthologizing the works of celebrated poets (frequently, Chaucer, Gower, and Lydgate), that is, a contemporary offshoot that sprouted on its own, in its own way, rooted in chantry prayers for the named dead and next-world ambitions of the named living.[4] From what we know of Audelay's existence, it combined (incongruously, it might seem) public infamy in 1417, as accessory to an act of sacrilege in the metropolis of London, and illness-ridden monastic seclusion as a deaf and blind chantry priest in and perhaps somewhat after 1426, both events assumed in the line of duty as secular chaplain to Lord Richard and Lady Joan Lestrange of Knockin, in Shropshire.[5]

We have only a smattering of clues as to how the book moved about and was used subsequent to its making. Presumably for a while after Audelay's death it stayed within the dominion of Haughmond Abbey, where its first audience dwelled,[6] though it might possibly have then become the property of Audelay's patron, Lord Lestrange, who died in 1449. Eventually, yet still in the fifteenth century, the book was acquired by William Wyatt, a minstrel from Coventry, who in turn gave it to John Barker, an Augustinian canon from the Priory of St. John the Baptist, in Launde, Leicestershire.[7] A gap then exists in its ownership record from roughly 1500 to 1780. Its earliest known modern owner was Richard Farmer (1735–97), who writes his description of it on a vellum flyleaf included with its modern binding:[8]

R. Farmer

I have not found any Account of this *old & blind* Poet, *John Audelay:* He calls himself *Capellanus*. His book consists of *metrical Divinity* & pious Legends—S^t. Gregory, S^t. Brigitt &c. &c.

Farmer was master of Emmanuel College, Cambridge, as well as, eventually, the university librarian. A great collector of black-letter books, he was esteemed by Samuel Johnson, Thomas Percy, and other men of letters in his day for his exceptionally deep study of Shakespeare's learning, a subject on which he published in 1767. Farmer's proclivity for reading widely and collecting books was nurtured in his youthful days in Leicester by the Reverend Gerrard Andrewes (d. 1764), a classical scholar and Farmer's grammar school master, and also by John Simmons (d. 1788), an avid book collector and vicar of the Church of St. Mary de Castro. Farmer's biographer notes how Leicester "had a distinguished group of literary men and book collectors,"[9] and Farmer was counted as one of Andrewes's protégés. He evidently maintained close ties to Leicester, for he was known to be gathering materials for writing the history of Leicestershire, a project he eventually abandoned, passing his papers on to John Nichols. It seems likely that the Audelay Manuscript remained in Leicestershire from the time that the canon John Barker acquired it until Farmer, an inveterate frequenter of bookshops, became its owner.[10]

When Farmer's large collection of books was auctioned off after his death, there were 8,267 lots. The sale itself lasted for thirty-six days in May and June of 1798 and netted only £2,216. 18s. 6d., which, as Arthur Sherbo notes, is "not a princely sum, and one wonders why he did not leave all or some of his books to Emmanuel College."[11] London antiquary and bibliophile Francis Douce (1757–1834) picked up many bargains at the sale, among them the Audelay Manuscript, which he purchased for 5s. 6d., as part of lot 8084.[12] Douce ordered the book's current modern binding, which was completed in November 1803; the title on the spine, "Audelay's Poems MS," agrees with Douce's notebook notation and was surely assigned by him. Douce is no doubt responsible, too, for the woodcut of three nobles engaged in hunting that is pasted inside the back cover.[13] Although Douce had once been a keeper of manuscripts at the British Library (1807–11), he chose to bequeath his vast collection of 393 manuscripts, 98 charters, 17,000 books, and other antiquarian holdings to the Bodleian Library, where he was assured they would retain the name "Douce collection."

Among the treasures amassed by Douce, which were transferred to the Bodleian in 1834, there were a finely illustrated *Roman de la Rose*, a *Piers Plowman*, a *Brut*, the Ormsby Psalter, and the Douce Apocalypse. For a long while the Audelay Manuscript, a slim volume in modern binding, drew little notice. Almost a hundred years passed before there was an Early English Text Society edition of the manuscript, published in 1931 and edited by Ella Keats Whiting. Unfortunately, this edition omitted many important features and portions of the book.[14] Whiting left out the prose texts and the original item numbers, and she did not translate the many Latin passages, which are critical for understanding the manuscript and its individual texts. She also neglected to provide Audelay's works with their titles, a move that sealed their obscurity. Now, some seventy-eight years after the appearance of the EETS volume, Middle English scholars still have little general knowledge of the book's contents, and Audelay's position as a writer remains largely unexamined.

It is hoped that the essays in this volume will begin to fill in these gaps. The TEAMS edition of John the Blind Audelay, *Poems and Carols*, which serves as companion to this book, remedies the omissions of the EETS edition by showcasing Audelay's devotional sequences, as well as his metrical versatility and his attentive instructiveness to readers. It also provides titles for Audelay's works (often given by the scribes), presents translations of Audelay's Latin, and details his biblical allusions and other borrowings. With Audelay's oeuvre rendered more accurately, readers will readily discover a writer of far more interest than has been assumed. Audelay's sensibilities resonate with the politics and ecclesiastical controversies of his day. His signature idiom in thirteen-line stanzas conveys his own distinct voice, and when these poems are combined with the more lyric carols and salutations, a nuanced portrait accrues, of a man's character, his personal proclivities and attitudes, and his religious practice. On the aesthetic side, Audelay's arrangements of salutations and carols seem no less than the forerunner of a familiar generic mode—the lyric sequence—appearing here long before we would normally ascribe it a place in the vernacular tradition. The moment has therefore come to bring John the Blind Audelay into the ambit of other fifteenth-century English authors. To spur the process along, the essays in this book delineate issues central to the study of this writer and his unusual book. Before summarizing the nature of these issues, I will offer a brief description of the manuscript itself and also provide an overview of its reception from the nineteenth century until now.

The Manuscript: Organization, Contents, Critical History

The first bibliographic notice of the Audelay Manuscript appeared in 1840 in the Douce manuscripts catalogue compiled by Bodley Librarian H. O. Coxe.[15] This list of contents illustrates how the book's idiosyncratic structure and organization have continuously eluded attempts at taxonomy. Indeed, mistaken perceptions regarding how the items are divided and sequenced have handicapped subsequent bibliographers and editors. While perhaps crudely done, the Audelay Manuscript is thoughtfully ordered and reader-directed. Its compiler[16] uses a variety of means to highlight individual items and interrelated parts: rubrics (mostly in Latin); red-ink underlinings; ornamental initials in two sizes and colors (either in red alone or in red and blue); scribal numbers at the tops of columns; visual indicators directed to the reader (pointing hands, faces and quatrefoils in initials, a meditative drawing); marginal English couplets to instruct the reader on how or when to pray, or how to read or use what follows; and even stanzas embedded within English poems designed to do the same.

Coxe bravely labored to tally the contents of MS Douce 302, noting them to be "[s]acred poems and legends by John Awdelay, a blind and deaf monk, of the monastery of Haghmond, co. Salop."[17] Though he misinterpreted many divisions and sequencings, he was first to record the important colophon on fol. 22v, which appears to relegate all leaves to this point to *The Counsel of Conscience*, a distinct section named by Audelay and labeled a "book" by both Audelay and his own compiler.[18] For this portion of the manuscript (complicated by the absence of several folios), Coxe's *Catalogue* differentiates just thirteen items, while Whiting in her EETS edition was later to count and print eighteen distinct pieces. Set against these counts is the separate numbering system inserted by the second scribe.[19] We now recognize that several scribal numbers mark off devotional sequences containing more than one item, usually as a mix of English verse, Latin prayers, and English instructions. In actuality, there are thirty-seven items in *The Counsel of Conscience*, eleven that stand alone and twenty-six that belong to one of five sequences.

The compiler of the Audelay Manuscript, and certainly Audelay himself, was much occupied by the sequencing of texts for devotional effect. Coxe's *Catalogue* records (unnumbered) the "Day of Dome" marginal rubric found on fol. 2r, beginning "The Day of Dome shuld come in here," and this is our first sign that someone with clerical aims cared deeply that items be presented to a reader in order. The instruction tells a reader to seek the missing Doomsday text thirteen leaves before, explaining that on account of the "defawte of the wrytere" (referring either to Audelay or a scribe), it was copied in the wrong place.[20] Signposts like this one occur throughout the codex, usually as instructions to a pious reader or congregant, and they underline Audelay's creative engagement with the making of the book. To ask what Audelay represents as a poet of the fifteenth-century requires, therefore, that we continually perceive his authorial activities beside his professional commitments. He was, foremost, a practicing chaplain, whose duties entailed the fashioning of worshipful textual programs—and often their recasting, as a matter of course, from other sources. His professional object was to deliver reforming religious experiences to others, who would thereby be moved to enact or strengthen their faith.

Sometime in Audelay's career he came to conceive of the fruits of his authorial/clerical career as a book—an anthology comprised of a combination of his own compositions with works he had freely adapted and re-metered, as well as a few direct borrowings brought in to cap his plan for a spiritually meaningful book. These works he set in order and in demarcated generic sections. In respect to the book's display of order by sequence and genre, and its firm identification of an author, the Audelay Manuscript is exceptional among medieval English literary manuscripts. At the same time, however, much about its contents resemble that vast, ubiquitous ocean of anonymous religious verse in the Middle English corpus of surviving texts. Because of this resemblance, there is another striking value to studying the Audelay Mansucript: it allows us to observe, in a specific place and under a specific identity, just how it was that innumerable anonymous religious lyrics and verse expositions came to be composed, for they often survive as related yet freely individual variants from manuscript to manuscript, having been adapted by curates, friars, and monks for practical occasions conducted in specific settings, and for either communal or private use. To have such a large and varied body of devotional lyric poetry by a named medieval writer situated in an exact context offers us an illuminating case study of liturgical, pastoral practice as a motive for poetic innovation.

The first twenty-two folios of the manuscript, which contain John the Blind Audelay's lengthy but incomplete *Counsel of Conscience*, stand as the first of what comprise the book's four sections:

1) *The Counsel of Conscience*, (fols. 1r–22v)
2) salutations and prayers (fols. 22v–27v)
3) twenty-five carols (fols. 27v–32r)
4) a meditative close (fols. 32r–35r)

Each of these parts forms an anthology unto itself, and together they make up the more fully structured anthology of MS Douce 302. These four divisions were delineated only recently, in 2003,[21] and in the absence of this understanding—indeed of any general recognition of an overriding logic in the make-up of MS Douce 302—scholarship on Audelay has proceeded uncertainly over the years. More than anything, I believe, the scheme imposed by Whiting's EETS edition, which assigned numerals 1 to 55 to an incomplete set of contents (i.e., "Poem 1," "Poem 2," etc.) while failing to provide titles, has very much obstructed the process of scholars coming to a shared perception of Audelay's *wrytyng* and *wyl*—that is, what Audelay wrote and what he planned to accomplish with a book. *The Counsel of Conscience*, for example, contains the increasingly studied alliterative *Marcolf and Solomon*,[22] *Virtues of the Mass* (a variant of a Vernon Manuscript poem), *The Vision of Saint Paul*,[23] *Our Lord's Epistle on Sunday*,[24] and *God's Address to Sinful Men*, as well as many poems and prayers dedicated to worship of Christ's Blood, Passion, Body at the Levation, and Words on the Cross, before closing with Audelay's loosely autobiographical and petitionary *Epilogue*, where he expounds on his vocation as a blind, suffering prophet called to save sinners. In this part of the manuscript Audelay's distinctive thirteen-line poetic idiom chimes insistently, sounding with metrical variations in seven long poems: *True Living, Marcolf and Solomon, The Remedy of Nine Virtues, Visiting the Sick and Consoling the Needy, Our Lord's Epistle on Sunday, The Vision of Saint Paul*, and *Epilogue*. Only two modern studies, by Eric Gerald Stanley (1996) and Oliver Pickering (in this volume), have examined *The Counsel of Conscience* as a whole entity.[25] As this is the section that most fully showcases the particularities of Audelay's own sense of his vocation as chaplain, penitent, and prophet, it is certainly to be hoped that many more studies will build productively on their pioneer work.

For the salutations section the situation of critical neglect is even more of a hindrance. The two studies to date are each dedicated to particular hagiographies, so the make-up of the whole section and Audelay's particular interest in the genre have never been fully addressed. Melissa Jones's article (1997) examines two adjacent poems, a carol and a legend, that hail Saint

Winifred—for Audelay, a local saint—whose fourteenth-century effigy survives with others between the still-standing arches of the chapter house in the ruins of Haughmond Abbey.[26] The other study of a salutation is by Martha W. Driver, who looks closely at Audelay's lengthy poem in honor of Saint Bridget (her essay appears in the present volume). Driver shows how Audelay witnesses in intimate ways to the cult of Saint Bridget in England in the early fifteenth century.[27] The remaining salutations composed by Audelay are little known, though as a complete, sequenced collection they represent an important literary endeavor produced in a climate of early fifteenth-century monastic devotionalism.[28]

In fact, Audelay's poems in honor of the saints are often compelling on aesthetic grounds. For example, *Gabriel's Salutation to the Virgin* is composed in an exquisite, hymnodic twelve-line stanza that editors (following scribal mistakes) have misrepresented.[29] With its metrical form restored, an annunciation hymn of fine emotional delicacy is revealed:

> The angel to the vergyn said,
>   Entreng into here boure,
> Fore drede of quakyng of this mayd,
>   He said, "Haile," with gret honour.
>   "Haile be thou, quene of maidyns mo.
>   Lord of heven and erth also
>   Consayve thou schal,
>   And bere withale
>   The Lord of myght,
>   Hele of al monkyn.
>   He wil make thee the gate of heven bryght,
>   Medesyne of al our syn."
>   (1–12)

Both scribes labored to record this piece, a translation of the *Angelus ad virginem*, and Scribe B ultimately contributed more than Scribe A, a circumstance found elsewhere only in a few isolated places, for example, in the copying of the *Circumcision Carol*.

Another salutation deserving close attention is the first poem of the section, *Salutation to Jesus for Mary's Love*. Here a joyous address to Jesus is embedded inside one to the Virgin Mother, as if a poem of praise has been modeled on Mary's bodily form, with direct approach and address of the Holy Infant being made possible only through the Holy Mother.[30] By the logic of Incarnation, this opening Ave to Virgin and Son tacitly balances the section's final salutation, which is based in Christ's Passion and directed to Christ's face imprinted upon the Veronica *sudarium*. With accompanying instructions, prayer, and even a drawing of God's Holy Face, the poem petitions for the beatific vision, a fervent hope that brings a pious penitent's own life and afterlife into the temporal arc of Christ's birth, death, and reign in heaven.[31]

In turning to the next section, we find Audelay's best-known work, his grouped collection of twenty-five carols. Reviewing how these carols came to light becomes again an excursus on neglect broken by brief moments of curiosity. Here, a short outline of the manuscript's publication history is in order. Coxe's 1840 *Catalogue* inspired the first partial publication of Audelay's poems, an edition in 1844 of just seven items, all from *The Counsel of Conscience*, produced for the Percy Society by James Orchard Halliwell.[32] To Halliwell can probably be credited the standard modern spelling of Audelay's name: "His name was John Audelay, or Awdlay, as the name is spellt different ways in the same manuscript."[33] In the preface Halliwell gives a sampling of Audelay's self-identifying signatures, which he draws from the likeliest sources (the *Finito libro* colophon, Audelay's *Epilogue*, and Audelay's *Conclusion*), and he prints in full the *Henry VI Carol*. After culling these tidbits, Halliwell dismisses the book as chiefly a dialectal specimen: "[T]he MS. is scarcely worthy of being published entire, and is, indeed, principally valuable as exhibiting a faithful specimen of the Salopian dialect at so early a period."[34] With so little encouragement, efforts at understanding the book lay dormant for more than fifty years, until German scholar J. Ernst Wülfing provided, in 1896, a systematic description of its contents and what could be known of John Audelay. Some years later J. K. Rasmussen undertook a philological description of MS Douce 302 for a Bonn dissertation that was published in 1914.[35]

It was during this period of fresh activity, in 1910–11, that the third section of MS Douce 302, Audelay's carols, was edited for the first time by R. W. Chambers and F. Sidgwick in a two-part article in *Modern Language Review*.[36] In MS Douce 302 the carols comprise a discrete, ordered sequence of twenty-five poems, headed by Scribe B's rubric—a couplet of instruction: "I pray yow, syrus, boothe moore and las, / Syng these caroles in Cristemas"—and closed by the last stanza of the final carol (written by Scribe A):

I pray youe, seris, pur charyté,
Redis this caral reverently,

> Fore I mad hit with wepyng eye,
> Your broder Jon the Blynd Awdlay.
>
> (*St. Francis Carol* 73–76; italics mine)

Knowing and planning from what Scribe A had already written, and wishing to identify the carols as an organized set, Scribe B inserted the opening couplet as a title ("these caroles in Cristemas"), an instruction ("Syng"), and a frame now completed.[37] The last signature by the penitent John the Blind Audelay thus seems to embrace the entire group retrospectively.[38]

Much of Audelay's modest acclaim has accrued largely by virtue of his carols, with a few having been singled out for real critical praise and, occasionally, for anthology selection. Chief of these are *Dread of Death, Childhood, Love of God, Henry VI, Four Estates,* and *Tree of Jesse*.[39] Five carols exist in other manuscripts, leaving Audelay's original authorship of them in doubt,[40] but in two instances his versions are the earlier and better ones. So it may be that negative views of Audelay's originality deserve to be balanced with discriminating studies that look at the carols' circulation, musical settings, and purposeful effect in being so grouped.

It is hardly surprising, moreover, to find that for some carols Audelay probably borrowed or adapted pre-existing texts. Proof of Audelay's dependence on external sources appears often in MS Douce 302, in, for example, *The Vision of Saint Paul,*[41] *Virtues of the Mass,* and the unattributed inclusion of the Richard Rolle extract at the end of the book. Indeed, one value of the book is how it allows a keyhole glimpse into a regional cleric's reading interests and literary practices in the 1420s. Lord Lestrange's personal chaplain considered the devotional texts within his reach to be his own professional working materials. They were tools for Christian redemption, highly efficacious for his cure of souls and therefore not to be wasted. Thus, he borrowed from them freely—sometimes to adapt, re-meter, or translate, and sometimes to construct quasi-liturgical moments of worship and prayer—all in the fervent belief that he was performing his divine duty to save souls and aid in the remission of sins. Among the most engrossing aspects of John the Blind Audelay, poet and self-proclaimed prophet, is how he charged this workaday priestly vocation of reading and making and remaking with incessant metrical experimentation, infused with his own personality and topics selected to reflect a particular response to the events and pressures of his time.

In this regard, the carol sequence brings Audelay the chaplain most to life. It stands out as distinctly unified and literary, and as the probable cause for a minstrel's later possession of the manuscript. In social terms, the collection seems to evoke the secular lord's hall, with men and women joined in song, even as we might well suppose that the carols were also sung later within the monastery walls to which Audelay had retired. Audelay's plan for the sequence appears to depend on a program of pastoral teaching (the articles of faith), liturgical observance following the church calendar, devotion to Mary, and some personal views of the Christian life: mourning loss of childish innocence, honoring king, upholding the social order, staying chaste, emulating Saint Francis, and dying well.[42]

After the carols comes the fourth and final section of MS Douce 302, the closing meditation on last things. This portion of the book has been treated unevenly by scholars. Some items remain obscure, for they have never or only recently been edited, while others have borne the forensic scrutiny of exhaustive philological analysis. Because this section mixes styles, its unified logic has escaped general notice. It is comprised of two short prose treatises; two alliterative poems (a prayer and a moral narrative); a Latin poem on worldly vanity; and a signature poem by Audelay, his final farewell, which closes the manuscript by declaring it to be his "wyl" and "wrytyng" (*Conclusion* 33). While Coxe's 1840 *Catalogue* recorded this section's opening four lines of reading instruction (probably a preface to the prose items only), it got nearly all other elements wrong. For the prose section it listed four items, dividing Rolle's *Sins of the Heart* and *An Honest Bed* into two parts each and neglecting to mention the shift to prose. For the alliterative poems *Paternoster* and *Three Dead Kings*, it printed erroneous opening lines and did not flag their important metrics. The Latin poem *Cur mundus* was properly listed, but Coxe detected two poems instead of one in Audelay's *Conclusion*. He did, however, quote the last stanza in its entirety because it signs off the manuscript with a name, profession, and locale. Here "Jon the Blynde Awdelay" (48) reveals his station in service to Lord Lestrange and his lingering illness in a west England abbey. Four years later, following the clues as laid out in *Catalogue*, Halliwell highlighted this passage and linked it to Audelay's *Epilogue*. Both Coxe and Halliwell thus correctly pinpointed these sites (at fols. 22v and 35r) as critical for understanding the book's provenance and its representation of an author.

In the period when the carols were first edited (1910–11), intense interest began to attach to one item in the fourth section, the alliterative poem headed by Scribe B "De tribus regibus mortuis" and later designated "Poem 54" in Whiting's system. At a time of ardent philological attention to Middle English survivals, Willy F. Storck and Richard Jordan latched onto this remarkable piece at the end of the MS Douce 302, with Storck setting in broad context its treatment of the Three Living and Three Dead folk motif, and Jordan providing the first lexical analysis.[43] What stands out about *Three Dead Kings* is its virtuoso display of artful diction, metrical intricacy, and tonal subtlety, features shared more quietly by *Paternoster*, its partner poem in the Audelay Manuscript. These important works are stylistically distinct from others in the book, and this observation led Whiting to question directly whether Audelay exhibits sufficient artistic power to have composed them.[44] Following Whiting's assessment, a sense that the answer must be "no" has taken on the air of assured fact, with scholars Bruce Dickins (1932), Thorlac Turville-Petre (1974, 1989), Angus McIntosh (1977), and Ad Putter (2003) forming a chorus of negative opinion.[45]

On this issue, the only strenuous dissent has come from Stanley, who expressed his objections in an essay published in 1997 and offers further argument in a detailed essay on the language of *Three Dead Kings* printed here.[46] Stanley points out, astutely, that a general tendency (led by Whiting) to see Audelay's abilities as distinctly limited is lamentable because it does not do justice to the range of evidence found at other points in the manuscript. To this argument I would add our uncertainty as to what poetic powers Audelay held in his youth, in what might have been a headier West Midland or London literary milieu than what surrounded him in his days of professional chaplaincy and later infirm retirement in a secluded abbey. We also must face squarely the meaning and import of the modern value placed on "originality" and unshared authorship for an age in which borrowing, recopying, and adaptation were normal practice. As Stanley shows, for all its richness, elements of Audelay's standard didactic idiom have seeped into *Three Dead Kings*, as they do in *Paternoster* and that curious bit of alliterative verse in the fourth section, *Over-Hippers and Skippers*, which seems a relic sprung directly from Audelay the preacher's memory. And two of these works are in Audelay's own favorite thirteen-line stanza.[47]

Despite the broad controversies of authorship and authorial intentionality broached by the presence of the book's final section, this section, omitted from the Whiting edition, remains virtually unknown to modern readers. The first two items introduce English prose into the manuscript, establishing a meditative mood before the solemnity of alliterative verse. The first is an extract from Richard Rolle's *Form of Living*, and the second is an allegory on death as the soul's restful achievement upon a bed of virtues. Both pieces remained unprinted until 1994, and only then was the interpolated alliterative stanza discovered.[48] The absence of the prose from

Whiting's EETS volume has kept it out of view and impeded assessment of the section.[49] At the same time, the insertion of a Latin moral poem after the alliterative poems has been also ignored. The meaning of these items needs to be evaluated because it is in this section of the Audelay Manuscript that the cumulative meanings of Audelay's several endings converge.[50]

Overview of Issues

The issues to be faced in assessing the significance of the Audelay Manuscript are perpetually two-pronged: on the one hand, there is the book itself, and on the other, there is the man it names and gives voice to: John the Blind Audelay. I will here briefly survey a few broad areas in need of attention, and, in doing so, I will leave aside local matters of subject, style, and relationships among items, which do, of course, demand future investigations with comparative and critical detail.

To begin, the structure of the book still needs considerable study, especially as our perception of it is fairly new. Audelay's *wyl* exists in the order as well as the content of items. It is clear that his anthology is a planned affair, with a "workshop" of at least two scribes—most likely Haughmond monks—enlisted to pull it off. The interlocking logic of units within sections and sequential groupings requires more analysis, especially in terms of liturgical evocations, use of sources, and purposes we would call literary. While metrical markers, Latin rubrics, and scribal numbers do demarcate different works, there is often a fluidity of boundary, as when the carols are given a title-instruction by Scribe B, playing off a last stanza that rests *inside* one of the carols. Elsewhere, Audelay's *Instructions for Reading 2* (underlined in red by Scribe B) prefaces three works—*On the World's Folly*, *Pope John's Passion of Our Lord*, and *Seven Hours of the Cross* (W12–W14)—by explaining how they are to be read, that is, first by ruminating upon the false world and only then contemplating the Passion narrative. Audelay claims this sequence as his own original, vernacular work, giving it the title *Blind Audelay's English Passion*.[51] Throughout the manuscript, the moments of instruction, usually in English couplets, are metrically distinct from surrounding matter, but as Whiting's confusions indicate, they are sometimes not visually differentiated from the sequences of poems and prayers that they punctuate. Indeed, in a variation of this phenomenon, the important *Epilogue* at the end of *The Counsel of Conscience* departs metrically from the preceding *God's Address to Sinful Men*, but there is no large initial to demarcate its first stanza. Instead, the initial is delayed, appearing (only by scribal notation) at its third stanza, the one that opens as a dream vision, "Fore as I lay seke, in my dremyng" (*Epilogue* 27). Does this mean that lines 1–26 preface the *Epilogue* proper? The placing of the initial certainly does highlight a narrative frame made of Audelay's sickness (and with it, the dreaming and the bookmaking), named at line 26 and opening the penultimate stanza at line 482:

> As I lay seke in my langure,
> In an abbay here be west,
> This boke I made with gret dolour
> When I myght not slep ne have no rest.
> Offt with my prayers I me blest,
> And sayd hilé to Heven Kyng:
> "I knowlache, Lord, hit is the best
> Mekelé to take thi vesetyng,
>   Ellis wot I wil that I were lorne."
> Of al lordis be he blest!
> Fore al that ye done is fore the best,
> Fore in thi defawte was never mon lost,
>   That is here of womon borne.
>   (482–94)

The point to be observed is that Audelay's intentionality of structure is everywhere evident, and it is complex, individualistic, adroit, and subtle.

Such structural intentionality is of a piece with Audelay's metrical variations, which also ought to be more fully recognized and studied. We are beginning to grasp the idiosyncratic quality of his supple thirteen-line stanza—not an easy medium for narration or pastoral care, but Audelay uses it again and again, sometimes building it from blocks he has used elsewhere, as if it has reached a mnemonic, formulaic status in his own delivery of it. He can apparently move it into alliterative long lines (as in *Marcolf and Solomon*), or not. A rather good specimen bursts out when triggered by the word *rabuld* in the Rolle extract; it seems that both it and the prose belong to the chaplain's reflexive storehouse of oratory.[52] Less well recognized is the fact that Audelay's carols favor two distinctive meters, a seven-line stanza ($abab_4C_2CC_4$, with a two-line tetrameter burden, introduced by a tag-refrain) used for nine carols, and a six-line stanza ($aaabBB_4$, with a two-line tetrameter burden) used for ten carols and varied in three more. He is also adept at many other forms, some common, such the eight-line refrain poem, and some very uncommon, such as the beautiful twelve-line stanza in *Gabriel's Salutation*. Whether he wrote the pararhyming, densely alliterative lines of *Paternoster* and *Three Dead Kings* remains a question, but one must credit Audelay for the acumen shown in how he positions them in his book. A chaplain so thoroughly engrossed in the metrical setting and formal sequencing of religious experience would have responded profoundly to the remarkable technical achievements these poems represent.

Matters of authorship and originality surely do have importance, but Audelay studies would improve if we were to look beyond those questions and, within the metrical versatility, examine nuances of tone, voice, and language. Audelay punctuates many texts with Latin (often from the Vulgate Bible), creating a style that recalls Langland, but it may derive foremost from a habit of preaching from Scripture and precept. Not all the Latin appears as incipits, explicits, and stanza headings. Much of it emerges as prayers in verse and prose, and sometimes a long prose passage like the *Finito libro* colophon allows a natural-sounding (though still clerical) speaking voice to enter the book, as if Audelay (through his scribes, and especially Scribe B) momentarily drops the prophet's rhyming mask to simply tell the reader what needs to be known. With the Latin passages not translated in Whiting's edition, it seems little surprise that we have not attended to the Audelay Manuscript in this way. But reading the instructional voice, in and out of Latin, in margins, in headings, and within stanzas—sometimes preserved by Scribe A, sometimes by Scribe B—is important to our recovery of Audelay's particular manner and purpose.

The essays in this volume will help to define directions that future studies of Audelay might profitably take. Michael J. Bennett's discovery, reported in 1982, of Audelay's role in his patron's sacrilegious crime in 1417 has impacted subsequent scholarship on the poet by providing the only life record that exists outside the manuscript. Here Bennett reviews that record and refines his analysis in terms of additional court evidence and the recorded lives of Lord Richard Lestrange and his wife. He also probes how the document from 1417 informs the manuscript from 1426, and vice versa: "[T]hey give the participant in the affray in the London church a future and the poet at Haughmond a past." Bennett's work continues to lay the foundation for investigations of Audelay's social relations, political alliances, audiences, and cultural milieu. To give a particular instance: his new findings on Lady Joan Lestrange's testament bring to light an analogous, seemingly related instance of a book owner transferring spiritual purpose to her book after her own death.

Robert J. Meyer-Lee's interest lies in the poet's relation to his book, and his book's relation to the reader, and he pays special attention to Audelay's modes of self-representation. He sees an intriguing similarity to Langland's *Piers Plowman*, for which "self-referentiality, and the pseudo-autobiography . . . this entails, constitute the poem's most profound formal apparatus for seeking the reform of its readers' souls and the institutions of the world." His essay opens up a host of avenues by which to view Audelay and his book, ranging from how the manuscript formally functions as a chantry for perpetual prayers to how modern trauma theory may illuminate Audelay's obsessive habit of naming himself. Meyer-Lee's work exposes the cultural rationales and ambivalences that reside in the poet's oeuvre, and especially in his plan to make a codex.

Susan Powell offers another way to view Audelay biographically by setting the poet beside his older contemporary from Shropshire, John Mirk, a nearby priest tied to a neighboring Augustinian house. Here we gain a glimpse of Audelay the cleric in his study and at his pulpit, composing on orthodox topics in ways that parallel Mirk's own pastoral agenda. The similarities make the differences all the more striking. John Audelay's sermons—doubtless there were many—do not survive. Whereas Mirk's work addresses a public audience, Audelay's poems and devotions suggest more private contexts and indulge in a higher degree of subjectivity. Like Bennett's examination of Audelay's political and social affiliations, in and out of London, Powell's essay moves us toward more investigations of Audelay, the chaplain-turned-ascetic, in his West Midland ecclesiastical environs.

The next essay shifts the focus to specific parts of Audelay's book. Oliver Pickering offers a new study of Audelay's *Counsel of Conscience*, noting that while we know where it ends, because of the decisive colophon on fol. 22v, we cannot know precisely where it begins. We also must acknowledge the fact that the original manuscript held much material now lost, so that a good deal of the Audelay corpus is gone. Noting the metrical tautness of the book's acephalous first poem, *True Living*, which Audelay mined for the making of several later poems and carols, and the robust originality of *Marcolf and Solomon*, Pickering speculates that what is now lost might have shown Audelay's talents to be considerable. He also offers the first purposeful comparison of Audelay's metrics beside Audelay's signatures, demonstrating that Audelay's claims for authorship are more commonly attached to his thirteen-line poems. Pickering's essay gives us much to ponder as we come to understand *The Counsel of Conscience* as an organized anthology.

The essays by Derek Pearsall and Richard Firth Green treat Audelay's important poem *Marcolf and Solomon*. Each essay marks a substantial contribution to recent debates on how Audelay's impassioned alliterative warning to those in ecclesiastical orders falls within broader strains of Langlandian poetics and the cultural anxieties generated by the prosecution of Lollards. Pearsall removes the poem from *Piers Plowman*'s direct influence, hearing their similar cadences as generic and idiomatic, while he provides a much-needed scrutiny of the poem on its own terms, laying out its major components and arguments. He sees it as crucially different from Langland in its gentler acceptance of the orders, including friars, and in its orthodox determination that religious brothers reform themselves and reach internal accord. Green, in contrast, maintains that Audelay shows clear indebtedness to Langland, nowhere more so than in his Lady Mede references, and that several of Audelay's favorite alliterative formulas find their closest analogues in *Piers Plowman*. In some cases, they appear nowhere else in the Middle English corpus. Taken together, these two scholars in debate exemplify a very wide swath of *Marcolf* studies yet to be cultivated and mown.

Even as the scholarly community continues to inspect *Marcolf* more closely, Robert Easting's essay on John Audelay's *Vision of Saint Paul* shows us how we have barely begun to peer beneath the surface regarding other works in *The Counsel of Conscience*. More studies of Audelay's sources are needed, and Easting remedies that situation for this interesting poem, which turns the apostle Paul's gaze upon startling punishments doled to those damned in hell. While Audelay's exact exemplar does not survive, one can still gauge some embellishments and some inherited errors, as in the fast-breakers damned to ride camels with fruit perpetually out of their reach (a picturesque detail deriving from a mistranslation that preceded Audelay). By the same token, Audelay does care about appropriate detail, making punishments for certain sins affect the offending body part, inveighing strongly against free will abused, and adding, at one point, manslaughter to a list of sins, perhaps in pointed remembrance of his patron's crime.

Addressing the second section of MS Douce 302, Martha W. Driver offers the first focused study of John Audelay's salutation in honor of Saint Bridget, approaching its genre and poetics, its witness of miracle (the "re-virginized" saint, who was a wife and mother), and its testimony to a saint's cult in Britain. Driver shows how Audelay evinces familiarity with some fairly obscure Bridgettine traditions not otherwise known in English sources. Audelay was conversant with lyric formulas of address to saints, especially the anaphoric "haile" prevalent to the genre, and even more he was bound to a fervent belief that such poems can operate as indulgences. A tradition of obtaining pardon by pilgrimage to Syon Abbey for its Lammas Day festival ties a reference in Audelay's poem to Margery Kempe's weeping, swooning acceptance of that pardon in 1434. Driver's study sets Audelay's devout engagement with saintly immanence in high relief.

The next pair of essays tackles the third section of Audelay's book, the carols. Julia Boffey approaches the group of twenty-five carols as a planned collection and notes how remarkable this fact is because most carol manuscripts are later, dating from the late fifteenth or early sixteenth century. Her careful assessment thus locates MS Douce 302 among late medieval books that preserve numerous carols, sometimes with musical settings, sometimes not. The order of Audelay's arrangement is of special interest, with its closure seeming to allude to death's approach. Boffey addresses the highly fluid concept of authorship for writers of lyrics and songs, and thus implicitly refutes overly restrictive notions of Audelay's originality.

John C. Hirsh examines John Audelay's one unabashedly political poem, the carol in honor of Henry VI, which gives much space to celebrating Henry V's victories and marriage, and thus to honoring Henry VI's lineage. Hirsh contextualizes the poem in terms of Lancastrian poetics, setting it beside "The Agincourt Carol," a comparable celebratory poem by John Lydgate entitled "Praise of Peace," and other lyrics by anonymous writers. Seeing in both Lydgate and Audelay a concern for peace, Hirsh proposes that we acknowledge Audelay to be more socially engaged and nuanced than previously thought. He also views the Lydgate influence as strong. Opinions will differ on this question, as they do for the Langland influence, but it is good to have the issue broached. Bennett, for example, takes a cautious approach in his comparisons of Audelay to Lydgate. Clearly, there is work ahead in this area.

The final two essays in this volume attend to the Audelay Manuscript's last section. Eric Gerald Stanley takes on the critics and lexicographers in performing a word-by-word analysis of the dense vocabulary found in *Three Dead Kings*. His essay is the newest member of a distinguished lineage, detailed above, of commentary on this austere and beautiful poem. Though Stanley stands virtually alone in his vigorous defense of Audelay's possible authorship of this virtuoso performance, he makes it difficult for others to ignore the sheer volume of philological data amassed here to prove that conclusions otherwise are not ironclad. Behind his work rests the evidence of the dictionaries and especially the *Middle English Dictionary*, completed after the earlier studies by Jordan, Dickins, Turville-Petre, and McIntosh. It is appropriate that this volume of new essays on John Audelay should include not only essays on *Marcolf*, the piece generating the most controversy, but also one on *Three Dead Kings*, the piece that has garnered the most esteem.

The last essay is one I have contributed upon the multiple endings of the Audelay's Manuscript's last and final section. Examination of the two hands reveals that the book closes three times, which I believe happened after different intervals, while Audelay was still alive. *Three Dead Kings* marks the first ending. The Latin *Cur mundus* marks the second. Audelay's *Conclusion* marks the third. The distance in style, mode, and effect among these three endings is meaningful. The conflation of ending and not-ending with Audelay's own dying and not-dying closes Audelay's book with intriguing serial remnants of his purpose to die well.

The collective fruits of this book allow John the Blind Audelay to assume his rightful place among his early fifteenth-century peers. The book of the blind chaplain may be something of an oddity, but, like Margery's *Book*, its self-referential author conveys depths of psychological complexity, while bearing, like Lydgate, professional witness to many poetic genres of his day: visions, passions, carols, lyrics, saints' legends, devotions, and *pastoralia*. His range within alliterative traditions is impressive, with sincere admiration for, if not authorship of, *Three Dead Kings*, and definite authorship of a thirteen-line alliterative poem fluent in the loosely styled line of *Piers Plowman*. He was a witness to historical events and cultural changes that he wrote about as an orthodox, patriotic, essentially conservative churchman: the founding of Syon Abbey, the promulgation of the Lancastrian dynasty, the perils of Lollard dissent, the decline of English lineage through lapses in chastity. And, importantly, he oversaw the making of an anthology of his works, craftily produced, interspersing other texts with his own, but acting, it seems, as editor-interpolator as he did so. That he made a book to record his own name, to petition prayers in perpetuity, to preserve his poetic oeuvre, to save the souls of others, and, in overall scope, to imitate the eternal book of heaven in which the names of the saved are inscribed—to have attempted all this is a matter of compelling literary and cultural import. If we are to understand the age that produced the writings of Hoccleve, Kempe, and Lydgate, then we need to understand what motivated Blind Audelay as well.

Notes

1. For up-to-date overviews of these writers (with good preliminary bibliographies), see John M. Bowers, "Thomas Hoccleve," Sarah Salih, "Margery Kempe," and John M. Bowers, "John Lydgate," in *The Oxford Encyclopedia of British Literature*, ed. David Scott Kastan, 5 vols. (Oxford: Oxford University Press, 2006), 3:62–65, 3:194–97, and 3:340–43, respectively. On the social background of these authors, see esp. Paul Strohm, "Hoccleve, Lydgate and the Lancastrian Court," in *The Cambridge History of Medieval English Literature*, ed. David Wallace (Cambridge: Cambridge University Press, 1999), pp. 640–61; Kathleen Ashley, "Historicizing Margery: The Book of Margery Kempe as Social Text," *Journal of Medieval and Early Modern Studies* 28 (1998): 371–88; and Lynn Staley, *Margery Kempe's Dissenting Fictions* (University Park: Penn State University Press, 1994).

2. In this regard, sensitive readers have occasionally likened him to George Herbert. See Rosemary Woolf, *The English Religious Lyric in the Middle Ages* (London: Oxford University Press, 1968), pp. 7, 222, 296, 336; and Elizabeth Salter, *Fourteenth-Century English Poetry: Contexts and Readings* (Oxford: Clarendon Press, 1983), pp. 17–18.

3. Audelay's references to "Mede, that swet maydyn" (*World's Folly* 17; W12.11; cp. *Marcolf* 705) seem to recall *Piers the Plowman*, while the vocabulary and style of *Paternoster* and *Three Dead Kings* are redolent of the *Gawain* poet's verse. In citing works from MS Douce 302, I am using the system of assigned titles listed in "The Audelay Manuscript: Table of Contents," pp. xv–xix. Quotations of works in MS Douce 302 are taken from John the Blind Audelay, *Poems and Carols (Oxford, Bodleian Library MS Douce 302)*, ed. Susanna Fein (Kalamazoo: Medieval Institute Publications, 2009).

4. On how Audelay's role as chantry priest nurtures the making of MS Douce 302, see Robert J. Meyer-Lee's essay in the present volume, pp. 54–85. On anthologies of the period, see A. S. G. Edwards, "Fifteenth-Century Middle English Verse Author Collections," in *The English Medieval Book: Studies in Memory of Jeremy Griffiths*, ed. A. S. G. Edwards, Vincent Gillespie, and Ralph Hanna (London: British Library, 2000), pp. 101–12. Susan Powell's essay in the present volume, pp. 86–111, looks at the clerical/literary milieu in which Audelay worked, close in locale to that of Mirk, an older man. On further similarities between Audelay's book and Mirk's *Instructions for Parish Priests* (ed. Edward Peacock, EETS o.s. 31, 2nd ed., rev. F. J. Furnivall [1902; repr. New York: Greenwood, 1969]), see my introduction in Audelay, *Poems and Carols*, pp. 1–24.

5. Michael Bennett, "John Audley: Some New Evidence on His Life and Work," *Chaucer Review* 16 (1982): 344–55; and his essay in the present volume, pp. 5–6.

6. The first portion of the manuscript, *The Counsel of Conscience*, is said to have been compiled (*compositus*) "ad exemplum aliorum in monasterio de Haghmon" (as a model for others in the Monastery of Haughmond), on fol. 22v.

7. Falconer Madan et al., *A Summary Catalogue of Western Manuscripts in the Bodleian Library at Oxford*, 7 vols. (Oxford: Clarendon Press, 1897), records the early

ownership notes scribbled and erased on the final leaf, after Audelay's *Conclusion* (fol. 35rb): "'Iste liber pertinet haue thys in mynde / To William Vyott bothe kurteous and kynde / A minstrall yn Coventr there yow schall hym fynde' (15th cent.): 'The owner of thys boke who lyst to demawnd / Jhon Barkre hyt ys a chanon of Lawnde / Gyvyn to hym hyt was with a gud mynd / By on Wyatt a minstrel bothe curtess & [kynd] / Hyt ys fre for all . . . hyt to rede [?] / But he that steyls hyt may the Devyl . . .' (15th cent.)" (6:585–86 [p. 586]). This transcription, legible only by ultraviolet light, is credited to N. R. Ker in Richard Leighton Greene, ed., *A Selection of English Carols* (Oxford: Clarendon Press, 1962), 179; see also Richard Leighton Greene, ed., *The Early English Carol*, 2nd ed. (Oxford: Clarendon Press, 1977), p. 317.

8. This modern leaf was bound with the manuscript when Francis Douce sent the book to "Bohn" on 4 May 1802, along with fourteen others, to be rebound. The modern binding consists of boards of marbleized paper, with the corners and spine bound in brown leather. The leather spine is embossed in gold: "Audelay's Poems MS." The bookbinder held Douce's books for an inordinately long time, and Douce was irritated by the delay, writing in his notebook: "This fellow kept my books 19 months, bound them badly & charged extravagantly" (Oxford, Bodl. Lib. MS Douce e.71, fol. 1v). Apparently the bound book was retrieved in November 1803. "Bohn" is probably bookseller Henry George Bohn, mentioned in *The Douce Legacy: An Exhibition to Commemorate the 150th Anniversary of the Bequest of Francis Douce (1757–1834)* (Oxford: Bodleian Library, 1984), p. 28, as Douce's source for an eleventh-century Gospel book from Liége. The inserted descriptive note in Farmer's hand is typical of his manner of book cataloguing (L. J. Lloyd, "Dr Richard Farmer 1735–97: Portrait of a Bibliophile XXI," *The Book Collector* 26 [1977]: 524–36 [p. 525]).

9. Arthur Sherbo, *Richard Farmer, Master of Emmanuel College, Cambridge: A Forgotten Shakespearean* (Newark: University of Delaware Press, 1992), p. 18. On the influence of Andrewes and Simmons on Farmer, see pp. 18–20. Simmons also encouraged Farmer in the historical project, and his large library was open to Farmer (p. 84). See also Arthur Sherbo, "Farmer, Richard (1735–1797)," *Oxford Dictionary of National Biography* (Oxford: Oxford University Press, 2004), 1–4, http://www.oxforddnb.com/view/article/9169 (accessed 23 November 2006).

10. Lloyd notes Farmer's forays among Leicester booksellers "in his early days" ("Dr Richard Farmer," p. 526). The sale of Simmons's books on 6 July 1779 was not Farmer's source for the Audelay MS; according to the sale catalogue, Simmons's library consisted solely of printed books. A copy of the catalogue is preserved in the British Library (shelfmark 128.k.10(3); see A. N. L. Munby and Lenore Coral, *British Book Sale Catalogues 1676–1800* [London: Mansell, 1977], p. 77).

11. Sherbo, "Farmer," p. 4; see also Sherbo, *Richard Farmer*, pp. 106–7. The sales catalogue lists 8,155 lots. A copy of it in the British Library (shelfmark 124e.16.) is annotated with the prices fetched by each book. See also Lloyd, "Dr Richard Farmer," pp. 524, 533 n. 5; and Sydney Roberts, *Richard Farmer (1735–1797)* (Letchworth, Hertfordshire: The Garden City Press, 1961), pp. 14–16.

12. *The Douce Legacy*, p. 148. On Douce, see also Laurel Braswell, *The Index of Middle English Prose. Handlist IV: A Handlist of Manuscripts Containing Middle English Prose in the Bodleian Library, Oxford* (Woodbridge: Brewer, 1987), pp. ix–x; and C. Hurst, "Douce, Francis (1757–1834)," *Oxford Dictionary of National Biography*, pp. 1–4 (accessed online 23 November 2006). On Douce's acquaintance with Farmer, see Arthur Sherbo, *Shakespeare's Midwives: Some Neglected Shakespeareans* (Newark: University of Delaware Press, 1992), p. 133. Some of the other books purchased by Douce at the Farmer sale are now MSS Douce 216, 258, 288, 301, and 311.

13. Reproduced and discussed in my article "Life and Death, Reader and Page: Mirrors of Mortality in English Manuscripts," *Mosaic* 35 (2002): 69–94 (pp. 90–91). Douce's high interest in the mortality motif of *Three Dead Kings* in MS Douce 302 is evident in his book *The Dance of Death Exhibited in Elegant Engravings on Wood, with a Dissertation on the Several Representations of That Subject* (London: William Pickering, 1833). Douce reproduces the same woodcut in his book (unnumbered page after p. 32), and he also gives here the first printed notice of the Audelay MS: "In a manuscript collection of unpublished and chiefly pious poems of John Awdelay, a blind poet and canon of the monastery of Haghmon, in Shropshire, anno 1426, there is one on the 'trois vifs et trois morts,' in alliterative verse, and composed in a very grand and terrific style" (p. 230). On Douce's unfortunate willingness to sometimes cut illustrations out of his books, see *The Douce Legacy*, p. 135. Martha W. Driver identifies the source of this woodcut as Guy Marchant's edition of the *Danse Macabre* (Paris, 1491); see her essay in the present volume, p. 215 n. 43.

14. Ella Keats Whiting, *The Poems of John Audelay*, EETS o.s. 184 (1931; repr. Oxford: Oxford University Press, 2006). The table on pp. xiii–xviii charts the item numbers inserted by Scribe B (see n. 16, below), Whiting's numbering system, and the works omitted by Whiting.

15. [H. O. Coxe], *Catalogue of the Printed Books and Manuscripts Bequeathed by Francis Douce, Esq., to the Bodleian Library at Oxford* (Oxford: Oxford University Press, 1840), pp. 50–52. For Douce's printed notice in 1833, see n. 13, above.

16. By use of the term *compiler*, I refer to Scribe B, who by all appearances acts on Audelay's wishes. Both scribes labored to execute Audelay's plan. Scribe A copied almost all the contents in continuous order, leaving gaps for Scribe B's work. Scribe B later inserted incipits, explicits, numbers, initials, and other details, and he proofread and corrected Scribe's A's copy. The scheme for MS Douce 302 was fashioned before Scribe A's work began, but it is Scribe B who controlled the finishing details. On Scribe B as "compiler," see Susanna Fein, "Good Ends in the Audelay Manuscript," *Yearbook of English Studies* 33 (2003): 97–119, esp. 103. An earlier theory that three hands redacted MS Douce 302 (Whiting, *Poems*, p. viii) has been refuted and now replaced by an understanding that there were only two scribes; see A. I. Doyle, "'Lectulus noster floridus': An Allegory of the Penitent Soul," in *Literature and Religion in the Later Middle Ages: Philological Studies in Honor of Siegfried Wenzel*, ed. Richard

G. Newhauser and John A. Alford (Binghamton, N.Y.: Medieval & Renaissance Texts & Studies, 1994), pp. 179–90 (pp. 181–82 n. 15).

17. Coxe, *Catalogue*, p. 50, col. b.

18. The *Finito libro* colophon, and compare *Epilogue* 417–18. For a good while, this colophon was taken as an initial endpoint for the manuscript, but paleographic evidence disproves this theory; see Fein, "Good Ends," p. 104, and n. 16.

19. See the table in the present volume, pp. xiii–xviii. Scribe B numbered the items before fol. 22v as a sequence, "[X]–XXVII" (I–IX and XII–XIV are missing, and so are the openings of numbers X and XV). A record of the scribal numbers was first provided in Fein, "Good Ends," p. 111.

20. Oliver Pickering observes that this note probably tells the reader that the proper ending to the preceding poem, *True Living*, was inadvertently copied out of place. To judge by the content of *True Living* at this point, Pickering's explanation makes good sense; see his essay in the present volume, pp. 112–37.

21. Fein, "Good Ends," p. 99. I have further refined the contents listed there (pp. 111–19); see the table in the present volume on pp. xiii–xviii.

22. See esp. Richard Firth Green, "Marcolf the Fool and Blind John Audelay," in *Speaking Images: Essays in Honor of V. A. Kolve*, ed. R. F. Yeager and Charlotte C. Morse (Asheville, N.C.: Pegasus, 2001), pp. 559–76; James Simpson, "Saving Satire after Arundel's *Constitutions*: John Audelay's 'Marcol and Solomon,'" in *Text and Controversy from Wyclif to Bale: Essays in Honour of Anne Hudson*, ed. Helen Barr and Ann M. Hutchison, Medieval Church Studies 4 (Turnhout: Brepols, 2004), pp. 387–404; and, in the present volume, Derek Pearsall, pp. 138–52, and Richard Firth Green, pp. 153–69. The poem has recently attracted notice in Mishtooni Bose, "Religious Authority and Dissent," in *A Companion to Medieval English Literature and Culture c. 1350–c. 1500*, ed. Peter Brown (Oxford: Blackwell, 2007), pp. 40–55 (pp. 50–51).

23. This is examined by Robert Easting in his essay in the present volume (pp. 170–90).

24. *Our Lord's Epistle* is the only work in *The Counsel of Conscience* to be selected for separate study in the early period of criticism. See R. Priebsch, "John Audelay's Poem on the Observance of Sunday and Its Source," in *An English Miscellany Presented to Dr. Furnivall in Honour of His Seventy-fifth Birthday*, ed. W. P. Ker, A. S. Napier, and W. W. Skeat (1901; repr. New York: Blom, 1969), pp. 397–407.

25. Eric G. Stanley, "*The True Counsel of Conscience*, or *The Ladder of Heaven:* In Defence of John Audelay's Unlyrical Lyrics," in *Expedition nach der Wahrheit: Poems, Essays, and Papers in Honour of Theo Stemmler*, ed. Stefan Horlacher and Marion Eslinger (Heidelberg: Carl Winter, 1996), pp. 131–59; and Pickering's essay in the present volume.

26. Melissa Jones, "'Swete May, Soulis Leche': The Winifred Carol of John Audelay," *Essays in Medieval Studies* 14 (1997): 1–7 (available online at http://www.luc.edu/publications/medieval); and Gill Chitty, with contributions by N. J. Palmer, J. J. West, and R. Gilyard-Beer, *Haughmond Abbey: A Brief Guide* (London: English

Heritage, 1992), the English Heritage brochure distributed at the Haughmond Abbey ruins: "The chapter house . . . where the canons of Haughmond met daily to regulate their religious duties and business . . . has three magnificent richly decorated arches dating from the late twelfth century. In the fourteenth century the areas between the shafts of the arches were carved with figures of saints beneath canopies." The eight surviving figures are, from left to right: "*a* St Augustine of Hippo, with his mitre and crozier, on whose writings the canons based their 'rule' which governed their life. *b* St Thomas Beckett, with his mitre and archbishop's cross-staff. *c* St Catherine with her wheel and sword, standing on the crown of the head of the Emperor Maxentius who had her martyred. *d* St John the Evangelist [the patron saint of Haughmond] with a palm branch and scroll, standing on his emblem, the eagle. *e* St John the Baptist, to whom the abbey is dedicated, with a lamb and flag (much eroded) on a roundel, and standing on the remains of the crowned head of King Herod. *f* St Margaret of Antioch standing on a dragon and piercing it with her cross. *g* St Winefred, whose shrine was in Shrewsbury, standing on the head of her would-be murderer, Prince Caradog. *h* St Michael with feathered wings holding a shield and a cross-staff with which he pierces a dragon at his feet." See also Marjorie M. Chibnall, "The Abbey of Haughmond," in *Victoria History of the Counties of England*, ed. R. B. Pugh, vol. 2, *A History of Shropshire*, ed. A. T. Gaydon (London: Oxford University Press, 1973), pp. 62–70; and G. C. Baugh and D. C. Cox, *Monastic Shropshire* (Shewsbury: Shropshire Libraries, 1988), pp. 17–24. The Augustinian houses of Shropshire were Haughmond Abbey, Wombridge Priory, and Lilleshall Abbey, each with a history dating from the twelfth century.

27. See Martha W. Driver's essay in the present volume, pp. 191–217.

28. For further comment on the salutations as a unified group, see the introduction in Audelay, *Poems and Carols*, pp. 13–15. As with the other sections, Scribe B's numbers and Whiting's numbers do not correspond. Twice where the scribe assigns a single number, Whiting assigns two (XXIX = W20, W21; XXXII = W24, W25). In this section, five of the seven places marked by a scribal number denote devotional sequences.

29. Whiting prints it as a ten-line stanza (*Poems*, pp. 159–60), and Karen Saupe follows the error in her anthology *Middle English Marian Lyrics* (Kalamazoo: Medieval Institute Publications, 1998), pp. 47–48, 174–76 (no. 4). *Gabriel's Salut.*, a translation of the hymn *Angelus ad virginem*, is the only Audelay salutation to have been printed in a modern anthology.

30. See my edition of Audelay, *Poems and Carols*, pp. 13–14, 278–79. For *Salut. to Jesus*, Whiting does not detect that the poem ends where a prayer rubric of two English couplets (written in red by Scribe B) begins (at W19.160, in her edition). A prayer on the Joys of the Virgin follows the rubric, and the sequence closes with one more instructional couplet.

31. On the drawing's probable origin in the artwork common to indulgence rolls, see Audelay, *Poems and Carols*, p. 292.

32. James Orchard Halliwell, ed., *The Poems of John Audelay: A Specimen of the Shropshire Dialect in the Fifteenth Century*, Percy Society 47 (London: T. Richards, 1844). The poems printed by Halliwell are selected from fols. 1r–12r: *True Living, Marcolf, Remedy, Seven Bleedings, Prayer on Christ's Passion, Seven Words, Virtues of the Mass* (= W1–W5, W7, W9). Note, too, that the spelling "Audelay" had already been used by Farmer (on the flyleaf) and Douce (on the book spine).

33. Halliwell, *Poems*, p. v.

34. Halliwell, *Poems*, p. vi.

35. J. Ernst Wülfing, "Der Dichter John Audelay und Sein Werk," *Anglia* 18 (1896): 173–217; and J. K. Rasmussen, *Die Sprache John Audelay's (Laut- und Flexionslehre)* (PhD diss., Bonn University, 1914).

36. R. W. Chambers and F. Sidgwick, "Fifteenth-Century Carols by John Audelay," *Modern Language Review* 5 (1910): 473–91; 6 (1911): 68–84.

37. Coxe's 1840 *Catalogue* records the couplet but does not take note that a carol sequence commences here (p. 51, nos. 21–42); moreover, it groups four carols (carols 2–5; W29–W32) under one heading and therefore records only twenty-two of the carols. Whiting recognizes the carols as a planned group (*Poems*, pp. xvii–xviii).

38. The carol collection contains three Audelay signatures: one at the end of the central carol on Henry VI and one each at the end of the last two in the collection, *Dread of Death Carol* and *St. Francis Carol*.

39. For favorable assessments of individual carols, see Woolf, *English Religious Lyric*, pp. 7, 222, 296, 336; Philippa Tristram, *Figures of Life and Death in Medieval English Literature* (New York: New York University Press, 1976), p. 222; Salter, *Fourteenth-Century English Poetry*, pp. 17–18; and Karl Reichl, "The Middle English Carol," in *A Companion to the Middle English Lyric*, ed. Thomas C. Duncan (Cambridge: Cambridge University Press, 2005), pp. 160–70 passim. See also the essays in the present volume by Julia Boffey (pp. 218–29) and John C. Hirsh (pp. 230–48). The carols are edited in Greene, *Early English Carol*, nos. 324, 325, 326, 328, 327, 7A, 97, 102, 108, 113, 117a, 428, 347, 412, 112A, 311, 172a, 230b, 177, 397, 398, 411, 272, 369, 310; and Audelay, *Poems and Carols*, pp. 175–210. Anthologies containing some of Audelay's carols include (in chronological order): Rolf Kaiser, ed., *Medieval English: An Old and Middle English Anthology*, 3rd ed. (Berlin: Rolf Kaiser, 1958), 295 (nos. 148, 149); Rossell Hope Robbins, ed., *Historical Poems of the XIVth and XVth Centuries* (New York: Columbia University Press, 1959), pp. 108–10 (no. 41); R. T. Davies, ed., *Medieval English Lyrics: A Critical Anthology* (London: Faber and Faber, 1963), 170–73 (nos. 81, 82); Greene, *Selection*, pp. 55–56, 79–80, 83–84, 122–23 (nos. 2, 22, 25, 61); Celia Sisam and Kenneth Sisam, eds., *The Oxford Book of Medieval English Verse* (Oxford: Clarendon Press, 1970), pp. 386–93 (nos. 157–60); Theodore Silverstein, ed., *English Lyrics before 1500* (Evanston: Northwestern University Press, 1971), pp. 105–6 (no. 84); and John C. Hirsh, ed., *Medieval Lyric: Middle English Lyrics, Ballads, and Carols* (Oxford: Blackwell, 2005), pp. 193–99 (nos. B8, B9).

40. The carols with versions in other manuscripts are: *Nativity Carol* (London, BL MS Sloane 2593); *Circumcision Carol* (Cambridge, TCC MS O.3.58 and Oxford,

Bodl. Lib. MS Arch. Selden. B.26); *Epiphany Carol* (MS Sloane 2593 and Oxford, Balliol College, MS 354); *Tree of Jesse Carol* (Balliol MS 354); and *Joys of Mary Carol* (Balliol MS 354). Copied in the sixteenth century, Balliol MS 354 postdates MS Douce 302. Greene sees Audelay's authorship of *Nativity Carol* as "doubtful" (p. 344).

41. See Robert Easting's essay in the present volume, pp. 170–90.

42. See further discussion of the carols in the introduction to my edition of Audelay, *Poems and Carols*, pp. 15–19.

43. Willy F. Storck and Richard Jordan, eds., "John Awdelays gedicht 'De tribus regibus mortuis': Eine englische fassung der legende von den drei lebenden und den drei toten," *Englische Studien* 43 (1911): 177–88; and Wülfing's brief description of *Three Dead Kings* ("Der Dichter John Audelay," pp. 213–14), predating Storck and Jordan by a few years. On Storck and Jordan's division of expertise, see E. G. Stanley's essay in the present volume, pp. 249–93.

44. Whiting, *Poems*, pp. xxiv–xxviii.

45. Bruce Dickins, "The Rhyme-Schemes in MS. Douce 302, 53 and 54," *Proceedings of the Leeds Philosophical and Literary Society* 2 (1932): 516–18; Thorlac Turville-Petre, "'Summer Sunday', 'De Tribus Regibus Mortuis', and 'The Awntyrs off Arthure': Three Poems in the Thirteen-Line Stanza," *Review of English Studies*, n.s. 25 (1974): 1–14; Thorlac Turville-Petre, ed. *Alliterative Poetry of the Later Middle Ages: An Anthology* (Washington, D.C.: Catholic University of America Press, 1989), pp. 148–57; Angus McIntosh, "Some Notes on the Text of the Middle English Poem *De tribus regibus mortuis*," *Review of English Studies* n.s. 28 (1977): 385–92; and Ad Putter, "The Language and Metre of *Pater Noster* and *Three Dead Kings*," *Review of English Studies*, n.s. 55 (2004): 498–526. See, too, Robert J. Menner, "Middle English 'Lagman' (*Gawain* 1729) and Modern English 'Lag,'" *Philological Quarterly* 10 (1931): 163–68. In my own critical work on *Three Dead Kings*, I have viewed its authorship as anonymous and its date as considerably earlier than the Audelay MS (ca. 1426). Ultimately, one cannot verify any hypothesis about the origin of this alliterative poem, though it is reasonable to assume that the same poet wrote *Pasternoster*. If both poems derive from Audelay, they were composed long before other works in the MS, in a style redolent of fourteenth-century alliterative verse. There is qualitative and dialectal variability in the accepted Audelay oeuvre, and writers do change over time. Thus the matter of ascription must remain open. I have addressed the question of authorship or dating in the following articles: "A Thirteen-Line Alliterative Stanza on the Abuse of Prayer from the Audelay MS," *Medium Ævum* 63 (1994): 61–74 (p. 64); "The Early Thirteen-Line Stanza: Style and Metrics Reconsidered," *Parergon*, n.s. 18 (2000): 97–126 (102–3 and nn. 23–24); "Life and Death, Reader and Page," pp. 70, 89; and "Good Ends," p. 108 n. 22.

46. E. G. Stanley, "The Verse Forms of Jon the Blynde Awdelay," in *The Long Fifteenth Century: Essays for Douglas Gray*, ed. Helen Cooper and Sally Mapstone (Oxford: Clarendon Press, 1997), pp. 99–121.

47. The stanza of *Over-Hippers and Skippers* is identical to that of *Marcolf*. The thirteen-line stanza of *Three Dead Kings* is much more finely wrought; in vocabulary

and stylistic effect, it bears close resemblance to the eleven-line stanzas of *Paternoster*. In my view, it demonstrates the sort of high-style model that caused Audelay to revere the thirteen-line form.

48. Fein, "A Thirteen-Line Stanza," pp. 61–74; and Doyle, "Lectulus noster floridus," pp. 179–90; Doyle prints the text found in University College Oxford MS 123, fols. 74v–75v.

49. A description of the unpublished prose texts appeared in 1987 in Braswell, *Handlist IV*, 70–71. See also Wulfing's description, "Der Dichter John Audelay," 211–12; and Whiting's mention, *Poems*, pp. x–xi.

50. See my essay in the present volume, pp. 294–306.

51. See *Instr. for Reading 2* 3 and *Prayer Explicit* 2–3.

52. See Fein, "A Thirteen-Line Stanza," pp. 61–68.

JOHN AUDELAY
LIFE RECORDS AND HEAVEN'S LADDER

Michael J. Bennett

The life records of Geoffrey Chaucer run to nearly five hundred items that provide documentation of his life over forty years.[1] They have been brought together in a stout volume that can be set alongside the substantial corpus of poetry and prose that can firmly be ascribed to him. They provide chronological framework for Chaucer's life and a good sense of the social and cultural milieus within which he lived and wrote. There are more than the makings of a biography, at least when the writer has the sureness of touch of Derek Pearsall.[2] Nonetheless it remains the case that the life records and the literary works do not greatly inform each other. With regard to John Audelay, a more obscure and less accomplished poet, the matter is wholly different. There is a modest body of work, surviving in a unique but incomplete manuscript, Oxford, Bodlein Library MS Douce 302.[3] Nonetheless much of the verse and indeed the very conception of the codex bear a strong authorial stamp. Audelay's name and his role as author-compiler are constantly restated, indeed some eighteen times. Only one notice of his life outside the text has been discovered: a reference to him in the King's Bench records in 1417.[4] This single reference to his participation in a bloody affray in a London church on Easter Sunday 1417, though, speaks to his verse and his compilation pointedly and illuminatingly.[5]

The origins of John Audelay are entirely obscure. The court record and the codex are at least consistent in describing him as a priest in the service of Richard, Lord Lestrange of Knockin (d. 1449),[6] first in his household in London in 1417 and then at the Lestrange chantry in Haughmond Abbey in Shropshire. The Lestranges of Knockin had lands stretching from the Welsh Marches through Shropshire to Middlesex,[7] and Audelay, though described as "of Knockin, in Wales" may have come to them from elsewhere. The surname is toponymic and probably derives from the village of Audley in northwest Staffordshire. It was not uncommon for clerks to be known by their place of birth. Equally, he may have been associated with the noble and gentry families of this name. After all, Audelay found his niche in aristocratic service and, prior to 1417 at least, appears to have shared their mores and values. Finally, the dialect of the author of almost all the verse in MS Douce 302 appears to be Shropshire. The two alliterative poems *Paternoster* and *Three Dead Kings*, probably not composed by Audelay, were written in a more northerly dialect, though still from within the northwest Midlands region.[8]

It is not known when Audelay was born, but it was before 1392. He was at least twenty-four years old, the canonical age for entry to the priesthood, in 1417. He was probably substantially older. He was ill and contemplating his demise—though perhaps prematurely—in 1426. His ordination records would be revealing, but so far have not been discovered. They do not appear in the registers of the bishops of Lichfield, Hereford, or London.[9] He may have been ordained by the bishop of St. Asaph, in whose diocese Knockin lay, but the registers have not survived. It is possible that he was ordained under another name, though his identification with John Borewell, another chaplain involved in the affray of 1417, is to be doubted.[10] A reasonable assumption is that Audelay was slightly older than the lord whom he served, for better or worse, for over a decade. Richard Lestrange was born in 1381 and was thirty-six at the time of the affray. If Audelay were born in the mid-1370s, he would have been around forty in 1417, and around fifty when, in 1426, he identified himself as "blind and deaf" and submitted himself to the grace of God.[11] Audelay's first editor, by way of a response to the penitential gloom of his poetry, speculated on a misspent youth.[12] It is tempting to see in Audelay's pen-portrait of "Oure gentyl Ser Jone" (*Marcolf* 144), a bad priest but a jolly good fellow, as the portrait of the poet as a younger man.[13] The revelation of Audelay's involvement in the affray of 1417 lends weight to this sort of speculation, but in important respects makes it redundant.

A focus on the career of Richard, Lord Lestrange of Knockin provides some perspective on Audelay's world. He was born in London and baptized in St. Bartholomew's the Less in Broad Street on 1 August 1381.[14] It was a city in which order was only slowly returning after the Peasants' Revolt in the summer. His father, John, sixth Lord Lestrange, came from a line of marcher lords who had latterly moved in more urbane circles. John's marriage to Maud, one of the three daughters and coheiresses of John Mohun, second Lord Mohun, brought his son not only the prospect of greater landed wealth but also important connections at court. Richard's maternal grandmother, Lady Joan Mohun, was a great favorite of Richard II.[15] His mother's sister was married to the king's cousin Edward, duke of Albemarle, later duke of York. Though his father was not very active politically, perhaps constrained by his connection with the disaffected Richard Fitzalan, earl of Arundel,[16] Richard may have been brought up to see himself as a courtier. After his father's death in July 1397, his wardship and marriage were granted to the duke of Albemarle, who granted them in trust to Richard's mother.[17] The dowager Lady Lestrange's remarriage to Sir Nicholas Hauberk, and her subsequent death in 1400, briefly brought Richard under the tutelage of one of Richard II's knights who had successfully accommodated himself to the Lancastrian regime.[18]

As he approached manhood, Richard found himself at the center of a political maelstrom. In the summer and autumn of 1397, Richard II struck out at his noble opponents. A prominent casualty was the earl of Arundel, the most powerful nobleman in the neighborhood of Knockin, cousin of the lords of Knockin and godfather of young Richard.[19] Richard II's incorporation of the Fitzalan marcher lordships into his new principality of Chester transformed the local political scene. In 1398 the king was twice in the neighborhood of Knockin, holding parliament at Shrewsbury in February and spending time in the region, using Holt Castle on the Dee as his main base, in June and August.[20] In the summer of 1399, Henry of Bolingbroke advanced through Shrewsbury into Cheshire. Prominent in his host was Thomas Fitzalan, earl of Arundel, who was now restored to his father's lordships in the Welsh Marches. After the surrender of Richard II at Chester and Henry IV's seizure of the throne, the region remained a flashpoint. The revolt of Owain Glyndŵr not only laid bare deep ethnic wounds, but also opened up divisions within the English marcher community. In their rebellion against Henry IV, the Percies made common cause with Glyndŵr and raised Ricardian loyalists in Cheshire. John Kynaston, steward of the Lestrange lordships, led the tenants to join the insurrection.[21] Henry IV moved decisively to confront and defeat the rebels at the Battle of Shrewsbury in 1403. Over the following five years, the region was the frontline in the future Henry V's campaigns to subdue the principality of Wales.

Richard Lestrange came of age during this turbulent time. The rebellion probably delayed his entrance into his patrimony. In August 1404 he reimbursed his stepfather in London, proved his age before the mayor of London, and entered into his inheritance.[22] In 1408 he secured a papal dispensation to marry Joan, who is described as the daughter of Lord

Grey.[23] In a subsequent papal letter she is described as Joan alias Constance, the name under which she was later known.[24] The new lord of Knockin was slow to make his mark on the public stage. The likelihood is that he was financially embarrassed: the minority, the losses incurred in the rebellion, and litigation over the Mohun inheritance all sapped his reserves. He may have spent more time in the capital than at Knockin. In 1409 he was ordered to repair to his castles on the Welsh Marches to counter renewed insurgency.[25] He doubtless attended the coronation of Henry V in 1413 and the first parliaments of the reign. In 1414 the king convened parliament at Leicester and heard complaints about disorder in Shropshire, which, it was alleged, "abounds in these days in homicides and rapines far beyond the rest of the counties of England."[26] A powerful judicial commission arrived in Shrewsbury to punish malefactors and restore order. In the wake of the Sir John Oldcastle conspiracy, the king was also concerned to root out heresy in the region. Lord Lestrange was appointed to a commission to search out and arrest Lollards in Shropshire.[27] He may not have been especially active. All in all, he was one of the least consequential members of the lower nobility.

In spring 1417 London was exceptionally busy. Henry V was planning a major expedition to France, and many magnates came to the capital to give counsel, raise funds, and order equipment.[28] Lord and Lady Lestrange, who seem to have divided their time between London and Knockin, were among their number. The Lestrange household was a rather modest establishment. Of the fifteen men recorded as retainers and servants in 1417, three were squires, two chaplains, and one a clerk. The rest were yeomen, including men named for their duties in the chamber, the stables, and the kitchen. Eleven were described as "of Knockin," including John Audelay, chaplain, with the remainder described as "of London."[29] With many of his manors in other counties in the hands of lessees, Lestrange seems to have been largely reliant on the resources of his estates in Shropshire and the Welsh Marches. Though he had inherited manors in Middlesex and a property at Holborn, he seems to have had lodging in the city. From his use of a box in the church, he would appear to have been a regular worshipper at St. Dunstan's in the East, close to the river at Billingsgate. In residence in the same parish were Sir John Trussell and his wife. The Lestranges and the Trussells were evidently not on good terms. Apart from the fact that they attended the same parish church, it is not known how they came to know each other and what was the source of the animosity between them. The quarrel erupted and escalated rapidly on Easter Sunday, culminating in a bloody affray in the church that left several men wounded and one dead. In addition to brief notices in several London chronicles,[30] two detailed accounts survive, one the record of an inquest held by the archdeacon of London on April 21, and the other the King's Bench record of Trussell's action against his assailants. It is the former account, provided by a jury of Londoners, incorporating eyewitness testimony, that provides the most compelling and vivid narrative.[31] It professed to recall the words actually used, and indeed in their dialect form.

On Easter Sunday, April 11, Lord Lestrange went early to Mass. Emerging from "le closette" in which he had heard the divine office, Lestrange saw Trussell at prayer and strode across the church to confront him over some matter. An altercation took place, in which he called him a "lewd knave." Trussell said that Lestrange lied and declared that he was a knight like him. Fearing violence, a number of parishioners moved to separate them. Lestrange was persuaded to withdraw, but he shouted menacingly, "Thou lewyd hegge knight, thou shall aby!" Three aldermen of London, informed of the fracas, sought out the two men in their lodgings and obtained pledges from them to keep the peace. Later in the day the two knights returned to the church. Trussell was back at church for vespers when in burst Lestrange and a group of squires and yeomen "with swords, daggers and shields, and helmets on their heads." They were immediately followed by Lady Lestrange, who hissed, "Herst thou, Trussell! Thou shall aby! This bargane thou bouthist never none so dere!" Thomas Fitzhuwe, who had entered with Lady Lestrange, seized Trussell by the throat and threw him to the ground. With a sword in one hand and a dagger in the other, Lestrange then shouted, "Steke him, sle him!" and his men hacked at Trussell, severely maiming him and wounding his son Geoffrey Trussell. One valiant parishioner, Thomas Petwardyn, wishing to avert the fighting and sacrilege, was dealt a mortal blow and died at his home a short while afterwards.[32]

In his appeal of mayhem in King's Bench, Trussell told essentially the same story, though with an appropriately sharper focus on the assault on him.[33] He alleged that his assailants seized him by the neck, threw him to the ground, struck him on the elbow of his left arm, cut his "whirlebone," and sliced the tendons so that he lost the life in two fingers. Though Trussell named Thomas Fitzhuwe as one of the party, he did not give him the principal role. He alleged that it was John Boorne who first attacked him and Peter Brereton who joined in the assault. Trussell was better informed about the names of his assailants than the jury in the archdeacon's court. Boorne and Brereton did not deny their role, but they claimed that it was Lady Trussell who brought armed men to the church and that they had merely acted to protect their lord and lady. Trussell's statement that Audelay was present in the company of Lord and Lady Lestrange—a point omitted in the church record—thus seems entirely creditworthy. Throughout the proceedings Trussell was insistent that his assailants were in the company of Lord Lestrange, Lady Lestrange, and John Audelay, chaplain, and acting on their procurement. He would have appealed them as well, he declared, if they had been present in court.[34]

The source of so bitter a dispute remains obscure. It was believed in London that the quarrel arose between or in relation to Lady Lestrange and Lady Trussell.[35] Lady Lestrange's reference to a "bargain" that Trussell would live to regret may indicate a business transaction, perhaps a loan. In terms of Lord Lestrange's animus against Trussell, a man in his late sixties, there is the possible issue of religion.[36] In his prime, Trussell had been one of a group of knights who were believed to be Lollards. Lestrange, who had been appointed to a commission to arrest Lollards in the wake of Oldcastle's rising, may have shared the government's exaggerated concern with the threat of heresy. In 1417 Oldcastle was still at large, seemingly under the protection of men like Trussell.[37] According to Paul Strohm, the month of April "was the absolute peak of Oldcastle's celebrity as arch-heretic and arch-fugitive."[38] Although it is easier to imagine that the quarrel in church originated as a dispute over precedence or in relation to parish business than over matters of faith or worship, it was specifically noted that the violence erupted at sermon time or, as the chronicler reports it, "in the preching tyme." If he retained his Lollard tendencies, Trussell might have been especially attentive—perhaps provocatively so—during the sermon. Lestrange presumably knew Trussell's reputation, and may have thought less of him on that account. In calling him a "hedge-knight," he may have sought to associate Trussell with Lollard "hedge-priests" and the fugitive Oldcastle.[39]

After the outrage Lestrange and his men fled into the city streets. There was a hue and cry in Tower ward and the neighboring wards, and Trussell played a part in rounding up his assailants.[40] Lestrange and his men were brought before the sheriffs of London at the Counter in Poultry.[41] The lord of Knockin obtained leave to submit to higher authority and was soon safely lodged in the Tower of London. Audelay was probably handed over to the bishop of London. Immediately after the affray, the bishop had suspended services in the polluted church and ordered his clergy to lay the great curse, with bell, book, and candle, on the malefactors in services the following Sunday.[42] The archdeacon of London held an inquest into the affray on Wednesday, April 21, and ordered the Lestranges to make their submission at St. Paul's Cathedral within ten days. On April 25, Henry V himself rode from Westminster to St. Paul's, to take "his leve of all maner of peple, as welle of pore as of rich," seek their prayers for his expedition, and charge the mayor to maintain order in the city.[43] On Saturday, May 1, the Lestranges made their appearance in the cathedral. The date had almost certainly been arranged to ensure maximum publicity for the submission and public penance. Lord and Lady Lestrange were ordered to walk barefoot with their men, in their shifts and with candles in their hands to St. Dunstan's in the East. Following the reconsecration of the church, they were required to make offerings to the value of 15 pounds. Thus the once-proud lord and lady, downcast and humiliated, trudged through the mocking May Day crowds along Cheapside to the scene of the scandalous affray.[44] If their chaplain were not there in body, he would have been there in spirit. It was an event long remembered in London, and presumably in Shropshire.

Lord Lestrange and his men returned to their respective prisons. The records show that, on April 20, some fourteen of Lestrange's men were in the custody of the sheriffs of London, probably at Newgate. One of their number, John Borewell, chaplain, was mainprised.[45] The remaining thirteen were transferred to the Marshalsea, the prison of the King's Bench, to respond to Trussell's appeal of mayhem. In another proceeding, one of their number, Philip Knockin, cook, was indicted for the death of Thomas Petwardyn.[46] Even though he was released from the Tower on May 10, Lestrange was able to keep himself at arm's length from the proceedings in King's Bench, though he presumably helped to organize, at some cost, bail for his servants.[47] In pursuing the case in person and by appeal, Trussell was obviously less interested in having Lestrange's men strung up as felons than in securing damages. On June 25, the jury found Boorne and Brereton guilty of the assault, and Lord and Lady Lestrange guilty of inciting it. It also found Audelay and the other servants guilty of "aiding, inciting, procuring, comforting, abetting, and ordering" the assailants. The jury awarded Trussell the substantial sum of 600 marks damages and 200 marks costs. Exhibiting his wounds, Trussell managed to have the damages increased to 800 marks, raising the total to 1,000 marks.[48] For Philip Knockin, it was not the end of the matter. He languished in the Marshalsea through July and perhaps cheated the gallows only by succumbing to the pestilential air in the prison.[49] Presumably the Lestranges bore the crippling burden of the compensation claim damages. The bad blood between them and the Trussells continued. In December 1417, Lord Lestrange entered a bond not to do or procure harm to Lady Trussell, and in March 1418, Lady Lestrange entered a bond to appear before the king to answer Trussell's appeal for mayhem.[50] On the anniversary of the assault in 1418, Trussell appeared in King's Bench to declare that the damages had been paid.[51]

After the outrage on Easter Sunday, John Audelay vanished from the scene. In all likelihood he was in the custody of the bishop, who would have sought to suppress his role in the assault and sacrilege. Audelay was not defrocked, but he was assuredly disciplined. Heavy penance would have been imposed, though of a private rather than a public nature. At some stage Audelay retired to Shropshire. A cure of souls in a country parish, however, does not seem to have been an option. Lord Lestrange presented other priests to two parsonages in his gift in 1418 and 1419.[52] It is possible that Audelay's initial claustration at Haughmond was part of the disciplinary process. The Augustinian abbey, a few miles from Knockin, was the natural choice. Earlier lords of Knockin had been great benefactors of the abbey, and there were longstanding plans for a Lestrange chantry in the convent.[53] An agreement between Lestrange and the abbot in 1424 almost certainly cleared the way for the formal establishment of the chantry, with Audelay as its first chaplain.[54] By this stage Audelay was probably already in ill health and losing his sight. Still, it should not be seen as an ordinary retirement. He was committed to an austere life of penance and prayer, and to the composition of a body of writing and the compilation of a book that would show others the way to salvation and solicit prayers for his own soul.

Audelay's book, now MS Douce 302, is organized into four main sections. The first part appears to be the heart of the enterprise. Audelay saw it as a book in its own right. In its extant form it lacks the first twenty-four folios, but in the Latin colophon at the end of the first part (fol. 22v), dated 1426, Audelay writes, "The book is finished. Praise and honor to God" (Finito libro. Sit laus et gloria Christo). He goes on to name it: the book is called *The Counsel of Conscience* or *The Ladder of Heaven and Life of Eternal Safety* ("Concilium conciencie" or "Scala celi et vita salutis eterni"). The poems of this part are earnestly didactic, seeking to inculcate an awareness of sin and to set the readers on the path to repentance and grace. The second part of the codex comprises a number of salutations and prayers, and the third part a series of carols. Audelay would seem to be the author of them all, but they were almost certainly written over a longer time frame than the poems in *The Counsel of Conscience*. The fourth and final part is an anthology of writing that relates to the final things. Throughout the work, but especially in the first and fourth parts, there is continuous reference to Audelay as the author and compiler. The codex is in two hands, with one consciously shaping the whole collection. If Audelay himself did not assume this role, the scribe-compiler seems to have faithfully executed Audelay's design for the enlarged book.

This codex provides the only known record of Audelay's life after 1417. His references to himself and the work as a whole provide evidence as to his position, his health, and his preoccupations around 1426. He is serving the Lestrange chantry at Haughmond; he is in failing health and contemplating death, and indeed "deaf and blind"; he is writing verse, calling on his readers to turn from sin and worldly concerns, and to do penance and be devout in their observances; he is organizing his verse into a book that will set his readers on the path to salvation. The record of 1417 and the codex of 1426 obviously inform each other in a biographical sense: they give the participant in the affray in the London church a future, and the poet at Haughmond a past. They also raise interesting new issues and possibilities with regard to the interpretation of his life and work. The man of 1417 was more complex than one would have any right to infer from the King's Bench record. The poet of 1426 had a background markedly different from that assumed by his earliest critics. There is continuity in identity—the name, the regional provenance, the priesthood, and the connection with the Lestranges—but there is radical discontinuity. The key issue in relation to the understanding and interpretation of his life and work is the role of the events of 1417 in the formation of "blind John Audelay," priest and poet, and in the conception of MS Douce 302.

Age and ill health account for some of the distance between the men of 1417 and 1426. Even without the outrage at St. Dunstan's in the East, Audelay might well have moved from service in the household to the position at Haughmond Abbey. The deterioration in his health alone could well have dictated the change. In his work Audelay certainly attests to his illness and specifically says that he is "deaf and blind." Though he makes figurative play of his blindness, his description of himself as "John, blind Audelay" suggests some real affliction. It is possible that he had been blind for some time.[55] The man whom Trussell counted among his assailants in 1417, however, appears to have been all too able-bodied. Even in the early 1420s, his disability seems not to have been entirely incapacitating. Near the end of the *The Counsel of Conscience*, he describes the circumstances of its production:

> As I lay seke in my langure,
> In an abbay here be west,
> This boke I made with gret dolour
> When I myght not slep ne have no rest.
>
> *(Epilogue 482–85)*

If Audelay, when ill and unable to sleep, was still able to work on his book, he cannot have been wholly blind. The crucial point to note is Audelay's belief that his affliction, presumably sudden and recent, was a visitation of God. He continues:

> Offt with my prayers I me blest,
> And sayd hilé to Heven Kyng:
> "I knowlache, Lord, hit is the best
> Mekelé to take thi vesetyng,
>   Ellis wot I wil that I were lorne."
>
> *(Epilogue 486–90)*

In the Latin colophon to this poem, he describes himself without ambiguity as "blind and deaf on his [Christ's] visitation" (secus et surdus in sua visitacione).[56]

Audelay was a man with an unusually morbid and exaggerated sense of his own sinfulness. He did, however, have a sin on his conscience that more than justified his belief that his affliction was a visitation of God. Less than a decade earlier he had been involved in a mortal sin and a felony in a church on "the most sacred Sunday of the resurrection."[57] Of course, he did not shed blood himself, and the jury may have been wrong to find him guilty of aiding and abetting the assault. Whatever the technical degree of his guilt at law, the enormity of his offence before God was all too evident. The events of 1417—the initial outrage, the humiliation and ruin of the Lestrange household, and the shame and punishment he would have experienced—may well have been deeply traumatic. The collapse of his health, sudden and debilitating, intensified the crisis but in the end brought catharsis. Like Saul of Tarsus struck blind on the road to Damascus, Audelay took his blindness as a sign of God's grace. Audelay saw some identity with the man who became Saint Paul. One of his most substantial pieces is a metrical translation of a Latin work known as *The Vision of Saint Paul of the Pains of Hell*. In the last stanza Audelay restates his belief that God has chastised him for his living, gives heartfelt thanks for "his gracious vesityng" (*Vision of St. Paul* 358–60) and concludes with a warning to his readers:

> Beware, serys, I you pray,
> And your mysdedis loke ye amend
> Betyme, lest ye be chamyd and schend!
> Fore al is good that hath good end.
>   Thus counsels youe the Blynd Audlay.
>   (361–65)

Audelay attached considerable importance to his book, both *The Counsel of Conscience* and the extended work that survives as MS Douce 302. He wrote it, according to the Latin colophon, "for the example of others in the monastery of Haughmond" (ad exemplum aliorum in monasterio de Haghmon).[58] He cannot have been thinking exclusively or primarily of the monks. There were other clerks, priests, and lay brothers associated with the convent. There were the local gentry and other visitors to the abbey. Above all, Audelay, who served the Lestrange chantry, must have had daily in his mind his lord and lady and the members of the household in which he served. Lord Lestrange himself may have lived among the monks himself for a time. Since they do not appear to have had any children, he and his wife may have lived separately. In 1438 Lady Lestrange was living a quiet and pious life in London.[59] When Audelay describes himself as "In an abbay here be west," he is seeing himself in the mind's eye of his former friends in the capital. The key point is that Audelay was writing for people who would have known about the outrage of 1417. The Lestrange chantry at Haughmond Abbey, like the chantry newly built on the site of the Battle of Shrewsbury, a few miles away, was a site of memory. In counseling and warning his readers, Audelay derived authority from his own sinful past and from the "visitation" that had set him on "heaven's ladder." He presents himself as an example to others. In his book he may even have made fairly direct reference to the event that had brought shame and ruin on the Lestrange household, prompted the establishment of the chantry, and set him, through God's grace, on the path to salvation. It needs to be borne in mind that the first half of *The Counsel of Conscience*, including the preface that Audelay assuredly wrote, is missing from the codex.

In what is left of his book, Audelay often touches on matters that would have had special resonance to readers who knew about his past. The extant codex begins in the middle of a long rambling poem about righteous living, with reflections on noblemen who had been shamed and punished for their sins:

> In hel ne purgatoré non other plase,
> Thes synnes wold make you schamyd and schent,
> And lese your worchyp in erth and grace.
> Al day, with ene, sene thou has
> Hou men bene slayne fore dedlé synne
> And han vengans fore here trespace;
> Both lyve and goodes they lesyn then,
> > Bi londys law.
> Yif thai had kept Cristis comaundment,
> Thai schuld never be schamyd ne chent,
> Ne lost here lyfe ne lond ne rent,
> > Nouther hongud ne draw.
> > > (*True Living* 1–12)

Other works in MS Douce 302 present chillingly apposite lessons from a priest with his particular past. *Virtues of the Mass* and *Our Lord's Epistle on Sunday* are lengthy perorations on how to attend Mass and the need to respect the Sabbath. In *The Remedy of Nine Virtues* Audelay rehearses (as from God's own voice) the nine virtues, including the sixth "to say no word of backbiting."[60] The connection between a row with a neighbor and public penance, though derived from Richard Rolle's *Novem virtutes*, seems all too pointed:

> To thi neghbour fore love of me,
> To make debate ny dyscorde,
> And thou dust me more cumford,
> Then thagh thou wentust barefote in the strete,
> For love of me that ys thi Lorde,
> That stremus of blood folewed thi fete.
> > (*Remedy of Nine Virtues* 1–6)

Audelay's additions to his sources, like his inclusion of backbiting in his *Ten Commandments Carol*, line 10,[61] are even more telling. His version of Saint Paul's vision of the pains of hell contains much that is distinctive. His first interpolation is a stanza on proper behavior in church (*Vision of St. Paul* 93–105),[62] which includes this advice:

> A, synful mon! Hereof have mynd:
> In Holé Cherche, nothyng thou say,
> Bot with holé prayers to God ye pray.
> > (101–3)

In another original stanza Audelay affirms that hell is not ordained for righteous people:

> No more than is a preson of lyme and stone
> Bot fore hom the lawis offend.
> Cursid dedis makis men al day eschend
> And theffys on galous on hye to hyng.
> (*Vision of St. Paul* 342–45)

It may be that where Audley is most intense and original in his handling of homiletic commonplaces, as in his *Dread of Death Carol*, such themes assert themselves most compellingly.[63]

In 1426 Audelay evidently believed that his life had been transformed. He saw his earlier life as one of sin and folly. His own experience and example give authority to his calls for reform and repentance. Audelay shows himself to be conscious of the special responsibilities of the clergy, and like other moralists of the time he is highly critical of their failings. He is somewhat unusual, however, in his empathetic understanding of the manner in which the clergy were diverted from or obstructed in their pastoral work by the expectations and estimations of the laity. In consecutive stanzas he draws pen-portraits of two priests. First there is the priest who lives up to his vocation, but is little regarded:

> Yif ther be a pore prest, and spirituale in spiryt,
> And be devoute with devocion, his servyse syng and say,
> Thay lekon hym to a Lollere and to an epocryte.
> Yif he be besé in his bedus, the Prince of Heven to pay,
> And holde hym in Holé Cherche, dulé uche day,
> Oute of the curse of cumpané, and kepe his concyans clene,
> He ys a nything, a noght, a negard, thai say.
> (*Marcolf* 131–37)

Then there is "Oure gentyl Ser Jone":

> He is meré mon of mouth among cumpané.
> He con harpe! He con syng! His orglus ben herd ful wyd!
> He wyl noght spare his purse to spend his selaré—
> Alas, he ner a parsun or a vecory!
> Be Jhesu, he is a gentyl mon, and jolylé arayd—
> His gurdlis harneschit with selver, his baslard hongus bye.
> (*Marcolf* 144–50)

Audelay the poet obviously empathized with the poor priest, and it is natural to assume that he saw some identity with him. Conversely, it has been imagined that "our gentle Sir John" was someone known to Audelay, but a man of an entirely different character. In fact, it is hard not to see in "our gentle Sir John" the priest who kept company with the Lestranges in London in 1417. Like Audelay, he did not serve a parish but was companionable and fashionably arrayed. He wore a "baslard," or short sword, all too reminiscent of the chaplain in the assault on Trussell. He was valued for his ability to sing and play the harp, accomplishments that the poet of 1426 probably shared. Audelay's portrait of the poor priest, if not an image of himself as he might have been, may reflect his more recent experience. Embracing poverty and the holy life, but outspoken in his condemnation of sin, he may have found himself accused of hypocrisy and Lollardy. The reference to Lollardy has special interest. It was all too easy to dismiss men who spoke out against immorality and license by calling them Lollards. Given the prohibition on religious writing in the vernacular in 1409, however, Audelay needed to tread warily. He was wholly orthodox in his beliefs, but his enterprise attests to a strong belief in the validity of vernacular instruction and reformist criticism.[64]

Audelay concluded *The Counsel of Conscience* or *The Ladder of Heaven and Life of Eternal Safety* in 1426. The verse in this book was probably written in the year or so before, and very much in the shadow of the events of 1417. The second and third sections were presumably added in or shortly after 1426. Though the authorial presence is less intrusive, they seem to be original to Audelay. It is not clear, however, when he wrote them. The likelihood is that Audelay had been writing verse for some time and that most of them were written before *The Counsel of Conscience*. "Our gentle Sir John" could well have written love lyrics. The *Childhood Carol*, though not a work of youth, was probably written in more complacent times. Audelay's presence in a noble household in London in 1417 must caution against the assumption that his cultural milieu was wholly monastic and provincial. In any case, there was a great deal of coming and going between Shropshire and the capital, and cultural influences ran in both directions. Audelay's *Salutation to Saint Winifred* is cited as an example of local patriotism, but Richard II elevated her cult to national level after spending time in Shrewsbury in early 1398.[65] Conversely, Audelay, who may have been in London at the time of Henry's foundation of the Bridgettine convent at Syon in 1415, is the first writer to show himself aware of the valuable indulgences that became available from the house in 1419.[66]

Some of the items in the second and third sections, though, were certainly written after 1417. The *Salutation to Saint Bridget* must have been written after 1419, and the *Henry VI Carol* after 1422. Still, there is no reason to suppose that either work is later than 1426. Even after his retirement at Haughmond, Audelay was able to keep in touch with developments in the realm at large. In March 1421, Henry V came to Shrewsbury, settled a reward on the captors of Sir John Oldcastle, and almost certainly visited the shrine of Saint Winifred.[67] In his *Henry VI Carol*, Audelay combines a loyal, romanticized view of the late king and his wife with an almost avuncular interest in the boy king. It has been remarked that Audelay's verse bears comparison with the work of John Lydgate. Audelay certainly matches Lydgate in his warm endorsement of the Lancastrian monarchy.[68] There are a number of parallel projects in respect of metrical translations of prayers and devotional works. It should not be assumed, though, that Audelay followed Lydgate's lead, and indeed there is no evidence that he was influenced by him. The point is that Audelay was as contemporary in his interests and concerns as the poet laureate. Even the inclusion in his codex of the older piece, *Three Dead Kings*, can be seen as a response to the same tastes that prompted Lydgate to translate the *Danse Macabre*.[69] In 1426, as Audelay finished the first part of his book at Haughmond Abbey, Lydgate embarked on a translation of Guillaume de Deguileville's *Pilgrimage of the Life of Man*.[70] Homespun but authentic, Audelay's *Counsel of Conscience* met similar needs.

The final section of Audelay's codex is a sustained meditation on death and the life to come. It comprises prose and verse, including an extract from Richard Rolle's *Form of Living* and two anonymous and otherwise unknown poems, *Paternoster* and *Three Dead Kings*. The balance of opinion is that Audelay was not the author of these two poems, both written in an older, alliterative style and in a more northerly dialect. Still, it needs to be borne in mind that the language and literary fashion changed significantly in the two decades either side of 1400 and that Audelay's own speech and style may have changed over his life as he moved around the northwest Midlands and between the Welsh Marches and London.[71] The whole codex ends with a final petition to his readers for prayers for his soul:

> To pray for hym specialy
> That hyt made your soules to save,

> Jon the Blynde Awdelay.
> The furst prest to the Lord Strange he was,
> Of thys chauntré, here in this place,
> That made this bok by Goddus grace,
> Deeff, sick, blynd, as he lay.
> (*Conclusion* 46–52)

Cuius anime propicietur Deus.[72]

It is as if Audelay were speaking from the grave. There can be little doubt that he intended the final lines of his book to be his epitaph.[73]

The likelihood is that John Audelay did not long survive the completion of *The Counsel of Conscience* in 1426. It is possible that it was the second scribe who brought the larger work to completion, collecting together the more suitable of the poet's literary remains, including the final valedictory poem. Audelay intended that the codex remain "here in this place," that is the chantry chapel at Haughmond, "for the example of others." His recognition that people might read or copy only parts of the book may help explain his repetition of his name and multiple requests for intercession. In the final poem he even expressed a concern that someone might steal the book or rip out pages, and he issued a stern warning:

No mon this book he take away,
Ny kutt owte noo leef, Y say forwhy,
For hit ys sacrelege, sirus, Y yow say!
Beth acursed in the dede truly!
(*Conclusion* 40–43)

The curious use of the term *sacrelege* again seems to bear witness, implicitly if not explicitly, to the scandal of 1417.

Lord and Lady Lestrange survived him. For another decade and more, Audelay lived on in the memory, and perhaps in the prayers, of his lord and lady and others who knew him. The Lestranges lost a great deal through the outrage of 1417. The fines and compensation alone would have been ruinous to a couple whose means seem always to have been straitened. Above all, they must have found it hard to recover their reputation after the sacrilege and the public penance in London. Lady Lestrange may have found it hardest. In her failure to bear children, she may have shared Audelay's sense of "visitation." When she made her will in 1438, she was living modestly in London. Her reference to her husband, whose permission to make the will she acknowledged, is affectionate but distant. Interestingly, one of the men in her service in 1417, Thomas Fitzwalter, and seemingly the wife of another, Alice Fitzhuwe, received bequests. Her will attests to a piety that was by no means conventional or superficial. She left her soul to God the omnipotent Creator, to the Virgin Mary, and to all the saints. She sought burial in a church to be specified by her husband. She left money for masses at two friaries in London and at three friaries in Shrewsbury. There was no reference to Haughmond Abbey, though there was a gift for the vicar of Oswestry. Her individuality is best attested in the gift of her robes to make altar cloths embroidered with the name of Jesus; in her sisterhood with the Franciscans; in her gift to a bachelor of theology, perhaps a favorite preacher; in her provision for a priest to celebrate a trental in *scala coeli* in Rome; and in her ownership of two religious books.[74]

It is the ownership of the books and her disposition of them that again links her to John Audelay and makes it likely that they were in contact in the mid-1420s. One book is simply described as "my English book with devotions and prayers" (meum bonum librum Anglicum cum devocionibus et oracionibus). There is every reason to suppose that it was a book of verse, not unlike some of the material in the second and third sections of MS Douce 302. She bequeathed it to one of her friends. The other item is simply called *Graciam Dei* (Grace of God). This obscurely titled work may be a personal compilation, not unlike *The Counsel of Conscience*. The greater likelihood, though, is that it was a translation of Deguileville's *The Pilgrimage of the Soul*, generally known under the title *Grace Dieu*.[75] Her wishes with respect to this work are very remarkable. She requested that her book be kept in the church or chapel in which she would be buried and placed "on a desk with a metal chain to be available for reading with the intent that chaplains, clerks, and laymen can read and learn from it lessons for their salvation" (super unum dext cum cathena ferrea legendum ea intencione ut capellani, clerici et homines laicali in eodem legere et addiscere possunt bona exempla in eorum salvacionem). Considered in isolation, her bequest might be seen to fit with the growing fashion in London of leaving books to churches for "common profit."[76] Lady Lestrange's scheme, however, was different. The book was not for loan and would remain close to her tomb. The people who chose to read it would, necessarily, remember her in their prayers. It served similar ends to Audelay's book in the Lestrange chantry at Haughmond Abbey.

The memory of Audelay, and perhaps the fate of his book, now depended on Lord Lestrange. Richard Lestrange may have found it easier than his wife and chaplain to put the past behind him. After Lady Lestrange's death he rapidly remarried, and, approaching seventy, he finally sired a male heir. At some stage, probably not long after 1426, MS Douce 302 appears to have been the victim of the sacrilege that Audelay had feared. Twenty-four folios have been lost from the beginning of the codex, and other folios have been taken from two other places in the first section. It seems very likely that the folios were torn out on account of their reference to the events of 1417. The first nine poems and whatever preface Audelay chose to write have been lost. The extant codex begins in the middle of what would have been the tenth poem, where Audelay is discussing the shame and punishment of sinful noblemen:

> In hel ne purgatoré non other plase,
> Thes synnes wold make you schamyd and schent,
> And lese your worchyp in erth and grace.
>   (*True Living* 1–3)

The second excision occurs in the middle of Audelay's peroration against backbiting immediately before the lines associating neighborly discord with public penance. In the neighborhood of Haughmond, there would be many people, notably the lord of Knockin himself, who would prefer the scandal of 1417 to be forgotten. The Lestrange chantry survived into the late fifteenth century, and prayers continued for the seventh lord and his two wives, but for want of resources the work of the chantry had devolved on the canons. By this stage Audelay's book was probably no longer at Haughmond. Prior to the dissolution of the monasteries in the 1530s, it had passed through the hands of a minstrel of Coventry to Launde Priory.[77]

NOTES

I would like to thank my colleague Dr. Jenna Mead for her insightful comments and suggestions on an earlier draft of this paper.

    1. Martin M. Crow and Claire C. Olson, ed., *Chaucer Life-Records* (Oxford: Clarendon Press, 1966).

    2. Derek Pearsall, *The Life of Geoffrey Chaucer* (London: Blackwell, 1992).

    3. For editions of the manuscript, see Ella Keats Whiting, ed., *The Poems of John Audelay*, EETS o.s. 184 (1931; repr. Oxford: Oxford University Press, 2006); and

John the Blind Audelay, *Poems and Carols (Oxford, Bodleian Library MS Douce 302)*, ed. Susanna Fein (Kalamazoo: Medieval Institute Publications, 2009). Citation of MS Douce 302 texts are from Fein's edition and follow the titles and divisions used there (see the table in the present volume, pp. xiii–xviii).

4. TNA, PRO, KB 27/624, mm. 76–76d.

5. For the first notice of this record and discussion of its implications, see Michael Bennett, "John Audley: Some New Evidence on His Life and Work," *Chaucer Review* 16 (1982): 344–55.

6. For accounts of Richard Lestrange, seventh Lord Strange of Knockin, see George E. Cokayne, ed., *The Complete Peerage of England, Scotland, Ireland, Great Britain, and the United Kingdom*, 2nd ed., 13 vols. (1910–59; repr. New York: St. Martin's, 1984), 12(1):355–56; and Hamon Le Strange, *Le Strange Records: A Chronicle of the Early Le Stranges of Norfolk and the March of Wales A.D. 1100–1310* (London: Longmans, Green, 1916), pp. 339–43.

7. In 1397 Richard, aged fifteen years and more, was found to be heir to the manor of Myddle and the castle and lordship of Knockin in Shropshire and the march of Wales; a manor in Holborn, London; the manors of Colham and Uxbridge in Middlesex; and manors in Berkshire, Buckinghamshire, Cambridgeshire, Lincolnshire, Northamptonshire, Oxfordshire, and Staffordshire: *CIPM*, 17:397–99 (nos. 1095–1104).

8. Angus McIntosh, "Some Notes on the Text of the Middle English Poem *De tribus regibus mortui*s," *Review of English Studies*, n.s. 28 (1977): 385–92 (p. 386); Ad Putter, "The Language and Metre of *Pater Noster* and *Three Dead Kings*," *Review of English Studies*, n.s. 55 (2004): 498–526, esp. 500–11.

9. Lichfield Joint Record Office, B/A/1/6, fols. 140r–58v, and B/A/1/7, fols. 212r–36v; R. N. Swanson, ed., *The Register of John Catterick, Bishop of Coventry and Lichfield, 1415–1419*, Canterbury and York Society (Woodbridge: Boydell, 1990); Virginia Davis, *Clergy in London in the Late Middle Ages: A Register of Clergy Ordained in the Diocese of London Based on Episcopal Ordination Lists*, CD-Rom (London: Institute of Historical Research, 2000); and William W. Capes, ed., *The Register of John Trefnant, Bishop of Hereford (A.D. 1389–1404)*, Canterbury and York Society (Hereford: Wilson and Philips, 1914).

10. A "Richard Audeley" was ordained priest in the diocese of Lichfield in 1390 (Lichfield Joint Record Office, B/A/1/6, fol. 146r–v). Dr. Maureen Jurkowski discovered a writ relating to the arrest of Lestrange's men that does not mention Audelay, but includes a reference to John Borewell, chaplain: TNA, PRO, C 250/10, no. 24. The discovery was noted in Susanna Fein, "Good Ends in the Audelay Manuscript," *Yearbook of English Studies* 33 (2003): 97–119 (p. 100 n. 7). From Borewell's ordination, however, it would appear that he was substantially younger than Audelay and a Londoner. He was ordained acolyte by the bishop of London in December 1413 and expressly described as "of the diocese of London": London, Guildhall Library MS 9531/4 (Register Clifford), fol. 67r.

11. *Finito libro* colophon, MS Douce 302, fol. 22v (Whiting, *Poems*, p. 149).

12. J. O. Halliwell, ed., *The Poems of John Audelay: A Specimen of the Shropshire Dialect in the Fifteenth Century*, Percy Society 47 (London: T. Richards, 1844), p. v; Fein, "Good Ends," p. 101 n. 11.

13. E. K. Chambers was so tempted, but exercised scholarly restraint. He admitted once suggesting that Audelay "might have had a goliardic youth," but in the end doubted whether the penitential phrases "were more than those of conventional piety" (*English Literature at the Close of the Middle Ages* [Oxford: Oxford University Press, 1945], p. 93).

14. *CIPM*, 18:320 (no. 944).

15. Nigel Saul, *Richard II* (New Haven: Yale University Press, 1997), pp. 318 note, 370 note.

16. John Lestrange was the son of Roger Lestrange, fifth Lord Lestrange of Knockin, and Aline, daughter of Edmund Fitzalan, earl of Arundel: see Cokayne, *Complete Peerage* 12(1):354.

17. *CPR, 1399–1401*, p. 424.

18. Cokayne, *Complete Peerage* 12(1):355. Hauberk paid 400 marks for Richard's wardship and marriage (*CPR, 1401–1405*, pp. 271, 506–7).

19. *CIPM,* 18:320 (no. 944).

20. Saul, *Richard II*, p. 473; Michael J. Bennett, *Richard II and the Revolution of 1399* (Stroud: Sutton, 1999), pp. 116–21, 129–31.

21. *CPR, 1401–1405*, p. 253.

22. *CCR, 1402–1405*, p. 351. Lestrange had to reimburse Hauberk the amount he had paid for his marriage. He did so by a preferential lease of his manors in Middlesex and counties in the southern Midlands; see *CCR, 1402–1405*, p. 376.

23. *CPL, 1404–1415*, p. 140. Her family background cannot be established. If she were a daughter of Reginald Grey, third Lord Grey of Ruthin, she would have been Richard's second cousin. But there is no evidence that she belonged to that family. She may have been the daughter of Henry Grey, Lord Grey of Wilton (d. 1396) and Elizabeth, daughter of Sir Gilbert Talbot. In the papal dispensation she is described as "of the diocese of Lincoln." The Greys of Wilton, like the Greys of Ruthin, were marcher lords with lands elsewhere in England. The dowager Lady Grey of Wilton (and presumably her daughter) appears to have lived in Buckinghamshire (in the diocese of Lincoln) after her husband's death (Cokayne, *Complete Peerage,* 6:177–78). In her will in 1438, Lady Lestrange acknowledged Lord Talbot and Joyce Tiptoft, née Charlton, as her cousins (TNA, PRO, PROB 11/3, fol. 195r–v).

24. *CPL 1404–1415*, pp. 345, 387. She made her will under the name of Constance (TNA, PRO, PROB 11/3, fol. 195r–v).

25. *CCR, 1409–1413*, p. 15.

26. G. O. Sayles, ed., *Select Cases in the Court of King's Bench under Richard II, Henry IV and Henry V* (London: Quaritch, 1971), p. 227. For an account of the disorder in Shropshire, divided between factions headed by the earl of Arundel and Lord Talbot,

see Edward Powell, *Kingship, Law and Society: Criminal Justice in the Reign of Henry V* (Oxford: Clarendon Press, 1989), esp. pp. 216–24.

27. *CPR, 1413–1416*, pp. 177–78.

28. Christopher Allmand, *Henry V* (Berkeley and Los Angeles: University of California Press, 1992), p. 113; James Hamilton Wylie and William Templeton Waugh, *The Reign of Henry V*, 3 vols. (Cambridge: Cambridge University Press, 1914–29), 3:41–47.

29. The fifteen servants of Lestrange recorded in three sources, namely in Trussell's charges in King's Bench [A], the inquest of the archdeacon of London [B], and the chancery writ of *habeas corpus cum causa* [C], are, with sources and variants in brackets: Lawrence Estwyk of Knockin, esquire [ABC, of London, yeoman]; Thomas Fitzhuwe of Knockin, esquire [ABC, of London]; John Boorne of Knockin, esquire [ABC, of London]; Thomas Fitzwalter of Knockin, yeoman [ABC, of London]; Henry Holbache of London, yeoman [ABC]; Robert Came of Knockin, clerk [ABC, Robert Clerk of London, yeoman]; John Draper of Knockin, yeoman [ABC, of London]; John Bever of London, yeoman [AB, Bebere, C]; Peter Brereton of Knockin, yeoman [ABC, Peter Chambre of London]; Philip Knockin of Knockin, cook [ABC, Philip Cook of London]; John de la Chaumbre of Knockin, yeoman [ABC, John Spen of London]; John de Stable of Knockin, yeoman [John Coke of London]; Roger Chatton of Knockin, yeoman [ABC, of London]; John Audeley, chaplain, of Knockin [A]; John Borewell, chaplain [C]: TNA, PRO, KB 27/624, mm. 76–76d [A]; E. F. Jacob, ed., *The Register of Henry Chichele, Archbishop of Canterbury, 1414–1443*, Canterbury and York Society, 4 vols. (Oxford: Clarendon Press, 1938–47), 4:173–74 [B]; and TNA, PRO, C 250/10, no. 24 [C].

30. For chronicle accounts, see A. H. Thomas and I. D. Thornley, eds., *The Great Chronicle of London* (London: Jones, 1938), p. 96; James Gairdner, ed., *The Historical Collections of a Citizen of London in the Fifteenth Century*, Camden Society, n.s. 17 (Westminster: Camden Society, 1876), pp. 115–16; and Mary-Rose McLaren, *The London Chronicles of the Fifteenth Century: A Revolution in English Writing, with an Annotated Edition of Bradford, West Yorkshire Archives MS 32D86/42* (Woodbridge: Brewer, 2002), p. 193.

31. Jacob, ed., *Register of Henry Chichele*, 4:168–75.

32. Jacob, ed., *Register of Henry Chichele*, 4:173–74.

33. The appeal of mayhem was extremely rare in the fifteenth century. Mayhem was conceived as the infliction of a wound that diminished the victim's fighting capacity, and was a somewhat archaic felony. Action by appeal was likewise an old-fashioned and heavy-handed process, but had the advantage, if successful, of securing damages for the victim (Powell, *Kingship, Law and Society*, pp. 50–51 n. 19). I thank Professor Anthony Musson for clarification of this matter.

34. TNA, PRO, KB 27/624, m. 76.

35. Lestrange and Trussell "felle at debate for here wyves" (Thomas and Thornley, eds., *Great Chronicle of London*, p. 96).

36. For his career, see K. B. McFarlane, *Lancastrian Kings and Lollard Knights* (Oxford: Clarendon Press, 1972), pp. 154–59.

37. In January 1417, Henry V repeated his offer of lavish rewards for Oldcastle's capture (*CPR, 1416–1422*, p. 83).

38. Paul Strohm, *England's Empty Throne: Usurpation and the Language of Legitimation, 1399–1422* (New Haven: Yale University Press, 1998), p. 130.

39. The exact force of the term *hedge-* is unclear. It can probably be taken to mean 'common' or 'base' (literally, 'of such a kind as is met with by the wayside' or even 'conceived under a hedge': *OED*, s.v. "hedge," sb. 8). Since Lollard preachers were sometimes called *hedge-priests*, it is possible the term *hedge-knight* had similar connotations.

40. TNA, PRO, KB 27/624, m. 76.

41. Thomas and Thornley, eds., *Great Chronicle of London*, p. 96. For a discussion of the jurisdiction of the sheriffs of London and their prisons, see Caroline M. Barron, *London in the Later Middle Ages: Government and People, 1200–1500* (Oxford: Oxford University Press, 2004), pp. 159–71.

42. Thomas and Thornley, eds., *Great Chronicle of London*, p. 96.

43. Friedrich W. D. Brie, ed., *The Brut, or the Chronicles of England, Part II*, EETS o.s. 136 (London: Kegan Paul, Trench, Trübner, 1908), p. 382.

44. Jacob, ed., *Register of Henry Chichele*, 4:175. For a discussion of public penance, less common in the fifteenth century than in earlier and later times, see David Postles, "Penance and the Market Place: A Reformation Dialogue with the Medieval Church (c. 1250–c. 1600)," *Journal of Ecclesiastical History* 54 (2003): 441–68.

45. TNA, PRO, C 250/10, no. 24. I thank Dr. Jurkowski for providing me with her notes on this manuscript.

46. TNA, PRO, KB 27/624, m. 76.

47. Lestrange was released on a bail of 1,000 marks (*CCR, 1413–1419*, p. 393). The men who stood bail included Thomas Corbet, a Shropshire squire, and gentlemen from five other counties.

48. TNA, PRO, KB 27/624, m. 76 d.

49. TNA, PRO, KB 9/210, m. 39. I am again indebted to Dr. Jurkowski for sharing her notes on this manuscript.

50. *CCR, 1413–1419*, pp. 447, 458. There was a seemingly related bond in December 1417 that Lady Margaret Trussell "shall do or procure no harm to John Shawe or any of the people" (*CCR, 1413–1419*, p. 447).

51. TNA, PRO, KB 27/624, m. 76 d. The date given in the record is the quindene of Easter, strictly Sunday, April 10.

52. Swanson, ed., *Register of John Catterick*, pp. 19, 22.

53. The scheme went back to the 1340s. It was then held up by a dispute over the advowson of the Church of Hanmer, seemingly resolved in 1412. Canon Lee, "Gift of the Church of Hanmer to Haghmond Abbey, A.D. 1166–77," *Transactions of the Shropshire Archaeological and Natural History Society*, 2nd ser., 2 (1890): 194–209.

54. Marjorie M. Chibnall, "The Abbey of Haughmond," in *A History of Shropshire*, ed. A. T. Gaydon, vol. 2 of *Victoria History of the Counties of England*, ed. R. B. Pugh: (London: Oxford University Press, 1973), pp. 62–70 (65).

55. There was "a blind priest" in Cheshire in 1401–02, coincidentally the recipient of Lestrange charity. He appears in the household account of Thomas Neville, Lord Furnival, husband of Ankaretta Lestrange, heiress of the Lestranges of Blackmere: Shrewsbury, Shropshire Records and Research Centre, Bridgewater Collection 212, Box 75.14. I owe this reference to Dr. Philip Morgan.

56. *Finito libro* colophon (fol. 22v). He had made the same point earlier in the codex: "God hath me chastest for my levyng. / I thonk my God, my Grace trewly, / Of His gracyouse visetyng, / Ellus were Y lore" (*Remedy of Nine Virtues* 82–85).

57. Jacob, ed., *Register of Henry Chichele*, 4:170.

58. *Finito libro* colophon (fol. 22v).

59. TNA, PRO PROB 11/3, fol. 195r–v.

60. Whiting, *Poems*, p. 233. The sixth would have appeared in the portion of the poem now missing.

61. Richard Leighton Greene, ed., *The Early English Carols*, 2nd ed. (Oxford: Clarendon Press, 1977), p. 428.

62. Whiting, *Poems*, p. 241.

63. This poem is generally regarded as the most intensely personal treatment of this theme; see Whiting, *Poems*, p. 442; and Rosemary Woolf, *The English Religious Lyric in the Middle Ages* (London: Oxford University Press, 1968), pp. 335–36.

64. James Simpson, "Saving Satire after Arundel's *Constitutions*: John Audelay's 'Marcol and Solomon,'" in *Texts and Controversy from Wyclif to Bale: Essays in Honour of Anne Hudson*, ed. Helen Barr and Ann M. Hutchison, Medieval Church Studies 4 (Turnhout: Brepols, 2004), pp. 387–404.

65. Michael J. Bennett, "Richard II and the Wider Realm," in *Richard II: The Art of Kingship*, ed. Anthony Goodman and James Gillespie (Oxford: Clarendon Press, 1999), pp. 187–204 (p. 200).

66. F. R. Johnston, "Syon Abbey," in *Victoria History of the Counties of England*, ed. R. B. Pugh, vol. 1, *A History of Middlesex*, ed. William Page (Oxford: Oxford University Press, 1969), pp. 182–91.

67. Wylie and Waugh, *Reign of Henry V*, 3:270; James Doig, "Propaganda and Truth: Henry V's Royal Progress in 1421," *Nottingham Medieval Studies* 40 (1996): 167–79 (p. 169).

68. Christopher Cannon, "Monastic Productions," in *The Cambridge History of Medieval English Literature*, ed. David Wallace (Cambridge: Cambridge University Press, 1999), pp. 316–48 (p. 344).

69. Derek Pearsall, *John Lydgate* (London: Routledge and Kegan Paul, 1970), pp. 177–79.

70. F. J. Furnivall and Katharine B. Locock, eds., *The Pilgrimage of the Life of Man, Translated by John Lydgate*, EETS e.s. 77, 83, 92 (1899, 1901, 1904; repr. as 1 vol.,

Millwood, N.Y.: Oxford University Press, 1975), p. 5; Pearsall, *John Lydgate*, pp. 172–76.

71. There is evidence that Audelay was very familiar with the technique of alliteration; see Susanna Greer Fein, "A Thirteen-Line Stanza on the Abuse of Prayer from the Audelay MS," *Medium Ævum* 63 (1994): 61–74 (p. 62).

72. On whose soul may God be propitious.

73. Fein, "Good Ends," pp. 108–9.

74. TNA, PRO, PROB 11/3, fol. 195r–v.

75. Rosemarie Potz McGerr, ed., *The Pilgrimage of the Soul: A Critical Edition of the Middle English Dream Vision* (New York: Garland, 1999), pp. xxii–xxiii. I owe this reference to Mishka Góra. The title *Grace Dieu* was also sometimes applied to *The Pilgrimage of the Life of Man*, the first book of Deguileville's triology.

76. Wendy Scase, "Reginald Pecock, John Carpenter and John Colop's 'Common-Profit' Books: Aspects of Book Ownership and Circulation in Fifteenth-Century London," *Medium Ævum* 61 (1992): 261–74.

77. Greene, *Early English Carols*, p. 317.

The Vatic Penitent
John Audelay's Self-Representation

Robert J. Meyer-Lee

"The circumstances behind the making of the Audelay Manuscript are something of a puzzle": so pronounces Susanna Fein at the opening of one of her recent studies of Oxford, Bodleian Library MS Douce 302, the sole surviving collection of verse attributable to early fifteenth-century poet John Audelay.[1] Fein then proceeds to identify and resolve many of this manuscript's puzzles, and yet even as the insights begin to accumulate, certain mysteries inevitably deepen. One of the most significant of these is how a poet responsible for verse that seems, in many respects, profoundly ordinary could also be responsible for a manuscript that, in comparison with prior or contemporary English codices, is so unprecedented. MS Douce 302 is, simply put, the most authorially invested collection of English verse of its day. Completed in or shortly after 1426, this compilation of original, translated, and copied poems and two prose pieces in many respects represents the first fully conscious effort in English to triangulate authorship and authority with the production of not just a single literary work but a self-described "book."[2] In her study Fein shows how, among other things, the codex is organized into four distinct functional and thematic sections, how each of these possesses its own internal design, how instructional verses and other paratextual matter have been included to alert the reader to the manner in which the codex is intended to be used, and how the entirety has been carefully revised by a second scribe who was quite conscious of the relation between the authority of the poet and the unity of the book. Although continental authors such as Guillaume de Machaut and Christine de Pizan had earlier produced similarly authorially invested codices of vernacular writing, MS Douce 302 far outstrips contemporary collections of English verse in this regard—quite eclipsing, for example, Thomas Hoccleve's much more loosely organized anthologies of his own verse, which he produced in almost precisely the same period.³ What one would like to know are the circumstances that impelled, in a period in which notions of English vernacular authorship and book production were still in their infancy, the sudden appearance of a codex possessing extraordinary book-consciousness, centered to a large degree around a named *auctor-compilator*.

That the evidence of the unique qualities of the Audelay Manuscript has so long been available but until recently so little investigated indicates well, I think, the negative half of my mystery: the apparently rigorously uninteresting nature of so much of Audelay's verse, which has enticed few readers to make their way through the entire collection. For long stretches didactic, conventional, and repetitive, the collection has, with the exception of its carols and the alliterative tour de force *Three Dead Kings* (which is probably not by Audelay), tended to hide its several treasures of formal ingenuity to all but the most patient investigators. Even Eric Stanley, one of the most patient, concludes in a recent study that Audelay's poems "are sermonic rather than lyrical" and, seeking to end his essay on a positive note, declares Audelay's style "comfortable."⁴ This style frequently resembles that of the refrain poems in the Vernon Manuscript (ca. 1390), which, whatever their degree of craft, read often as workmanlike exercises in sacerdotal homily.⁵ Because of verse such as this, for too long it has been too easy to assimilate what is truly unusual about Audelay's book to the conventional and dull. And, more importantly, if we therefore simply dismiss his verse as unremarkable, we miss an opportunity to encounter the deep-seated ambivalence and constitutive indeterminacy that lie beneath the surface calm of late medieval English culture in its most predictable forms.

In an attempt to limn this ambivalence and indeterminacy, I take for my point of departure one of the most unusual features of Audelay's book: his rather obsessive habit of naming himself. Audelay's surname appears eighteen times in the codex, and sixteen of these signatures occur in the English verse itself.⁶ Given the total of 6,400 or so surviving lines of verse in the collection, this rate of explicit versified self-naming far exceeds that of any other medieval English poet, including those inveterate self-namers, Audelay's contemporaries Hoccleve and John Lydgate. Moreover, since these acts of self-naming are distributed across the collection and occur within a codex possessing many marks of intentional design, they create an impression of authorial consciousness reaching from one end of the manuscript to the other, forging a claim for unity based on the authority of the biographical.⁷ And yet, that such an otherwise apparently conventional medieval poet would be so assertive of his empirical, historically specific individuality has seemed to many unlikely, and hence the critical tendency has been to marginalize his self-naming as a quaint curiosity or somehow to assimilate it to the normative.

How the latter may be done will be evident to many readers through a brief examination of the signature stanza characteristic of the first section of the codex. Here are the final eight lines of the instance appearing at the end of this section:

> God hath me chastyst fore my levyng;
> I thong my God, my Grace, treuly,
> Fore His gracious vesityng.
>   Beware, seris, I youe pray,
>   Fore I mad this with good entent,
>   In the reverens of God Omnipotent.
> Prays fore me that beth present—
>   My name is Jon the Blynd Awdlay.
>   (*Epilogue* 500–507)

In the context of his self-derogating assertion, "God hath me chastyst fore my levyng," and his concluding request for prayers, his self-naming seems plainly to be an act of penance. In exchange for the homiletic good work he has performed for his readers, he asks for their help in saving his soul. Furthermore, since we learn little else about Audelay other than what is revealed in these acts of naming (specifically, that he is blind and, elsewhere, that he is deaf or near-deaf and sick), the sudden intrusion of his historical particularity in these acts may plausibly be construed as paradigmatic as well as penitential. That is, in these lines he names himself not only to seek the spiritual benefit of his reader's good will but also, by not occluding the reader's identification with too much personal detail, to use his person to represent the appropriate attitude and actions of a sinful, penitent Christian in general. As these lines suggest, then, the codex operates through three distinct and related discursive modes: homiletic, exemplary, and petitionary, with the exemplary mode Janus-faced in respect to the spiritual functions enacted by homily and petition (by at once instructing readers in regard to their penance and exhibiting Audelay's own).[8] As a result, penitential autobiography converges with iconographic homily, and even Audelay's stated blindness may be understood as more essentially a sign of spiritual blindness, the state of sin that contrition, confession, and satisfaction—as both exemplified and realized by this stanza—may redress. Hence, what seemed to be remarkable, Audelay's repeated self-naming, is, in this view, another example of his repetitive use of a conventional feature of late medieval vernacular poetry, in this case that of the representative penitent familiar from much devotional verse.

    This explanation of Audelay's self-naming no doubt accords with much of Audelay's design.[9] And yet, this explanation is *so* plausible that one wonders why more poets did not follow a similar strategy. That is, one wonders why, among the many earlier and contemporary manuscripts filled with English devotional verse, one does not find other authors inserting their names into their verse as beneficiaries of their readers' prayers. In many ways, such self-naming would seem to be natural to the form—the obvious thing to do at the conclusion of a poem that has been premised upon, and voiced, a theology of penance and intercession. Nonetheless, that the bulk of this sort of verse—such as, for example, the devotional poems in the Vernon Manuscript—entirely lacks such authorial self-designation suggests, rather, that authors of this verse and their readers found such self-naming not at all natural to the form. Even Hoccleve, who shows no compunction about naming himself in such secular works as the *Regiment of Princes* (ca. 1412), excludes all definite signifiers of his historically specific person from his devotional lyrics. The sheer consistency of this anonymity begs explanation, for which one might wish to invoke Leo Spitzer's influential notion of the generic medieval poetic "I"; and yet self-designating practices in other literary contexts, as Hoccleve's in the *Regiment*, makes this theory rather awkward.[10] Instead (and without raising the hoary specter, upon which Spitzer's theory depends, of the supposed medieval allergy to individuality), one may observe more simply that, when turning to the devotional lyric, authors no doubt realized that the penitentially practical and homiletically shrewd nature of this verse militated against their identifying themselves. On the one hand, if this verse was intended to be used as a penitential model for any given Christian, it would not have been especially helpful for the speaker to identify himself or herself as a particular and likely unknown individual. On the other hand, if the aim of this verse was to represent humility before God, then it would be suspiciously contrary to call attention to one's act of authorship, since spiritual pride in one's acts of penance, as any cleric would know, negates the efficacy of those very acts. Thus Audelay's repeated acts of self-naming, while explicable according to one set of norms, remain inexplicable according to another set. He names himself for what appear to be conventional reasons, but he does so within the sort of verse least likely to encourage such authorial self-designation. The puzzle thus remains.

In the remainder of this essay, I present a solution to this puzzle that consists of three interlocking pieces, which together provide an answer for why Audelay, in particular, would designate himself in the fashion that he does. These puzzle pieces are, in the order I investigate them, the influence of Langland's *Piers Plowman*, the institutional conditions of Audelay's final occupation as chantry priest, and Audelay's blindness.[11] As we will see, along with the poetic inspirations these influences supply, they also cloud Audelay's poetic practice with problems of ambivalence and indeterminacy—problems which ultimately both originate and culminate in the traumatic impact of the third influence, Audelay's blindness. The resulting explanation of Audelay's self-naming possesses implications for his achievement as a whole and also, I suggest in my conclusion, for a more general consideration of the underpinnings of late medieval devotional culture. Audelay's anomalous habit, I believe, proves to be one of those exceptions to the rule that helps make visible some of the cracks and seams of its encompassing culture.

Langlandian Poet

Over the years several scholars, and most recently James Simpson, have noticed that Audelay's verse, despite failing to alliterate consistently, nonetheless appears to emulate *Piers Plowman* in aspects of attitude, concerns, and style.[12] I believe that this influence extends even deeper and that, in particular, Audelay possesses an acute appreciation for how Langland's masterpiece is suffused with, organized around, and places its greatest literary aims within a notion of authorial biography. In contending this, I have in mind the understanding of *Piers Plowman* developed by Anne Middleton in a series of illuminating articles.[13] In this view of the poem, the work's self-referentiality, and the pseudo-autobiography of its poetic *maker* this entails, constitute the poem's most profound formal apparatus for seeking the reform of its readers' souls and the institutions of its world. *Piers Plowman* (especially the long versions) proceeds as an evolving representation of charity that is at the same time a thoroughgoing (but ultimately, and necessarily, incomplete) defense of itself as a material instance of charity. Langland's very description of what *do-well* means, in other words, seeks to include itself as an act of doing well, and thus the poem, as a labor of authorship, attempts to perform before our very eyes (or at least show the results of) the ideal life of penitential labor that the poem advocates. The story of the life of the poem's "maker" thereby becomes central to the question of the poem's salvific efficacy: if the labor of creating *Piers Plowman* defines a life of charity, then the life of the poem's *maker* necessarily becomes a paradigm for that of the reader. And yet, conversely, for this life story to operate in this fashion, it must be interpreted by the reader as a good work and responded to accordingly: that is, only through the reader's construal of this story as an instance of *do-well*, and corresponding proper response, does the poem, in fact, become such an instance. If instead, say, the reader merely enjoys the poem's colorful personifications of sins and is thereby distracted from its message of penance—or if the reader finds Langland to be the unregenerate "loller" that the poem repeatedly charges him to be—Langland's life of poetic making can be neither paradigmatic nor a labor of charity. This is the great wager and genius of Langland's poem: that the spiritual statuses of text, author, and reader are mutually and reciprocally constituted. In this design, if one reads the poem correctly, one has redeemed the poem, its labor of authorship, and—at least potentially—one's own soul.

At first glance, the Audelay codex would seem to share little with this design. Most prominently, instead of the extended narrative that is the design's fundamental armature, Audelay's book consists of a collection of relatively short poems on a variety of topics, not unified by any readily apparent narrative frame nor even containing individual poems (with the exception of *Three Dead Kings*) of an especially narrative character. Nonetheless, there is an *implied* overall narrative in the codex—a narrative which, much like that of *Piers Plowman*, provides the literary work with both an organizing principle and overall spiritual function. This is the narrative of the author's death and, in particular, his attempt to die in as much of a state of spiritual beatitude as possible. As Fein demonstrates, the topic of dying well pervades the codex, and it is especially closely tied to Audelay's methods of formal closure. Each of the codex's four major sections, for example, concludes with either a meditation upon dying or a petition in regard to death's spiritual determination, and the final section is wholly devoted to "matters pertaining to readiness for death."[14] Audelay thus uses the supposedly imminent occurrence of his own death as the basic spiritual challenge the work seeks to overcome, the paradigmatic manner of overcoming it, and the organizing formal principle of the collection. Audelay, that is, seeks to die well by deploying his final energies on creating a codex that systematically urges his readers, through his own example, to die well.

One illustration—from the two stanzas preceding the signature stanza quoted above (viz., *Epilogue* 469–94), which together conclude the first section of the codex—will have to suffice to illustrate these aspects of Audelay's design. In the first of these stanzas, Audelay—as a conclusion to a section of verse that has been monitory, homiletic, and in a few instances visionary in nature—petitions the "Treneté" for the "grace" to die well, to achieve a "good endyng" by forsaking his "syn" and "foly" in this world before leaving it, and to experience "purgatory" as worldly "payne" before he dies. In itself, the sentiment of this stanza, with its closing petition, "To grawnt me grace of good endyng," would supply a fitting finale to this poem and section. Yet, to execute his overall design, in the next stanza Audelay supplements this conclusion with an autobiographical context for this petition, an image of the poet lying "seke" in "an abbay here be west," producing, "with gret dolour," the very "boke" that we are reading, during moments when he "myght not slep ne have no rest" (presumably the result of his earthly "payne"). He continues by recording his prayer to "Heven Kyng," in which he "knowlache" that "hit is the best / Mekelé to take" the "vesetyng" of his suffering, and this prayer both culminates this mini-narrative and serves as further instruction for the poem's readers—as the proper response to the misery of terminal illness. Along with the signature stanza that follows, the effect of these stanzas is to transform the didactic verse that preceded them into the implicit story of Audelay, on his deathbed, forsaking his life of sin and folly by doing the good work of warning others to so forsake this life. Together with other such references to the relation between the making of this book and the spiritual status of the author's death (the final one of which I discuss next), these three stanzas point the reader to a narrative frame in which the largely non-narrative material of the codex may be triply understood: as at once the story of a historically specific author's deathbed penance, the actual product of that penance, and a implicit paradigm for the actions readers should take before dying.

Just as Langland's poem seeks to instruct its readers to *do-well* by defending its own making as a labor of doing well, then, Audelay's codex seeks to instruct its readers to die well by providing the representation and actual product of the labor of dying well. For both authors, the biographical fact of the particular author's life is essential to the paradigmatic function of author and work. Moreover, in both cases the most crucial method by which this biographical fact is activated is through what Middleton has termed for Langland's work its signature system.[15] The eighteen repetitions of Audelay's surname operate as a simplified version of such a system. Although most of them are not accompanied by the autobiographical contextualization supplied at the end of *Epilogue*, their sheer repetition ensures that the fact of the author's circumstances are kept in view as the codex evolves its meditation on dying well through its four sections.

This evolution culminates, naturally, in the last stanzas of the codex, in which one witnesses the final pointer to the quasi-narrative frame and, as well, some of the potential problems this literary strategy entails. In the penultimate stanza, Audelay declares,

> Herfore Y have dyspysed this worlde,
> And have overcomen alle erthely thyng.
> My ryches in heven with dede and worde
> I have ypurchest in my levyng,
> With good ensampul to odur gefyng.
> Loke in this book; here may ye se
> Hwatt ys my wyl and my wrytyng.
> All odur by me war for to be!
>   Bewarre, brether, Y yow pray,
>   Yowre mysdedes that ye amende
>   Owte of thys worlde or that ye wende,
>   For alle ys good that hath good ende.
>   Thus conseles Jon the Blynde Awdelay.
>   (*Conclusion* 27–39)

As the labor of his book-making reaches an end, Audelay insists that, by despising "this worlde" and overcoming "alle erthely thyng," he has led his life to a good end; he has "ypurchest" postmortem "ryches in heven" through his mode of "levyng"—which, most germanely in this context, consists of the "dede" of book-making, the "worde" of its text, and the "good ensampul" he has thereby given his readers throughout the codex. Next, to bring to final fruition the triple role these lines suggest for the codex—as instructions to the reader, as a depiction of his own good work, and as a material instance of that work—he turns, at this crucial moment, to a direct command: "Loke in this book; here may ye se / Hwatt ys my wyl and my wrytyng" (32–33). The reader's response to the book, inscribed by this command at that book's very end, completes the book's design: in the very act of looking "in this book," the reader transforms a neutral material artifact into a relic of the penitential labor of "Jon the Blynde Awdelay"; in the reader's subsequent discernment of the "wyl" or intent of the book's "wrytyng" to be the desire for others to be "war" by the author's example, that penitential labor obtains potential spiritual value; and if the reader indeed does "amende" his or her "mysdedes" before death and thereby obtain a "good ende," that potential value is fully realized. With the reader's "good ende," the spiritual intent of the work is activated, Audelay's claim for the book is borne out, and his good end is reciprocally constituted by the ends of our act of reading and of our own lives.

All this depends, of course, on the reader in fact doing what he or she is commanded to do in this stanza. In other words, the final intent of the work exists in the work itself only as a surmise—as a fiction, in the imperative mode, of its own completion. Whether the work actually ends well—and thus whether Audelay's labor of authorship achieves its spiritual value and Audelay himself ends well (to the extent that the penitential labor of this book is decisive in the matter of his soul)—is finally left open as an imagined possibility. And that there are alternatives to this possibility is evident in the rather different command Audelay issues at the opening of the next and final stanza of the codex:

> No mon this book he take away,
> Ny kutt owte noo leef, Y say forwhy,
> For hit ys sacrelege, sirus, Y yow say!
> Beth acursed in the dede truly!
> (*Conclusion* 40–43)

Considered in isolation, the anathema voiced in these lines appears fairly conventional—a common sentiment, along with the request for prayers that follows, of bookplates.[16] But in the context of a codex in which the biographical and the bibliographical are so intertwined, the anxiety of the bookplate, here embedded within Audeley's thirteen-line stanza, is one and the same as the anxiety of authorship. In particular, with the command to "kutt owte noo leef," Audelay fears that the reader may fail even to be a reader. He or she may fumble at the first step—"Loke in this book"—and, instead of transforming a neutral artifact into a relic of Audelay's labor, treat that artifact as merely matter, cutting out a "leef" to serve as material for some other purpose. Obviously, failing this first step, the reader will be unable to discern Audelay's intent and respond to it accordingly, and therefore none of the imagined good ends will be achieved. Seeking to counter this outcome, Audelay insists, in his shrewd adaptation of the bookplate anathema, that the artifact possesses spiritual value independent of the reader's actions: since it would be "sacrelege" to treat the artifact as mere matter, subject to physical reappropriation, it must already be, before the failed reader encounters it, a reified relic of Audelay's holy endeavor. That is, because the failed reader, in place of achieving a good end, will be "acursed in the dede," the author escapes the tyranny of reader response in the determination of his book's meaning and value: the book has the power to save if the reader responds appropriately, and it has the power to damn if the reader does not. In either case, the book ends well, and hence so does, presumably, Audelay's life.

And yet, as with the command to the reader in the previous stanza, this command to refrain from physical desecration of the book and that act's threatened consequences are a fiction of reader response, imagined by the author and inscribed as an element of the good end he seeks for his work. As such, this fiction is itself subject to reader response. Indeed, for readers to recognize the very terms of Audelay's threat, they must already have looked into "this book" and recognized it as an object for which the category of sacrilege is relevant; only at this point, and after they have reached the end of the work, can it be said that they possess the intent to perform sacrilege and may thus be "acursed" for it. But at this point, readers are also in position to judge the work, and if they choose to cut leaves from the manuscript, it may be because they judge the codex less spiritually valuable than it supposes itself.[17] And if this judgment is correct, the threatened curse redounds back upon the work's author, whose assertions of spiritual value become deathbed exhibitions of pride, error, or both.

In sum, if Audelay's labor of authorship is to have any value—and thus bearing on his soul—it must be judged worthy of continued material existence, and this existence is, quite literally, in the hands of the reader. Because the mutually constituted good ends of author, text, and reader may also be bad ends, the literary strategy Audelay inherits from Langland carries with it a profound ambivalence and indeterminacy. These qualities are the reason why Langland's poem, at its end, rather than obtaining resolution, famously opens out into a continued search for truth. Recognizing the inherent indeterminacy of his literary strategy, Langland inscribes narrative indeterminacy into the poem's terminus. Audelay, without the same type of narrative, and having pointed throughout to his own imminent death, instead concludes his book in perhaps the only way possible—with an epitaph that takes the form of an open-ended petition to the only reader that finally matters: "Cuius anime propicietur Deus" (May God have favor on his soul).

Chantry Poet

The influence of *Piers Plowman* thus helps to explain the pervasiveness and centrality of the historical person of John Audelay in MS Douce 302. But mysteries remain. In particular, if Langland wields such a powerful influence over the literary strategies of this verse collection, then why, indeed, is it a collection and not, like Langland's poem, a single extended narrative? Relatedly, and more to the point of this essay, why does Audelay's signature system take a form—frequent, repeated versifications of his full name in the first-person—that has no precedent in Langland? (Notoriously missing from *Piers Plowman* is any unqualified assurance that William Langland is its author.) The answer to these questions is, I think, rather obvious, even if some of its implications are not. Audelay's inspiration was, simply put, his profession as chantry priest, which supplied, I shall argue, the theological, structural, and material premises upon which Langland's influence could become operative.

As we know from the final stanza of MS Douce 302, Audelay served as the "furst prest to the Lord Strange . . . / Of thys chauntré, here in this place" (*Conclusion* 49–50), that is, initial priest to Richard Lestrange, Lord of Knockin, at his newly established chantry chapel at Haughmond Abbey, Shropshire. From external evidence, we know that Lord Lestrange, after long negotiations, established this chantry in 1424.[18] From other external evidence, unearthed by Michael Bennett in an important study, we know that Audelay earlier held the position of household chaplain in Lord Lestrange's traveling retinue, as in this role he accompanied the baron in 1417 to a notorious ambush in a London church.[19] Since Audelay dated the first section of MS Douce 302 to 1426, we may thus assume that, for about two years before this date, he had been retired from his duties as household chaplain and had been occupied with the less onerous ones of a chantry. This retirement was most likely necessitated (as I suggest below) by the onset of the blindness, deafness, and sickness that he repeatedly mentions in his verse, although the post may have also, or instead, been compensation for long service—perhaps for poetry already written. Although a chantry was in most instances a financially humble benefice, for an old and decrepit priest it was a very desirable post, one that many younger priests waited years to obtain.[20] Moreover, since after Audelay the chantry seems to have been held by canons at the abbey—the more typical arrangement for chantries established at religious houses—the initial presentation of the benefice may well have signified some special recognition.[21]

The timing and possible significance of Audelay's benefice raise the question of the chronology of the compositions that make up MS Douce 302. Given 1426 as the date of the above-mentioned colophon, we know that Audelay was, at least, actively compiling the manuscript during his time at Haughmond. Fein suggests the codex to be an authorially directed "memorial collection" that contains material written over the course of his career, a suggestion that I find likely.[22] Yet plainly some of the items—such as the *Henry VI Carol* (Henry ascended in 1422)—must have been written closer to the date of manuscript compilation, which leads one to wonder how much of the codex represents a single, sustained creative effort, rather than a systematic orchestration of mostly already written compositions. Bearing strongly on this question, in turn, is the related one of when Audelay went blind (presuming this blindness is not only figurative), since, as illustrated in the passage from *Epilogue* quoted above, many of the manuscript's items explicitly record this condition.[23] We may, I think, safely assume that he was not born blind, as this circumstance would have made his clerical training and profession rather difficult. Richard Firth Green, arguing that *Marcolf and Solomon* was composed sometime in the period 1410–13, dates Audelay's blindness to this period or before, based on the present tense of the line "Blynd as Y am" (503).[24] Yet Green's argument about the date of *Marcolf and Solomon* is not definitive (depending as it does, for example, upon the uncertain identification of the addressee Solomon with Henry IV). Simpson, whose reading of the same poem emphasizes its vexed rendering of orthodox reformist critique in an age when such critique could be mistaken for political subversion, believes that "the poem was written in the ambience of the Oldcastle Rising of 1414" but admits that the date could lie anywhere between 1409, when Thomas Arundel's *Constitutions* appeared, and 1426.[25] I find it difficult to imagine Lestrange maintaining a blind priest in his traveling retinue, and it seems to me especially unlikely that he would make provision for a blind man at the London ambush of 1417. Audelay's retirement to Haughmond Abbey reflected, I believe, his growing inability to continue his position in his lord's household because of the increasing severity of his disability. Therefore, I would date the onset of Audelay's blindness (if not total loss of sight) in the period between 1417 and 1424.

This dating does not, however, necessitate that the entire contents, or even any of the individual poems in which Audelay mentions his blindness, were first composed during this period. If Fein's argument about Audelay's personal direction of not just the compilation of MS Douce 302 but also its revisions is correct, then it is quite possible that, in the process of producing the codex, Audelay added new material to old poems, including material relating to his blindness. This supposition, then, suggests an additional approach to the mystery of Audelay's self-designating practice. For of the eighteen acts of self-naming in the codex, only two do not also mention Audelay's blindness, and, in both of these cases, the poet's blindness is stated elsewhere in the poem.[26] If, as I think is likely, all mention of Audelay's blindness represents material added during the compilation of the codex, then it follows that virtually all acts of self-naming were also included during this process. (This assumption receives further support from the fact that all but three of these acts of self-naming occur in the final stanza of a poem or in the colophon following *Epilogue*. Of these three, one each occurs in *Epilogue* and *Conclusion*, both of which were plainly composed with the codex in mind, and the third appears in the penultimate stanza of *Visiting the Sick and Consoling the Needy*, the final stanza of which is an extension of the ideas of the preceding one.) Before his retirement to Haughmond, then, Audelay may well have written versions of many of the poems in the codex that would have appeared much like the sort of freestanding, anonymous sacerdotal efforts that populate such anthologies as the Vernon Manuscript. His collection, and likely revision, of this verse into a book formally and thematically unified by an implied autobiographical narrative, anchored by repeated acts of explicit self-naming, thus coincides with his assumption of duties as a chantry priest.

For Audelay, who in these years was probably becoming gradually both blind and deaf and hence increasingly cut off from experience of the external world, these duties must have had profound internal resonance. Unlike other chantry priests, his disabilities would have prevented him from fulfilling most of the nondevotional duties often included in the position, such as the maintenance of the estates that make up the chantry's endowment. Audelay's entire professional life, then, would at this point have been devoted to saying daily masses and prayers for the soul of Lestrange and likely also those of Lestrange's wife, relatives, and ancestors, as well as those of any others whom the baron may have included in the chantry's foundation charter.[27] Audelay would have understood this activity, moreover, as spiritually efficacious not only for these souls but also for his own, as saying such prayers would, on the face of it, appear to be charitable labor. Indeed, what could better offer an old priest the opportunity to die well than to expire while petitioning God's (or a saint's) aid for another to die well—or, for those already dead, to mitigate the consequences of the state of their death?

In its function, its verbal form, and the physical space of its practice, this activity provides a straightforward analogy to the Audelay codex. In regard to function, Audelay's collection seeks to perform precisely the chantry priest's double purpose of saving the souls (or lessening their punishment) of both himself and the subjects of his speech. In regard to verbal form, Audelay's poems, like the masses and prayers of the chantry priest, are pre-scripted utterances composed according to pre-established forms, ordered systematically, and, in theory, infinitely repeatable. And in regard to physical space, in parallel with the discrete physical space that houses the repeatable performances of the chantry priest, MS Douce 302 provides a discrete textual space housing the repeatable performances of Audelay's poems—a parallel reinforced by the traditional association of architectural tropes not only with the reading of sacred and devotional texts but also with their composition.[28] Audelay's book, therefore, in aim, literary form, and material realization may be understood as the codicological equivalent of a perpetual chantry chapel, although with two crucial changes: in the codex, he takes the place of Lord Lestrange, and the reader takes his place. In other words, if Audelay's book is structured like, and functions as, a chantry, then Audelay himself is the chapel's founder, the form and contents of the poems are the foundation charter—that is, the determining textual structures of behavior and thought—and readers are the successive chaplains who animate these structures, thereby bringing about spiritual alms for the author and incurring spiritually productive labor for themselves. Although these correspondences may seem somewhat overly sophisticated, they in fact follow directly from the convergence of the straightforward understanding of the codex as penitential memorial with the consideration that it was compiled during the very period in which Audelay was taking up his duties as chantry priest. However consciously intentional this design may be, Audelay, with this codex/chantry, seeks to save his soul (or mitigate its punishment) by having his readers/priest perform labor that also saves their souls. From the perspective of this analogy, the peculiarities of MS Douce 302, rather than being inexplicable, appear instead—as the work of a blind chantry priest and Langlandian poet anxious about dying well—almost inevitable.

In particular, the mystery regarding Audelay's acts of self-naming would seem to be entirely dispelled. Unlike the intentions of normative penitential verse, which, as I have mentioned, encourage anonymity, the basic intention of the perpetual chantry requires the naming of its founder—indeed, it requires the daily repetition of the founder's name, *ad infinitum*, and not just for the benefit of his or her particular soul but also as a *memento mori*, the concrete signifier to the living of the universal inescapability of death.[29] This is, as we have seen, precisely the effect of Audelay's self-designation: as "founder" of the codex, he compels the repeated recollection of his name for both the benefit of his soul and as a paradigm for the reader, who will one day face death as Audelay represents himself facing it.

The poem perhaps most essentially chantry-like is, fittingly, the final one in the codex, which begins,

> Here may ye here now hwat ye be.
> Here may ye cnow hwat ys this worlde.
> Here may ye boothe here and se
> Only in God ys all comforde.
> (*Conclusion* 1–4)

The repeated, anaphoric deictic opening the first three lines refers readers most immediately to the image of death evoked by the preceding poem, *Three Dead Kings*, but—given that these lines inaugurate the conclusion of the codex—they also refer to the concern with death of the collection as a whole, which thereby is conceived as a book-length reminder to readers of the inescapability of their deaths. After more instruction in this regard, the poem continues with the passage quoted above, asserting the good end that Audelay has achieved, offering the author as model for readers, and then, at the beginning of the codex's final stanza, expressing anxiety toward proper reader response. Such anxiety, since it adapts a bookplate anathema, may seem particular to a literary work, but in fact it also rather closely parallels that which is evident in the detailed instructions founders left regarding their chaplains' qualifications, required activities, and even how they ought to live the minutiae of their lives—such as the food they may eat, the apparel they may wear, and the places and times in which they were allowed to see women (if at all).[30] The founders' concerns were quite rational: they had paid for prayers to be said dutifully and with dignity; anything less would be both a financial setback and spiritually ineffective. For a chantry chapel to be at all efficacious—for it to be not simply a lavish, wasted expenditure—it must possess a priest whose labor consists of unequivocal works of holiness. Audelay, in the final stanza of his poetic chantry, conceives of his reader's response in a parallel manner:

> No mon this book he take away,
> Ny kutt owte noo leef, Y say forwhy,
> For hit ys sacrelege, sirus, Y yow say!
> Beth acursed in the dede truly!
> Yef ye wil have any copi,
> Askus leeve and ye shul have,
> To pray for hym specialy
> That hyt made your soules to save,
>   Jon the Blynde Awdelay.
> The furst prest to the Lord Strange he was,
> Of thys chauntré, here in this place,
> That made this bok by Goddus grace,
>   Deeff, sick, blynd, as he lay.
>   (*Conclusion* 40–52)
> *Cuius anime propicietur Deus.*

Instead of somehow harming the codex through ignorance or improper response, the reader ought to obtain a "copi": he or she ought to be presented, like a new chantry priest, to the chapel and its charter—that is, to Audelay's "bok" and its contents—receiving thereby both instructions for, and a material object of, holiness. As a cantarist/reader, then, one's fundamental duty is "To pray for hym specialy," that is, the founder/author, "Jon the Blynde Awdelay," who made this poetic chantry not just for his own soul but also for the souls of those who act the part of cantarists. If the concluding five lines, with their past-tense verbs ("was," "made," "lay"), strike us, as Fein suggests, as Audelay somehow speaking from beyond the grave, then this may well be the poet's intent, as this impression so precisely conveys the relation between founder and chantry chaplain.[31] And, as if to ensure that we do not mistake this intent at this crucial moment, Audelay leaves us with a visual cue for it, the image of himself as "prest" of Lord Lestrange's "chauntré," providing a final model for how we, having completed the book, ought to respond.

Audelay's duties as chantry priest thus provide a powerful overall framework for his codex and, as well, a legitimate reason to depart from the convention of anonymity. But this influence, like Langland's, brings with it some problems. Already evident in the above discussion is the problem of indeterminate reader response, which we have seen also attends Langland's influence. The twofold anxiety evoked by this indeterminacy—that readers may not respond to the work in a manner that justifies its spiritual aims, and (less apparent in Langland) that reader neglect or hostility may spell the very historical demise of the work—is duplicated in the historical vicissitudes of the chantry chapel. Chaplains may not perform their duties as prescribed, and, as often happened, chantries may fail to be perpetual because of institutional or economic difficulties or—as was in fact the case for all English chantries with the Edwardian Chantries Act of 1547—a major shift in how they are culturally interpreted. Audelay, becoming increasingly disabled in his years as chantry chaplain, was no doubt aware of the fragility of the institution, a recognition that shows up, by analogy, in his closing plea to "kutt owte noo leef" but instead obtain a "copi" and thereby help make his literary effort perpetual. For both chantry and codex, founders/authors must confront the inevitable fact of their deaths; the chaplains/readers whom they seek to control through the detailed prescriptions of charters/texts, and upon whom their souls depend, will soon be radically out of reach, their chantries/codices subject to the flux of history in which they are no longer active participants.

In addition, in his specific chantry position, Audelay faced the different but equally far-reaching problem of the vitiating potential of worldly glory and material self-interest. Chantries, just like the private chapel in which he earlier served, were at once spiritual institutions and secular, socioeconomic status symbols.[32] And they were especially so the latter when, like that of Lord Lestrange, they were established by a still-living founder. To be able to afford a perpetual chantry—in comparison with the much less costly obits or lights—was a conspicuous, material statement of one's wealth, stature, and influence; chantries like Lestrange's were in this respect an institutional monument to the baronial family's heritable nobility, joining ancestors and successors, the living and the dead, in a perpetual public display of privilege.[33] Such a patent mixture of the sacred and profane was, as one might expect, objectionable to some reformists of the time, as evident in Wycliffe's charge that chantry founders "were seldom if ever free from the pride of Lucifer in wishing to perpetuate their name in the world."[34] Criticism like this would have underscored to Audelay the fact that, although beneficed, he was still very much beholden to Lord Lestrange financially, especially since the latter was still alive. Indeed, in Audelay's new position, the relation between his income and his loyalty to his secular lord was perhaps even more pointed then it was in his prior role as household chaplain. While in that role he likely had administrative duties and oversight of the spiritual needs of various household members, his basic occupation in his new role was singularly devoted to the baron—his fundamental responsibility being to pray for Lestrange's soul in an institution that provided the baron not only potential spiritual rewards but also considerable cultural capital. Audelay was, in short, an agent as well as recipient of Lestrange's wealth, and hence his labor in this capacity, as spiritually selfless as it sought to be, was inescapably to some degree both worldly and self-interested: as Lestrange's chantry priest, his petitions to God were always also instruments of personal income and vehicles of aristocratic splendor.

It is perhaps the very desire to transcend this self-interest and worldliness that, paradoxically, helps to make the codex so self-regarding. By taking on the role of Lestrange as "founder" of the codex, Audelay substitutes his spiritual self-interest as penitent Christian for his own and his lord's worldly self-interest. As an object of his readers' prayers, he potentially evades the taint that may come from being the subject who prays for the soul of the man who pays him precisely for that purpose. Yet, even so, perhaps because he was aware that Lord Lestrange remained his patron in this very project, he cannot but end his codex, as we have seen, by inscribing his actual relation to this patron. This concluding visual cue to his general readership is thus, in addition, a final acknowledgment to a *specific* reader that, whatever else Audelay may be, he was Lord Lestrange's "furst prest."

These problems—of the ambivalence and indeterminacy associated with self-interest and reader response—are so deeply inherent in the chantry analogy in Audelay's case that one might conclude that it is these, rather than their containing literary model, that initially motivated Audelay's adoption of the analogy.[35] That is, Audelay, in the compilation of this codex, may have turned to the analogy of the chantry chapel not, initially, for poetic inspiration but as a means to negotiate the spiritual challenges inherent in his occupation. Whether or not this was his conscious intent, however, the codex that he produced under the aegis of his new position gives urgent spiritual questions a discrete material form, one that stands as an attempt to resolve these questions even after his spiritual destiny is fixed by death.

Blind Poet

What remains to be understood, at this point, is why Audelay in particular, among the many readers of Langland and chantry priests in the early fifteenth-century, would have felt compelled to resolve these questions in this form—that is, to respond to this nexus of influences and their attendant problems by *recapitulating* them in the form of a book. Why, in other words, would Audelay write and collect verse at all, rather than just devote himself to the seemingly less equivocal duties of prayer? Although with this question we enter the murky waters of authorial motivation, I believe we must venture thither, since to answer only how the codex came to take its peculiar form, without exploring what motivated its creation in the first place, does not fully explain its unprecedented status.

Fortunately, in respect to the motivation behind his self-designating practice, Audelay has left us with one major clue: as mentioned above, each of Audelay's acts of self-naming are somehow associated with his blindness, and most often his surname is formulaically adjoined to the epithet "blind." Indeed, from the sheer repetition of this formula, one might be inclined to dismiss it as merely formulaic, but instead of leaving this habit of Audelay's thereby undisturbed I would like to call attention to it as, precisely, a habit—that is, as a repetition compulsion. If my supposition is correct about the coincidence of the onset of Audelay's blindness, his composition of the self-naming stanzas, and the compilation of the codex, then this repeated declaration of his condition would seem to possess considerable interpretative bearing. But even if my supposition does not hold, Audelay's codex-wide self-characterization as blind remains a stylistic tic, which, with each iteration, recalls the onset of his blindness. Part of the grammar of his identity, these repetitions are not merely habitual but symptomatic of this onset as a traumatic event.

Without invoking the entire machinery of psychoanalysis associated with trauma theory, I believe that some of this theory's insights help make visible the motivations behind Audelay's production of MS Douce 302.[36] In this theory, trauma is an overwhelming psychological (and often also physical) event for which an individual lacks the psychic infrastructure needed to process it. As a result, the individual does not, in a sense, experience the event; it remains latent in the individual's psyche as a sort of unrecognized open wound. This latency persists until a second, somehow analogous event, occurring in the context of a more developed psychic infrastructure, catalyzes the effects of the first. As Jean Laplanche observes, "it always takes two traumas to make a trauma," with the later trauma emerging as an ambiguous sign of the earlier one, bringing it belatedly into the foreground in some unresolved state, where it may become the mysterious center around which aspects of the psyche, including conceptions of one's identity, organize themselves.[37] For Audelay, the later, catalyzing trauma is the onset of blindness. The earlier, catalyzed trauma must, of course, remain a matter of speculation; for the purposes of my argument, it is enough to assume that some such trauma was psychically extant. But a good, if not certain, candidate for this trauma is Audelay's presence at and possible participation in the aforementioned London ambush.[38] This event occurred on Easter Sunday, 1417. After an earlier, verbal altercation in the Church of St. Dunstan's in the East between Lord Lestrange and one Sir John Trussell—causing a disturbance that provoked the intervention of three London aldermen—Lord Lestrange foreswore his pledge of peace and returned to the church at vespers with belligerent intent. Bennett's description of what follows, following various contemporary sources, captures vividly the grossness of the ensuing attack:

> Sir John Trussell was back at church and busy in his devotions when in burst Lord Lestrange and a group of squires "with swords, daggers and shields, and helmets on their heads," shortly followed by Lady Lestrange. . . . Her husband then unsheathed his sword, and shouted to his retainers, "Steke him, sle him!" His followers threw Trussell to the ground, hacked into him with their swords, severely maiming his left arm and viciously wounding his son and a number of servants who attempted to defend their lord. One valiant parishioner, wishing to avert the fighting and sacrilege, was dealt a mortal blow, and died at his home a short while afterwards.[39]

According to Trussell's later charges in the court of King's Bench, "John Audelay, chaplain . . . had assisted, abetted and procured the defendants [the squires who directly inflicted the violence] for the perpetration of the felony"; and Audelay was, apparently, convicted of this charge, although no record of his sentence has been found.[40] While this conviction, as Bennett notes, does not necessarily entail that Audelay committed the crimes of which he was accused, at the very least it means that he was present at, and failed to prevent, this bloody ambush of a sixty-eight-year-old, unarmed fellow Christian, who was praying in God's house on the most sacred of days.[41] This crime, universally condemned by ecclesiastical and temporal authorities, was such a patent desecration of holiness that one as evidently pious as Audelay was must have wondered, at times, if it could be forgiven.

As readers of MS Douce 302 at least as far back as Ella Keats Whiting have noticed, Audelay plainly considers his blindness to be a chastisement from God, one which he not unlikely associated, as Bennett suggests, with such a grave and public sin.[42] The repeated acts of self-identification, then, as "John the Blind Audelay," are precisely what trauma theory would expect: they are miniature reenactments of the catalyzing traumatic event, the onset of his blindness, which he is compelled to repeat in some figural fashion because the earlier, catalyzed event remains incompletely assimilated in his psyche. Or, perhaps it would be more accurate to say that the earlier event has been assimilated, but in the form of an unresolved question at the center of Audelay's identity, "the story of a wound that cries out, that addresses us in the attempt to tell us of a reality or truth that is not otherwise available."[43] For Audelay, this "reality or truth" is that of damnation, and the "story" of his "wound" is the question of the referential status of his blindness. In contrast to the patients Freud saw, Audelay lived within a culture that possessed a relatively well-defined, unquestioned theodicy, one in which psychic wounds were always also theological signifiers. His blindness, in catalyzing the trauma of the ambush (or other earlier event), therefore necessarily evokes the urgent psycho-theological question—the unfinished story—of the precise meaning that this physical trauma to his body lends to the spiritual trauma of his misdeed. Is his blindness, that is, a mark of continued divine disfavor for the deed, a physical affliction either bestowed as a goad toward more complete contrition or imposed as a sign to others of the consequences of sin? Does his loss of sight, in other words, parallel and signify a more fundamental—and more traumatic—loss in his soul?

In this regard, one may observe how very frequently blindness is mentioned in other contexts in the codex. Stanley has produced a useful compendium of many of these references, toward the aim of suggesting that they, as well as the ones adjoined to his name, lack necessary autobiographical valence: "There is nothing," he concludes, "to suggest that Audelay thinks of blindness other than as an affliction common to fallible humanity."[44] And yet, noticing how invariably these references to blindness possess negative connotations, one might just as well read the "affliction common to fallible humanity" back into the signifying field of Audelay's personal physical trauma. With blindness everywhere in his book signifying humanity's fallen nature, the empirical "John the Blind Audelay" becomes himself a concrete universal for fallible humanity. In this way, Audelay brilliantly fuses the conventional and the autobiographical—or the iconographical and the empirical—but in so doing he necessarily raises dark implications for the status of his soul.[45]

Alternatively, Audelay's blindness may represent his earthly purgatory and thereby signify, rather than disfavor, divine forgiveness—or even special election, the elevation of a returned prodigal son to an esteemed position of exemplarity. His blindness may, that is, signify in its very physical loss a compensatory fullness, a bodily imperfection that indexes, through its imagined complement, a spiritual becoming-perfect.[46] In this regard, we may notice that purgatory—that realm of becoming-perfect par excellence—is, as one might expect, a topic of very frequent interest in the codex, several instances of which consider not just the purgatory after death but also the possibility of serving one's sentence while still on earth.[47] In particular, in *Visiting the Sick*, Audelay advises the reader that "hit is fore the best / To have thi payne, thi purgatorye, / Out of this word or that thou dye" (126–28), a phrase that he tellingly repeats, as we have seen, in the highly self-conscious conclusion of the first section of the codex, only modifying it to be part of a petition to God and to refer specifically to himself: "To have my payne, my purgatory, / Out of this word or that I dy" (*Epilogue* 478–79). These two statements, when combined with that moment at the end of the codex in which he declares, "My ryches in heven with dede and worde / I have ypurchest in my levyng" (*Conclusion* 29–30), create a mini-narrative in which Audelay offers advice, takes that advice himself, and realizes its fruition. At the conclusion of the codex, the implication is that the petition that he made at the end of its first section has been granted, and hence, by the mediation of the production of this codex itself, his earthly "payne" has indeed preempted his postmortem sentence.

This divine recognition of his suffering, garnered as it is through the medium of authorship, necessarily elevates the codex and its labor of construction into something themselves almost sacred. If, that is, his blindness becomes, through the auspices of the codex, a sign of compensatory fullness, then that codex and his own role as its maker correspondingly obtain a fullness of divine meaning. This quality is evident in the more visionary items in the collection (such as *The Vision of Saint Paul*), but it is especially suggested by the lines that begin, with slight variations, several of the signature stanzas in the first section. Here is the version from *Epilogue*:[48]

> Mervel ye not of this makyng,
> Fore I me excuse—hit is not I;
> This was the Holé Gost wercheng,
> That sayd these wordis so faythfully,
> Fore I quoth neuer bot hye foly.
> (495–99)

In these lines Audelay claims to inscribe into his text divine language, and although he ostensibly denies his own agency in this action, the very syntax of this denial reinforces the impression of authorial presence. In the second line of the quotation, the pronoun "hit" refers simultaneously to two gerunds, one human and one divine: it refers backward to the "makyng" that is understood to be the product of a named, human author, and forward to the "wercheng" of the "Holé Gost." By encasing this third-person pronoun within a linear space delimited by opening and closing first-person pronouns (the variation in *The Remedy of Nine Virtues* even drops the "Fore," reading, "I me excuse, hit ys not Y"; 78), the human *maker* of this verse, with the appropriate humility, tacitly identifies himself with the divine worker. In the context of this identification, the subsequent signature, "Jon the Blynd Awdlay" (*Epilogue* 507), takes on a well-defined meaning, one with a long tradition in literary history: it is the designation of the blind prophet, the suggestion that Audelay, in this codex, has been given the gift of divine vision at the mere cost of his earthly sight. In a word, blindness signifies his vatic powers as poet, and, in this function, it represents the greatest claim a poet can make. If carried through consistently throughout the codex, this representation of blindness would implicitly declare his trauma healed (or becoming-healed), the physical wound having taken the place of the psychotheological one, serving as a sign of Audelay's salvation and model for, and agent of, the salvation of others.

Few if any readers, however, find this representation consistently expressed in the codex, and this faltering may well signify Audelay's recognition that, in fact, this representation is merely that: a marker of the desire for vatic status, but necessarily not the vatic status itself. (In the same fashion, the codex as a whole marks Audelay's desire for a good end but does not, by itself, produce it.) Audelay's anxiety about his soul inevitably recurs, as attested by many of the quotations given above and insinuated even in this very stanza, in the request for prayers from his readers in its penultimate line, just before his signature: "Prays fore me that beth present" (*Epilogue* 506). Like Milton in the opening of book 3 of *Paradise Lost* (but, of course, quite a bit less grandly), Audelay counterpoints assertions of the vatic significance of his blindness with implications of divine disfavor, and it is the ceaseless *agon* between these two poles—for Audelay, between the vatic and penitential—that is at once the basic motivation of the literary effort and its impelling force.

One may wonder, at this point, why Audelay would not have successfully overcome his spiritual anxiety in the manner that was (unlike for Milton) available to him: through, that is, the very penitential mechanisms that he devotes so much of the codex to explaining and advocating. Indeed, by instead publicizing the uncertain status of his blindness in verse, he risks exacerbating his situation by committing the sin of spiritual pride (in the assertion of vatic stature) or of doubting God's justice (in lamenting his condition).[49] The answer to this question takes us back to the problem of self-interest and thus to the crucial link between the referential ambiguity of Audelay's blindness and the codicological form of his response to it. One may fairly presume that Audelay confessed the sins pertaining to his earlier trauma (be it the the London ambush or other event), was absolved, and performed whatever penance was required of him. (Lord and Lady Lestrange were required, as Bennett reports, "to lead their retainers, barefoot and in their shifts, with candles in their hands, in abject penitence through the streets of London from St. Paul's to St. Dunstan's";[50] we do not know if Audelay was among this group.) Whatever anxiety he may have still possessed—that is, what would have prevented his trauma from being assimilated—must therefore derive from incomplete contrition. As Audelay himself warns,

> Trust ye not to esy penans
> That the prest injoyns you to;
> But yif ye have veré repentans,
> And thynke never more so to do.
>   (*God's Address* 113–16)

If the earlier trauma was the London ambush, we may be sure that Audelay never thought "more so" to accompany Lord Lestrange into a church with the intent of slaying a man. But had he truly repented of all the dispositions and prior actions that led him to that point? In particular, did his manner of life at the time he compiled the codex reflect sincere, comprehensive sorrow for the full scope of his misdeed? For years he had been in service to Lord Lestrange, for which employ his role in the ambush (whatever it consisted of) was an expected duty. Later, as chantry chaplain, he was still being paid by Lestrange, still benefiting from the service that led to his crime, still assisting in the production of cultural capital (albeit within an accepted spiritual institution) for a man who had led him into profound sacrilege. In this capacity, Audelay was not unlike Claudius in act 3, scene 3, of *Hamlet*, who realizes that, as long as he continues to benefit from the results of his crime, he is not capable of true repentance: "May one be pardon'd," he wonders, "and still retain th' offense?" (56). And the plain answer is that he cannot.

Audelay's crime, obviously, was not of the same severity as Claudius's, and his absolution not nearly as unequivocally impossible, and yet his professional circumstances did not lend themselves toward fully resolving his situation in the other direction. Only by reconceiving his vocational identity in terms that would fully justify it could he seek to heal the traumatic wound still open in his soul. And it is this reconception that motivates the production of MS Douce 302, which, in this view, is an attempt to redeem his profession. To this end, the mimetic relation between chantry and codex becomes, notionally, the reverse of its likely cognitive genesis: the chantry architecture of the manuscript becomes the authentic space of spiritual labor; the actual, physical chantry at Haughmond Abbey, with its taint of self-interest, becomes the book's vitiated, fallen shadow. At the center of both is John the Blind Audelay, who is either unrepentant sinner or divinely elected vatic poet. Upon this question hangs Audelay's trauma and his soul, and the aim of the codex is to put into motion the healing of the former and the corresponding saving of the latter. But because Audelay could neither save his own soul nor heal his own trauma, he seeks to evoke—just as Langland does—the signs of grace in the completion of this motion, the determination of its outcome, by reader response. If in this response the reader concludes Audelay's blindness to be a mark of divine vision, then that reader ought to follow Audelay's instructions, which will in principle entail his or her own salvation—and this latter event would indeed confirm Audelay's vatic powers. In the end, the truth of Audelay's blindness is one and the same as the truth of the salvific power of his book.

Yet for readers of Audelay's book, as for Audelay himself, certain knowledge of this truth, outside that granted by revelation, lies only in Hamlet's "undiscovered country." The trauma of Audelay's blindness, notwithstanding the penitential armature in which it is encased, must for the living thus remain traumatic, and hence Audelay is compelled in his acts of self-naming to reenact the trauma throughout the codex, and readers are compelled to reanimate these recapitulations as they work their way through the text. Moreover, for Audelay's contemporary readers—and for any others shaped by a culture that shares an Augustinian apprehension of the human condition—these repetitions are ultimately symptoms of the trauma that lies behind all others: the trauma of the Fall. If the onset of Audelay's blindness catalyzes the traumatic effects of an earlier crime, those effects, in turn, bring to the surface the impact of the originary crime that, while constitutive of his culture and serving, in one sense, as the basis for human knowledge, must, in a deeper sense, remain unassimilable.[51] For the Fall, like the referential status of Audelay's blindness, is an unfinished story of a wound, the end of which fundamentally determines the nature of the present but which also lies out of reach, in eternity. Against this backdrop, the peculiarities of Audelay's verse dissipate, since all penitential verse—or, even more generally, late medieval devotional culture—in some way evokes the trauma of the Fall. From this perspective, MS Douce 302 is just one of many species of psycho-cultural repetition compulsion, ceaselessly recapitulating the Fall in miniature, forging an individual and cultural identity out of a traumatic loss that must be kept ever before one's eyes precisely because it cannot truly be experienced.

With this conclusion, I have in a sense returned full circle and declared that Audelay's self-designating practice is, after all, fully understandable within the normative conventions and functions of late medieval devotional verse. But to reach this conclusion, I have sought to explain how this anomalous feature of the Audelay codex complicates and broadens our understanding of the literary, historical, and psycho-cultural parameters of this verse. The poet's acts of self-naming as "John the Blind Audelay" are, I have argued, indeterminately both urgent reaffirmations of his election and ineluctable repetitions of his curse. The soteriological suspense provoking this indeterminacy is the impelling motivation of the codex; his work as chantry priest lends this motivation its physical and literary form, to which Langland's influence adds an implied autobiographical narrative. Together, these pieces go a long way toward solving the literary historical puzzle of Audelay's self-naming, and yet that self-naming itself seeks to solve a puzzle that has no earthly solution. Audelay's idiosyncrasy is thus explicable as the cross-product of the known and the unknowable, demonstrating that apparently ordinary, didactic, repetitive verse by a provincial chantry priest is, upon closer examination, riven by ambivalence and indeterminacy native, rather than alien, to normative late medieval English devotional culture. For Audelay, the potential for defusing this ambivalence and clarifying this indeterminacy rests upon the interpretation of his blindness as compensatory fullness—an interpretation that depends, in turn, upon the spiritual and material fullness of the codex that represents that blindness in its cultural context. His concluding plea not to cut leaves from this codex is thus, in addition to its other meanings, a plea for his own and his readers' souls, one that merges past and present, living and dead, subjects and objects, and material and spiritual in a single imperative: a command that was, as the missing leaves attest, unheeded.

NOTES

1. Susanna Fein, "Good Ends in the Audelay Manuscript," *Yearbook of English Studies* 33 (2003): 97–119 (p. 97). The findings and rich suggestions of this study have greatly inspired the present essay. A preliminary version of this paper read at the "Books, Authors, and Authority" session at the International Congress of Medieval Studies at Kalamazoo (5 May 2005) garnered helpful feedback; I thank Olivia Remie Constable for organizing this session.

2. For example, from Audelay's *Conclusion*, "Loke in this book; here may ye se / Hwatt ys my wyl and my wrytyng" (32–33). Citations of MS Douce 302 are from John the Blind Audelay, *Poems and Carols (Oxford, Bodleian Library MS Douce 302)*, ed. Susanna Fein (Kalamazoo: Medieval Institute Publications, 2009). The date 1426 is supplied in the Latin prose colophon (*Finito libro*) following Audelay's *Epilogue* to *The Counsel of Conscience*. Fein believes this dates only the first section of the codex, which she takes to be an earlier book incorporated into MS Douce 302, and thus the date of the latter falls sometime after this (see "Good Ends," p. 104).

3. Between 1422 and 1426 (the year of his death), Hoccleve collected his shorter poems into two holograph manuscripts, now San Marino, Huntington Library MSS HM 111 and HM 744. For full descriptions and reproductions, see J. A. Burrow and A. I. Doyle, introduction to *Thomas Hoccleve: A Facsimile of the Autograph Verse Manuscripts*, EETS s.s. 19 (Oxford: Oxford University Press, 2002).

4. Eric G. Stanley, "*The True Counsel of Conscience*, or *The Ladder of Heaven:* In Defence of John Audelay's Unlyrical Lyrics," in *Expedition nach der Wahrheit: Poems, Essays, and Papers in Honour of Theo Stemmler*, ed. Stefan Horlacher and Marion Islinger (Heidelberg: Carl Winter, 1996), pp. 131–59 (p. 155). In another article—"The Verse Forms of Jon the Blynde Awdelay," in *The Long Fifteenth Century: Essays for Douglas Gray*, ed. Helen Cooper and Sally Mapstone (Oxford: Clarendon Press, 1997), pp. 99–121—Stanley argues for Audelay's authorship of *Three Dead Kings*, but Fein persuades me to the opposite view ("Good Ends," p. 108 n. 22).

5. For just one example, see Audelay's versification of the Ten Commandments in *True Living* 143–55 and the Vernon lyric "Keep Well Christ's Commandments," in *Religious Lyrics of the XIVth Century*, ed. Carleton Brown, 2nd ed., rev. G. V. Smithers (Oxford: Clarendon Press, 1957), pp. 148–51 (no. 102; *IMEV, NIMEV* 1379). Such resemblance is perhaps not merely coincidental. Ella Keats Whiting, ed., *The Poems of John Audelay*, EETS o.s. 184 (1931; repr. Oxford: Oxford University Press, 2006), notes several other poems that echo or even parallel ones in the Vernon MS: *Virtues of the Mass, Prayer of General Confession, Vision of St. Paul, Salut. to Mary, Five Senses Carol*, and *Seven Gifts Carol* (pp. 235, 238, 241, 244–45, 249–50); and Derek Pearsall, *Old English and Middle English Poetry* (London: Routledge and Kegan Paul, 1977), noting a further echo, speculates that Audelay "may have used" the Vernon MS (p. 249).

6. For a list, see Whiting, *Poems*, p. xv n. 5.

7. Whiting prints 6,377 lines of verse from the imperfect Audelay MS, which, as Fein estimates, may have contained additionally "as many as nineteen leaves before the first folio and five more internally" ("Good Ends," p. 98). Whiting does not print the two pieces of English prose and a Latin poem, as Fein also notes. Although half the signatures occur in the first section, this section comprises over two-thirds of the verse in the surviving folios (4,331 lines in Whiting's edition), which suggests that Audelay may have begun to name himself with slightly more frequency in the latter sections, thereby strengthening the continuity in this regard. For Hoccleve's and Lydgate's habits and frequency of self-naming, see my *Poets and Power between Chaucer and Wyatt* (Cambridge: Cambridge University Press, 2007).

8. This analysis of the interlocking spiritual functions of the manuscript largely follows Fein, "Good Ends," pp. 100–103. See also Whiting's comments in *Poems*, pp. xv–xvi.

9. Stanley, *"True Counsel,"* pp. 131–43, voices this view, which elaborates comments of Tim William Machan, *Textual Criticism and Middle English Texts* (Charlottesville: University of Virginia Press, 1994), pp. 103–4.

10. For just one example of Hoccleve's devotional lyrics, see poem 4 in part 2 of Frederick J. Furnivall and I. Gollancz, eds., *Hoccleve's Works: The Minor Poems*, 2nd ed., rev. Jerome Mitchell and A. I. Doyle, EETS e.s. 61, 73 (London: Oxford University Press, 1970), pp. 283–85 (*IMEV, NIMEV* 4233). For Spitzer's widely adopted (although, of late, oft-criticized) formulation of the medieval poetic "I" as "representative of mankind," see his "Note on the Poetic and the Empirical 'I' in Medieval Authors," *Traditio* 4 (1946): 414–22.

11. A fourth puzzle piece, which possesses somewhat less bearing, and which for reasons of scope I do not discuss, pertains to Audelay's earlier occupation as household chaplain and the parallels that this occupation has with those of contemporary Lancastrian poets Hoccleve and Lydgate.

12. See James Simpson, "Saving Satire after Arundel's *Constitutions*: John Audelay's 'Marcol and Soloman,'" in *Text and Controversy from Wyclif to Bale: Essays in Honour of Anne Hudson*, ed. Helen Barr and Ann M. Hutchison, Medieval Church Studies 4 (Turnhout: Brepols, 2004), pp. 387–404.

13. In particular, Anne Middleton, "The Audience and Public of 'Piers Plowman,'" in *Middle English Alliterative Poetry and Its Literary Background: Seven Essays*, ed. David Lawton (Cambridge: Brewer, 1982), pp. 101–23; "Making a Good End: John But as a Reader of *Piers Plowman*," in *Medieval English Studies Presented to George Kane*, ed. Edward Donald Kennedy, Ronald Waldron, and Joseph S. Wittig (Woodbridge: Brewer, 1988), pp. 243–63; "William Langland's 'Kynde Name': Authorial Signature and Social Identity in Late Fourteenth-Century England," in *Literary Practice and Social Change in Britain, 1380–1530*, ed. Lee Patterson (Berkeley and Los Angeles: University of California Press, 1990), pp. 15–82; and "Acts of Vagrancy: The C Version 'Autobiography' and the Statute of 1388," in *Written Work: Langland, Labor, and Authorship*, ed. Steven Justice and Kathryn Kerby-Fulton (Philadelphia: University of Pennsylvania Press, 1997),

pp. 208–317. Middleton's argument about *Piers Plowman* is complex and wideranging; my characterization of Langland's poem in what follows, while it derives from hers, is necessarily narrower.

14. Fein, "Good Ends," p. 107.

15. Middleton, "William Langland's 'Kynde Name,'" p. 38 and passim.

16. See, for example, the items collected as numbers 89–94 in Rossell Hope Robbins, ed., *Secular Lyrics of the XIVth and XVth Centuries*, 2nd ed. (Oxford: Clarendon Press, 1955). I owe this observation to Andrew Cole.

17. For speculation that some of the actual damage to MS Douce 302 may indeed be the result of motivated suppression (for political rather than spiritual reasons), see Michael Bennett, "John Audley: Some New Evidence on His Life and Work," *Chaucer Review* 16 (1982): 344–55 (pp. 352–53). I take up in more detail the findings of this revealing study in the final section ("Blind Poet") of the present article.

18. See Marjorie M. Chibnall, "The Abbey of Haughmond," in *Victoria History of the Counties of England*, ed. R. B. Pugh, vol. 2, *A History of Shropshire*, ed. A. T. Gaydon (London: Oxford University Press, 1973), pp. 62–70 (p. 65).

19. See Bennett, "John Audley," p. 348.

20. See K. L. Wood-Legh, *Perpetual Chantries in Britain* (Cambridge: Cambridge University Press, 1965), pp. 231–33, and, for additional evidence suggesting that chantries as retirement sinecures were the exception to the rule, Alan Kreider, *English Chantries: The Road to Dissolution* (Cambridge, Mass.: Harvard University Press, 1979), pp. 26–28. In the following discussion, all general information about chantries and their chaplains, unless otherwise specified, I take from Wood-Legh.

21. For the Haughmond canons, see Chibnall, "Abbey of Haughmond," p. 65; for the religious as the usual chaplains of chantries in their houses, see Wood-Legh, *Perpetual Chantries*, p. 130.

22. Fein, "Good Ends," p. 109.

23. The manuscript also mentions Audelay's deafness, although much less frequently: I count just four times in verse—*Epilogue* 20, *Salut. to St. Bridget* 202, *Dread of Death Carol* 8, and *Conclusion* 52—and once in the *Finito libro* colophon. Since the instance in *Epilogue* puts this condition in future tense—"blynd, def to be" (20)—Fein, seeking to explain how a deaf poet could communicate his ideas about the codex and the details of revision to his scribes, credibly supposes Audelay's hearing to be "failing but not lost" ("Good Ends," p. 98 n. 2).

24. Richard Firth Green, "Marcolf the Fool and Blind John Audelay," in *Speaking Images: Essays in Honor of V. A. Kolve*, ed. Robert F. Yeager and Charlotte C. Morse (Asheville, N.C.: Pegasus, 2001), pp. 559–76 (pp. 566–67).

25. Simpson, "Saving Satire," p. 391.

26. These two cases occur, respectively, in *Marcolf* 1008, which is complemented by the aforementioned earlier reference to Audelay's blindness in the poem, and in the Latin heading to *Salut. to St. Bridget*, at the end of which poem the poet characterizes himself as "both blynd and def, the sinful Audelay" (202).

27. Unfortunately, this charter has not survived. Whiting quotes a later prescription for the chantry's recipients of prayer, apparently made by Richard Lestrange's son John in 1476, that requires "a daily mass to be said at the Altar of St. Anne, Mother of the Virgin, for the souls of the said John and Jacinta, of Richard, late Lord Strange, and Elizabeth his wife, parents of John, and of Constancia, former wife of the said Richard" (*Poems*, p. xv).

28. For this traditional association, see Mary Carruthers, "The Poet as Master Builder: Composition and Locational Memory in the Middle Ages," *New Literary History* 24 (1993): 881–904. In emphasizing the influence of the late medieval English chantry on the composition of vernacular devotional verse, my argument here dovetails with the one Ann R. Meyer makes about *Pearl* (*Medieval Allegory and the Building of the New Jerusalem* [Cambridge: Brewer, 2003], esp. the book's final chapter, pp. 155–86).

29. For example, in the chantry for Sir Thomas Lovell (d. 1524) in Holywell Priory Church, Shoreditch, windows were once inscribed with verse that might be considered a doggerel equivalent to Audelay's signatures: "All ye nuns of Holywell / Pray ye both day and night / For the soul of Sir Thomas Lovell / Whom Harry the Seventh made Knight"; see G. H. Cook, *Mediaeval Chantries and Chantry Chapels* (London: Phoenix House, 1947), p. 33. Such features of chantries as *transi* tombs are striking indicators of their *memento mori* function.

30. For founders' prescriptions pertaining to their chaplains, see chap. 10, "The Chantry Priests' Daily Life," in Wood-Legh, *Perpetual Chantries*, pp. 234–70.

31. See Fein, "Good Ends," pp. 108–9.

32. For private chapels and their chaplains, see Kate Mertes, *The English Noble Household 1250–1600: Good Governance and Politic Rule* (Oxford: Blackwell, 1988), especially chap. 5, pp. 139–60. For the socioeconomic function of chantries, see Wood-Legh, passim, and the comment in her conclusion: "That the love of ostentation played no small part in inspiring and shaping the founder's designs is manifest" (p. 305). See also the corroborating findings in P. W. Fleming, "Charity, Faith, and the Gentry of Kent 1422–1529," in *Property and Politics: Essays in Later Medieval English History*, ed. Tony Pollard (New York: St. Martin's, 1984), pp. 36–58; and for more background, Cook, *Mediaeval Chantries*, chaps. 1–2, pp. 7–39; and Kreider, *English Chantries*, chaps. 1–3, pp. 5–92.

33. For a convenient description of the lesser intercessionary institutions of obits and lights, see Kreider, *English Chantries*, p. 8.

34. Qtd. in Wood-Legh, *Perpetual Chantries*, p. 305.

35. Langland's influence, too—as best illustrated in the famous authorial *apologia* in Passus 5 of the C version—also brings with it the problem of self-interest, although on this point I cannot here elaborate.

36. Reaching back to the beginnings of Freud's career—see, for example, Joseph Breuer and Sigmund Freud, *Studies in Hysteria* [1895], trans. A. A. Brill (Boston: Beacon, 1950)—and much elaborated since, trauma theory has in the last decade or

so attracted considerable attention from literary scholars. For the modes of reading and sets of problems this theory introduces into the interpretation of literary texts, a frequent touchstone is Cathy Caruth, *Unclaimed Experience: Trauma, Narrative, and History* (Baltimore: Johns Hopkins University Press, 1996)

37. Jean Laplanche, *New Foundations for Psychoanalysis*, trans. David Macey (Oxford: Blackwell, 1989), p. 88; qtd. in Heather Hirschfeld, "Hamlet's 'first corse': Redemption, Trauma, and the Displacement of Redemptive Typology," *Shakespeare Quarterly* 54 (2003): 424–48 (p. 425). (Hirschfeld's wide-ranging, provocative essay on *Hamlet* has inspired my application of trauma theory to Audelay.) See also the formulation by psychoanalyst Juliet Mitchell, "Trauma, Recognition, and the Place of Language," *Diacritics* 28 (1998): 121–33 (p. 121).

38. I assume here, once again, that Audelay's blindness postdates 1417. But my argument does not depend on this sequence, since the opposite one would simply switch the roles of catalyzing and catalyzed trauma. Or, for an alternative explanation, see n. 42, below.

39. Bennett, "John Audley," p. 347.

40. Bennett, "John Audley," p. 348.

41. For some of the details here, see the account of the event in K. B. McFarlane, *Lancastrian Kings and Lollard Knights* (Oxford: Clarendon Press, 1972), pp. 157–58. Trussell is one of the supposed Lollard knights whom McFarlane shows to be a rather unlikely candidate for that label.

42. Although Bennett's claim about Audelay's interpretation of his blindness is made more convenient by the assumption that the chaplain became blind after 1417, the flexible temporality of sin, punishment, and God's foreknowledge—as well as the logic of trauma—would enable Audelay to recognize an earlier onset of blindness as punishment for the disposition toward sin that he would later commit, and perhaps even as God's unheeded attempt to help him forestall it.

43. Caruth, *Unclaimed Experience*, p. 4.

44. Stanley, "In Defence," p. 140.

45. For a perceptive discussion of how, in medieval literature, the categories of conventional and autobiographical may overlap rather than oppose each other, see J. A. Burrow, "Autobiographical Poetry in the Middle Ages: The Case of Thomas Hoccleve," *Proceedings of the British Academy* 68 (1982): 389–412.

46. This point derives in part from ideas about the semiotic properties of relics developed by Seeta Chaganti, "'A Form as Grecian Goldsmiths Make': Enshrining Narrative in Chrétien De Troyes's *Cligés* and the Stavelot Triptych," *New Medieval Literatures* 7 (2005): 163–201.

47. I count nineteen times alone in which purgatory is mentioned by name: *True Living* 1; *Marcolf* 928, 933; *Virtues of the Mass* 250; *Visiting the Sick* 102, 121, 127, 138, 143, 154, 358, 364; *Vision of St. Paul* 222; *God's Address* 119, 142; *Epilogue* 331, 478; *Salut. to Jesus* 108; and *St. Francis Carol* 22.

48. See also *Remedy of Nine Virtues* (where the signature is in the following stanza), *Visiting the Sick*, *Lord's Epistle*, and *Vision of St. Paul* (listed by Fein, "Good Ends," p. 101 n. 10).

49. These sins were, incidentally, among those that were regarded as especial temptations at the end of one's life: see Dennis Siy, "Death, Medieval Moralities, and the *Ars Moriendi* Tradition" (PhD diss., University of Notre Dame, 1985), pp. 63, 67.

50. Bennett, "John Audley," p. 347.

51. For a full development of this point, which I merely summarize here, see Hirschfeld, "Hamlet's 'first corse,'" p. 432 and passim. Although Hirschfeld's argument pertains specifically to the early modern English culture that inspired *Hamlet*, this culture, especially as mediated by Shakespeare in this particular play, has much bearing on that of late medieval England, as has been recently shown by Stephen Greenblatt, *Hamlet in Purgatory* (Princeton: Princeton University Press, 2001).

John Audelay and John Mirk
Comparisons and Contrasts

Susan Powell

Since so few medieval writers can be both identified by name and positioned in a sociocultural and geographic context, there is some value in considering John Audelay and John Mirk. The fact that they lived within a generation of each other in time and wrote their extant works within fifteen miles of each other in space links them further. The fact that both were priests and that they shared an association with the order of Austin canons provides sufficient points in common to justify this essay, which will investigate the comparisons and interrogate the contrasts between the two men.

The present volume provides much material on John Audelay.[1] The facts that are relevant now are as follows. His name is known (although the spelling varies).[2] He was alive, but sick, blind, and deaf, in 1426, when he was chaplain to the chantry of Richard Lestrange, lord of Knockin, at the Austin canon house of Haughmond Abbey in Shropshire.[3] He had previously served as Lestrange's household chaplain and had been implicated in a notorious case of murder and sacrilege instigated by Lord Lestrange on Easter Sunday 1417 in St. Dunstan's in the East, London.[4]

Less is known of John Mirk, but it is of some interest, amongst the large number of writers of sermons and pastoral manuals, that his name is known.[5] There is no precise date associated with his work, unlike that of Audelay, but he is likely to have written his three known works, the *Instructions for Parish Priests*, the *Festial*, and the *Manuale Sacerdotis*, perhaps in that order, from the late 1380s on.[6] The *Festial* explicit, in a part of the manuscript that appears to be late fourteenth or early fifteenth century, refers to him as dead ("cuius anime propicietur deus").[7] From the available evidence, he was canon and later prior of Lilleshall Abbey in Shropshire, not far from Haughmond, another Austin canon house.[8]

The two men clearly led different lives. As chaplain to Lord Lestrange, Audelay will have travelled with his retinue (as is clear from his presence in the London church on Easter Sunday 1417) and will have led a more social, even worldly, life than was available to Mirk in his small and remote abbey. He will have had regular duties which involved performing the various offices required daily of a priest, some at least in the presence of his master and entourage, of which the most important was the celebration of the Eucharist, rarely performed daily and certainly not received by the laity frequently.[9] He is likely to have been confessor to Lord Lestrange and/or various of his family. His pastoral duties will have involved the education of the household in the main tenets of the church and in their duties to God and to their neighbor.

As for Mirk, he lived in an altogether more humble milieu. Lilleshall Abbey was typical of Austin canon houses in being small. Shropshire was at the time remote, governed by major landlords, of whom Richard Arundel was chief (Lestrange was a powerful tenant of his), but far from the metropolis, the seat of power and culture.[10] As a royal foundation (traditionally founded by Æthelflæd, queen of Mercia), it was not without status, and in January 1398, when parliament was held at Shrewsbury, John of Gaunt and a large retinue stayed at Lilleshall, but that was an unusual event, with which the abbey simply could not cope.[11] As an Austin canon, Mirk led a life midway between that of the regular (monk) and the secular (parish priest), and it may be that he served as parish priest to one of Lilleshall's endowed churches at some time in his career, perhaps St. Alkmund's, Shrewsbury.[12] He was not, therefore, entirely enclosed but, if he indeed had a cure of souls at any time, it was to a poor parish of largely illiterate men and women.

All three of Mirk's works are highly pedagogic in intent and focus. His aim is to provide the basic knowledge to be taught to the people by their parish priests or curates (in the *Instructions*), to provide ready-made sermons for the ill-equipped priest or curate (in the *Festial*), and to guide a fellow priest in how to live a life appropriate to his sacred calling (in the *Manuale*).[13] The *Instructions* is a 1,934-line pastoral manual in rhyming couplets,[14] which offers the parish priest guidance on his duties, particularly in relation to pastoral instruction (69–535), hearing confession (675–1698), the sacraments of baptism and confirmation (536–674), and the performance of the last rites (1699–1838). In the course of the work, Mirk deals with the Paternoster and Ave Maria (404–25), the Creed (426–53), the articles of the faith (454–525), the seven sacraments (526–35), the Ten Commandments (849–972), the seven deadly sins (973–1302), the seven deeds of mercy (1355–64), and the seven virtues as remedies for the seven deadly sins (1551–1624).

The *Instructions* therefore covers material which it had long been the duty of the priest to teach, but which had acquired greatest importance through the 1281 Lambeth *Constitutions* of Archbishop Pecham of Canterbury, and, more recently but for the other province, through the 1357 injunctions of Archbishop Thoresby of York, the vernacular version of which is known today as *The Lay Folks' Catechism*.[15] As chaplain to the Lestranges, Audelay will have had the same duty of teaching as Mirk, and many of his poems present, in different forms, the same tenets as the *Instructions*, for example, the essential basics of the Paternoster, Ave, and Creed;[16] the threefold rule of penance: contrition, confession, and satisfaction;[17] the Ten Commandments of the Old Testament and two precepts of the New Testament;[18] the multiple sevens of the seven deadly sins, the seven deeds of mercy, the seven sacraments, and the seven petitions of the Paternoster.[19] In particular, *True Living* and *Virtues of the Mass* offer comprehensive verse instructions not dissimilar to Mirk's much longer treatise, while the carols of the third section of the manuscript provide discrete versified teaching on the Ten Commandments, the seven deadly sins, the seven works of mercy, and the seven gifts of the Holy Ghost. An alliterative item in the fourth section offers a versified exposition of the Paternoster directly comparable with Mirk's *Festial* sermon on the subject (Erbe no. 69).

Other instructional material in Audelay is part of the general religious culture of the period and can be replicated in Mirk's three works, for example, the importance of the sacrament of marriage,[20] the correct behavior in sickness and at the point of death,[21] how to comport oneself during the elevation of the Host[22] and the various benefits incurred by seeing the Host at this moment,[23] details of fasting,[24] and so on. The only medieval authority cited by Audelay is one of the two main sources used in Mirk's *Festial*, John Beleth, author of the *Rationale divinorum officiorum*, a compendium on the feast days and ritual of the church year.[25] Even minor and seemingly idiosyncratic details, such as the fact that the rich need to be charitable to the poor since the latter will judge the former at the Day of Judgment, or that the souls in hell are released from suffering from Saturday noon to the first hour of Monday, are part of a common pool of pastoral material.[26] Other material, such as the warning to treat the book with care and to let others read it, is also conventional.[27]

The *Festial* is a collection of sermons from Advent Sunday to the Dedication of a Church, intended for preaching on all the major feasts in the church calendar, both *temporale* and *sanctorale*.[28] Notable (and after the Reformation, notorious) are the plentiful *narrationes*, narratives or stories, serving as exempla, examples or illustrations. In some cases these overbalance the doctrinal content of the sermon, as in, for example, the sermon for Corpus Christi Day (Erbe no. 41), which has five *narrationes*, or the sermon for the fourth Sunday in Lent, where, after dealing with the Old Testament lesson of Moses and the Ten Commandments, Mirk gives over the rest of the sermon to two long and circumstantial *narrationes* of dubious spiritual benefit, separated by a brief passage of exposition.[29] Where Audelay too illustrates his teaching by a *narratio*, it is a common one, replicated in the *Festial*, such as the Saint Gregory Mass, the devil recording the chattering women in church, or the legend of Saint Martin, who cut his cloak in half to give to a beggar.[30]

The *Manuale* is a five-part Latin text of between twelve and twenty chapters in each part. Broadly it offers guidance on what makes a good and what a bad priest, following the priest through a typical day from sunrise to sunset.[31] It is specifically addressed to a fellow priest, offering seemingly personal as well as general advice and criticism, but it is also intended for wider clerical consumption, as are his *Instructions*. The *Festial* (apart from some interventions not for lay ears)[32] is for a lay audience. Audelay's audience is at first appearance not dissimilar but it is much less clearly delineated. To look at only one poem (*Epilogue*), he addresses "ye curatis" and "ye prestis," and also "breder" and "seris."[33] The exact import of "brothers" and "sirs" is unclear but is likely to refer to the canons with whom he was living, who were certainly priests (and so would be known as "sir" or "dominus") and who also lived together as monastic brothers.[34] *Epilogue* is the last poem of the first section of the manuscript and is followed by the explicit saying that this part was written "ad exemplum aliorum in monasterio de Haghmon" (as a model for others in the monastery at Haughmond).[35] Audelay also, however, addresses "Al Cristyn men" and "al . . . / That heryn or redin in this boke" (*Epilogue* 430 [cp. 235], 404–5). Indeed, he seems reluctant to pinpoint any one target, particularly in this poem, where he wakes from sleep with the unenviable task of the Old Testament prophet (like Job in *Patience*) who is obliged by God to warn men of their sins. In the following lines, for example, he moves swiftly from accusation to apology:

> I say you, breder, in Cristis name,
> To me hit were a hy slawnder
> To lye apon my blessid breder;

> Y wold youe fayne here forther,
>   Bot your wyckid dedus thay don you fame.
>   . . .
> Thagh I say soth, blamys not me—
> I blustur forth as Bayard blynd.
>   (*Epilogue* 373–77, 380–81)

The matter of Audelay's audience deserves much greater scrutiny than I can afford here,[36] but, in short, his criticism of parish priests, curates, canons, and friars together is such that might at one time have been read by scholars as Lollard in tone (although he himself warns that it is too easy to label any decent priest a Lollard).[37] So too of Mirk's criticism of priests (in the *Manuale*). For example, the first of the five parts (eighteen chapters) focuses on the priest himself: What makes a good priest? And, rather more detailed, what makes a bad priest? Good priests have due reverence for the priesthood and live unworldly lives: they avoid litigation, they despise the world, and they have not been promoted falsely. Bad priests prefer archery to contemplating the wounds of Christ, and playing ball to using the quill; they chant feebly in church but sing cheerfully enough in the pub; they are silent in the pulpit but noisy following the hounds; they chase after witticisms but are slow to look into manuscripts; they are illiterate, worldly drunks and gluttons, gamblers, fornicators, and businessmen.[38]

While this might be seen as at least para-Lollard, neither Audelay nor Mirk has the least leaning toward Lollardy, and both condemn it. Audelay's principal locus for Lollard criticism is *Marcolf and Solomon*.[39] Mirk makes only two references to Lollardy in the *Festial*, one of which is generalized and oblique,[40] but in the *Manuale* he goes into greater detail, warning against celebrating the Eucharist anywhere other than in church and explaining precisely the Lollard heresy with relation to the sacrament of the altar.[41] Criticism of bad priests and criticism of Lollards are not, however, incompatible. What in a different context might be termed anticlericalism is found amongst even the most orthodox priests of the Middle Ages, who do, however, reserve such criticism for internal airing (which is why the *Manuale* is Mirk's only work critical of the clergy and his only work written in Latin). Audelay is writing somewhat outside the narrow confines of priest to parish, or priest to priest, which identify Mirk, and his multiple (and partly imagined?) audience allows him greater scope for comment and criticism. James Simpson, for example, writes interestingly of *Marcolf and Solomon*, which preserves "a double face, both critical of heretical belief yet sharing Lollard criticisms of ecclesiastical practice."[42]

There is perhaps a certain slipperiness about Audelay which Mirk (in a less compromised and compromising position) had not needed to acquire. There are other ways too in which Audelay and Mirk differ, and this essay will move now into an exploration of the contrasts (rather than points in common) that are identifiable in Audelay compared with Mirk. I will deal here with only two, one in relation to the general content of his oeuvre, the other in relation to Audelay's own intruded presence within his writing.

First, pragmatically, much of Audelay's material (verse and prose)[43] has a private context which Mirk's does not have. It very commonly fits into the category of lay devotional reading, a focus easily explained by his career in a noble household.[44] Mirk, on the other hand, is writing for the common people in his sermons, addressing them through the medium of much the same ill-educated curate that he addresses in his *Instructions*;[45] in the *Manuale* he addresses a higher class of priest.[46] All three works are pragmatic and didactic, intended for preaching and teaching. Audelay covers similar material, as we have seen, but he also includes material that is characteristic of the late Middle Ages—meditative, devotional, directed at private reading rather than public declaration or dissemination, targeted at a middle-class lay audience. None of Audelay's prose sermons survives, although we may assume he delivered such sermons. Instead of a series of Christmas sermons, however, the manuscript has a series of carols for the Christmas period from December 25 through to January 6, that is, Christmas Day to Epiphany, again presumably for use in an informal lay context.[47]

Audelay's devotional material includes poems like those that treat of the seven bleedings of Christ, the seven words from the Cross, or the Hours of the Passion. Typically, such material encourages meditation on Christ's Passion through a recitation of his sufferings, as in *Prayer on Christ's Passion*, which ends with an invocation to "Say this oreson everé day" (38); or the multi-item *Psalter of the Passion* (W6) containing the hymn *Anima Christi sanctifica me*, a Latin prayer *O Deus qui voluisti* (W6.29–58)—parallel to the preceding *Prayer on Christ's Passion*—and a closing Latin prose prayer to release the sinner who recites the hymn from the pains of hell and lead her/him "quo perduxisti latronem tecum crucifixum" (whither thou brought the thief crucified with thee); or the versified *Prayer of General Confession* (W10), which opens with the Saint Gregory Mass and the pardons attached to it and ends with a prayer to Christ on the Cross. These poems often conclude with multiple recitations of the Paternoster and Ave, and with the promise of pardon, even specific numbers of days of remission. For example, *Seven Bleedings of Christ*,[48] begins each of fifteen stanzas (like the popular prayer, the Fifteen Oes) with the invocation to the Holy Name ("O Jhesu") and ends with fifteen Paternosters and fifteen Aves.[49] Rather like the round robins which have today metamorphosed into e-mail messages, the poem ends with the promise that good things (in this case, the bliss of heaven) will come to the person who passes the message on: "He that techis another mon this, / He schal be sekyr of heven blis" (*Seven Bleedings* 134–35). So too the *Salutation to Jesus for Mary's Love*, where all but the last stanza of lines 91–159 invoke in their first lines "O Jhesu." Eventually this sequence ends with the encouragement: "Wel ys hym that wil and may / Say this prayere every day" (*Instr. for Prayer 8* 1–2; W19.177–88).[50] In the multi-item *Devotions at the Levation of Christ's Body* (W8), one is to say a prayer on both knees in adoration of the sacrament of the altar as a way to gain pardon:

> Of that sacrament,
>   He schal have this pardon
> Of his synns, remyssione;
> Thus I fynd ewretyn
>   Of Pope Enocent.
>   (*Instr. for Prayer 5* 4–8; W8.67–70)

Such poems often have Latin rubrics, commonly at the start of the poem, as in *God's Address to Sinful Men*: "Hec . . . Domini docebit vos" (These things says the Lord God: "Return to me, for I have redeemed thee. I do not wish the death of a sinner, but rather that he turn and live." For he called the Cananaean and the publican to repentance, and also the one who wept for [her, i.e., Mary Magdalene's] sin. And so you also, unbelievers, come and hear, because I will teach you the fear of the Lord).[51] The longer poems, like this one, are intercalated with Latin subheadings (largely scriptural), rather in the manner of *Piers Plowman*, which are then translated and expounded in the following stanzas, for example, between lines 8–9, "Ego . . . sua," (I am God, Judge and Just, and I give to each one according to his deeds); between lines 24–25, "Non . . . penitenciam" (I came not to call the just, but sinners to repentance); between lines 32–33, "Magis . . . unum" (There is more joy in heaven over one man); and so on. Sometimes the Latin rubric at the beginning is more than just a title to the poem, as in *Our Lord's Epistle on Sunday*, which translates as "Hear these things, all peoples: the Lord Jesus

Christ wrote this letter with his own hands and sent it to the city of Gaza where I, Peter, accepted the first episcopate," or *The Vision of Saint Paul*: "[Here] begins the narration in which Michael led Paul to hell. It must be inquired who first asked that souls have rest in hell, i.e., the apostle Paul and the archangel Michael. The day of the Lord is the chosen day." Sometimes the poem ends with a lengthy rubric, as in the much-quoted ending to Audelay's *Epilogue* at the close of the first section of the manuscript, *The Counsel of Conscience* proper:

> The book is finished. Praise and glory be to Christ. The book is called *The Counsel of Conscience*, thus it is named, or *The Ladder of Heaven and the Life of Eternal Salvation*.[52] This book was composed by John Audelay, chaplain, who was blind and deaf in his affliction, to the honor of our Lord Jesus Christ and to serve as a model for others in the monastery of Haughmond. In the year 1426 A.D. May God be propitious to his soul.

Sometimes the Latin serves as refrain, as in "Magnificat anima mea dominum" (my soul doth magnify the Lord) in the *Song of the Magnificat*, or the changing refrains of the *Joys of Mary Carol*.

Prominent in this genre, poems to be read and prayed privately, involving meditation on the sufferings of Christ or on his life and that of his saints, are the salutations of the second part of the manuscript (W19–W27; cp. too W8 and the carols W44–W46). So called because they begin "Hayle" (Latin *salve*), three salutations—*Salutation to Mary*, *Gabriel's Salutation*, and *Mary Flower of Women Carol*—are addressed to the Virgin Mary, the object of a memorable salutation, when the angel Gabriel at the Annunciation addressed her: "Ave Maria" (Hail, Mary).[53] Another focuses on her response to the angel, the words of the Magnificat. These poems invoke the angelic salutation and call on the Virgin with familiar terms and metaphors, such as "maid and moder," "mayd and wife,"[54] "rose without thorne," or "rose of/on ryse."[55] They are often incantatory and exhortatory as they call on the Virgin in familiar tropes: by her five joys;[56] by the lily which traditionally stood between her and the angel at the salutation;[57] by her titles of lady of earth, queen of heaven, and empress of hell.[58] Other salutations focus on the Host itself (*Salutation to Christ's Body*), Saint Bridget, Saint Winifred, the Virgin's mother Saint Anne, and the Holy Face.[59] Amongst the carols of the third section are similar prayers for the Virgin, her mother Saint Anne, Saint Francis (seemingly written for friars),[60] and Henry VI (later to be prayed to, rather than for, when he became a putative saint and the focus of a cult).[61]

The *Salutation to the Holy Face* deserves a little more scrutiny as an example of lay devotion, since it is not just intended for declamatory recitation (each stanza begins with the Latin *salve*), nor just for prayerful repetition of each stanza, nor is its significance that it offers plenary remission when recited over twenty days (as the Latin rubric promises), but it is also accompanied by a visual aid in the form of a drawing of the Holy Face inserted between the Latin indulgence and the English poem.[62] Here we have a typical example of lay devotion: the visual image to accompany the text in order to focus meditation and empathy.[63] We may compare the face drawn in the initial *O* at *Pope John's Passion*, line 89, and *Salutation to Jesus for Mary's Love*, line 91 ("O Jhesu"), and in the initial *D* ("Deus") of the Latin prose prayer that concludes the *Salutation to Saint Anne*.

Finally, in terms of lay interest in the late Middle Ages, must be mentioned those poems that deal with the art of dying well, *ars moriendi*.[64] As I shall argue later, this was of fundamental concern to Audelay at this stage of his life. *Visiting the Sick and Consoling the Needy* dissects the art of dying in an analysis of the deathbed; in the *Dread of Death Carol* Audelay faces head-on his—and Everyman's (31–33)—dread of death; and the alliterative poem *Three Dead Kings* develops an important trope, serving as a *memento mori* to the living and a reminder of the leveling of estates by death, amongst other themes. *Dread of Death Carol* is, in particular, so highly personalized, with its references to Audelay's blindness, deafness, and the numbing of his senses of taste and smell, that it transcends the conventionality of the refrain "Timor mortis conturbat me," which Audelay translates as: "Dred of deth, sorow of syn, / Trobils my hert ful grevysly" (1–2).[65] Indeed, while Audelay announces the theme with the conventional text, the refrain of the subsequent stanzas is more esoteric, taken from the prayer at Mass, *Anima Christi*, attributed to Saint Ignatius: "Passio Christi conforta me" (Passion of Christ, comfort me), a reminder that mankind was redeemed from death by Christ's Passion:

> Lerne this lesson of Blynd Awdlay:
> When bale is hyest, then bot may be,
> Yif thou be nyd nyght or day,
> Say "*Passio Christi conforta me.*"
>   (*Dread of Death Carol* 61–64; W51.42–45)

Much more might be said about the manuscript as a compendium of late medieval devotional writing, but I move on now to my second point of comparison and contrast between Audelay and Mirk, that is, their status within their own writings. Mirk intrudes fairly frequently in his work in the role of author and teacher. Usually his presence is silent, signaled only by the imperatives of command (italicized below):

> Wharefore þou preste curatoure,
> That wolt plese thy sauyoure,
> ʒef thow be not grete clerk,
> *Loke thow moste* on thys werk.
> (Mirk, *Instructions* 11–14)

Furst, yf a man aske why Schere Þursday ys called soo, *say* þat in holy chyrch hit is called our Lordys supperday. (Mirk, *Festial*; Erbe, 125/3–4)

Tu igitur, karissime, . . . noli effiminari ocio et mollicie. (You, therefore, dearest, *do not* become effeminate in ease and soft living; Mirk, *Manuale*; MS Bodley 632, fol. 69r)

Often, however, he intrudes in the first person (italicized below):

> ʒet *I* wole wryte more . . .
> Fyrst se, prest, as *I* þe mynne,
> Þat þow be out of dedly synne.
> (Mirk, *Instructions* 1749–54)

Wherfor, ryght as Seynt Paule monyscheþe hys dyscypuls, ryght soo *I* monyssch you þat ben *my* chyldyr yn God, þat ʒe take not þys grace of God yn vayn. (Mirk, *Festial*; Erbe 86/17–18)

Ecce, karissime, qualiter manu solicitudinis te ad uigilandum et in uinea Dei laborandum pulso, atque ut in bonis operibus te exerceas peropto. (See, dearest, how *I* press you with the hand of solicitude to be vigilant and labor in the vineyard of God, and how *I* desire you to exercise yourself in good works; Mirk, *Manuale*; MS Bodley 632, fol. 68v)

In almost no case is Mirk subjective in his use of the first person (the only example might be in the prologue, with its conventional, though not necessarily insincere, modesty topos).[66] Audelay, on the other hand, while he uses the imperative mood and the first person in the conventional mode of preacher/teacher to the preached/teached (as Mirk does), is remarkable for his subjective and introspective use of the first person and his self-naming intrusion into his own poems.[67] I will concentrate here, as others have before me, on the penitential stanza that occurs in five poems, all in the first section of the manuscript, *The Counsel of Conscience, Ladder of Heaven, or Way of Eternal Salvation*.[68]

The first eight lines of what is always a thirteen-line stanza (rhyming *ababbabacdddc*) preserve certain lines each time they appear. I will quote the first occurrence:

> Mervel ye not of this makyng;
> I me excuse, hit ys not Y.
> Hit ys Goddus worde and His techyng,
> That he taght a salutary,
> For Y kowthe never but hye foly.
> God hath me chastest for my levyng.
> I thonk my God, my grace, trewly,
> Of his gracyouse visetyng.
> *(Remedy of Nine Virtues* 77–84)

In the other occurrences of this eight-line discrete stanza, it is the third and fourth lines only which vary. As quoted above and in *Our Lord's Epistle on Sunday* (196–203), Audelay is the instrument of God's words; in *Visiting the Sick* (378–85), he is the instrument of the words of Saint Anselm; in *The Vision of Saint Paul* (353–60), he repeats the words of Michael who led Paul to hell "be Goddis bedyng" (355); and in *Epilogue* (495–502), it is the explicit working of the Holy Ghost that enables him to speak as he does. For so seemingly self-effacing a penitent, Audelay is remarkably confident in the divine source of his inspiration.

This ambivalence, or even schizophrenia, manifests itself in this stanza: his audience must not be amazed that he can speak as he does. (Perhaps even, they must not be surprised at his impudence to speak as he does, given his own past life: "Y kowthe never but hye foly"?) Audelay is now the conduit of the word of God, a status attained by the visitation of God.[69] In striking him blind and deaf (depriving him of two of the five senses that impede man's salvation),[70] God has shown him special grace and has granted him spiritual insight. *Epilogue* records the circumstances in which he attained this status of God's prophet: "as I lay seke, in my dremyng" (27; cp. 482). As Audelay lay sick at Haughmond,[71] unable to sleep and presumably wallowing in torpor and self-pity,[72] the emissary of God appeared to him (as he had to the Old Testament patriarchs and prophets) and ordered him to save his people ("Methoght a mon to me con say"; 28). It became clear to Audelay that there was reason for his afflictions. God had visited him in order to bring him physically and spiritually to the status of the prophets (we may compare Eli in the Old Testament and Zacharias in the New Testament)[73] who prophesied in their affliction: "Thus prophecis the Blynd Awdlay" (*Henry VI Carol* 94; W39.66), "Lerne this lesson of Blynd Awdlay" (*Dread of Death Carol* 61; W51.43).

It is indeed a peculiar combination of self-aggrandizement and self-effacement. One can imagine how the realization of his role must have comforted Audelay. It would give him a new status amongst the Haughmond canons, no longer a cuckoo in their midst, looked at askance, but set there by God as an example to them ("ad exemplum aliorum in monasterio de Haghmon").[74] It was to spur him to write his book:

> And grawnt me, Lord, throgh thi gret grace,
> Sum good word that I may say
> To thi worchip, Lord, I thee pray,
> To help mon soule, that hit may,
>   That hit heren in honé plase!
>   (*Epilogue* 48–52)

> This boke I made with gret dolour
> When I myght not slep ne have no rest.
> Offt with my prayers I me blest,
> And sayd hilé to Heven Kyng:
> "I knowlache, Lord, hit is the best
> Mekelé to take thi vesetyng,
>   Ellis wot I wil that I were lorne."
>   (*Epilogue* 484–90)

Not only does Audelay recognize a new role by which he can save others, a *memento mori* to the world, for "as I was so shalt thou be":

> Here may ye here now hwat ye be.
> Here may ye cnow hwat ys this worlde.
> Here may ye boothe here and se
> Only in God ys all comforde.
>   (*Conclusion* 1–4)

He also recognizes in that role his own salvation: "God hath me chastest for my levyng" (*Remedy of Nine Virtues* 82).[75] The sins of his past (of which there were perhaps more than his known collusion in murder and sacrilege) are to be redeemed in his own lifetime, not paid for in hell. Indeed, perhaps the thinking is that he will not even see purgatory, since he is suffering his purgatory here on earth:[76] "To have my payne, my purgatory, / Out of this word or that I dy . . ." (*Epilogue* 478–79).[77] To return to the five-times-iterated stanza of penitence: the final five lines of each thirteen-line stanza function as a bob and wheel (as in *Sir Gawain and the Green Knight*) and read differently at each occurrence:

> Ellus were Y lore.
> Ever that Lorde, be he blest!
> Al that he duth ys for the best,
> Ellus were ye lyke to be lost,
>   And better unbore.
>   (*Remedy of Nine Virtues* 85–89)

> Ye curatis here, I you pray,
> That han mon soule in your kepyng,
> Let red this treté fore oné thyng
> To the seke at here endyng.
>   Thus counsels you the Blynd Audley.
>   (*Visiting the Sick* 386–90)

> Beware, serys, I you pray,
> Fore I mad this with good entent,
> Fore hit is Cristis comawndment;
> Prays fore me that beth present—
>   My name hit is the Blynd Awdlay.
>   (*Lord's Epistle* 204–8)

> Beware, serys, I you pray,
> And your mysdedis loke ye amend
> Betyme, lest ye be chamyd and schend!
> Fore al is good that hath good end.
>   Thus counsels youe the Blynd Audlay.
>   (*Vision of St. Paul* 361–65)

> Beware, seris, I youe pray,
> Fore I mad this with good entent,
> In the reverens of God Omnipotent.
> Prays fore me that beth present—
>   My name is Jon the Blynd Awdlay.
>   (*Epilogue* 503–7)

Different as they are, these five iterations have common themes: they urge the audience to penitence by Audeley's own example, and they ask for prayers for Audelay, the man marked out as special by his blindness ("My name is Jon the Blynd Awdlay"). He writes to save souls and by doing so will save his own soul—his role, as Susanna Fein has said, is dual, "at once priestly and petitionary."[78] The eight lines that precede the bob and wheel address the outside world ("Mervel ye not of this makyng"; 495), but then turn to focus inward on Audelay himself and his special relationship with God ("*I me* excuse, hit ys not *Y*. / . . . / For *Y* kowthe never but hye foly. / God hath *me* chastest for *my* levyng; / *I* thonk *my* God, *my* Grace, trewly, / Of his gracyouse visetyng"; *Remedy of Nine Virtues* 78, 81–84; my italics). In the bob and wheel, Audelay addresses his audience again, warning them of their twofold duty: to listen to his words and to pray for him. Again, despite the outward address, the focus is inward, self-referential and subjective: the first-person pronoun is present in each stanza and in four of the five the title is displayed as a badge (of pride?): "the Blynd Audley" (*Visiting the Sick* 390).

As a way of returning to the links between Audelay and Mirk, let us look at one of these five stanzas in particular, at the lines "Fore al is good that hath good end. / Thus counsels youe the Blynd Audlay" (*Vision of St. Paul* 364–65). The lines "al . . . end" appear tautologous and trite: everything is good that has a good end, Candide's "all is for the best in the best of all possible worlds." They occur again at the end of the manuscript: "For alle ys good that hath good ende. / Thus conseles Jon the Blynde Awdelay" (*Conclusion* 38–39). I would suggest, however, that there is more to the lines than is immediately obvious and that the lines are a variant of the proverb frequently used by Mirk in the *Festial*: "who so lyueth a fowle lyfe, he may be sure of a foule ende" (Erbe 56/20–21).

The proverb itself is a familiar one.[79] Mirk cites it three times in all, in the sermons for the Conversion of Saint Paul (Erbe 56/20–21) and Good Friday (Erbe 120/10–16), and in the life of Nero (Erbe 194/20–22, 28–29). In each case a wicked life is shown to result in a terrible death: a wicked man becomes insane, is tied up in his madness, and is torn apart by three black dogs; Pilate kills himself with his own knife and his body is thrown into the Tiber; Nero gnaws a sharp stake with his own teeth and impales himself on it, whereupon, before he expires, he is torn apart by wolves. (Mirk goes on to make comparison with the evil lives and deaths of Herod, Pilate, and Simon Magus.) The message is clear: an evil life will have an evil end.

I would suggest that Audeley takes a different spin on the proverb (which he might himself have used in his own preaching). He reads it as: a good end cancels out the evil of the earlier life:

> al is good that hath good end.
> Thus counsels youe the Blynd Audlay.
> (*Vision of St. Paul* 364–65)

> alle ys good that hath good ende.
> Thus conseles Jon the Blynde Awdelay.
> (*Conclusion* 38–39)

His past evil life has been redeemed by his blindness, by his newfound role as prophet, by his example to others. As noted above, he is suffering purgatory here on earth:

> Fore him I thonke specialy,
> That wit and wysdam to me hath broght
> To foresake my syn and my foly.
>   In this word here levyng,
> To have my payne, my purgatory,
> Out of this word or that I dy,
> A, gracyus God, gramarsy,
>   To grawnt me grace of good ending!
>   (*Epilogue* 474–81)

The "him" to whom Audelay prays at line 474 here is the Holy Ghost, the one who has brought to him (as to the apostles at Pentecost) the wit and wisdom to forsake the world and evangelize others.[80] The Holy Ghost is to be thanked for permitting Audelay to suffer his penance, his purgatory, in this world, before he dies out of this world. Audelay thanks God ("gramarsy") for granting him the grace of a good ending, not an ending to come but the one he is experiencing now in that abbey in the west at Haughmond. May God grant the same grace of a good ending (whatever the past life) to those who follow his counsel of conscience and who pray for his soul:[81]

> Here I conclud al my makyng,
> In the mercé of God, I have sayd before;
> God grawnt ham grace of good endyng

> That done theraftir, both lasse and more,
> And let ham never, Lord, be forelore,
> That prayn for Jon the Blynd Audlay.
>   . . .
> > For in heven thou wilt hem reward,
> >   That here mysdedis here wil amende.
> >   (*Epilogue* 1–6, 12–13)

These last lines are telling: the kingdom of heaven is the reward for those who amend their sins here on earth. In other words, whoso lives a foul life may not necessarily have a foul ending. Audelay is the proof of this:

> My ryches in heven with dede and worde
> I have ypurchest in my levyng,
> With good ensampul to odur gefyng.
>   (*Conclusion* 29–31)

I may appear to be cynical about Audelay and to have presented him as self-aggrandizing and even self-deluding, but his belief that penitence through the proper channels of contrition ("with wepyng eye"; *St. Francis Carol* 75), confession (which we must assume), and satisfaction (blindness, deafness, and the "makyng" of MS Douce 302) redeems a man's soul is, in fact, more in keeping with the teaching of Christ and the Christian Church than Mirk's insistence that a foul life has a foul ending. Certainly Audelay knew that it was sometimes the case that a foul life had a foul ending, as he has the Virgin Mary (anachronistically) say of Robert of Sicily, for example:

> Thenke on Kyng Robart Sesel:
> He went no lord had be bot he,
> Yet sodenlé downe he felle
> And was put into a folis degré!
> An angel was set apon his se,
> Fore he had these verse in his scornyng—
> *Deposuit potentis de sede*—[82]
> And sayd in heven ther was no Kyng.
>   (*Magnificat* 49–56)

But Audelay (and Mirk, and indeed every medieval Christian) knew that the grace of Christ's forgiveness and the power of his redemption of mankind through his Passion were sufficient to cancel out all sins and ensure a place in the kingdom of heaven, provided the sinner demonstrated penitence. As Mirk himself says at the end of his sermon on the Conversion of Paul (a foul life that did not end foully): "Wherfor ych man take good ensampull, whyll he ys here, by Saynt Paule, and amende hym will he hath space and tyme of amendyng. And he þat soo doþe, he schall come to Saynt Paule and haue þe ioye þat euer schall last. To þe whech ioye God bring vs all, yf hyt be his wyll. Amen" (Erbe 56/22–28).

Let me end with a *jeu d'esprit* to link Audelay and Mirk. The priest to whom Mirk addresses his *Manuale Sacerdotis* is also called John: "Amico suo karissimo domino [Iohanni] . . . Iohannes, dictus prior de Lylleshull, salutem in auctore salutis" (to his dearest friend, *dominus* John . . . John, entitled prior of Lilleshall, [sends] greetings in the name of the author of salvation).[83] He was also, it seems, related to Mirk by blood.[84] Mirk refers to this other John constantly in the *Manuale*—he makes a statement and adds: "Ecce, *karissime*" (See, dearest); he gives a good example and adds: "Tu igitur / ergo, karissime" (therefore, you, dearest); he gives a bad example and adds: "Tu autem, karissime" (but you, dearest). He addresses him at greatest length, however, at the beginning of the *Manuale* and at the end. I will concentrate here on the preface.

Mirk's role in the *Manuale* preface is comparable to that of Audelay: he presents himself as one who has taken on the task of drawing the draught of doctrine from the well of charity for the benefit of others, and as such he is confident that he in turn will taste the draught of eternal life from the springs of the Savior. As the apostle James says (James 5:19–20), the man who turns the sinner back from his sin will save a soul from death and hide a multitude of sins. Mirk soon moves from the general to the specific to complain about those clergy who live undisciplined lives and for whom he has taken on himself "medicinam correccionis eorum uulneribus apponere" (to apply the medicine of correction to their wounds; MS Bodley 632, fol. 68r). This he will do with a strong will, with some learning, but mostly with the grace of God, and he will write to John for his benefit and that of others, as well as for his, Mirk's, own eternal merit (the terms are those in which Audelay writes, as discussed above). Those who flatter John do not love him tenderly, and those who call him "blessed" are in fact his seducers. Mirk will not be like them.

Thereafter Mirk launches into part 1 of the *Manuale* with its description of derelict priests, unsuited for their position, who have been ordained or preferred for money or for frivolous reasons (fols. 68v–69r); who have attached themselves to a worldly magnate in the hope of preferment; who are guilty of simony; and who in their appearance and manners are more like knights than priests (fols. 73v–74r). He denies the link with the other John, but with the ominous parenthesis "ut spero" (as I hope),[85] as indeed he does, pointedly, at the end of the work: "See now, dearest, how much and how tenderly I love you, when I write such friendly things to you for the use of your soul, often admonishing you by the deeds of others, never addressing you personally, wishing and desiring greatly that you should live in this perfect way in the priesthood, in so far as you may laudably receive your reward from the high priest Jesus Christ."[86]

I am not suggesting that the wayward priest John to whom John Mirk addressed his *Manuale Sacerdotis* was John Audelay. That is most unlikely, and the manuscripts anyway vary in the details of the introductory salutation.[87] It is, however, too intriguing not to fantasize briefly about the links between the two men, the one by this stage an older man, experienced, pragmatic, an Austin canon all his life, now prior of his remote abbey in the West Midlands, the other his relative and (as he says) friend, young, inexperienced, perhaps frivolous, certainly not sufficiently impressed by the gravity of the sacred order of priesthood entrusted to him. John Mirk's means of directing the other John to the correct path is partly by instruction and example, partly by the fear of God: "But because it is written, 'The fear of God is the beginning of wisdom,' therefore I want you first of all to be frightened, because fear leads to all good."[88] Mirk says this in the first chapter of the first book of the *Manuale*, following it with a *narratio* from Bede which he also uses (in the first sermon of the *Festial*), in which a man reforms his life after being taken to hell, purgatory, and heaven (Mirk deals only with hell).[89] In the last chapters of the *Manuale*, too, where he turns back to address John directly, he offers a graphic and highly rhetorical vision of hell, designed to terrify and reform. He also, however, offers the vision of heaven: "But because I have terrified you with the pains of the impious, listen now to the rewards of the just."[90] The final chapter offers then a vision of the joys of heaven: "[W]hatever we desire we shall have at once, and whatever we shall see we shall love. . . . But who will be suitable for this joy? Indeed, the true penitent, the humble obedient man, the kind friend, the faithful servant."[91]

The first in the list is the true penitent "who is always grieving for his sins, since true penitence is to grieve for one's sins without intermission."[92] It can hardly be that John Mirk had John Audelay in mind when he wrote this, nor would I even suggest that Audelay read the *Manuale* (although he might have read it). There is no need to stretch a point: the common culture of the late Middle Ages means that we can be sure that John Audelay had just such thoughts in mind when he undertook the making of his counsel of conscience:

> *The Cownsel of Conseans* this boke I calle,
> Or *The Ladder of Heven*, I say, forewy:
> Ther is no mon may clym up a walle
> Without a ladder, sekyrly;
> No more may we to heven on hye
> Without treu cownsel of consians.
> . . .
> Clyme up this ladder—then may ye se
> What joys in heven that ther be,
> And what payns in hel and turmentré.
> Then chese yourselve weder to go.
>   (*Epilogue* 417–22, 426–29)

Notes

1. An excellent lucid introduction to Audelay is provided in Susanna Fein, "Good Ends in the Audelay Manuscript," *Yearbook of English Studies* 33 (2003): 97–119. For brief mentions of both Audelay and Mirk, see Ralph Hanna, "Augustinian Canons and Middle English Literature," in *The English Medieval Book: Studies in Memory of Jeremy Griffiths*, ed. A. S. G. Edwards, Vincent Gillespie, and Ralph Hanna (London: British Library, 2000), pp. 27–42.

2. For the spellings used in the single manuscript, Oxford, Bodl. Lib. MS Douce 302, see Ella Keats Whiting, ed., *The Poems of John Audelay*, EETS o.s. 184 (1931; repr. Oxford: Oxford University Press, 2006), p. xv. (Audelay, the conventional spelling, is in fact least commonly found in the manuscript.)

3. See, in particular, the colophon to Audelay's *Epilogue*, beginning *Finito libro* (quoted below), and Audelay's *Conclusion*. For Haughmond, see Marjorie M. Chibnall, "The Abbey of Haughmond," in *Victoria History of the Counties of England*, ed. R. B. Pugh, vol. 2, *A History of Shropshire*, ed. A. T. Gaydon (London: Oxford University Press, 1973), pp. 62–70.

4. The details of this incident, unknown to Whiting, were uncovered by Michael Bennett, "John Audley: Some New Evidence on His Life and Work," *Chaucer Review* 16 (1982): 344–55. The revelation of Audelay's involvement has led to a re-evaluation of the poet and his writings of which this present volume is the culmination to date.

5. See the (Latin) explicits to his *Festial* and *Instructions for Parish Priests* in London, BL MS Cotton Claudius A.ii., fols. 125v, 154v; and to his *Manuale Sacerdotis* in, e.g., Oxford, Bodl. Lib. MS Bodley 632, fol. 98v.

6. See Susan Powell, "A New Dating of John Mirk's Festial," *Notes & Queries*, n.s. 29 (1982): 487–89; and Alan J. Fletcher, "John Mirk and the Lollards," *Medium Ævum* 56 (1987): 217–24.

7. The dating is not very precise, since the style of hand might have been acquired at an earlier stage of the scribe's career. A full discussion of the hands in MS Cotton Claudius A.ii will be provided in my edition of the *Festial* to be published by the Early English Text Society.

8. For the explicits to the *Festial* and *Instructions* that provide the evidence of his being a canon there, see n. 5, above. Mirk refers to himself as prior in the incipit to the *Manuale* (see, e.g., MS Bodley 632, fol. 68r).

9. In his *Manuale*, Mirk says that a priest is not expected to celebrate the Eucharist daily (see, e.g., MS Bodley 632, fol. 88r). To compare Lestrange with another aristocrat (although further points of contact are hard to find between them), it is worthy of note that at a later date Henry VII's mother, Lady Margaret Beaufort, received the sacrament "ful nye a dosen tymes euery yere" (John E. B. Mayor, ed., *The English Works of John Fisher*, EETS e.s. 27 [1876; repr. New York: Kraus Reprint, 1975], p. 295 [lines 25–26]).

10. For neighboring Cheshire as a cultural center, see K. B. McFarlane, *Lancastrian Kings and Lollard Knights* (Oxford: Clarendon Press, 1972), passim, and, on the Arundels and Lestranges, pp. 64–65 and 152–59, respectively.

11. For the details in this paragraph, see Marjorie M. Chibnall, "The Abbey of Lilleshall," in *A History of Shropshire* (see n. 3, above), pp. 70–80. For the 1398 visit, see further in Susan Powell, "The *Festial*: The Priest and His Parish," in *The Parish in Late Medieval England: Proceedings of the 2002 Harlaxton Symposium*, ed. Clive Burgess and Eamon Duffy (Donington: Shaun Tyas, 2006), pp. 160–76.

12. Fletcher, "John Mirk and the Lollards," pp. 220–22. See too the discussion by Powell in "The *Festial*."

13. There are two editions of the *Instructions*: Edward Peacock, ed., *Instructions for Parish Priests by John Myrc*, EETS o.s. 31, 2nd ed., rev. F. J. Furnivall (1902; repr. New York: Greenwood, 1969); and Gillis Kristensson, ed., *John Mirk's Instructions for Parish Priests* (Lund: Gleerup, 1974). For the *Festial*, see Theodor Erbe, ed., *Mirk's Festial: A Collection of Homilies, by Johannes Mirkus (John Mirk), Part I* [text and glossary only], EETS e.s. 96 (1905; repr. New York: Kraus Reprint, 1975) (hereafter cited as Erbe). For a new EETS edition of the *Festial*, see n. 7, above. The *Manuale* has not been published, but I am currently preparing a text with translation based on James Martin Girsch, ed., "An Edition with Commentary of John Mirk's *Manuale Sacerdotis*" (PhD diss., University of Toronto, 1990). All translations of Mirk appearing in this essay are my own.

14. Mirk's choice of the verse form is undoubtedly for mnemonic reasons, whereas with Audelay the reasons may be multiple and may include, e.g., personal preference or aptitude, and the comparative ease for a blind man of committing verse, rather than prose, to memory before dictation. (Milton, famously, composed at night and was "milked" [his own word] in the morning.)

15. On *pastoralia* and its origins, see Marion Gibbs and Jane Lang, *Bishops and Reform, 1215–1272: With Special Reference to the Lateran Council of 1215* (1934; repr. London: Cass, Oxford University Press, 1962), esp. pp. 94–179; R. M. Haines, "Education in English Ecclesiastical Legislation of the Later Middle Ages," *Studies in Church History* 7 (1971): 161–75; Vincent Gillespie, "*Doctrina* and *Praedicacio:* The Design and Function of Some Pastoral Manuals," *Leeds Studies in English*, n.s. 11 (1980): 36–50; and Leonard E. Boyle, *Pastoral Care, Clerical Education and Canon Law, 1200–1400* (London: Variorum Reprints, 1981). *The Lay Folks' Catechism* has been edited by Thomas Frederick Simmons and Henry Edward Nolloth, EETS o.s. 118 (1901; repr. Millwood, N.Y.: Kraus Reprints, 1973).

16. Cp. *True Living* 225; *Seven Bleedings* 110–15; *Seven Words* 97–102; *Virtues of the Mass* 114–19, 126–37, 372–83; *St. Gregory's Indulgence* 11–16; *Visiting the Sick* 289–325; etc. (The Creed is known as the *beleue*; see, e.g., *Virtues of the Mass* 32.) Reference to verse contained in MS Douce 302 is to John the Blind Audelay, *Poems and Carols (Oxford, Bodleian Library MS Douce 302)*, ed. Susanna Fein (Kalamazoo: Medieval Institute Publications, 2009).

17. Cp. *Virtues of the Mass* 150–55, *God's Address* 105–12, etc.

18. Cp. *True Living* 143–59, *Virtues of the Mass* 138–43, etc., for the former, and *Epilogue* 222–47.

19. Cp. *True Living* 160–85, *Seven Words* 1–12, *Virtues of the Mass* 120–25, 144–49, *Visiting the Sick* 23–26, 261–86, etc.

20. Cp. *True Living* 65–116 with Erbe no. 70. On the relative paucity of *pastoralia* in the *Festial*, see Susan Powell, "John Mirk's *Festial* and the Pastoral Programme," *Leeds Studies in English*, n.s. 22 (1991): 85–102.

21. Cp. the whole subject matter of *Visiting the Sick* with Mirk's *Instructions* 1699–1838 (Kristensson, *Instructions*, pp. 163–70).

22. Cp. *Devotions at the Levation of Christ's Body* and *Virtues of the Mass* (W8, W9), and *Manuale*, pt. 4 (see, e.g., MS Bodley 632, fols. 87v–92r passim). Audelay writes of lay comportment, and Mirk writes of priestly comportment.

23. Known as the *merite misse*, the merits of the Mass. Cp. *Virtues of the Mass* 1–65 with Erbe 169/31–170/2 (references to Erbe are by page and line).

24. Cp. *God's Address* 49–64 with Erbe 82/10–26.

25. *Epilogue* 321.

26. Cp. *God's Address* 197–248 with Erbe 4/33–5/11, and *Vision of St. Paul* 288–313 with Erbe 80/1–26.

27. Cp. Audelay's *Conclusion* 40–43 with Mirk's *Instructions* 1917–26 ("Rede þys ofte, and so let oþer; / Huyde hyt not in hodymoke"; Kristensson, *Instructions*, p. 175), and *Manuale:* "libellum istum semel a te lectum in angulum camere non proicias . . . sed assidue illum legens, de manibus non dimittas" (having read this book once, you should not throw it into a corner of the room . . . but reading it assiduously, you should not let it out of your hands; MS Bodley 632, fol. 68v).

28. These are service-book terms, the *sanctorale* referring to saints' feasts and the *temporale* to the other days celebrated throughout the church year. In Erbe's edition, there are seventy-four sermons (a few of which are not intended for preaching to the people or are not properly worked up).

29. Erbe 104/1–106/3.

30. *St. Gregory's Indulgence* 1–4 (cp. Erbe 173/11–28); *Virtues of the Mass* 264–341 (cp. Erbe 279/34–280/7); *God's Address* 233–40 (cp. Erbe 272/7–12).

31. Little has been written on the *Manuale*, but see Alan J. Fletcher, "The Manuscripts of John Mirk's *Manuale Sacerdotis*," *Leeds Studies in English*, n.s. 19 (1988): 105–39. See too W. A. Pantin, *The English Church in the Fourteenth Century* (Cambridge: Cambridge University Press, 1955), pp. 215–17; G. R. Owst, *Preaching in Medieval England: An Introduction to Sermon Manuscripts of the Period c. 1350–1450* (Cambridge: Cambridge University Press, 1926), pp. 47 n. 1, 245, 297; and Peter Heath, *The English Parish Clergy on the Eve of the Reformation* (London: Routledge and Kegan Paul, 1969), pp. 1–4.

32. E.g., Erbe nos. 28 and 46.

33. Cp. *Epilogue* 267 ("ye curatis"), 326 ("Ye prestis"), 54, 61, 87, etc. ("seris"), and 373, 375, 379 ("breder").

34. Austin canons were part-monk, part-priest (unlike other regular or secular clergy), so that both "breder" and "seris" would have been appropriate for them. They would all have been ordained (and so "prestis") and may additionally have held cures of souls ("curatis"), as noted above.

35. Cp. *Conclusion*, where Audelay says specifically that he has made the book "your soules to save, / . . . here in this place" (47–50).

36. For a discussion of the numerous addressees of *Marcolf*, see James Simpson, "Saving Satire after Arundel's *Constitutions*: John Audelay's 'Marcol and Solomon,'" in *Text and Controversy from Wyclif to Bale: Essays in Honour of Anne Hudson*, ed. Helen Barr and Ann M. Hutchison, Medieval Church Studies 4 (Turnhout: Brepols, 2004), pp. 387–404, esp. p. 392.

37. Cp. *Marcolf* 131–33, 669–88, and *Epilogue* 248–60.

38. Cp. MS Bodley 632, fols. 68v–76v passim.

39. See Simpson's discussion in "Saving Satire," pp. 392–401, and Derek Pearsall's discussion in the present volume.

40. For the references, see Erbe 164/14–35, 171/12–29. See also Fletcher, "John Mirk and the Lollards," pp. 218–20, and Susan Powell, "Lollards and Lombards: Late Medieval Bogeymen?" *Medium Ævum* 59 (1990): 133–39.

41. See esp. *Manuale*, pt. 4, chap. 11 (cp. MS Bodley 632, fols. 90v–91r).

42. See Simpson, "Saving Satire," p. 396, who contends that this shows Audelay's "attempts to preserve a space for orthodox yet trenchant vernacular ecclesiological satire and theology in unpropitious circumstances," i.e., after the promulgation of Archbishop Arundel's *Constitutions* in 1409 (p. 389).

43. For editions of the prose, see Susanna Greer Fein, "A Thirteen-Line Alliterative Stanza on the Abuse of Prayer from the Audelay MS," *Medium Ævum* 53 (1994): 61–74

(appendix, pp. 65–70, an extract from Rolle's *Form of Living*); and A. I. Doyle, "'Lectulus noster floridus': An Allegory of the Penitent Soul," in *Literature and Religion in the Later Middle Ages: Studies in Honor of Siegfried Wenzel*, ed. Richard G. Newhauser and John A. Alford (Binghamton, N.Y.: Medieval & Renaissance Texts & Studies, 1994), pp. 179–90 (an allegory on the chamber of the soul).

44. For an excellent overview, see Eamon Duffy, *The Stripping of the Altars: Traditional Religion in England, c.1400–c.1580* (New Haven: Yale University Press, 1992), chaps. 6–8, which deal with lay prayer, the devotions of the primers, charms, pardons, and promises. Duffy provides an excellent introduction to the context of lay piety in the late Middle Ages. For private devotional reading amongst women (both lay and religious), see, e.g., Carol M. Meale, ed., *Women and Literature in Britain, 1150–1500* (Cambridge: Cambridge University Press, 1993); Mary C. Erler, *Women, Reading, and Piety in Late Medieval England* (Cambridge: Cambridge University Press, 2002); and Denis Renevey and Christiania Whitehead, eds., *Writing Religious Women: Female Spiritual and Textual Practices in Late Medieval England* (Toronto: University of Toronto Press, 2000). For the relationship between lyrics and private devotion, see Rosemary Woolf, *The English Religious Lyric in the Middle Ages* (London: Oxford University Press, 1968); and Douglas Gray, *Themes and Images in the Medieval English Religious Lyric* (London: Routledge and Kegan Paul, 1972).

45. In his prologue (not in Erbe), Mirk says that he has compiled the *Festial* for "othur that bene in the same degre that hauen charge of soulus" and " suche mene clerkus as I am myselff" (MS Cotton Claudius A.ii, fol. 3v). For the full prologue, see Powell, "John Mirk's *Festial* and the Pastoral Programme," p. 86. In the *Instructions*, he addresses "þou preste curatoure" (11), "dere prest" (1913), "leue broþer" (1917) (Kristensson, *Instructions*, pp. 68, 174, 175).

46. He is referred to throughout as "karissime" (dearest), the usual term of address between religious.

47. The sequence from *Nativity Carol* to *Circumcision Carol*, plus *Epiphany Carol* (W33–W38, W42). They cover Dec. 25: Nativity of the Lord; Dec. 26: St. Stephen's Day; Dec. 27: St. John the Evangelist's Day; Dec. 28: Holy Innocents' Day; Dec. 29: St. Thomas of Canterbury's Day; Jan. 1: Circumcision of the Lord; and Jan. 6: Epiphany. These are the same days for which Mirk provided sermons in the *Festial* (cp. Erbe nos. 6–12).

48. For the five bleedings of Christ, cp. Erbe 45/25–46/2.

49. Cp. *Salut. to Jesus* 91–177. On the Fifteen Oes, see Duffy, *The Stripping of the Altars*, pp. 249–56, and Claes Gejrot, "The Fifteen Oes: Latin and Vernacular Versions with an Edition of the Latin Text," in *The Translation of the Works of St Birgitta of Sweden into the Medieval European Vernaculars*, ed. Bridget Morris and Veronica O'Mara, The Medieval Translator 7 (Turnhout: Brepols, 2000), pp. 213–38.

50. This salutation to Jesus is said to be "embedded" (Fein, "Good Ends," p. 115 [no. 34]) in *Salut. to Jesus*, although it gives every impression of being a separate poem.

51. The Latin is largely a gloss on the poem's refrain "Nolo mortem peccatoris" (I do not want the death of a sinner) and the first stanza (*God's Address* 1–8).

52. On Audelay's chosen titles, see *Epilogue* 416–29 and further below.

53. Cp. "Hayle, Maré, to thee I say" (*Salut. to Jesus* 1); "The angel to the vergyn said" (*Gabriel's Salut.* 1); "Ave, Maria, now say we so" (*Joys of Mary Carol* burden); and "'Hayle' to thee was swettlé sayd" (*Mary Flower Carol* 13 [W46.11]).

54. Cp. *Salut. to Mary* 2; *Joys of Mary Carol* 2, 37; and *Mary Flower Carol* 4. See too the repetition of *moder* and *mayd* in the ninth line of the first nine stanzas of *Salut. to Jesus*.

55. Cp. *Salut. to Jesus* 61; *Salut. to Mary* 74; *Tree of Jesse Carol* 35; and *Joys of Mary Carol* 36.

56. *Salut. to Jesus* 81–91; *Salut. to Mary* 166–75. For the Virgin's five joys, see the poem in an Assumption sermon in the *Festial*, with its (common) association with Saint Thomas of Canterbury (Erbe 232/22–233/31). Cp. too the repeated first phrase of the burden, "Gaude, Maria" (Rejoice, Mary), in the *Joys of Mary Carol*.

57. *Tree of Jesse Carol*; see the *narratio* in the *Festial* Annunciation sermon (Erbe 108/25–109/16).

58. *Salut. to Jesus* 21, 154–55; *Salut. to Mary* 37–39; *Mary Flower Carol* 25; and cp. Erbe 109/32–33, 224/22–23, 297/10–17. There is much useful and stimulating material on devotion to the Virgin Mary in Marina Warner, *Alone of All Her Sex: The Myth and Cult of the Virgin Mary* (London: Weidenfeld and Nicolson, 1976).

59. Mirk provides sermons for Saint Anne (Erbe no. 51), whose feast day had been honored officially since only 1383, and Saint Winifred (Erbe no. 43), whose shrine was at nearby Shrewsbury and whose cult was in his day becoming nationally as well as locally important (see Anne F. Sutton, "Caxton, the Cult of St Winifred, and Shrewsbury," *The Fifteenth Century* 5 [2005]: 109–26). He was too early (and provincial) to know much if anything about Saint Bridget, and Henry VI certainly reigned after his death.

60. We have no record of Audelay's associations with friars, and he is critical of them (admittedly, as of everyone) elsewhere. But cp. "Saynt Frances, . . . / Save thi breder" and "Pray we to Frawnses, that beth present, / To save his breder and his covent" (*St. Francis Carol* burden, 67–68).

61. See John W. McKenna, "Piety and Propaganda: The Cult of Henry VI," in *Chaucer and Middle English Studies in Honour of Rossell Hope Robbins*, ed. Beryl Rowland (Kent, Ohio: Kent State University Press, 1974), pp. 72–88.

62. See Fein, "Good Ends," p. 105 n. 18, and the reproduction of the image on p. 202 of this volume.

63. There is much useful material on the use of images at a slightly later date (in early printed books) in Martha W. Driver, *The Image in Print: Book Illustration in Late Medieval England and Its Sources* (London: British Library, 2004).

64. See Nancy Lee Beaty, *The Craft of Dying: A Study of the Literary Tradition of the Ars Moriendi in England* (New Haven: Yale University Press, 1970).

65. On such poems, see Woolf, *English Religious Lyric*, pp. 333–36, which includes a sensitive discussion of Audelay's poem.

66. See n. 45, above.

67. Audelay names himself eighteen times in all. A name very close to that of Audelay appears in the *Festial* MS Cotton Claudius A.ii., where the sermon for Saint George ends on fol. 62v: "A[m]en (sub)scripsi addeley" (I, Addeley, wrote Amen below). The name Addeley may come from Hadley in Shropshire, a few miles from Lilleshall, or might conceivably be a variant of Audelay (which itself derives from Audley in Staffordshire).

68. See n. 47, above. While the colophon *Finito libro* has "vita salutis eterni" (life of eternal salvation), the preceding poem has "the way of salvacion" (*Epilogue* 416). The confusion between Latin *vita* (life) and *via* (way) is explicable, and *via* seems the more logical lexeme.

69. Cp. colophon *Finito libro*: "in sua visitacione" (in his visitation).

70. Cp. *Five Senses Carol*.

71. "In an abbay here be west" (*Epilogue* 483).

72. The man in his dream advises him to "Let be thi slouth and thi slomeryng!" and Audelay complains of lying sick "in my langure" (*Epilogue* 29, 482). Cp. *Dread of Death Carol* 43–46 (W51.31–34).

73. For the blindness of Eli, see 1 Sam. 3:2, and for the dumbness and subsequent prophecies of Zacharias (father of John the Baptist), see Luke 1:5–25, 57–80.

74. See above and n. 35.

75. Cp. *Visiting the Sick* 383, *Lord's Epistle* 201, *Vision of St. Paul* 358, and *Epilogue* 500.

76. The belief that one might suffer purgatory already on earth is most familiar in the exasperated response of Justinus in Chaucer's *Merchant's Tale* to January's infatuation with May ("I shal have myn hevene in erthe heere," IV 1647): "Paraunter she may be youre purgatorie" (IV 1670). Cp. *The Wife of Bath's Prologue:* "By God! in erthe I was his purgatorie" (III 489; see the note in F. N. Robinson, ed., *The Works of Geoffrey Chaucer*, 2nd ed. [Boston: Houghton Mifflin, 1961], pp. 700–701).

77. Cp. *Visiting the Sick* 126–28.

78. Fein, "Good Ends," p. 102.

79. Bartlett Jere Whiting, with Helen Wescott Whiting, *Proverbs, Sentences, and Proverbial Phrases* (Cambridge, Mass.: Harvard University Press, 1968), B199.

80. For the collocation "wit and wisdom," cp. Mirk's Pentecost sermon: "Goode men and woymen, as ȝe knowen wele all, þys day ys called Whitsonday, for bycause þat þe Holy Gost as þys day broȝt wyt and wysdome ynto all Cristes dyscyples, and soo by hor prechyng aftyr ynto all Cristys pepull" (Erbe 159/3–6).

81. It is noteworthy that there is no mention of praying for the souls of the Lestranges, for which purpose Audelay was employed at the time, nor are they anywhere mentioned amongst his addressees.

82. He has cast down the mighty from their seat (Luke 1:52, from the Magnificat, the subject of the poem).

83. MS Bodley 632, fol. 68r. In fact, this manuscript reads "domino B" (another reads "N," i.e., *nomen* 'name'), but "iohanni" or "i." is the usual reading, and a later reference in the text makes plain that the recipient was indeed called John: "Disce igitur et tu, Iohannes, Sanctum Iohannem diligere, et pro Deo et Sancti Iohannis amore elemosinas erogare" (learn therefore, you too, John, to love Saint John and to bestow alms in the name of God and for love of Saint John; fol. 95v). Although John may have been a common appellation for "Everypriest"—cp. "oure gentyl ser Jone" (*Marcolf* 144)—it seems to me that (apart from the incipit) Mirk writes in too specific terms not to have had a single individual in mind, in the first instance, at least.

84. The rubric to part 5, chapter 16, reads: "qualiter alloquitur prior cognatum suum de obseruancia premissorum" (how the prior addresses his relative concerning the observance of the previous matters; MS Bodley 632, fol. 97r).

85. "Tu igitur, karissime, quia sacerdotale officium legitime, ut spero, suscepisti" (you, however, dearest, because you have undertaken the priestly office lawfully, as I hope; MS Bodley 632, fol. 69r).

86. "Attende iam, karissime, quantum et quam tenere te diligo, qui tam amicabilia tibi ad anime tue utilitatem scribo, sepe per aliorum facta te admonens, nonnunquam teipsum alloquens, optans et multum desiderans te ita perfecte in sacerdocio uiuere, quatinus summo sacerdoti Ihesu Christo possis laudibiliter racionem reddere" (MS Bodley 632, fol. 97r).

87. I have used dots of omission above where MS Bodley 632, fol. 97r, reads "uicario de A" (for the suggestion, with which I do not concur, that the addressee was vicar of St. Alkmund's, Shrewsbury, see above and n. 12). In those manuscripts that describe John beyond his Christian name, three read "domino iohanni de s," another "i. de s.," another "N. uicario de c." Only one has "iohanni A.," which would fit the name John Audelay (York, York Minster Library MS XVI.O.11).

88. "Sed quia scriptum est, "Inicium sapiencie timor Domini," ideo uolo te primum esse timidum, quia timor ad omne bonum ducit" (MS Bodley 632, fol. 69r).

89. Bertram Colgrave and R. A. B. Mynors, eds. and trans., *Bede's Ecclesiastical History of the English People* (Oxford: Clarendon Press, 1969), pp. 488–99. Cp. Erbe 5/12–36. The *narratio* is in the tradition of visions of the afterlife that have their origin in Saint Paul's vision in 2 Cor. 12:2–4 (cp. Audelay's version in MS Douce 302).

90. "Sed quia impiorum penis te terrui, de premiis iustorum modo audi" (MS Bodley 632, fol. 98r).

91. "Quicquid desideramus, statim habebimus, et quicquid uidebimus amabimus. . . . Sed ad hoc gaudium quis erit idoneus? Profecto uerus penitens, humilis obediens, amabilis socius, fidelis seruus" (MS Bodley 632, fol. 98r–v).

92. "Uerus penitens, qui semper est de peccatis dolens, quoniam uera penitencia est sine intermissione temporis de peccatis dolere" (MS Bodley 632, fol. 98v).

THE MAKE-UP OF JOHN AUDELAY'S *COUNSEL OF CONSCIENCE*

Oliver Pickering

John Audelay, seemingly close to death in Haughmond Abbey, Shropshire, appears to claim much for himself by way of authorship. "Loke in this book; here may ye se / Hwatt ys my wyl and my wrytyng" (32–33), he commands in his *Conclusion*, the final poem in Oxford, Bodleian Library MS Douce 302,[1] and he names himself as author in as many as fourteen different poems distributed throughout the manuscript. The main rubricator, writing earlier in the volume at the end of a poem beginning, "Here I conclud al my makyng" (*Epilogue* 1), concurs: "Iste liber fuit compositus per Johannem Awdelay, capellanum" (This book was composed by John Audelay, chaplain) (*Finito libro* colophon; fol. 22v). But Audelay, other than saying he was Lord Lestrange's chantry priest (*Conclusion* 49–50), and that he lay sick "In an abbay here be west" (*Epilogue* 483), presents himself as no more than a suffering example of mankind for others to learn from, and a conduit for divine teaching:

> Mervel ye not of this makyng,
> Fore I me excuse—hit is not I;
> This was the Holé Gost wercheng,
> That sayd these wordis so faythfully.
>   (*Epilogue* 495–98)

His repeated insistence on his physical infirmities (blind, deaf, sick in body) makes us wonder how the book ever came to be written, but otherwise personalizes him no more than if these features were additions to his name, which is indeed the usual context in which they appear (for example, "My name is Jon the Blynd Awdlay"; *Epilogue* 507). Tim William Machan goes so far as to describe Audelay's self-references as depersonalization: their formulaic quality, he writes, "furthers the lack of specificity, which in turn enables readers sharing the meditative experience to recognize the same recalcitrant traits of a sinner in themselves."[2] In such circumstances, authorship does not necessarily equate to responsibility for original composition. The book's purpose, we are told, is to save souls, and the act of selecting, assembling, and editing the right material for the good of others—in this case, "ad exemplum aliorum in monasterio de Haghmon" (as a model for others in the Monastery of Haughmond), as the redactor puts it[3]—can be argued to be the essence of medieval authoring.

The presence in the manuscript of English and Latin poems found elsewhere, the great variety of verse form, the inconsistency with which Audelay attaches his name to poems, and the presence, too, of material undoubtedly not by Audelay: all these factors argue for MS Douce 302 being a compilation rather than a single-author anthology in the modern sense. Audelay's claims in the final poem are in practice diminished by its position at the end of a non-Audelaian sequence comprising two meditative prose pieces (one by Richard Rolle), the two highly wrought rhymed alliterative poems *Paternoster* and *Three Dead Kings* (which in their artistry are greatly superior to anything else in the manuscript, and which have recently been shown to have been composed in a different dialect), and the well-known Latin poem *Cur mundus militat sub vana gloria*.[4] The fact that Audelay's final, personal poem is in the hand of the rubricator rather than that of the principal scribe complicates the matter further, adding to the impossibility of knowing the extent of Audelay's input into the book's manufacture or the rationale and decision-making that lay behind it.

Yet there is little doubt that Audelay was a poet in his own right. He clearly wanted his name preserved (and for the book to be regarded as his), and several of his apparent compositions, notably his carols, have been praised by modern critics.[5] Susanna Fein, in her indispensable survey of the contents of the Audelay Manuscript, has distinguished four groups of material, and the first of these, referred to by recent scholars as *The Counsel of Conscience*,[6] is the subject of the present study. Questions to be addressed in the essay include the homogeneity of this portion of the manuscript and the extent to which its contents can be said to be original compositions by Audelay.[7]

The title *Counsel of Conscience* is Audelay's own, and in using it he is clearly referring to a body of material—a book—that is now finishing: "*The Cownsel of Conseans* this boke I calle, / Or *The Ladder of Heven*" (*Epilogue* 417–18). The starting point of the book is, however, unstated.[8] The phrase "counsel of conscience" is repeated by the rubricator shortly afterward in a Latin passage with which he in turn marks the end of what he clearly regarded as a definable body of work, separate from what was to follow:

> Finito libro, sit laus et gloria Christo. Liber vocatur Concilium conciencie, sic nominator, aut Scala celi et vita salutis eterni. Iste liber fuit compositus per Johannem Awdelay, capellanum, qui fuit secus et surdus in sua visitacione, ad honorem Domini nostri Jhesu Christi et ad exemplum aliorum in monasterio de Haghmon, anno Domini millesimo cccc visecimo [*sic*] vj. Cuius anime propicietur deus, amen. (fol. 22v)[9]

> (The book being finished, let there be praise and glory to Christ. The book is called the Counsel of Conscience, or it is called thus, the Ladder of Heaven and the Life of Eternal Salvation. This book was composed by John Audelay, chaplain, who was blind and deaf by divine affliction, to the honor of Our Lord Jesus Christ and as an exemplar for others in the monastery of Haughmond, AD 1426. May God have mercy on his soul, amen.)

In Whiting's edition the material preceding this rubric comprises eighteen poems, which Fein, carefully noting component parts and instructions for reading, subdivides into a total of thirty-two items. Any discussion of the sequence needs to bear in mind the three lacunae that affect this part of the manuscript, especially the major loss of leaves at the very beginning and the additional loss of four leaves after folio 7. It is clear from a scribal note on folio 2r, referring the reader to "the thirteenth leef afore" for material accidentally misplaced, that at least thirteen leaves have been lost from the beginning,[10] but on the basis of surviving leaf signatures (and the manuscript's norm of six-leaf gatherings), it is likely that as many as nineteen leaves have gone, for the first surviving leaf signature, on the present folio 3, is d iiij.[11] When we consider that the average number of verse lines to a page in the surviving part of the manuscript is 90 to 100, it is probable that at least 3,500 lines of verse have been lost from the beginning of the volume, and about 750 lines after folio 7.[12] The red roman numerals with which the rubricator numbered many of the poems provide an indication of how many items are now missing: the first such numeral now extant, XI, heads the first surviving complete poem (*Marcolf and Solomon*), showing that nine items have been wholly lost at the start. The next such numeral is XVI (*Seven Bleedings*), showing the loss of a further three items within the second lacuna.

The surviving contents of the manuscript before *The Counsel of Conscience* rubric are set out in the following table. Two numbering sequences are shown, namely the scribal numbering (far left) and the poem numbers in Whiting's edition (next left). The descriptive titles are those allotted in Fein's recent edition, boldface indicating those poems in which Audelay names himself as author. The length of the poems and their verse forms are also indicated.

	W1	*True Living*	
		Acephalous. 263 surviving lines. Thirteen-line stanzas.	
XI	W2	**Marcolf and Solomon**	
		1013 lines. Alliterative thirteen-line stanzas.	
	W3	**The Remedy of Nine Virtues**	
		Acephalous. 102 surviving lines. Thirteen-line stanzas.	
XVI	W4	*Seven Bleedings of Christ*	
		139 lines. Six-line tail-rhyme stanzas.	
XVII	W5	*Prayer on Christ's Passion*	
		42 lines. Six-line tail-rhyme stanzas.	
XVIII	W6	*The Psalter of the Passion* (mainly in Latin)	
		Includes twelve lines of English. Couplets.	
XIX	W7	*Seven Words of Christ on the Cross*	
		114 lines. Six-line tail-rhyme stanzas.	
XX	W8	*Devotions at the Levation of Christ's Body* (ends with Latin prayers)	
		88 lines of English. Six-line and eight-line tail-rhyme stanzas.	
XXI	W9	*Virtues of the Mass*	
		413 lines. Six-line tail-rhyme stanzas.	
XXII	W10	*For Remission of Sins* (three-part devotional sequence)	
		72 lines. Couplets.	

XXIII	W11	***Visiting the Sick and Consoling the Needy*** 403 lines. Thirteen-line stanzas.
	W12	***On the World's Folly*** Preceded by an English (couplets) and Latin introduction. 66 lines. Three-line tail-rhyme stanzas.
XXIIII	W13	***Pope John's Passion of Our Lord*** 124 lines. Eight-line refrain stanzas, ending with two couplets.
	W14	*Seven Hours of the Cross* 90 lines. Nine-line stanzas.
XXV	W15	***Our Lord's Epistle on Sunday*** 208 lines. Thirteen-line stanzas.
XXVI	W16	***The Vision of Saint Paul*** 365 lines. Thirteen-line stanzas.
XXVII	W17	*God's Address to Sinful Men* One leaf lost internally. 264 surviving lines. Eight-line refrain stanzas.
	W18	**Audelay's** *Epilogue* 507 lines. Thirteen-line stanzas.

Audelay's *Epilogue* is overwhelmingly hortatory, its main, repetitive preoccupations being the need for men and women to live well to ensure a place in heaven—"The hyeway to heven I wold ye toke, / To joy and blis without endyng" (410–11)—and Audelay's own sense of his mission to help his fellow Christians save themselves. This stress on salvation and how to achieve it is no more than we should expect from a body of work entitled "*The Cownsel of Conseans* . . . / Or *The Ladder of Heven*":

> Ther is no mon may clym up a walle
> Without a ladder, sekyrly;
> No more may we to heven on hye
> Without treu cownsel of consians.

>   Clyme up this ladder—then may ye se
>   What ye schul do to Godis plesans,
>   And weder ye wil have wele or wo.
>   (*Epilogue* 417–25)

The poem is of course intimately linked to some of those preceding it, most obviously through their shared use of a thirteen-line stanza rhyming *ababbcbcdeeed*, as indicated in the table above, and the near identity of their versions of Audelay's famous "signature" stanza.[13] But surveying (as we shall now do) the preceding part of the manuscript—containing some 4,270 lines of extant verse and perhaps 4,500 lines of verse now lost—can we be certain that the book entitled *The Counsel of Conscience*, with the distinctive homiletic concerns detailed in the *Epilogue*, really stretches back to the beginning (and beyond)?

The most obviously "different" poem of the sequence, Whiting's Poem 2, variously entitled *Counsels to Those in Religious Life* and *Marcol[f] and Solomon*, has recently been the most studied.[14] The poem stands out as by far the most ambitious of Audelay's extant compositions, in length (1,013 lines), in meter (alliterative long lines for the octave of the thirteen-line stanza), in subject matter (the "covetise" afflicting all parts of the Church), and in subtlety of approach: Audelay manages his theme of drawing attention to clerical abuses—and the need to reform them—by assuming the persona of Marcolf (or Marcol) the fool addressing King Solomon,[15] thus giving himself license to speak out satirically at a time when criticism of the church was associated with Lollardy. James Simpson analyzes the poem in detail, praising Audelay's achievement in preserving "a space for orthodox yet trenchant vernacular ecclesiological satire and theology in unpropitious circumstances"; the poem is, he declares, "a defence of the necessity of orthodox protest against ecclesiastical abuse, even when such protest might easily be confused with Lollardy."[16]

Simpson was one of the first to refer to the poem as *Marcol and Solomon*, but although it is a remarkable piece of writing, which deserves to be better known, there is little sense of Marcol and Solomon as participants or even as structural devices.[17] Throughout the poem it is essentially Audelay's own voice that we hear, usually addressing one or other body of clergy but sometimes the laity whose souls are being neglected. And although its poetic mode differs from that of Audelay's other compositions, it is not, despite Simpson's strong implication,[18] the only poem in which Audelay criticizes the behavior of curates and priests, or expresses concern about being taken for a Lollard. Criticism of the clergy for living sinfully is a feature of the first surviving poem, *True Living* (56–64), and of *Epilogue* (88–91). With the description in *Marcolf* (131–37) of the danger in which a devout priest can find himself simply for being devout—"Thay lekon hym to a Lollere and to an epocryte" (133)[19]—may be compared the following stanza from *Epilogue*, in which Audelay speaks about his own plight:

> I wot ryght wel I schal be chent
> Of Godis enmys—hit is no nay!—
> Fore to the treuth thai take no tent;
> The soth fore hem, Y dar not say;
> Herefore the Fynd he wil hem fray,
> Fore thay cal trew Cristyn men Lollard,
> That kepyn Cristis comawndmentis nyght and day,
> And don Godis wil in dede and worde.
>   Ayayns ham, I take Crist to wytnes;
>   Here is non error ne Lollardré,
>   Bot pistill and gospel, the Sauter, treuly;
>   I take witnes of the treue clargy
>   That han Godis lauys fore to redres.
>   (248–60)

But although there are some shared themes—and although the word *consyans* occurs several times in *Marcolf*—Audelay's long poem differs fundamentally from his *Epilogue* in not being directly concerned with individual salvation.

With *Marcolf* we can also begin to differentiate Audelay's poems by date. *Epilogue*'s explicit summation of his poetic message and mission, its repetitiousness, its apparent reuse of lines from *Marcolf*,[20] and its rather clumsy handling of the verse form (especially the ninth line of the stanza) all mark it as a composition of his later years; it probably dates from the mid-1420s. In contrast, the allusions in and preoccupations of *Marcolf* have led its two most recent commentators to date it to 1410–13 and ca. 1414, respectively, that is, after the issuing of Archbishop Arundel's repressive *Constitutions* (1409) and in or before the year of the Oldcastle rebellion (1414).[21] If a remark in line 503 ("Blynd as Y am") is taken literally and not figuratively, it would seem that Audelay had already lost his sight at the time the poem was written, or was at least close to doing so, but it is noticeable that he finally signs off not in the manner of later poems in the manuscript—for example, "My name hit is the Blynd Awdlay" (*Lord's Epistle* 208)—but simply as "Syr Jon Audlay" (1008), suggesting a lesser degree of disability.[22] This reinforces the likelihood of an earlier date of composition. Simpson draws attention to the evident influence of *Piers Plowman* on the style, poetic strategies, and concerns of *Marcolf*,[23] and it may be hypothesized that the latter dates from a period in Audelay's writing life when he was deeply interested in and influenced by alliterative and stanzaic alliterative poetry of the later fourteenth century, leading him to experiment with related styles and verse forms. If correct, this hypothesis may also explain the presence later in MS Douce 302 of *Paternoster* and *Three Dead Kings* (as admired compositions that he wished to preserve), and of the thirteen-line alliterative stanza buried in the manuscript's extract from Richard Rolle's *Form of Living*.[24] The clumsier and less ambitious thirteen-line-stanza poems for which he does claim authorship would, then, represent efforts at composition somewhat later in life, at a point when a diminution in his poetic skill coincided with an overriding concern for the salvation of souls.

Marcolf occurs, also, at a disjunctive point in MS Douce 302, where the notion of an organized *Counsel of Conscience* is hard to maintain on physical grounds. It ends, complete, at the foot of folio 7v, with the final line fitted into the lower margin. Four leaves are then lost, with the result that *The Remedy of Nine Virtues* (to be discussed shortly) begins imperfectly. Earlier, on folio 2r, *Marcolf* follows *True Living* without apparent physical disruption, but the latter poem ends with a marginal apology:

> The Day of Dome shuld come in here;
> Ver the defawte of the wrytere;
> At the thirtenth leef afore hyt ys;
> Seche hyt there, thou shalt nott mys.
>   (*Instr. for Reading 1* 1–4)[25]

True Living, which begins *in medias res* because of the loss of the first part of the manuscript, is also patently unfinished when it ends (not remarked on by recent commentators), and the lines on Doomsday referred to in the rhymed note must be its lost continuation, as that subject has just begun to be discussed. How the first scribe came to copy the continuation on a leaf subsequently positioned thirteen leaves earlier is now unanswerable, and we similarly cannot know whether *True Living* once concluded with an Audelaian signature stanza.

Fein calls this poem *True Living* in her edition, and it combines injunctions about right behavior with criticism of social and clerical evils.[26] It is more crisply written than *Epilogue*, with the ninth line of each stanza a short bob, and it features declaratory stanza openings (for example, "Kepe youre wedloke, ye weddid men"; 65), and some trenchant phrasing elsewhere (for example, "Nou a ladé wyl take a page / Fore no love bot fore fleschely lust"; 95–96). One reason for believing that it too dates from earlier rather than later in Audelay's writing career is the extent to which it was plundered by its author for material out of which to fashion his carols. The set of carols, occupying folios 27v–32r of the manuscript, begins with a sequence of five poems on elements of Christian doctrine (the commandments, the sins, the works of mercy, the five wits, and the gifts of the Holy Ghost), and large parts of the first, third, and fifth of these are lifted from *True Living* with little change.[27] Lines from *True Living* also reappear in the *Four Estates Carol* and furnish almost the whole of the *Chastity of Wives Carol*.[28] However, despite its likely earlier date, there is no question about *True Living*'s appropriateness for a compilation entitled *The Counsel of Conscience*.[29]

The acephalous poem *The Remedy of Nine Virtues*, another thirteen-line-stanza poem and the first in the manuscript to end with the declaration, "My name hyt ys the Blynde Awdelay" (102), also fits well into such a scheme.[30] If the virtues were its sole concern, it may have lost only five and a half stanzas at the beginning (excluding the likelihood of an introduction), for it begins in the middle of the sixth virtue, after which the seventh to ninth receive one stanza of discussion each; four concluding stanzas then follow. In style, the poem is similar to *True Living*, but it is isolated from it physically. Four leaves have been lost before the present folio 8r (on which it begins), and with them, in all probability, upwards of 750 lines of verse. The jump in the scribal numbering of the manuscript contents, shown in the table above, reveals that three complete poems are now missing.[31] It is idle to speculate about their nature, but there is no certainty that they resembled *Remedy* in style or subject matter. Even if they did, there is now discontinuity, for *Remedy* is followed by a sequence of poems of a quite different kind.

The sequence of texts from *Seven Bleedings of Christ* to *For Remission of Sins* (W4–W10; fols. 8r–12v) comprises a group of poems that are devotional as well as instructional, and which have the linked themes of the Passion of Christ and preparation for receiving the Eucharist. They are written in either six-line tail-rhyme (*aabccb*) or short couplets, and some of them, in whole or part, are well attested elsewhere in the extant corpus of Middle English verse. In addition, some parts of the sequence are in Latin. Audelay appears to claim none of these poems as his own, as none is signed, and it is unlikely that any of them originated with him.

Seven Bleedings (W4) is a prayer on the blood shed by Christ at his Passion, the prayer itself, lines 19–109, being preceded by three introductory stanzas and concluded by five others, which commend the prayer as a means of salvation. The simplicity of the tail-rhyme verse, as also in *Prayer on Christ's Passion* (W5), *Seven Words of Christ on the Cross* (W7), and *Virtues of the Mass* (W9), is reminiscent of the tail-rhyme prayers found in the late fourteenth-century Vernon Manuscript (Oxford, Bodl. Lib. MS Eng. poet. a.1),[32] and is quite different from Audelay's habitually more wordy style. Much of *Seven Bleedings* is in fact paralleled in the lyric "Ihesu, for þi blode þou bleddest" preserved in Oxford, Balliol College MS 316A, Oxford, Christ Church MS 151, and London, BL MS Cotton Caligula A.ii.[33] Lines 19–60 of *Seven Bleedings*, the part relating to the seven deadly sins, are equivalent to lines 1–42 of this forty-eight-line lyric, many of the stanzas being virtually identical, as with:

> O Jhesu, thi payns were ful strong,
> When the skorgis both scharp and long,
>   Mad thi body to bled;
> To thee, Lord, mercé I cry,
> Thou kepe me out of *Glotoné*,
>   And helpe me at my ned.
>   (31–36)[34]

It is probable that Audelay has reworked and expanded an existing poem, but quite possible that the longer version represented by *Seven Bleedings* had a previous existence.

Lines 112–13 of *Seven Bleedings* recommend reciting fifteen Paternosters and fifteen Aves in connection with Christ's Passion, and such a quasi-liturgical context is very much apparent in the case of "Ihesu, for þi precious blod," another tail-rhyme lyric on the same theme (and in exactly the same poetic mode), which is preserved in several late fourteenth- and fifteenth-century manuscripts. As Rosemary Woolf notes, the version of this poem found in Oxford, Bodl. Lib. MS Rawlinson liturg. g. 2 "is surrounded by Latin prayers, and each stanza is followed by a paternoster and ave."[35] The closeness of the liturgy is evident throughout the sequence W4–W10, with sinful man in need of salvation either enjoined to recite his devotions privately or to respond appropriately when in church.

The Psalter of the Passion (W6), which is headed "De psalterio passionis," is in fact mainly in Latin. In her article Fein subdivides it into five parts, but it has seven, comprising two instructional couplets in English (W6.1–4) introducing the well-known Latin verse prayer *Anima Christi sanctifica me* used at Mass (W6.5–16); another English couplet (W6.17–18) introducing a four-line Latin verse prayer *O pendens dudum* (W6.19–22); three further English couplets of instruction (W6.23–28) introducing the Latin verse prayer *O Deus qui voluisti* (W6.29–58); and a final short Latin prayer in prose, "Tu Domine per has sanctissimas penas tuas" (You, Lord, by these your most blessed sufferings).[36] The previous poem, *Prayer on Christ's Passion* (W5), another tail-rhyme prayer to Christ in his Passion, wholly in English, anticipates what follows in that its first twenty-four lines are closely modeled on the *O Deus qui voluisti* section.[37] One point of *The Psalter of the Passion* is apparently to provide devotional material that can be used in place of the Paternoster and Ave by more advanced worshippers able to say "the Sauter of the Passion" (*Instr. for Prayer 1* 2; W6.2).[38] Such a "Sauter" is not provided here, but later lines make clear that the penitent is expected to use the short Latin prayers in *The Psalter of the Passion* alongside other texts:

> And say on thi bedis in this manere
> As thou didist our Ladé Sautere;
> When the Sauter hit is edone,
> Then say thi Crede with hit anon.
>   (*Instr. for Prayer 3* 1–4; W6.23–26)

Two lengthy English poems of salutations to the Virgin, based on Latin verses related to the text of the Psalms, and headed "Psalterium b. Mariae" (Psalter of the Blessed Mary), are preserved in the Vernon Manuscript and may possibly be comparable to the "our Ladé Sautere" referred to here,[39] but it is more likely that the phrase refers to the Little Hours of the Virgin. Whatever the exact text, the liturgical or quasi-liturgical context is again apparent.

The following poem, *Seven Words of Christ on the Cross* (W7), is yet another Passion-related prayer, wholly in English and this time based on the seven utterances of Christ on the Cross. Like other Middle English compositions on this subject, it derives from a Latin prayer attributed to Bede. The prayer itself, lines 1–96, is followed by three stanzas urging the saying of Paternosters and Aves in anticipation of death and hoped-for salvation. The poem is in tail-rhyme, like *Seven Bleedings* and *Prayer on Christ's Passion*, and its final stanza promising remission—beginning "Welle is him that wil and may / Worchip these wordis everé day / With devocion" (109–11)—is very similar to the final stanza of *Prayer on Christ's Passion*—"Wele is him that wil and may / Say this oreson everé day / Of Cristis Passion" (37–39). Indeed the same locution opens *The Psalter of the Passion* ("Wele is him that wele can / Sai the Sauter of the Passion"; *Instr. for Prayer 1* 1–2; W6.1–2), showing the extent to which these poems interrelate.[40] Alexandra Barratt, in commenting on *Seven Words*, has pointed out that the author's immediate source was almost certainly the popular collection of prayers and liturgically derived texts for lay use known as the Primer, of which Bede's prayer (like the Psalms of the Passion and the Little Hours of the Virgin) was a common component.[41]

The next texts in the sequence—*Devotions at the Levation of Christ's Body*, *Virtues of the Mass*, and *For Remission of Sins* (W8–W10)—then move on to the related theme of the Mass. The English part of *Devotions at the Levation* has six subsections, of which the most important is a prayer in the form of a lengthy salutation, beginning "Hayle, gracious Lord in thi Godhede" (*Salut. to Christ's Body* 1–56; W8.7–62). This composition is similar in style to salutations found later in the manuscript, especially those addressed to the Virgin Mary and Jesus (W19–W20), and it is therefore possibly of Audelay's own making, always assuming the later poems are his. Unlike those, however, the salutation in *Devotions at the Levation* is in eight-line tail-rhyme stanzas (*aaabcccb*). Addressed to Christ in the sacrament, it is part praise, part Creed, and part preparation for receiving the Eucharist. Preceding it is an introductory six-line tail-rhyme stanza, giving instructions:

> When thou seyst the sacrement,
> Worchip hit with good entent.
>   Thus thou schalt begyn:
> Knele on thi kneys; then mekely
> Bececche him, of grace and mercy,
>   Foregifnes of thi synne.
>   (*Instr. for Prayer 4* 1–6; W8.1–6)

Afterward comes a tail-rhyme stanza of eight short lines introducing a second prayer, this time to be said "Afftyr the Levacion / Of that sacrement" (*Instr. for Prayer 5* 3–4; W8.65–66) and in anticipation of pardon promised by Pope Innocent. This second prayer—"O Lord Jhesu Crist, fore thi holé flesche most worthi" (*Prayer for Pardon* 1; W8.71–88)—is in longer-lined tail-rhyme stanzas, now of six lines. Unlike the series in *The Psalter of the Passion*, the sequence of instructions and prayers in the body of *Devotions at the Levation* is wholly in English, but, like there, Latin prayers follow at the end, beginning "Adoramus te Christe et benedicimus tibi quia per sanctam crucem tuam" (We worship you, Christ, and we bless you because of your Holy Cross).

Virtues of the Mass (W9) is different in that it is on a liturgical subject rather than being liturgical or quasi-liturgical in itself. Once again in simple six-line tail-rhyme stanzas, it is a version of an evidently popular Middle English poem on the merits of hearing Mass, including instructions on what to do during the service. A considerably longer version (684 lines) survives in the Vernon Manuscript, and there seems no doubt that the text in MS Douce 302 (413 lines) derives from this version or from an intermediate rewritten abridgment, for another version of 312 lines is found in London, BL MS Harley 3954.[42] An element of the poem found in all three texts is the well-known tale of a devil writing down the names of women chattering in church during Mass, the observer in this case being Saint Augustine (*Virtues of the Mass* 276–341), but the surrounding material is more divergent. About half the lines in MS Douce 302 equate to Vernon.[43] Much of the latter's text, notably its detailed account of the different stages of the Mass, is not taken over, while material in Douce but not in Vernon includes information about basic Christian doctrine (for example, lines 114–55) as well as the conclusion in which the sinner is given final instructions about prayer and observance before a final promise of pardon and salvation (lines 354–413), similar to lines elsewhere in W4–W10:

> Alle that han herd this sermon,
> A hundred days of pardon,
> > Saynt Gregoré grauntis you this.
> > > (*Virtues of the Mass* 409–11)

Whereas the stanzas on doctrine could conceivably be Audelay's own, the concluding lines are largely shared with the Harley text.[44] Overall, and because of the presence of the poem in the Vernon Manuscript, there is no doubt that Audelay adapted *Virtues of the Mass* from an existing composition.[45]

The final poem of the group currently under discussion, *For Remission of Sins* (W10), has three distinct sections, all of them in short couplets. The central element, *Prayer of General Confession* (W10.23–60), is a general confession beginning "Swete Jhesu Crist, to thee," well known from other manuscripts including Vernon.[46] It is preceded by a brief account of Christ's appearance to Pope Gregory at the Mass, once again holding out the promise of pardon if prayers, including the following confession, are recited. The confession itself is followed by a couplet introducing a final prayer asking Christ on the Cross for forgiveness (*Prayer for Forgiveness* 1–10; W10.63–72).

The absence of Audelay's name from poems W4–W10, coupled with their different verse forms, poetic style, and subject matter, and not least their textual associations with material preserved in other manuscripts, often earlier in date, makes it very likely that he considered them a separate sequence to which he had small claim as author. We cannot exclude the possibility that he considered them part of his *Counsel of Conscience*, but the poems in question generally do not instruct the sinner in the business of Christian living. They lead him instead, in the context of the Mass, to pray to Christ directly.

The shift back to normal Audelaian mode at W11, *Visiting the Sick and Consoling the Needy*, is very noticeable, as Audelay as author now apparently reasserts himself. Six out of the eight poems comprising the sequence W11–W18 contain his built-in signature, and it can be argued that only *Seven Hours of the Cross* is not in fact signed: the other unsigned item, *God's Address to Sinful Men*, leads directly into *Epilogue*, which is not signaled as a new poem other than by a change in verse form. *Epilogue* is signed in its first stanza as well as its last ("That prayn for Jon the Blynd Audelay"; 6), and this first stanza, beginning "Here I conclud al my makyng" (1), effectively rounds off the poem that precedes it. In addition, four of the eight poems—*Visiting the Sick*, *Lord's Epistle*, *Vision of Saint Paul*, and Audelay's *Epilogue* (W11, W15, W16, W18)—have, at their conclusion, a whole stanza in common, which is also shared with *The Remedy of Nine Virtues* (W3), that is, the stanza, quoted in part from *Epilogue* at the start of this essay, in which Audelay asserts that, in writing as he does, he is no more than a mouthpiece of God.[47]

Nevertheless W11–W18 do not form a homogeneous group, and the preoccupations of W4–W10 are, for a time, still evident. *Visiting the Sick* (W11), whose final *two* stanzas are largely shared with those of *Remedy*,[48] is typical enough: though headed "De visitacione infirmorum et consolacione miserorum" (Concerning the visitation of the sick and the consolation of the wretched), it ranges rather laboriously over many aspects of the need to repent of one's sins, hold to the Creed and the sacraments, and lead a good Christian life. *On the World's Folly* (W12), in contrast, though ending with Audelay's name, is not in thirteen-line stanzas, is not self-contained, and in its brevity, mixture of English and Latin elements, and anticipation of the next poem (once again on the Passion), recalls aspects of W4–W10. It begins with a six-line introduction telling the reader that "Here schul ye here a treu lessoun, / Hou fayth and charyté away is gon" (*Instr. for Reading 2* 5–6; W12.5–6), and that when he has read this lesson he should read *Pope John's Passion of Our Lord* (W13), which follows—stimulated by the subject matter of *On the World's Folly*, which is essentially a brief diatribe on the evil state of the world caused by mankind not having Christ's Passion in mind. The stanza form is a tight three-line tail-rhyme, directly modeled on the form of the six Latin lines that immediately precede the start of the evil-times complaint; indeed the opening English lines of the complaint are closely translated from them.[49] The English verses follow the Latin model in that the final lines of all twenty-two stanzas rhyme on essentially the same sound, with many of the couplet portions also rhyming across the stanzas, and it may be that the whole of the English is a translation. However, despite the similarities to aspects of poems W4–W10, in which Audelay may have had only a small hand, it seems certain that *On the World's Folly* should be attributed to him. Not only is there his signature, but there are references to the need to hold one's own counsel and the likelihood of being punished for speaking the truth, themes that occur also in *True Living* and in *Marcolf and Solomon*.[50]

The Passion to which *Instructions for Reading 2* refers, *Pope John's Passion of Our Lord*, is claimed by Audelay apparently entire ("That mad in Englesche this Passion"; *Prayer Explicit* 3; W13.123), though it consists of different elements, again recalling the methods as well as the themes of the W4–W10 group. There is an introduction of two stanzas, the first of them linking the devotion to Pope John XXII;[51] a Passion narrative of eight stanzas loosely based on Saint John's Gospel (which is said to be the source);[52] one stanza enjoining mankind to repent and pray; three stanzas of personal prayer to Christ; one stanza of final instruction in saying Paternosters, Aves, and the Creed, to gain Pope John's three hundred days of remission; and, unusually, a short envoi (containing Audelay's claim to authorship) in a different verse form. The poem is otherwise unified, however, by its use of an eight-line refrain stanza rhyming *ababbcbc*, found also in *God's Address to Sinful Men* (W17). Formally, this is no more than the first eight lines of Audelay's thirteen-line stanza (though with the refrain element added),[53] and no special significance need be attached to the occurrence of the author's name outside the main body of the poem. Audelay's phrasing in the *Prayer Explicit*—"That mad in Englesche this Passion" (3; W13.123)—may suggest another translation, but the sequence of different elements argues (as above) rather for the influence of the W4-W10 group, particularly as the text being attributed to Pope John XXII appears to be no more than the famous short prayer *Anima Christi sanctifica me*, which formed a component part of *The Psalter of the Passion* (W6) and whose fifth line, "Passio Christe conforta me" (Passion of Christ, comfort me), forms the opening line of *Pope John's Passion*'s second stanza.[54] Audelay used the same line as part of the burden for his *Dread of Death Carol* (W51), "Timor mortis conturbat me" (The fear of death disturbs me).

Pope John's Passion is headed, seemingly erroneously, "De passione Domini nostri Jhesu Christi et de horis canonicis" (Concerning the Passion of our Lord Jesus Christ and concerning the canonical hours), but the presence of the second element is explained by *Seven Hours of the Cross* (W14)—headed "Hic incepiunt hore canonice passionis Jhesu Christe" (Here begin the canonical hours of the Passion of Jesus Christ)—in which the Passion theme continues. Not given a separate scribal number, it was evidently regarded as a continuation of *Pope John's Passion*. In addition, it is unsigned, and although this might be explained by its status as an appendix to *Pope John's Passion*, it is also possible that *Seven Hours* had an independent origin. The verse form, a nine-line stanza not found elsewhere in MS Douce 302, at first resembles lines 5–13 of one version of Audelay's thirteen-line stanza in ending with a bob and wheel, but the quatrain section rhymes *aaaa*, giving an overall *aaaabcccb*. These first four lines are also noticeably long, with a marked caesura. The subject matter of the poem—Christ's Passion—also displays a close overlap with that of *Pope John's Passion*, and it is perhaps unlikely that Audelay himself would have undertaken the narrative a second time. *Seven Hours* is in fact an English version of the well-known Latin hymn *Patris sapiencia veritas divina*, familiar from liturgical contexts, which equates the stages of the Passion with the canonical hours. A number of Middle English versions are extant,[55] *Seven Hours* having limited but definite textual parallels with (once again) a poem preserved in the Vernon Manuscript, where the English verses are accompanied by their Latin originals (in *Seven Hours* only the first line of each Latin verse is given, as a stanza heading). Although the Vernon poem is organized into sixteen-line sections, the first four lines of each, which is where the parallels with *Seven Hours* occur, closely resemble the relevant parts of the latter in being long monorhyming quatrains.[56] It is therefore likely that Audelay is here borrowing, or at least adapting, an existing composition, and it is noticeable that the opening and closing stanzas, in which the sinner is first urged to pay attention and finally promised remission, have quatrains with generally shorter lines, suggesting separate composition.[57]

Following this second concentration on Christ's Passion (W12–W14), with its variety of verse forms, *Our Lord's Epistle on Sunday* (W15) returns to Audelay's normal method of discourse, the hortatory thirteen-liner. This poem on the proper observance of Sunday is a clumsy and unappealing piece of work, in which the ninth and thirteenth lines are sometimes hardly distinguished metrically from the rest of the stanza. It is a version of the text known as the Sunday Letter, purportedly written by Christ himself to teach his people to honor the Sabbath.[58] In the tradition represented by *Lord's Epistle* (which has been shown to be based on a known Latin redaction, preserved in London, BL MS Royal 8 F.vi),[59] the letter is said to have been sent to Bishop Peter of Gaza, who testifies to its authenticity in the first person in lines 144–56. Much of the poem is made up of dire threats of destruction against those who fail to observe Sunday properly or pay their tithes, and priests who fail to teach this lesson are similarly warned. Audelay ends the poem with the stanza he repeats elsewhere, beginning, "Mervel ye noght of this makyng— / Fore I me excuse, hit is not I" (196–97), and by stressing the divine origin of the poem—"Fore this of Godis oun wrytyng" (198)—and in choosing to include it in his *Counsel of Conscience*, he is presumably endorsing its message. The importance of Sunday is then underlined with a poem in the same meter but containing a large amount of narrative, so that it reads altogether more easily. This is a version of *The Vision of Saint Paul* (W16), in which the archangel Michael shows Saint Paul the torments of the variously damned, contrasting the pains of hell with the joys of heaven. The climax is God's gesture, in answer to appeals from the damned souls, Paul, and all the angels, in sparing those in hell from torment—

> Fro Setterday at non, Y say treuly,
> And al the fest of the Sununday
> Into the fyrst our of Monday.
>   (296–98)—

in lines that closely parallel *Lord's Epistle* 93–94. As Whiting points out, an apparent Latin source for *Vision* exists in MS Royal 8 F.vi, directly adjacent to the Latin source for *Lord's Epistle*, but *Vision* seems also to be related to the poem on the Vision of Saint Paul in the Vernon Manuscript, as she additionally notes.[60] The latter poem is in short couplets, with the result that few textual parallels are close enough to suggest direct influence, but the two English versions match very closely in terms of content.[61] Audelay, as often, fills out the poem at the end, inserting a reference to "dere breder that beth present" (*Vision of St. Paul* 323), which may indicate an audience at Haughmond Abbey. The final two stanzas display his habitual intertextuality: the last of all is, once again, the "Mervel ye not" formulation, adapted for the occasion, while the penultimate stanza reuses the memorable second stanza of *True Living* (13–25), which very likely years earlier had also touched on hell:

> Fore hel is not ordend fore ryghtwyse mon,
> Bot fore hom that serven the Fynd,
> No more than is a preson of lyme and stone
> Bot fore hom the lawis offend.
> Cursid dedis makis men al day eschend
> And theffys on galous on hye to hyng.
> Ther ryghtwys men, thai han good end,
> That servyn here God in here levyng.
>   Y pray you, seris! Trest wele hereto!
> Fore he that levys here ryghtwysly,
> On what deth ever he dey,
> His soule never paynd schal be,
>   Ne never after wit of wo.
>   (*Vision of St. Paul* 340–52)

In this later version the originally short ninth and thirteenth lines of *True Living*'s thirteen-line stanza—"Trust wel therto!" and "Ne never wyt of wo" (21, 25)—have been deliberately lengthened so as to achieve the more uniform meter of the rest of *Vision*, Audelay by this date apparently no longer liking the metrical contrasts provided by a true bob and wheel.

True Living, along with *Marcolf and Solomon*, also lies behind *God's Address to Sinful Men* (W17), the final poem before Audelay's *Epilogue* (W18). This is not, as might be expected from Fein's title, a devotional appeal from the Cross, blaming men for neglecting Christ's suffering on mankind's behalf; instead it is again instructional, and the speaking voice could as well at times be Audelay's own. As so often, the concern is to teach the right way to salvation, with a concentration on fasting and confession in Lent, on the works of mercy, and on meeting the needs of the poor. Other themes may have been lost with the leaf, containing up to 200 lines, which is now missing after line 189 (out of an extant total of 264 lines).

God's Address is written, like *Pope John's Passion*, in eight-line refrain stanzas rhyming *ababbcbc*, the refrain in this case being almost uniformly the Latin line "Nolo mortem peccatoris" (I do not wish the death of a sinner). The lines are relatively short, with the result that the verse moves swiftly, and Audelay's reliance on *Marcolf* for source material in the two stanzas comprising lines 137–52 (in which, as elsewhere in his work, he directly addresses those who have cure of souls) demonstrates the degree to which he has here cut down his earlier composition.[62] We may compare:

> I counsel ale youe, ale curators, that wyselé you wayt,
> That han the cure of mons soule in youre kepyng,
> Engeyne the not to yeesy penans, ne to strayt alegat,
> Lest ye slene both bodé and soule with youre ponyschyng,
> Fore better is a Paternoster with repentyng
> To send hem, to the mercé of God, to purgatoré.
> 						(*Marcolf* 923–28)

with:

> Ye curatours, wysely ye wayt,
> That han mon soule in your kepyng;
> Enjoyne ye not penance to strayt,
> Lest ye slen mon soule with ponyschyng!
> A Paternoster with repentyng
> To send ham to purgatoré, better hit is.
> 						(*God's Address* 137–42)

We can admire Audelay's skill in reducing the long, ruminative lines of *Marcolf* to the more directly didactic requirements of *God's Address*: a poetic development opposite to the lengthening of the short lines of *True Living* noted in *The Vision of Saint Paul*. The parallels with *True Living* itself follow after the lacuna in the middle of *God's Address*. Lines 197–202 and 213–20, on giving charity to the poor, closely match *True Living* 238–43 and 251–58, two passages that Audelay also reused in his *Seven Works of Mercy Carol* (W30).[63] Finally, the description of the seven works of mercy in *God's Address* 164–73 is likely to have derived from *True Living* 173–79, though the phrases are rearranged and the parallels not continuous.

What can be said about the make-up of John Audelay's *Counsel of Conscience* on the basis of the above analysis? First, there is too much variety in verse form, subject matter, poetic mode, poetic "origin," and likely date of composition for Audelay plausibly to have conceived poems W1–W18 as a book with a particular title from the start, especially when we consider that as much verse has been lost as has survived from the first part of the manuscript. But it was of course open to Audelay, as to any writer, to assemble poetic materials and call them by what collective title he chose, and it may be that he did indeed mean to encompass, within this naming, the whole of the extant manuscript up to the end of *Epilogue*. If so, the title he decided on, *The Counsel of Conscience*, fits his instructional poems best of all, the Passion and Eucharist material rather less well, and *Marcolf and Solomon* the least, although he himself, at the end of his life, would very likely not have wished to make such distinctions.

Second, the poems most likely to have originated with Audelay are, not surprisingly, those that he signed as his own and which have intertextual relations with other items in *The Counsel of Conscience*. As has been seen, the component parts of the main Passion and Eucharist sequence (W4–W10) can largely be related to extant compositions, English and Latin, in other manuscripts (though such relationships are not restricted to that sequence), and in several cases there is no doubt at all that Audelay borrowed or adapted other writings to which he had access. It is no coincidence that these "borrowed" items—which Audelay does not claim as his own—do not use the thirteen-line stanza form. Audelay was evidently happy to accept other verse forms when they suited his purpose, but thirteen-line stanzas were clearly his preference for his own compositions.

We do not know whether John Audelay had any readers other than his scribes, at Haughmond Abbey or elsewhere. Given the strength and sincerity of the didactic effort that characterizes his later writings, we must hope that he did. These are poems written with an overriding functional purpose. But on the basis of *The Counsel of Conscience* as a whole, it is apparent that Audelay's poetic abilities declined as his urge to save souls increased. There is a gulf between the tautness of *True Living* and the subtlety of *Marcolf*, on the one hand, and the poorly written, hard-line instruction of the Sunday Letter poem, on the other. Nevertheless, he evidently hung on to the poetic form he knew best, the thirteen-liner—despite its lack of appropriateness for hortatory purposes—while at the same time (we may guess) becoming more reliant on adaptations of existing compositions. Considering that *True Living* and *Marcolf*, arguably the best and the earliest written poems in *The Counsel of Conscience*, are also the first in the manuscript as it now survives, suggesting a chronological sequence, it may well be that the substantial body of verse lost from the front of MS Douce 302 comprised Audelay's most accomplished work, written closer to the beginning of the fifteenth century under the influence of later fourteenth-century styles. If so, then John Audelay may have been a much more considerable poet than he now appears.

NOTES

1. Audelay's poems are cited and quoted from John the Blind Audelay, *Poems and Carols (Oxford, Bodleian Library MS Douce 302)*, ed. Susanna Fein (Kalamazoo: Medieval Institute Publications, 2009). Poem numbers prefixed by "W" refer to the numbering of items in Ella Keats Whiting, ed., *The Poems of John Audelay*, EETS o.s. 184 (1931; repr. Oxford: Oxford University Press, 2006). Individual poems are normally referred to by title (see the chart above, pp. 115–16), but Whiting's system is retained where it helps to reference sequences of poems.

2. Tim William Machan, *Textual Criticism and Middle English Texts* (Charlottesville: University of Virginia Press, 1994), p. 104.

3. Whiting, *Poems*, p. 149, from *Finito libro*, the rubric at the end of *Epilogue*.

4. On the prose pieces, see Susanna Greer Fein, "A Thirteen-Line Alliterative Stanza on the Abuse of Prayer from the Audelay MS," *Medium Ævum* 63 (1994): 61–74; and A. I. Doyle, "'Lectulus noster floridus': An Allegory of the Penitent Soul," in *Literature and Religion in the Later Middle Ages: Philological Studies in Honor of Siegfried Wenzel*, ed. Richard G. Newhauser and John A. Alford (Binghamton, N.Y.: Medieval & Renaissance Texts & Studies, 1994), pp. 179–90. For the dialect and metrical skill of the rhymed alliterative poems, see especially Ad Putter, "The Language and Metre of *Pater Noster* and *Three Dead Kings*," *Review of English Studies*, n.s. 55 (2004): 498–526.

5. See, e.g., Rosemary Woolf, *The English Religious Lyric in the Middle Ages* (London: Oxford University Press, 1968), pp. 222, 296, 336; and Elizabeth Salter, *Fourteenth-Century English Poetry: Contexts and Readings* (Oxford: Clarendon Press, 1983), pp. 17–18.

6. See especially Eric G. Stanley, "*The True Counsel of Conscience*, or *The Ladder of Heaven*: In Defence of John Audelay's Unlyrical Lyrics," in *Expedition nach der Wahrheit: Poems, Essays, and Papers in Honour of Theo Stemmler*, ed. Stefan Horlacher and Marion Islinger (Heidelberg: Carl Winter, 1996), pp. 131–59; and Susanna Fein, "Good Ends in the Audelay Manuscript," *Yearbook of English Studies* 33 (2003): 97–199; but the use of the title *Counsel of Conscience* to refer to the first part of MS

Douce 302 as far as *Epilogue* goes back to J. Ernst Wülfing, "Der Dichter John Audelay und sein Werk," *Anglia* 18 (1896): 175–217 (p. 180).

7. Stanley, *"True Counsel,"* surveys some of the material, as does the same writer's "The Verse Forms of Jon the Blynde Awdelay," in *The Long Fifteenth Century: Essays for Douglas Gray*, ed. Helen Cooper and Sally Mapstone (Oxford: Clarendon Press, 1997), pp. 99–121, but neither study analyzes *The Counsel of Conscience* from the point of view of structure and contents.

8. And so it is not the case, as James Simpson asserts, that W1–W18 are "said to comprise a single, titled work"; see James Simpson, "Saving Satire after Arundel's *Constitutions*: John Audelay's 'Marcol and Solomon,'" in *Text and Controversy from Wyclif to Bale: Essays in Honour of Anne Hudson*, ed. Helen Barr and Ann M. Hutchison, Medieval Church Studies 4 (Turnhout: Brepols, 2004), pp. 387–404 (p. 390).

9. See Whiting, *Poems*, p. 149. In this case I have altered the punctuation and capitalization given by Whiting for the sake of the sense.

10. I.e., the twelve leaves preceding the present folio 1, which is the second leaf of a quire from which the first has been lost, plus a presumed additional leaf to make up two regular six-leaf gatherings before the acephalous one with which the manuscript now begins.

11. Fein, "Good Ends," p. 98 n. 3, gives the collation of the surviving part of the manuscript as: "d^6 (lacking 1–2), e^6 (lacking 3–6), f^6, g^6, h^6 (lacking 1; oddly, the scribe labels this gathering 'f'), j^6, k^6." However (and as her other calculations implicitly acknowledge), gathering d lacks only one leaf at the beginning, not two.

12. The collation of MS Douce 302 seems not otherwise to be of textual interest, for the book appears to have been through-written in a continuous and uniform manner, without gaps, with the result that the contents overlap the quire boundaries.

13. Cp. *Epilogue* (W18) 495–507 with *Visiting the Sick* (W11) 378–90, *Vision of St. Paul* (W16) 353–65, and esp. *Lord's Epistle* (W17) 196–208. Cp. also *Remedy of Nine Virtues* (W3) 77–89, though this version lacks Audelay's signature, which instead appears a stanza later, at line 102.

14. Fein, "Good Ends," p. 112 (no. 3); Richard Firth Green, "Marcolf the Fool and Blind John Audelay," in *Speaking Images: Essays in Honor of V. A. Kolve*, ed. Robert F. Yeager and Charlotte C. Morse (Asheville, N.C.: Pegasus, 2001), pp. 559–76; and Simpson, "Saving Satire." The poem is briefly discussed in Andrew Wawn, "Truth-Telling and the Tradition of *Mum and the Sothsegger*," *Yearbook of English Studies* 13 (1983): 270–87 (p. 281).

15. For a discussion of the tradition of Marcolf and Solomon, see Green, "Marcolf the Fool."

16. Simpson, "Saving Satire," pp. 389, 394.

17. Thus at *Marcolf* 988, we find "Thus Salamon hath sayd the soth, verement," but when he is supposed to have begun speaking is quite unclear. One possibility is as far back as line 430, in the stanza following that which begins "I say thee, broder Salamon, tel in thi talkyng" (417).

18. See Simpson, "Saving Satire," p. 388 ("It . . . belongs to a cycle of poems that are otherwise devotional and impeccably orthodox") and p. 390 ("the non-contentious matter in the rest of the collection").

19. The lines are quoted in Simpson, "Saving Satire," p. 398.

20. Cp. esp. *Marcolf* 504–6 and *Epilogue* 374–76; and *Marcolf* 952–56 and *Epilogue* 381–85. The notes to Whiting's edition remain valuable for their mapping of verbal parallels across Audelay's poetry, but the first of the above pairs is not noted there.

21. Green, "Marcolf the Fool," pp. 566–67; Simpson, "Saving Satire," p. 391.

22. Stanley posits that Audelay was not blind when *Marcolf* was written because of its numerical perfection in having 1,000 lines, achieved by the inclusion of one stanza of only twelve lines ("Verse Forms," p. 118 n. 49). His argument is not itself convincing (the stanza in question is not central, there is the possibility of scribal error, and there is a further stanza beyond line 1000), but it should be noted that there are several figurative uses of the word *blind* in Audelay's poems, referring to moral blindness—e.g., "These synnys a mon thai done blynde" (*True Living* 35)—opening the possibility that Audelay's references to his own disabilities are also figurative. In the case of *Marcolf*, it could be argued additionally that the phrase "Blynd as Y am" (503) is put into Solomon's mouth.

23. See especially Simpson, "Saving Satire," pp. 388–90, 402–4.

24. See Fein, "Thirteen-Line Alliterative Stanza," pp. 61–74.

25. Qtd. in Whiting, *Poems*, p. vii, and Fein, "Good Ends," p. 112.

26. Like *Marcolf*, *True Living* forms part of the argument in Wawn, "Truth-Telling," where it is associated with the truth-telling tradition (pp. 273–74), as are the refrain lyrics in the Vernon MS (a manuscript that preserves other poems with affinities to Audelay's).

27. Cp. *True Living* 143–55 with *Ten Commandments Carol* 1–18 (W28.3–17); *True Living* 173–79, 238–41, 251–58 with *Seven Works of Mercy Carol* 1–4, 8–11, 15–18, 22–25, 29–32 (W30.3–10, 13–16, 18–26); and *True Living* 212–15, 225–32 with *Seven Gifts Carol* 22–25, 29–32, 36–39 (W32.18–21, 23–26, 28–31).

28. Cp. *True Living* 130–33 with *Four Estates Carol* 1–4 (W40.3–6); and *True Living* 78–103 with *Chastity of Wives Carol* 8–42 (W49.8–37).

29. Another parallel arguing for later reuse of *True Living* and thus for its earlier date of composition is the virtual identity between its lines 13–25 (on the different deserved fates of evil men and good men) and *Vision of St. Paul* 340–52, discussed below.

30. See also the penultimate stanza (*Remedy of Nine Virtues* 77–89), which—in this case separated from the signature itself—is the one shared by several of these instructional poems; see n. 13, above.

31. As has been noted, two prose items, *Sins of the Heart* and *Honest Bed*, occur toward the end of the manuscript (see Fein, "Good Ends," pp. 118–19), but it is overwhelmingly probable that verse alone occupied the bulk of MS Douce 302.

32. See, e.g., items 15–17 in Carl Horstmann, ed., *The Minor Poems of the Vernon MS.*, part 1, EETS o.s. 98 (1892; repr. New York: Kraus Reprint, 1975), pp. 34–35 (*IMEV, NIMEV* 975, 1959, 1969).

33. The poem is printed from the Balliol College MS in Carleton Brown, ed., *Religious Lyrics of the XVth Century* (London: Clarendon Press, 1939), pp. 95–97 (no. 62; *IMEV, NIMEV* 292).

34. Cp. "Ihesu, for þi blode þou bleddest," lines 13–18 (Brown, *Rel. Lyr. XV Cent.*, p. 96). The only substantive differences exhibited by the Balliol text printed by Brown are "smert" in place of "scharp" (line 32); "On" rather than "To" (line 34); and "To clense" rather than "Thou kepe" (line 36).

35. Woolf, *English Religious Lyric*, p. 226. The poem is printed from the Rawlinson MS in Carleton Brown, ed., *Religious Lyrics of the XIVth Century*, 2nd ed., rev. G. V. Smithers (Oxford: Clarendon Press, 1957), pp. 218–19 (no. 123; *IMEV, NIMEV* 1708).

36. Fein, "Good Ends," p. 112. In her later edition, she prints *The Psalter of the Passion* as seven items, in agreement with my analysis here.

37. As Whiting notes in her edition (*Poems*, p. 234).

38. Cp. *Instr. for Prayer 2* 1–2 (W6.17–18): "Instid of thi Paternoster, this thou take, / And this thi Ave, fore Cristis sake."

39. See Horstmann, *Minor Poems*, pt. 1, pp. 49–105, 106–20 (*IMEV, NIMEV* 1060, 1057). Cp. N. F. Blake, "Vernon Manuscript: Contents and Organisation," in *Studies in the Vernon Manuscript*, ed. Derek Pearsall (Cambridge: Brewer, 1990), pp. 45–59 (pp. 46, 52).

40. It occurs again, in the form "Wel ys hym that wil and may / Say this prayere every day" (*Instr .for Prayer 8* 1–2; W19.176–77), as the closing couplet of one of the salutations that make up the manuscript's next poetic grouping. As will be seen, a salutation is a prominent feature of the grouping numbered XX by the rubricator (*Devotions at the Levation of Christ's Body*), next to be discussed.

41. Alexandra Barratt, "The Prymer and Its Influence on Fifteenth-Century English Passion Lyrics," *Medium Ævum* 55 (1975): 264–79 (pp. 276–78). For a valuable study of the knowledge and use of the Primer (or Book of Hours) by the laity, see Eamon Duffy, *The Stripping of the Altars: Traditional Religion in England, c. 1400–c. 1580* (New Haven: Yale University Press, 1992), pp. 209–32.

42. The Vernon text is printed in F. J. Furnivall, ed., *The Minor Poems of the Vernon MS.*, part 2, EETS o.s. 117 (1901; repr. Millwood, N.Y.: Kraus Reprint, 1987), pp. 493–511 (*IMEV, NIMEV* 4276). The text in Harley 3954, which is dated to the third quarter of the fifteenth century, remains unprinted (*IMEV, NIMEV* 1986).

43. Whiting, *Poems*, p. 235, tabulates by line number the most important parallel passages.

44. Harley begins, like Douce, at line 13 of Vernon, but remains close to the latter for far longer than Douce. Neither abridgment uses Vernon, lines 168–252 (which include simple forms of confession for lay use) or 397–684 (the account of the different stages of the Mass).

45. Putter, "Language and Metre," provides ample linguistic (including lexical) evidence that Audelay lifted lines in *Virtues of the Mass* from an existing source, and he draws particular attention to parallels with the Harley version of the poem. See esp. his pp. 506–7, 509–10.

46. See *IMEV, Suppl.*, and *NIMEV* 3233. The Vernon text can be found (as lines 1–44 of the poem there printed) in Horstmann, *Minor Poems*, pt. 1, pp. 19–20, and in Frank Allen Patterson, ed., *The Middle English Penitential Lyric* (New York: Columbia University Press, 1911), pp. 50–53.

47. The lines in question are *Remedy of Nine Virtues* 77–89, *Visiting the Sick* 378–90, *Lord's Epistle* 196–208, *Vision of St. Paul* 353–65, and *Epilogue* 495–507. There are also other textual parallels, e.g., *Visiting the Sick* 10–13, *Lord's Epistle* 179–82, and *Vision of St. Paul* 258–61.

48. Cp. *Visiting the Sick* 378–403 and *Remedy of Nine Virtues* 77–102.

49. The parallel texts begin: "Multis diebus iam peractis, / Nulla fides est in pactis; / Videte," and "Moné days now agone / Fayth ne covenant is ther non— / Behold and se!" (*World's Folly* 1–3, 7–9; W12.unnumbered, 1–3).

50. See "And trust not to another mon" and "Fore I say soth, I am escheent" (*World's Folly* 59, 70; W12.53, 64), and cp. particularly "Fore I have towchid the trouth, I trow I schal be schent" (*Marcolf* 1001). For discussion of the topos in relation to Audelay, see Wawn, "Truth-Telling," pp. 272–74, 281.

51. The scribe mistakenly writes "Pope Ion þe xij" (*Pope John's Passion* 1), but the reference to Avignon makes it clear that Pope John XXII is intended.

52. Some of the narrative material does not occur in John, notably the earthquake and eclipse at the moment of Christ's death (*Pope John's Passion* 57–64).

53. The refrain in *Pope John's Passion* varies but is normally a version of either "And on Cristis Passion had peté" (8) or "And al hit was fore love of thee" (16).

54. F. L. Cross, ed., *Oxford Dictionary of the Christian Church*, 3rd ed., rev. E. A. Livingstone (Oxford: Oxford University Press, 1997), s.v. "Anima Christi," notes that John XXII, though probably not its author, "enriched it with indulgences."

55. See Whiting, *Poems*, p. 240, and Woolf, *English Religious Lyric*, pp. 235–36.

56. The Vernon text is printed in Horstmann, *Minor Poems*, pt. 1, pp. 37–43 (*IMEV, NIMEV* 701). Cp. especially the following: *Seven Hours* 19–20 and Vernon 17–18; *Seven Hours* 28 and Vernon 33; *Seven Hours* 30–31 and Vernon 35–36.

57. It may also be noted that the Vernon poem's final promise of pardon is specifically attributed to Pope John (presumably John XXII), as is the pardon in *Pope John's Passion*.

58. For a valuable survey of OE and ME versions of the Sunday Letter (including this one) and an account of its origins, see V. M. O'Mara, *A Study and Edition of Selected Middle English Sermons: Richard Alkerton's Easter Week Sermon Preached at St Mary Spital in 1406, a Sermon on Sunday Observance, and a Nunnery Sermon for the Feast of the Assumption* (Leeds: School of English, University of Leeds, 1994), pp. 94–104.

59. Audelay's poem is printed alongside this closely similar text by R. Priebsch, "John Audelay's Poem on the Observance of Sunday and Its Sources," in *An English Miscellany Presented to Dr. Furnivall in Honour of His Seventy-Fifth Birthday*, ed. W. P. Ker, A. S. Napier, and W. W. Skeat (1901; repr. New York: Benjamin Blom, 1969), pp. 397–407.

60. Whiting, *Poems*, pp. 241–42. The existence of a Latin text of the Vision of Saint Paul in MS Royal 8 F.vi is noted in Priebsch, "John Audelay's Poem," p. 398 n. 2 (and see also the essay by Robert Easting in the present volume).

61. The short-couplet version is printed in Horstmann, *Minor Poems*, pt. 1, pp. 251–60 (*IMEV, NIMEV* 1898). For closer than usual parallels, cp. *Vision of St. Paul* 53–55 and Vernon 55–59; *Vision of St. Paul* 211 and Vernon 234; *Vision of St. Paul* 244 and Vernon 264. Whiting, *Poems*, p. 241, notes three stanzas within the body of the poem that are not represented in Vernon, of which the strangest in context is the one beginning "Holé Cherche is a house of prayere" (93–105), which looks to belong to another poem altogether.

62. These parallels do not appear to have been previously noticed. Besides the verses next quoted, *God's Address* 145–52 draw directly on *Marcolf* 936–40 (and more generally on 941–48).

63. See n. 27, above.

Audelay's *Marcolf and Solomon* and the Langlandian Tradition

Derek Pearsall

When I first came across John Audelay's poems thirty years ago, I was delighted to find an author who named himself (several times) and attached to himself a canon of writings in a unique manuscript that he himself supervised.[1] Scholars of Middle English literature have got used to managing without named authors and fixed canons, sometimes even claiming that it is a matter of no great moment. But in truth, anonymity is an exasperation, and, with the absence of a canon, prevents or inhibits much of the critical activity that we enjoy practicing. So Audelay's readiness to come out of the customary unknown was an unexpected pleasure. And not only did he have a name: he also had a local habitation, for he tells us that he was living at Haughmond Abbey, a house of Augustinian canons in Shropshire, as priest of the Lestrange family chantry, having previously served as chaplain in the retinue of Richard Lestrange, Lord of Knockin, in Shropshire. The discovery in 1982 that Audelay was one of those present at a notorious act of sacrilege in a London church in 1417, in which his patron was involved and in which a parishioner was killed, added an enigmatic penitential shadow to a life that was, he tells us, drawing to its close in sickness and blindness.[2]

All this would be of less interest if Audelay were not also a significant minor poet, author of some accomplished carols and of poems of prayer and devotion of a decidedly more than routine cast in a variety of meters, though probably not of the extraordinary bravura poem of *Three Dead Kings* which has penultimate place in MS Douce 302.[3] The first eighteen poems in the manuscript form a distinct group, a "boke," which Audelay at the end calls "*The Cownsel of Conseans*, . . . / Or *The Ladder of Heven*" (*Epilogue* 417–18), devoted chiefly to basic doctrinal instruction along with themes for more advanced meditation and prayer. It was a different kind of poem in this group, Poem 2 in Ella Keats Whiting's edition (here called *Marcolf and Solomon*), that compelled my particular attention when I first read Audelay. It is a long and sprawling anthology of reproof and exhortation to the clergy, written in a complex thirteen-line stanza consisting of an octave of four-stress alliterative and semi-alliterative lines rhyming like the balladestanza (*ababbcbc*) and five shorter lines, like a bob and wheel, largely non-alliterative, rhyming deeed. When I came to write of this poem, I spoke of it as "deeply penetrated by alliteration and alliterative rhythms . . . profoundly influenced by *Piers Plowman*, with mention of 'Mede the maydyn' (705) and constant echoes of cadence and phrasing."[4] I quoted the following lines (Audelay is addressing lords):

> Thagh ye be leders of the lond, gete you lovyng,
> And cale the clargé to your counsel, that beryn Cristis kay,
> And holdist up Holé Cherche, the Prinse of Heven to pay.
> Y dred lest dedlé sun this reeme wyl dystry.
> (*Marcolf* 237–40)[5]

It is the nature of this influence that I wish to reexamine in this essay.

The poem is loosely framed as the advice given by the fool "Marcol" (this is how Audelay spells the name throughout), "I, Marcol, the more fole mon, on my mad wyse" (66), to his brother "Salamon" (67). There is a long tradition of poems, though poorly represented in English, in which the cunning rustic "fool" Marcolf (the usual form of the name) outwits Solomon in a series of verbal duels.[6] What Marcolf says has the homely truth of the fool, whilst his foolishness enables him to evade censure. Audelay takes advantage of this conventional license:

> I reche never who hit here,
> Weder prest or frere,
> For at a fole ye ma lere,
>   Yif ye wil take hede.
>   (1010–13)

But in other respects his poem belongs only superficially within the tradition: it is a poem of complaint, satire, and exhortation, directed against the covetousness and neglectfulness of priests and friars, not a string of proverbial maxims that confound solemn wisdom, and it lacks completely the scatological element that is often a feature of the Solomon dialogues.

In fact, Audelay makes little use of the opportunities offered by the genre. There is no development of the speaking voice or persona of the fool, and the further references in the body of the poem to the supposed dialogue form, at lines 92 ("Dispise thou no pristhod, broder, I thee pray"), 391–92 ("My blessid broder, Salamon, spesialy I thee pray, / Meve this mater maysterfully to prest and to frere") and 417–18 ("I say thee, broder Salamon, tel in thi talking / Furst of the frerys"), do not build up in any significant way. At the end of the poem it appears that Solomon began to speak at some unspecified point in the preceding discourse, following Marcolf's exhortations: "Thus Salamon hath sayd the soth, verement, / As Marcol, the more fole, warned hym, I wene" (988–89). The voice of the "I" throughout is that of the orthodox cleric, John Audelay ("Blynd as Y am"; 503), and he names himself at the end ("Syr Jon Audlay"; 1008).

There is no way of knowing how long before 1426 (the date given in the *Finito libro* colophon) *Marcolf and Solomon* was written. James Simpson, whose excellent essay on the poem is chiefly engaged in elucidating Audelay's response to the persecution of Lollardy and the suppression of religious dissent, argues, surely correctly, that it must have been written after the promulgation of Arundel's *Constitutions* in 1409, while Richard Firth Green argues more specifically for a date between 1410 and 1413.[7]

The burden of criticism in the poem is directed against the secular clergy and friars who neglect their pastoral duties and are motivated only by covetousness and love of an easy life. Against this, there runs constantly the exhortation to laymen to obey their priests even though those priests may lead a sinful life, and not to do what they do but what they say (118–30, 780–818):

> I counsel youe, ale Cristun men, and comawnd in Cristis name
> That ye obey your curatis that ye ben boundon to;
> Yif oné be fallyn be frelté in ané febel fame,
> God graunt hem of his grace no more so to do.
>   (780–83)

> But do not as thai doun—therof take good hede!
>   (797)

Audelay places particular stress on the efficacy of the sacrament of penance and the sacrament of the altar, even when administered by a sinful priest:

> Fore God hath graunt of his grace to curatis his pouere—
> Thagh thai ben synful men—to asoyle youe of your synne,
> Thorgh vertu of the sacrementte, sothlé I yowe enseure.
>
> (806–8)

> Yif the prest unworthelé presume to syng his mas,
> Serus, Y say the sacrement enpayrd hit may not be.
>
> (832–33)

> The sacrement of the autere defoulyd mai not be.
>
> (852)

The repeated emphasis upon this orthodox point of doctrine is evidently a response to the denial by Lollards of the ministering power of sinful priests.

Most stanzas are prefixed by a Latin scriptural tag or common saying, and there are three stanzas with longer Latin prose colophons (754, 819, 962). The English stanzas sometimes offer a loose extended paraphrase of the Latin, but they are often related to it only obliquely or hardly at all. The Latin phrase that precedes the first stanza, written by Scribe B though Scribe A writes almost all the others, seems to act as a title for the whole poem and to state its main theme: *De concordia inter rectores fratres et rectores ecclesie*. Simpson, in the essay referred to above, speaks of it likewise as a title for the whole poem, and interprets it thus: "The Latin quotation that opens the entire text, indeed, focuses (as I read it) on lay/clerical relations as the key problem . . . 'Concerning harmony between (lay) brothers who govern (society) and the governors of the Church.' The poem addresses itself principally to those relations (between orthodox laity and all clerics), not to relations between orthodoxy and heresy."[8] I believe this interpretation to be mistaken. Though the need for priests to live truly and for laymen to respect them is an important recurring theme, it is not the main theme, and *rectores fratres* cannot possibly mean what Simpson visibly strains to make it mean. Further, he neglects the very specific relation of *concordia* and of the two kinds of *rectores* to the particularities of the poem. The main theme of the poem, as I believe is indicated by its title, is the desire that friars (*rectores fratres*) and secular priests (*rectores ecclesie*) should work together harmoniously for the benefit of those laymen who are in their care:[9]

> My blessid broder, Salamon, spesialy I thee pray,
> Meve this mater maysterfully to prest and to frere;
> Spare not to say the soth, and make a loveday.
>
> (391–93)

And further:

> Betwene prestis and frerys, ywys,
>   I make this loveday.
>   (973–74)

In the latter instance, Audelay goes on to allude at length to the kiss of peace of the Four Daughters of God as the model of such concord (975–87). There are several other occasions where "prest and frere" are jointly referred to or addressed (for example, lines 70, 818, 822), and "loveday" is clearly a popular translation of *concordia*. Audelay emphasizes that priests and friars "al thai beth breder" (620), and that "Thai schuld never be at dyscord" (622). Friars are called *rectores fratres* because the cure of souls was the office they often performed as preachers and confessors. It was indeed in this role that the possessioners traditionally saw the mendicants as usurping their own essential (and often lucrative) duties, a cause to them of bitter and jealous resentment. It is this age-old dispute that Audelay is addressing. Friars were often also quite literally the rectors of a parish, that is, the incumbents of its living, though Audelay mentions only their greed for salaries and trentals (470), in competition with chantry priests. The granting of papal permission to friars to hold benefices, which had been rare (and of course against the rules of the orders), became more common in the fifteenth century; often the benefice lay in the gift of a great lord, for whom the friar had officiated as chaplain or confessor.[10] The incumbency of the living that went with the benefice was customarily neglected or delegated to a poorly paid curate.[11]

Any attempt to summarize the content of a poem so loosely structured is bound to be inadequate, but some elements of its organization can be outlined as a context for what has been suggested to be the main theme, that of concord between priests and friars.

The introduction (1–66) affirms the necessity for Christians of following God's commandments if they are to stay on the path to salvation. There follows (67–169) criticism of those who neglect the souls in their care ("pryst and . . . frere"; 70) and cause "homlé hosbondusmen" (68) to cry out against them: "Thai are the lanternys of lyf, the leud men to lyght, / Bot thai be caght with covetyse, with consians unclere" (71–72). The criticism centers here on parish priests—Audelay shows an unexpected gift for traditional anticlerical satire in the wonderfully comic stanza on the local parson, "Oure gentyl Ser Jone" (144)—but combined with the criticism is the constant reminder that even a bad priest, if he speaks the word of God, must be obeyed and respected, in the hope that God will make him better (159–60). In the next section, a long digression (170–390), Audelay turns aside to the monks, for whose rule of life and witness of prayer he expresses unstinted admiration. Those who keep their rule and do not seek worldly advancement should continue to receive the patronage of great lords. Audelay turns next to the friars (391–546), whose life is seen as admirable if they keep to their rule—in fact, the poet goes so far as to say, later, that the realm would be ruined if it were not for the example that friars set by their life and teaching to secular priests (599–600). They were chosen by God to "be clene kalender, the sekelers on to see" (410). Their entitlement to beg is affirmed, as long as it is not a burden on the poor (510–11), but their covetousness is condemned (469–81), and there is some rather enigmatic irony apparently at their expense (456–68).

Audelay returns abruptly to the secular clergy (547–857).[12] He complains first against the simoniacal appointment of ignorant and neglectful priests, and then more generally against the covetousness of the clergy and their neglect of their duties, who should be "clene calender, the leud men on to se" (614, cp. 410, quoted above), "lanterns lyght in Holé Cherche to bren" (630, cp. 71, quoted above). Neglectful priests leave the people to go astray, and are content if they get their tithes and their "slus or schof" (693); they are maintained by "Mede the maydyn" (705), seek pluralities, and say masses for money. But even though they fail to practice what they preach, they should be obeyed, for they remain, despite all, true ministers of the sacraments (806–57). The poem ends (858–1013) with reflections on the Trinity, on the nature of the sacraments, on the necessity of penance, and with renewed exhortations to priests and friars to live truly so that the laity will respect and gladly obey them.

Before turning to the Langlandian connection, I should comment on the allusions to "Lolleres" (133, 670, 677), which provide such an important jumping-off point for Simpson's essay on "Saving Satire." In the first, Audelay complains about how a "pore prest, and spirituale in spyrt" (131), who truly and devoutly serves his office, is scornfully likened to "a Lollere and to an epocryte" (133) by ignorant and worldly men, including his fellow priests.[13] The use of "Lollere" here to mean someone who is unnecessarily and inconveniently religious, who somehow exhibits his devotion and piety in order to make others feel bad, seems a direct outgrowth of the use to which Chaucer put the word in the Host's scornful dismissal of the Parson's mild rebuke of his swearing ("'I smelle a Loller in the wind,' quod he") in the Epilogue to *The Man of Law's Tale*.[14] Such people are a nuisance and spoil everyone's fun, like Margery Kempe on pilgrimage. The other two references occur in a passage where Audelay warns of the dangers faced by laymen who speak out and tell the truth (669–76).[15] Such "leud men" are accused of being Lollers by worldy curates, which puts them in fear that their detractors may condemn them "To preche apon the peleré, / And bren hem after too" (675–76). Believe me, says Audelay, a real "Loller" is unmistakably known by his deeds: he refuses his obligations to the Church, to worship the Cross, or to attend services, does not believe in the presence of "God veray" (681) in the sacrament of the altar, and generally sets the sacraments at nought. "Take him fore a Loller, Y tel you truely!" says Audelay (684).

The clear purpose of these remarks is to preserve a space for genuine criticism of the clergy so that it will not be tagged thoughtlessly and maliciously as "Lollardy." Simpson has it exactly right, I think: "My primary argument is that Audelay's remarkable text attempts to preserve a space for orthodox yet trenchant vernacular ecclesiological satire and theology in unpropitious circumstances. . . . Audelay's is not principally an attack on Lollardy at all. It is, instead, a defence of the necessity of orthodox protest against ecclesiastical abuse, even when such protest might easily be confused with Lollardy."[16] Whether Audelay found the inspiration for his courageous outspokenness (for that it is, I think) in "harnessing the energies of *Piers Plowman* in his effort to preserve such a discursive space," as Simpson says,[17] is the matter that I now finally address.

Simpson argues vigorously for the Langlandian connection and makes some telling points. The strongest, for me, is in his comparison between the uses of "kynd" and "kyndly" in the two poems, and the inferences he draws from it, and between the two poets in their concern and understandable apprehension about speaking the truth out loud.[18] The other arguments seem to me less strong. "Both Langland and Audelay are, in my view," says Simpson, "orthodox critics of ecclesiastical covetousness, whose principal target is the friars, and whose principal solution to the problem of mendicancy is a 'fyndyng.'"[19] This is true of Langland, but certainly the friars are not the principal targets of Audelay's criticism, as I hope my summary of the poem has shown with sufficient clarity. Audelay criticizes them far less severely and insistently than Langland, and expresses admiration for their way of life, especially their begging, to which Langland gives only grudging approval (for example, C.16.355–56). As for the "fyndyng," it is indeed Langland's long-sought-after if never explicitly defined solution to the problem of mendicancy, but the term is introduced in Audelay only in the stanza of what I have called enigmatic irony (456–68), which begins thus:

> Yif ye wyle yef ham of your good without beggyng,
> Thai wold nowther begge ne borou, thus dare I say;
> And fynd hem here houshold and here housing,
> Nouther by ne byld—I red ye asay!
>
> (456–59)

This seems to mean, "If you give to them before they have to beg, then they will not have to beg; and (if you) find them their housing and sustenance, (then they will not have to) beg nor build." The remainder of the stanza is a puzzle. We are bid to look upon the friars' church, "Apon here bellys, on here bokys, and here byldyng, / Apon here prechyng, here prayes, her reverent aray" (461–62). Some of these aspects of their life look like the ostentation that is a common theme of antimendicant satire; others seem unobjectionable. It is a puzzle to me, but the next stanza is one of unequivocal condemnation—"I lekyn ham to Judas" (473)—and unless Audelay's tone is one of more than usual fluidity, I take it that he is deploring in the preceding stanza the consequences of providing the friars with a regular income, whether through fees for confessions and burials or through other unscrupulous dealings such as the sale of "letters of fraternity."[20] Where for Langland the friars' systematic practice of begging is what inevitably leads to scandalous abuse, for Audelay it is the proper traditional basis of their livelihood. Their poverty compels the charity of those who have the means—it is God's way of sending them succor (491, 540)—though friars should not beg from the poor (510–20).

On endowment generally, the two poets are totally opposed. Langland, who leans toward what became the Lollard position on this issue, urges lords not to break up their estates and alienate their heirs by giving to corrupt and wealthy religious and clergy (for example, C.5.163, C.17.55), while Audelay exhorts them to continue the practice of their fathers by endowing the Church (255, 274). On other issues that were contentious among reformists in the 1370s and 1380s and that were declared heretical after the condemnation of the Lollards, Langland, writing at an earlier date, gives expression at times to a degree of radical opinion—on disendowment, on priestly poverty, on secular lordship, on the necessity of oral confession—that was later dangerous and that he himself, in the C-text, may have modified in the direction of caution.[21] Audelay, by contrast, is strictly orthodox, as in his reproof to those lords who attempt to interfere in the affairs of religion, where he cites Saint Thomas as a martyr to the cause of the Church's independence (342), and in his assertion that oral confession to a priest or friar is necessary at least once a year (820). Simpson cites Anne Hudson for evidence that "ground," which is used in a number of phrases by Audelay, was perhaps part of a Lollard secret vocabulary, a kind of code word.[22] It may have had such a cachet for a time, among certain groups, but it was not removed from ordinary circulation, even in the phrases associated with the Lollards, as the *MED* shows.

Simpson also compares "the formal strategies" used by the two poets, in particular the invoking by Audelay of the voices of the "homlé hosbondusmen" (68) and of the fool Marcol, which he sets beside Langland's "lunatyk" (B.Prol.123–24) and "lunatyk lollares" (C.9.107–14).[23] But their practices are in truth very different. Langland's use of enigmatically nonauthoritative voices in order to position his criticism—not just those of the "lunatyk" and the "lunatyk lollares" but, more significantly, those of Will himself, Rechelesnesse (in the C-text), and a host of other witnesses—is a major strategy in the building of his poem's meaning, where for Audelay Marcolf is a flimsy mask, soon discarded and only momentarily reassumed. The voice of the poem is his own voice, critical of the faults of priests and friars but in the context of a repeated and explicit admiration for what they do. Audelay participates hardly at all in the general anticlericalism of the Langlandian tradition. He is not an "outsider," but belongs to the body of orthodox critical commentators on the religious scene, clerics such as John Mirk and William of Nassington (author of the *Speculum vitae*), as one might expect of a salaried chantry priest and adoptive canon.

Simpson mentions one or two other themes and topics that Langland and Audelay have in common, such as the image of heat to explicate the Trinity and the story of the Four Daughters of God.[24] These, though, are the commonplaces of medieval religious writing, as are the warnings against the untrustworthiness of executors (89, 258; *Piers Plowman* C.2.192, C.6.254, etc.); the comparisons between the wickedness of man and the obedience to natural law of animals (105; *Piers* C.13.143); the condemnation of priests who bear "baslardes" (150; *Piers* B.15.121, 124); the mention of "favele" (394; *Piers* C.2.passim); the condemnation of priests who "permutate" their pluralities (730–31; *Piers* C.3.33); the reference to the game of the "newe fayre" (728; *Piers* C.6.377); the image of the "penetawnsere" as a surgeon (899–902; *Piers* C.22.315). Both poets mention "lovedays" (390, 393, 974; *Piers* C.3.196, 197, C.5.158, C.11.17), but for Langland, as for Chaucer

(*General Prologue* 258), these are days of shifting and dubious arbitration, with friars sleazily involved, while for Audelay they are the symbol of true concord.

A writer could of course be influenced by *Piers Plowman* without fully sharing the poem's purposes and persuasions, and we return therefore to the impression created among readers of *Marcolf and Solomon* of a pervasively "Langlandian" idiom, despite the difference of meter.[25] There are a large number of alliterative phrases that the two poems have in common, but many are the ordinary currency of the language and nearly all are well attested in the poetry of the alliterative tradition, as J. P. Oakden's lists show.[26] Those for which other attestation has not been found (this does not mean there is none to be found) are very much subject-related, the alliterative revival not generally offering much scope for "put to poverty," "part with the poor," or "preach to the people." Beside this, many of Audelay's favorite alliterative phrases make no appearance in *Piers Plowman*.[27] Gnomic and proverbial-sounding expressions have sometimes a Langlandian ring, for example, "Whosoever sparys fore to speke, sparys for to spede, / And he that spekys and spedys noght, he spellys the wynd" (443–44). Compare "Spille hit, spare hit nat and thow shalt spede the bettere" (*Piers* C.3.425), and "Betere is that bote bale adoun brynge / Then bale be ybete and bote neuer the betere" (*Piers* C.4.88–89).[28] Others sound Langlandian, but have a wide currency in a variety of moralistic and minatory writings, for example, "He has wysdam and wyt, I tel yow trewly, / That can beware or he be wo and leve in clene lyve" (42–43).[29] The impression of Langland's presence remains intuitive, and the lack of hard evidence of Audelay's knowledge of *Piers Plowman*—with the exception of "Mede the maydyn" (705)[30]—creates a puzzle. By contrast, when a poem is clearly directly influenced by *Piers Plowman*, as is the case with *Mum and the Sothsegger*, the evidence is unmistakable.

The answer to the puzzle, I think, is that both Langland and Audelay draw upon a common body of popular complaint, satire, and prophecy, a body of phrase and idiom to which Langland himself contributed significantly. It was a largely oral tradition (that is, oral memory of written texts), nurtured also by popular preaching in the vernacular, where the alliterative tendency is often strong.[31] It appears in written form in scraps and fragments and enigmatic traces, such as "Thomas of Erceldoune's Prophecy" in London, BL MS Harley 2253, or the letters of John Ball, or the scraps of verse embedded in prose treatises and sermons, or the short poems of popular prophecy that offer a satirical criticism of the present under the guise of a cryptic vision of the future.[32] Bills, in the form of little parchment rolls and one-page pamphlets, played a part in the dissemination of such traditions, and their contents were often orally transmitted, but their ephemeral nature (posted, for instance, on doors and windows) means that they cannot be expected to survive (the letters of John Ball are exceptional).[33] They are mostly political and usually subversive, but Wendy Scase draws attention to a poem against those preachers who dress like gallants, one version of which "borrows from a quatrain that was thought to have been posted as a bill."[34]

Sometimes the tradition emerges in more worked-over literary form, as in our two poets here, or in anonymous moralistic refrain poems, or the more elaborate versions of such poems in the Vernon Manuscript, or in the religious-didactic poems of Oxford, Bodl. Lib. MS Digby 102, or in the poem of *The Simonie* ("On the Evil Times of Edward II"), which seems to be frequently echoed in *Piers Plowman*, perhaps again as the result of raids by both poets on the common stock of complaint and satire.[35] So the apocalyptic tone of prophecy in Audelay (for example, in lines 237–40, 990–91), though it sounds like an echo of *Piers Plowman*, is more likely an echo of this more widespread and resonant tradition—which Langland knew as well. The letters of John Ball, which achieved written form and survival only because of the diligent hostility of the chroniclers, is the most apt example for my purposes of the accidental outcropping of the popular tradition. I would venture, even, to suggest that the mention of "Mede the maydyn" in Audelay is itself of a kind with the allusion to "Peres Ploughman" in the letters. Piers is a character who has been heard of and has taken his place in a certain popular mythology. The person or people who wrote the letters did not have to have read Langland's poem to know what they wanted to make of his homely hero. Likewise, Audelay shows few signs, to me, of having known *Piers Plowman* directly or having been directly influenced by its procedures and strategies. He was simply dipping into the same pot.

What I have offered here is an alternative explanation of the resemblances between *Piers Plowman* and *Marcolf and Solomon*, other than that of direct influence. It is still a definite possibility that Audelay knew Langland's poem. But there is a wider implication that may give added significance to the inquiry. Perhaps our modern practice of deducing or establishing influences through the comparison of surviving written texts is not always appropriate to medieval literary culture.[36] Popular poems often circulated in essentially ephemeral form, on rolls and bits of parchment, and the odd scraps that remain are lucky accidents. Also, oral tradition was still strong, and there is a wealth of evidence for it in the well-documented comparisons of versions of popular romances and ballads. It is annoying to have to appeal to what can only be fragmentary evidence at best, but the alternatives are either a persuasion of the universality of the modern, that the only influences exerted are those for which written attestation can be produced, or a resort to the mysteries of the intertextual, where the relations between texts have only to be perceived, not explained.

Notes

1. The manuscript is Oxford, Bodl. Lib. MS Douce 302. Most of the contents are in Ella Keats Whiting, ed., *The Poems of John Audelay*, EETS o.s. 184 (1931; repr. Oxford: Oxford University Press, 2006). Whiting's edition, admirable for its day, is about to be superseded by that of Susanna Fein, and I am grateful to her for an advance copy of the text of *Marcolf and Solomon*, which I use for all reference and quotation in this essay.

2. See Michael Bennett, "John Audley: Some New Evidence on His Life and Work," *Chaucer Review* 16 (1982): 344–55.

3. For opposed views for and against Audelay's authorship of the poem, see, respectively, Eric G. Stanley, "The Verse Forms of Jon the Blynde Awdelay," in *The Long Fifteenth Century: Essays for Douglas Gray*, ed. Helen Cooper and Sally Mapstone (Oxford: Clarendon Press, 1997), pp. 99–121, and Ad Putter, "The Language and Metre of *Pater Noster* and *Three Dead Kings*," *Review of English Studies*, n.s. 55 (2004): 498–526.

4. Derek Pearsall, *Old English and Middle English Poetry* (London: Routledge and Kegan Paul, 1977), p. 249.

5. The closest parallel in *Piers Plowman* to this kind of apocalyptic admonition is C.Prol.62–65. The editions used here are those of George Kane and E. Talbot Donaldson, eds., *Piers Plowman: The B Version*, 2nd ed. (London: Athlone, 1988), and George Russell and George Kane, eds., *Piers Plowman: The C Version* (London: Athlone, 1997). Where the two versions have substantially the same text, I cite C.

6. See Richard Firth Green, "Marcolf the Fool and Blind John Audelay," in *Speaking Images: Essays in Honor of V. A. Kolve*, ed. Robert F. Yeager and Charlotte C. Morse (Asheville, N.C.: Pegasus, 2001), pp. 559–76. See also Francis Lee Utley, "Dialogues, Debates and Catechisms," in *MWME* 3:736–45.

7. James Simpson, "Saving Satire after Arundel's *Constitutions*: John Audelay's 'Marcol and Solomon,'" in *Text and Controversy from Wyclif to Bale: Essays in Honour of Anne Hudson*, ed. Helen Barr and Ann M. Hutchinson, Medieval Church Studies 4 (Turnhout: Brepols, 2004), pp. 387–404 (p. 391); Green, "Marcolf the Fool," pp. 566–67.

8. Simpson, "Saving Satire," p. 397.

9. Green likewise sees the poem as "lamenting the way avarice has driven a wedge between the friars and the secular clergy" ("Marcolf the Fool," p. 566).

10. See David Knowles, *The Religious Orders in England*, 3 vols. (Cambridge: Cambridge University Press, 1962–71), 2:171, 173.

11. Knowles, *Religious Orders*, 2:293.

12. Simpson speaks of Marcolf's voice as "fluid and mobile, suddenly changing the direction of address without warning" ("Saving Satire," p. 401), but it is possible to view such abrupt and unsignalled shifts of subject and register less generously.

13. Audelay recurs to this theme in *Epilogue* 248–60: "thay cal trew Cristyn men Lollard" (253).

14. *Canterbury Tales*, II 1173. The edition used is Geoffrey Chaucer, *The Canterbury Tales*, ed. Jill Mann (London: Penguin, 2005). For the characterization of "Lolleres," I draw on the brilliant essay by Anne Middleton, "Acts of Vagrancy: The C Version 'Autobiography' and the Statute of 1388," in *Written Work: Langland, Labor, and Authorship*, ed. Steven Justice and Kathryn Kerby-Fulton (Philadelphia: University of Pennsylvania Press, 1997), pp. 208–317 (p. 287).

15. Audelay speaks in similar terms in lines 500–503, but without actually mentioning Lollards.

16. Simpson, "Saving Satire," pp. 389, 394.

17. Simpson, "Saving Satire," p. 390.

18. Simpson, "Saving Satire," p. 403.

19. Simpson, "Saving Satire," p. 402.

20. I.e., documents entitling laymen to the benefits of prayer in religious houses. See the useful note by Janette Richardson in *The Riverside Chaucer*, ed. Larry D. Benson, 3rd ed. (Boston: Houghton Mifflin, 1987), p. 878 (note to *Summoner's Tale* III 2126–28).

21. See Derek Pearsall, "Langland and Lollardy: From B to C," *Yearbook of Langland Studies* 17 (2003): 7–23.

22. Simpson, "Saving Satire," p. 394, citing the essay by Anne Hudson, "A Lollard Sect Vocabulary?," in *So Meny People, Longages and Tonges: Philological Essays in Scots and Mediaeval English Presented to Angus McIntosh*, ed. Michael Benskin and M. L. Samuels (Edinburgh: Benskin & Samuels, 1981), pp. 15–30.

23. Simpson, "Saving Satire," p. 402.

24. Simpson, "Saving Satire," p. 403.

25. The difference of meter includes not only the use of the rhyming stanza instead of the unrhymed alliterative long line, but also the frequent presence of over-rich (*aa/aa*) and defective alliteration, both rare in *Piers Plowman*.

26. In the first group, e.g., "say . . . the soth" (5, 99, 393, 421, 669, 1002; *Piers* passim); "wele . . . ye wyt" (5; *Piers* passim); "kyndlé know" (59, 917; *Piers* passim); "love of thi Lord" (336, 353, 370, 967; *Piers* passim); "wele . . . woo" (385; *Piers* C.11.105, C.12.209, C.20.209, C.21.243); "borou . . . beg" (434; *Piers* C.7.35, C.16.372, C.16.374); in the second group, "matens and masse" (33, 680; *Piers*

passim); "mend here mysdedys" (33, 160, 278, 398, 489; *Piers* C.1.164, C.7.121, C.16.263); "mend that thai do mys" (38, 94, 585, 637, 985; *Piers* C.4.86, C.19.297); "schame . . . schent" (187, 411, 599, 616, 904, 922; *Piers* B.11.426); "worchip of this world" (202, 280, 316; *Piers* C.1.8); "lykyng ne lust" (203; *Piers* B.16.32, C.11.80, C.13.152, C.16.212); "trustis to tresoure" (369; *Piers* C.1.66, C.3.161, C.9.334); "pot hom to povert" (485; *Piers* C.13.8, C.21.67); "part with the pore" (522, 540, 768; *Piers* C.11.46, C.11.63, C.15.115, C.16.258); "preche the pepul" (433, 509, 771, 1006; *Piers* passim). Joseph S. Wittig, *Will's Visions of Piers Plowman, Do-Well, Do-Better and Do-Best: Piers Plowman Concordance* (London: Athlone, 2001), enables one to rifle through *Piers Plowman* with confidence. J. P. Oakden's lists of alliterative phrases, though notoriously inadequate (he does not, for instance, record several of the alliterative phrases cited above from *Piers*), give parallels for most of those listed: see his *Alliterative Poetry in Middle English*, 2 vols. (1930, 1935; repr. as 1 vol., Hamden, Conn.: Archon, 1968), 2:267–361. The lists can be supplemented from Barnet Kottler and Alan M. Markman, *A Concordance to Five Middle English Poems: Cleanness, St. Erkenwald, Sir Gawain and the Green Knight, Patience, Pearl* (Pittsburgh: University of Pittsburgh Press, 1966), and from other sources.

27. E.g., "obey obedyans" (32, 176, 288); "lanternys of lyf/lyght" (71, 630); "caght with covetyse" (72, 201, 314); "dedus wyl hem deme" (95, 356, 605, 999); "cursid covetyse" (77, 119, 354, 365, 405, 629); "cloystyr and . . . quere" (177, 196); "chasid away charyté" (357, 743); "leud . . . unleryd" (396, 422); "meryd and . . . mede" (381, 591, 796, 837); "houshold and . . . housyng" (190, 458, 567); "dredles out of dred" (231, 445).

28. It is worth noting that this last little bit of wisdom is spoken by a "wise" lawyer as he closes a very dubious deal with some neat wordplay.

29. The exhortation "Be war or ye be wo" appears in the letters of John Ball and in a number of poems cited in Whiting's edition of Audelay (*Poems*, p. 226, note to *Marcolf* 43), and in Green, "Marcolf the Fool," pp. 569–70. Audelay uses the expression elsewhere in *Epilogue* 218 and in the burden of the *Seven Deadly Sins Carol*. It does not appear in Langland.

30. There is another reference in *World's Folly*, "Mede, that swet maydyn" (17; W12.11).

31. See G. R. Owst, *Literature and Pulpit in Medieval England: A Neglected Chapter in the History of English Letters and of the English People* (Cambridge: Cambridge University Press, 1933), chaps. 5–7, "The Preaching of Satire and Complaint," pp. 210–470, e.g., p. 373; Gloria Cigman, ed., *Lollard Sermons*, EETS 294 (London: Oxford University Press, 1989), e.g., pp. 1–2, 23. Audelay's blindness would have given particular stimulus to his oral memory and his responsiveness to oral tradition. Susanna Greer Fein speaks of "the mixed oral/written quality" of MS Douce 302 in her comments on a thirteen-line stanza that she has detected, interpolated (perhaps from memory) in Audelay's text of Rolle's *Form of Living*: see "A Thirteen-Line Stanza on the Abuse of Prayer from the Audelay MS," *Medium Ævum* 63 (1994): 61–74 (p. 71).

32. For "Thomas of Erceldoune's Prophecy," see Rossell Hope Robbins, ed., *Historical Poems of the XIVth and XVth Centuries* (New York: Columbia University Press, 1959), p. 29 (no. 8; *IMEV, NIMEV* 3989); for the letters of John Ball, see the discussion (with an excellent text of the letters in an appendix) in Richard Firth Green, "John Ball's Letters: Literary History and Historical Literature," in *Chaucer's England: Literature in Historical Context*, ed. Barbara Hanawalt (Minneapolis: University of Minnesota Press, 1992), pp. 176–200; for scraps embedded in prose, see Elizabeth Salter, "Alliterative Modes and Affiliations in the Fourteenth Century," *Neuphilologische Mitteilungen* 79 (1978): 25–35 (pp. 28, 33–34); for popular prophecy, see Robbins, *Historical Poems*, pp. 113–21 (nos. 43–47).

33. See Wendy Scase, "'Strange and Wonderful Bills': Bill-Casting and Political Discourse in Late Medieval England," *New Medieval Literatures* 2 (1998): 225–47.

34. Wendy Scase, "'Proud Gallants and Popeholy Priests': The Context and Function of a Fifteenth-Century Satirical Poem," *Medium Ævum* 73 (1994): 275–86.

35. For the anonymous refrain poems, see Carleton Brown, ed., *Religious Lyrics of the XVth Century* (Oxford: Clarendon Press, 1939), e.g., pp. 280–82 (nos. 182–83); for the Vernon lyrics, see Carleton Brown, ed., *Religious Lyrics of the XIVth Century*, 2nd ed., rev. G. V. Smithers (Oxford: Clarendon Press, 1957), pp. 125–208 (nos. 95–120). Poems 8 and 9 in MS Digby 102, in J. Kail, ed., *Twenty-Six Political and Other Poems from the Oxford Mss. Digby 102 and Douce 322*, EETS o.s. 124 (1904; repr. Millwood, N.Y.: Kraus Reprint, 1975), pp. 31–40, concentrate on the duties of those who have cure of souls and on criticism of those who neglect their duties ("lanterns" is a common image for good priests in the poems of Digby 102, e.g., 8.62, 21.152, 23.7). Elizabeth Salter, "*Piers Plowman* and *The Simonie*," *Archiv für das neueren Sprachen und Literaturen* 203 (1967): 241–54, argues strongly for the direct influence of *The Simonie* on *Piers Plowman*, but a suggestion of their debt to a common traditional source is made in Derek Pearsall, "The Timelessness of *The Simonie*," in *Individuality and Achievement in Middle English Poetry*, ed. O. S. Pickering (Cambridge: Brewer, 1997), pp. 59–72 (pp. 60–61). Many poems of monitory precept, and others containing attacks on the clergy, are listed, respectively, by Cameron Louis, "Proverbs, Precepts, and Monitory Pieces," in *MWME* 9:3006–16; and by Rossell Hope Robbins, "Poems Dealing with Contemporary Conditions," in *MWME*, 5:1442–53.

36. Green, for instance, speaks of "oblique reference to John Ball's letters" in Audelay ("Marcolf and Solomon," p. 570) and a continued rumbling of political discontent, rather than the outcropping in the two writers of common phrases and idioms which they turn to their own purposes. But interestingly, in his essay on John Ball's letters, Green gives detailed evidence of just the kind I have been trying to assemble for the influence of "proverbs and scraps of vernacular verse" (p. 187) on the letters, "drawn from stock material" (p. 185), and circulated orally as well as in other ways (p.183).

Langland and Audelay

Richard Firth Green

William Langland and John Audelay had a number of things in common (at least insofar as we can rely on their poems for autobiographical information): both were west-country men (though Audelay probably by residence rather than by birth), both were chantry priests, both lived "yn London and opeland,"[1] and both survived long enough to feel themselves the victims of "Syre euele-tauȝt Elde" (*Piers Plowman* C.22.186). Audelay, of course, was writing a generation or so after Langland, but assuming that he cannot have been born much later than 1360, it is not impossible that the two men might have met one another.

James Simpson has recently drawn attention to the literary debt owed by John Audelay, particularly in his *Marcolf and Solomon*, to William Langland.[2] Ironically, however, since Simpson enlisted Derek Pearsall's support for the view that the poem was "profoundly influenced by *Piers Plowman*,"[3] Pearsall himself now entirely repudiates his earlier opinion (published nearly thirty years ago), so that the question remains far from resolved. While I freely concede that Pearsall's knowledge of *Piers Plowman* is far more profound than my own, and his ear for Langlandian cadences far sharper than mine, on this issue I find myself siding with Simpson.

The clearest (and I would say, virtually irrefutable) evidence that Audelay had read *Piers Plowman* comes from his two allusions to Lady Mede (or, as Langland himself routinely refers to her, "Mede the Mayde").[4] In *On the World's Folly* Audelay writes:

> Fore trew corexion is ther non,
> For love of Mede, that swet maydyn,
>   In non degré.
>   (16–18; W12.10–12)[5]

This in itself might not seem enough to establish any close familiarity since it is arguable that Mede the Maid had become a mere byword for bribery by the early fifteenth century,[6] but in *Marcolf and Solomon* Audelay includes her in an extended discussion of the corruption of ecclesiastical courts:

> Alas, that thes offecers of Holé Cherchis laue
> Lettyth these leud men lye in here syn,
> That dredun nothyng here domus hem to withdrawe,
> Fore Mede the maydyn mantens hem therin,
> Because of Ser Covetys, is neyre of here kyn,
> May do with mon of Holé Cherche hollé his entent;
> The wyf and the hosbond he mai part atwyn;
> Thagh thai be boundon togeder be the sacrement.
> (702–9)

Admittedly, Audelay is here concerned with divorce, rather than with marriage within the prohibited degrees of affinity, but the passage closely recalls, I believe, the abuses of Civil and Simony in Passus 3 of *Piers Plowman* B-text. And there are further details confirming Langland's influence: Sir Covetise, for instance, recalls "the countee of Coveitise" (B.2.86) that is included in Mede's marriage charter, and Audelay's pun on Mede's mercy (that is to say, both the legal fine and forgiveness) a little later—

> Thus oure blessud byschop, dene offecialle,
> Sofers thes sekelers in here syght to sun opynly,
> Thagh thai to here constri, hom to here court calle,
> Thai mercyn hem with moné and med prevely.
> (*Marcolf* 715–18)—

echoes a similar pun in Langland:

> And though ye mowe amercy men, lat mercy be taxour
> And mekenesse thi maister, maugree Medes chekes.
> (B.6.39–40)

Though Audelay's reference to "Mede the maydyn" is by far the strongest evidence that he had read *Piers Plowman* (or perhaps heard it read), there are a number of other allusions that he may well owe to the earlier poet.[7] He might well have taken his reference to "the new fayre" a few lines later, for instance, from Langland. Compare

> Ye curatis, fore your covetys ye castun in the new fayre
> The churches that ye byn chosun to, be Godus ordenauns.
> (*Marcolf* 728–29)

with

> Clement the Cobelere caste of his cloke,
> And to the newe feire nempned it to selle.
> (B.5.320–21)

Another possible instance is his reference to Favel, though it is equally possible that he knew the French *Roman de Fauvel*[8] as well as *Piers Plowman* when he writes, "Loke thou coré not favele ne be no flaterer" (*Marcolf* 394). It is clear that he is thinking of Favel as a horse—something one could hardly have guessed from *Piers* alone; indeed, it is one of Langland's wittier conceits to turn Favel from a horse into a rider: "And Favel on a flaterere fetisly atired" (B.2.166). Nevertheless, one might hear in Audelay's line, "Fore Favel with his fayre wordis and his flateryng" (*Marcolf* 1005), an echo of Langland's "Favel thorough his faire speche hath this folk enchaunted" (B.2.42). Finally, one might also hear Langland's lines:

> Ac there was wight noon so wys, the wey thider kouthe,
> But blustreden forth as beestes over ba[ch]es and hilles
> (B.5.513–14)

behind Audelay's

> Bot never honé whyl beware in here levyng,
> Bot al blustyrne furth unblest, as Bayard the blynd.
> (*Marcolf* 951–52),

or his later injunction: "Blust not furth unblest, as Bayard the blynd" (*Marcolf* 993). The expression was something of a favorite with Audelay, no doubt because it held a special resonance for him.[9] "As bold as blind Bayard" was an extremely popular proverb at the end of the Middle Ages (B. J. Whiting cites twenty-one examples of it), but only Audelay uses Langland's phrasal verb *bluster forth* in connection with it.[10] Indeed, it may well be that *Cleanness*, line 886, preserves the proverbial expression in something like its original form, and that it is Langland who has altered it in the process of shifting its referent to the plural.

One final passage is worth quoting at length because it might be argued to indicate which text of *Piers Plowman* Audelay knew. It is a description of a worldly priest:

> Oure gentyl Ser Jone—joy hym mot betide!—
> He is a meré mon of mouth among cumpané.
> He con harpe! He con syng! His orglus ben herd ful wyd!
> He wyl noght spare his purse to spend his selaré—
> Alas, he ner a parsun or a vecory!
> Be Jhesu, he is a gentyl mon, and jolylé arayd—
> His gurdlis harneschit with selver, his baslard hongus bye—
> Apon his pert pautener, uche mon ys apayd,
>   Both maydyn and wyfe.
>   (*Marcolf* 144–52)

If this owes anything to a similar passage in the B-text, it is worth noting that it is not one that Audelay could have found in either of the other versions:

> Sire Johan and Sire Geffrey, [ech] hath a girdel of silver,
> A baselard or a ballok-knyf with botons overgilte.
> Ac a porthors that sholde be his plow, *Placebo* to sigge,
> Hadde he nevere, [his] service to [h]ave,
> [And save he have] silver therto, seith it with yvel wille.
>   Allas, ye lewed men, muche lese ye on preestes!
> Ac thing that wikkedly is wonne, and with false sleightes,
> Wolde nevere wit of witty God but wikkede men it hadde —
> The which arn preestes inparfite and prechours after silver,
> Secutours and sodenes, somonours and hir lemmannes.
>   (B.15.123–32)

Of course Sir John was a common nickname for a priest (the Prioress's chaplain, for instance, is "this sweete preeste, this goodly man sir John," two fifteenth-century popular songs feature seducers called Sir John, and this is also the name of the lecherous priest who cuckolds John John in Heywood's farce); and to judge from John Mirk (another west-country man), the wearing of fancy daggers (*baselards*) by priests was conventionally regarded as an abuse.[11] Nonetheless, the resemblances between the passages are striking. On the other hand, most other such parallels between Audelay and Langland—for instance, their descriptions of the accord of the Four

Daughters of God or their treatments of confession as a healing of the wounds of sin—seem far too general and commonplace to establish any kind of direct influence.

It is no accident that most of the Langlandian echoes so far adduced come from *Marcolf and Solomon*, for along with *Paternoster* it shows Audelay experimenting with alliterative verse. Perhaps because of Chaucer's Parson's sharp division of verse into separate categories of rhyme and letter, we seem generally to feel that any blending of the two was unusual. In fact, there are enough examples to prove that this was far from being an exotic hybrid: *The Four Leaves of the Truelove*, *A Pistill of Susan*, *Somer Soneday*, *The Awntyrs off Arthure*, and *Three Dead Kings* are all written in thirteen-line stanzas of eight rhymed alliterative lines followed by a form of the bob and wheel.[12] Audelay employs this form for *Marcolf* and (with the substitution of a "bob and couplet") in *Paternoster*. The meter in these poems is considerably looser than in *Three Dead Kings*.[13] Indeed, in *Marcolf* Audelay's meter is looser even than Langland's: many more of his lines are hypermetrical—some, to use A. V. C. Schmidt's terminology, enriched or extended, others clustered or reduced;[14] while I have not attempted a statistical analysis, there seem to be far more mute staves than in *Piers Plowman*, and far more blank staves in other than final position. Audelay also has a number of defective lines with only three lifts, a situation that is very rare in Langland. For those who are interested, I have attempted to scan the first eight lines of a stanza (chosen at random):

Lókys, lórdus, to ʒoure lýffe || and to ʒour léuyng	*aaa/a*
For I am tóuchid vpon þe tóng || þe sóþ for to sáy;	*aa/bb*
Þaʒ ʒe be léders of þe lónd, || géte ʒou lóuyng,	*aa/xa*
And **c**ale þe **c**lárge to ʒour **c**óunsel, || þat béryn **C**ristis káy,	*(a)aa/x(a)a*
And **h**óldist vp **h**óle cherche || þe **p**rinse of **h**éuen to **p**áy;	*aa/(b)ab*
Y **d**réd lest **d**edle sún || þis réme wyl **d**ystrý	*a(a)x/x(a)x*
Fore þe láuys of þis lónd || ben lád a **w**rong **w**áy,	*aa/a(b)b*
Boþ témperale and spírituale, || Y tél ʒou tréuly,	*ax/aa*
Euen vp-so-doune.	
(*Marcolf* 235–43)[15]	

Eric Stanley has drawn attention to the high proportion of stock phrases in Audelay's verse, and a glance down his list shows that a considerable number of them alliterate.[16] Nevertheless, the proportion of such phrases that Audelay shares with Langland seems to me to be more than coincidental. It would be tedious to run through an inventory of them here, but I will mention a few of the more important ones. Noun doublets, and adjective-noun phrases are perhaps the most likely to be drawn from a common linguistic reservoir (after all, we still have a great many in use today),[17] but a couple seem worth noting. "True of [one's] tongue" occurs frequently in *Piers Plowman* and seems to be echoed in Audelay's

> Mon soul with mekenes to have in kepyng,
> With the treuth of here toung to teche hem the way,
> Throgh the seven sacrementis here soule to blis bryng.
> (*Marcolf* 643–45)

Much the same case might be made for the phrases "the worship of the world" and "the love of our Lord." To my ear, a number of Audelay's alliterating verb phrases sound even more Langlandian. One might compare, for example,

> Fore thou trustis more to thi tresoure and to thi catele
> Then in the love of thi Lord, that ale thi wele hath wroght.
> (*Marcolf* 369–70)

with the well-known lines at the end of Passus 7 of the B-text:

> Forthi I rede yow renkes that riche ben on this erthe:
> Upon trust of youre tresor triennals to have,
> Be ye never the bolder to breke the ten hestes.
> (B.7.182–84)

Again, a similar case might be made of such phrases as "(a)mend [one's] misdeeds," or "preach [to] the people," or "to kairen about the country" (see the appendix, below, for all these phrases). With very little effort, these kinds of examples might be multiplied several times; the force of my argument, however, depends less upon individual instances than their aggregative weight. Audelay shares with Langland, I claim, a kind of homiletic alliterative vocabulary that is quite distinct from that of most of the romances.

The mention of preaching brings me to broader aspects of style that both poets share. I will note three of these. The first is the tendency to address their audience directly, as if from the pulpit; this mode is often marked by the phrase "Look thou!" or "Look ye!" Compare, for instance, Audelay's lines,

> Then loke thou grounde thee in God and drede thi Saveoure
> That wyle cale thee to thi countus and to thi rekynyng.
> <div align="right">(<i>Marcolf</i> 330–31)</div>

with these lines from Langland:

> Forthi loke thow lovye as longe as thow durest,
> For is no science under sonne so sovereyn for the soule.
> (B.10.207–8)

Other passages suggest how common this form is in both poets, yet outside represented direct speech (particularly in the drama) and personal communications such as the *Paston Letters*, it is relatively rare elsewhere in Middle English. One consequence of their hortatory stance is the readiness in both authors to drop the persona they have adopted and to slip back into their authorial voice. Thus, after the dramatic intervention of Trajan in Passus 12 of Langland's C-text, it is impossible to decide whether the following lines are to be attributed to Will or to Rechelesnesse (who ends the speech, which may or may not begin at this point, some three hundred lines later):

> Lo, lordes, what leute dede and leele dome y-used!
> Wel ouhte ȝe lordes þat lawes kepeth this lesson to haue in mynde
> And on Troianes treuthe to thenke all tyme in ȝoure lyue
> And louye for oure lordes loue and do leute euermore.
> (C.12.86–90)

Similarly, as both Pearsall and Simpson note, Audelay slips in and out of his Marcolf persona, often without any clear markers.

A second stylistic trait is the way both poets work Latin passages into their verse. In *Marcolf and Solomon* Audelay commonly, if not invariably, introduces his stanzas with a line or more of Latin, generally from the Bible. But in some ways more interesting is the Langlandian way he sometimes runs English into Latin, either from line to line or within a single line. Here is an example of the first:

> *Ecce quam bonum et quam jocundum.*[18]
> Take tent to this tyxt, prestis, I you pray,
> *Habitare semper fratres in unum,*[19]
> Thus Davit in the Sauter, sothlé con he say.
> <div align="right">(<i>Marcolf</i> 638–41),</div>

while examples of the second are:

> What sayd your Soveren to his dyssiplis, when he dyd wasche hem,
> And knelud louly apon his knen tofore his blessid covent,
> And betoke hom this tokyn, *diligatis invicem*?[20]
>
> (*Marcolf* 266–68)

and

> *In Actibus Apostolorum*[21] ther may ye rede
> Hou the goodys of Holé Cherche sumtyme were isempde.
>
> (*Marcolf* 625–26)

   Finally, both Langland and Audelay share the preacher's aspiration to render abstract theological mysteries concrete and comprehensible. The Samaritan's attempts to embody the concept of the indivisible Trinity as, first, a hand and, then, a flaming torch in Passus 17 of the B-text of *Piers Plowman* might be compared with Audelay's exposition of the Trinity in terms of the sun:[22]

> I se, sothlé, in the sune knyt thre maner kynde,
> His clerté and his clerenes, what clerke can declare;
> Bohold the hete in thi hert, and have hit in mynd;
> The conselacion and the comford, thai thre what thai are.
> Fore al that levys in this lond, ful evyl schul hit fare
> Nere that gloreus Gleme that fro the heven glydis;
> Ho that servyth not that Soverayn, his hert may be ful sare,
> That lenus of his love seche a lyght that ale this word gladis.
>   . . .
> I declare the clerté to the Fader of myghtis most;
> The heete hylé therof to his onlé Sunne;
> The consolacion and the comford to the Holé Gost;
> Kyndly yknyt togeder, without devesioun.
>
> (*Marcolf* 858–65, 871–74)

Indeed, the Holy Ghost's solar comfort and consolation here almost merit being put alongside Langland's great lines,

> And as glowynge gledes gladeth noght thise werkmen
> That werchen and waken in wyntres nyghtes,

> As dooth a kex or a candle that caught hath fir and blaseth,
> Namoore dooth Sire ne Sone ne Seint Spirit togideres
> Graunte no grace ne forgifnesse of synnes
> Til the Holy Goost gynne to glowe and to blase.
> (B.17.218–23)

Enough has been said, I believe, to show that that Langland's influence upon Audelay, particularly in his *Marcolf* poem, was significant.

Such a claim chimes well with John Burrow's argument that the earliest readership of *Piers Plowman* was "an audience of clerks."[23] We might, indeed, speculate that Audelay could have encountered Langland's poem in an anthology something like the Vernon Manuscript. Versions of a number of Audelay's other poems—*Prayer of General Confession*, *Seven Hours of the Cross*, *The Vision of Saint Paul*, and *Salutation to Mary*—appear in Vernon, which also includes, of course, a copy of the A-text of *Piers Plowman*. Detailed comparison suggests that neither the Vernon nor its sister manuscript the Simeon (London, BL Addit. MS 22283) can have been Audelay's actual original, but some similar west-country monastic anthology of devotional poetry may well have been known to him.

On the other hand, Langland does not seem to have had a profound influence on Audelay's political views: Audelay has a far less jaundiced opinion of the friars, for instance, and he takes a far more sanguine attitude to the efficacy of lovedays. Above all, there is little of the proto-revolutionary that inspired the author of *Piers Plowman's Crede* about John Audelay. No doubt the progress of Wycliffism over the intervening years had made Langland's more extreme views seem dangerously radical to the Shropshire priest, who is rather conspicuously eager to assert his own orthodoxy and to distance himself from the Lollards. More interesting, and poetically more satisfying, however, is the literary sympathy between the two men—particularly, the way their autobiographies have become intertwined with their poetry, the way Long Will and Blind John have woven their own personas deeply into their respective works. Susanna Fein has argued convincingly that we should read Audelay's sequence of poems as a whole, as the record of a spiritual journey and a spiritual project: "Audelay," she writes, "loads his poems with appeals for repentance from his listeners and readers, and then petitions that they pray in turn for his own soul. The petitionary passages reveal an author who self-consciously and with evident sincerity fashions himself as both prophet and penitent."[24] And again, "the ending imposed by death and the anxieties bred thereof are fears that haunt

Audelay's verse; he is caught in the prickly state of petitioning for purgatory (at the least) as he openly wishes to avoid its pains, all the while maintaining gratitude to God for present afflictions."[25] If we accept this view of Audelay's quest as both a spiritual as well as a literary one, there is one obvious earlier model for him to have drawn on—Will's lifelong search for Saint Truth in *Piers Plowman*.

Appendix

Alliterative Phrases in Audelay, Langland, and an Alliterative Corpus

The following table represents a correlation made by Hoyt Duggan, of eight alliterating phrases in Audelay and Langland with a corpus of alliterative lines drawn from the Chadwyck-Healey electronic database,[a] augmented with his own corpus formed for the purposes of metrical analysis in 1986 (a total of over 38,000 lines in all).[b] My debt to Professor Duggan for running this electronic survey for me at a particularly busy time of year is very great, and it is a pleasure to acknowledge here so generous and collegial an act on his part. As a control, I have myself checked all these phrases in William of Nassington's non-alliterative *Speculum vitae*, available in electronic form from the Oxford Text Archive (a total of 16,096 lines in all). This search yielded no exact matches, and only one approximation — for *the worship of the world*: "Þan forsakes he þe werldes worshepe" (4174). Unless otherwise noted, phrases from Audelay are from *Marcolf and Solomon* and the Langland quotations are from the B-Text (ed. Schmidt).

[a] The corpus includes the following texts: *Alexander A* and *Alexander B*, in Francis Peabody Magoun, Jr., ed., *The Gests of King Alexander of Macedon; Two Middle-English Alliterative Fragments* (Cambridge, Mass.: Harvard University Press, 1929); Israel Gollancz, ed., *Death and Liffe*, vol. 5 of *Select Early English Poems*, 9 vols. (London: Milford, Oxford University Press, 1913–33); George A. Panton and David Donaldson, eds., *The "Gest Hystoriale" of the Destruction of Troy*, EETS o.s. 39, 56 (1869, 1874; repr. London: Oxford University Press, 1968, 1976); Edmund Brock, ed., *Morte Arthure*, EETS o.s. 8 (London: Trübner, 1865); Mabel Day and Robert Steele, eds., *Mum and the Sothsegger*, EETS o.s. 199 (1936; repr. Oxford: Oxford University Press, 1971); M. Y. Offord, ed., *The Parlement of the Thre Ages*, EETS o.s. 246 (1959; London: Oxford University Press, 1967); F. J. Amours, ed., *The Pistill of Susan*, in *Scottish Alliterative Poems in Riming Stanzas*, STS 27, 38 (1892–97; repr. New York: Johnson Reprint, 1966); Walter W. Skeat, ed., *The Romance of William of Palerne*, EETS e.s. 1 (1867; repr. New York: Kraus Reprint, 1973); E. Kölbing and Mabel Day, eds., *The Siege of Jerusalem*, EETS o.s. 188 (1932; repr. New York: Kraus Reprint, 2001); Walter W. Skeat, ed., *The Wars of Alexander, an Alliterative Romance*, EETS e.s. 47 (1886; repr. Millwood, N.Y.: Kraus Reprint, 1975); Stephanie Trigg, ed., *Wynnere and Wastoure*, EETS 297 (Oxford: Oxford University Press, 1990).

[b] Hoyt N. Duggan, "The Shape of the B-Verse in Middle English Alliterative Poetry," *Speculum* 61 (1986): 565–66.

Audelay (1):

> And callun hit permetacion, *cuntreys about to kayre* (730)

Langland (1):

> Coveiten noght *in contree to cairen aboute* (Prol.29)

Corpus:

> Only Audelay and Langland use the phrasal verb "to cairen about"; *The Wars of Alexander* has "kaires he *fra* þo contres" (1056); *William of Palerne* has "cairende *ouer* cuntreis" (1922; cp. 2714, 5324), and "caire wold þei *to* here cuntre" (5184; cp. 5190).

Audelay (5):

> Then fore *love of thi Lord* (336)
> Then lese *the love of youre Lord* and let down his laue (353)
> Then in *the love of thi Lord*, that ale thi wele hath wroght (370)
> Fore *the love of our Lord*, nouther lagh ne gren (967)
> And verefyus in a verse *the love of our Lord* (976)

Langland (6):

> Al for *love of Oure Lord* lyveden ful streyte (Prol.26)
> And noght for *love of Oure Lord* unlose hire lippes ones (Prol.214)
> Than for *love of Oure Lorde* or alle hise leeve seintes (4.39)
> But al for *love of Oure Lord* and the bet to love the peple (11.174)
> Fram *the love of Oure Lord* at his laste ende (14.133)
> *The love of Oure Lord* and his loore bothe (18.196)

Corpus:

> The corpus yields two other examples: *Mum and the Sothsegger* (428) and *Alexander B* (597); Oakden (2:292) provides one more: *Piers Plowman's Crede* (782).[c]

---

[c] J. P. Oakden, *Alliterative Poetry in Middle English*, 2 vols. (1930, 1935; repr. as 1 vol. Hamden, Conn.: Archon, 1968), 2:293.

Audelay (14):

        And *mend here here mysdedys*, and here matens and masse (33)
        Here mysse and *here mysdedus, to mend* here therfore (160)
        Y rede ye *mend your mysdedus* here wyle ye may (278)
        Bot yif thai *mend here mysdede* — Y lykyn hem be lorne (398)
        Here mys and here *mysdedis her to amende* (489)
        Here *mysdedis here to mende* (*Seven Words* 22)
        Thi *mysdedis betyme amend* (*Visiting* 63)
        And your *mysdedis, loke ye amend* (*Lord's Epistle* 37)
        Lest here *mysdedis thai wold amend* (*Vision* 143)
        That here *mysdedis thai nyl not mend* (*Vision* 331)
        And your *mysdedis loke ye amend* (*Vision* 362)
        That here *mysdedis here wil amende* (*Epilogue* 13)
        Lest your *mysdedis ye schuld amend* (*Epilogue* 128)
        Bot your *mysdedis that ye amend* (*Epilogue* 134)

Langland (2):

        Mekely for oure *mysdedes, to amenden* us alle (1.168)
        To *amenden us of oure mysdedes* and do mercy to us alle (5.480)

Corpus:

        The corpus yields one other example, from *Mum and the Sothsegger* (92); but cp. *Parlement of the Thre Ages* (359).

Audelay (6):

        To preche the pepul apert the Prince of Heven to pay (433)
        Preche the pepul pryncypaly the Prince of Heven to pay
        Pil not the pore *pepule with your prechyng* (509–10)
        Thus *ye prechyn the pepul* in the pylpit opynlé (771)
        He wyl *preche the pepul* apert hem for to pay (1006)
        To *preche the pepul* with good entent (*Lord's Epistle* 6)

  Cp.:

        Tofore *the pepul apart. Thus schuld he preche* (658)

Langland (7):

        Prechynge the peple for profit of [the] womb[e] (Prol.59)
        Preestes that *prechen the peple* to goode (3.223)
        That ye *prechen to the peple*, preve it on yowselve (5.42)

	That whan thei *preche the peple* in many places aboute (5.145)
	And *precheth to the peple* Seint Poules wordes (8.91)
	Poul *preched the peple*, that parfitnesse lovede (10.202)
	And *preched to the peple*, and prelates thei maden (20.127)
Cp.:	
	How pertly *afore the peple [to] preche* gan Reson. (5.23)
	And if he among *the peple preched*, or in places come (15.402)
Corpus:	
	The corpus yields one other example, from *The Siege of Jerusalem* (1153)

Audelay (1):	
	Mon soul with mekenes to have in kepyng,
	With *the treuth of here toung* to teche hem the way,
	Throgh the seven sacrementis here soule to blis bryng. (643–45)
Langland (4):	
	[For] whoso is *trewe of his tonge* and telleth noon oother, (1.88)
	For though ye be *trewe of youre tonge* and treweliche wynne, (1.179)
	And that thow be *trewe of thi tonge*, and tales that thow hatie, (6.50)
	Trewe of youre tonge and of youre tail bothe, (15.105)
Cp.:	
	That worth *Trewe-tonge*, a tidy man that tened me nevere. (3.322)
	And also *Tomme Trewe-tonge*-tel-me-no-tales (4.18)
	He tempreth *the tonge to trutheward*, that no tresor coveiteth (14.309)
Corpus:	
	The corpus yields no other examples.

Audelay (1):

> Fore thou *trustis more to thi tresoure* and to thi catele
> Then in the love of thi Lord, that ale thi wele hath wroght
> (369–70)

Langland (3):

> That *trusten on his tresour* bitrayed arn sonnest (1.70)
> In *trust of hire tresor* she t[en]eth ful manye (3.124)
> Upon *trust of youre tresor* triennals to have (7.183)

Corpus:

> The corpus yields no other examples.

Audelay (4):

> To *the worchip of this world*, thai wryn fro me away (202)
> Fore ale *the worchyp of this word*, hit wyl wype sone away (280)
> Fore *worldys worchip*, hit con hym blynd (298)
> Ellys *the worchip of this world*, hit wyle sone abate (316)

Langland (1)

> Have thei *worship in this world*, thei wilne no bettre (1.8)

Corpus:

> The corpus yields one other example: *The Parlement of the Thre Ages*, "And with the wirchipe of this werlde he went to his ende" (519; cp. 175); but cp. *Morte Arthure*, "My wele and my wyrchipe of alle this werlde ryche" (401, and 3963; cp. 541).

Notes

1. Derek Pearsall, ed., *William Langland, Piers Plowman: An Edition of the C-Text*, 2nd ed. (1978; repr. Exeter: University of Exeter Press, 1994), C.5.44.

2. James Simpson, "Saving Satire after Arundel's *Constitutions*: John Audelay's 'Marcol and Solomon,'" in *Text and Controversy from Wyclif to Bale: Essays in Honour of Anne Hudson*, ed. Helen Barr and Ann M. Hutchison, Medieval Church Studies 4 (Turnhout: Brepols, 2004), pp. 387–404, esp. 402–4.

3. Derek Pearsall, *Old English and Middle English Poetry* (London: Routledge and Kegan Paul, 1979); see Simpson, "Saving Satire," p. 389 n. 8, and Derek Pearsall's essay in the present volume.

4. I.e., B-text 2.20 and 235, and 3.1, 4, 36, 87, and 105. A. V. C. Schmidt, ed. *William Langland, The Vision of Piers Plowman: A Critical Edition of the B-Text*, 2nd ed. (London: Dent, 1995).

5. Quotations of Audelay's poems are drawn from John the Blind Audelay, *Poems and Carols (Oxford, Bodleian Library MS Douce 302)*, ed. Susanna Fein (Kalamazoo: Medieval Institute Publications, 2009). Poem numbers with the prefix "W" are from Ella Keats Whiting, ed., *The Poems of John Audelay*, EETS o.s. 184 (1931; repr. Oxford: Oxford University Press, 2006).

6. However, it is important to distinguish here between a generalized veniality satire (which is omnipresent in the Middle Ages) and the specific allegorization of veniality as a woman. John A. Yunck's *The Lineage of Lady Meed* (Notre Dame: University of Notre Dame Press, 1963) spends some time on English vernacular parallels to Langland's satire, but while he gives two fifteenth-century examples of a "Maister Meede" (pp. 268, 270) and alludes to a number of "Sir Penny" poems (p. 309), the earliest instances he has of a *female* Mede are from the sixteenth century: Spenser's Lady Munera and Barnwell's Lady Pecunia (p. 309), both clearly indebted to Langland himself. Yunck appears not to have noticed the two allusions in Audelay.

7. Several of the following examples are also given by Simpson in "Saving Satire," but since I wrote the first version of this paper before I had read his article —though after hearing him give a paper partially on this topic at the Third International Conference on *Piers Plowman* in Birmingham (2003)—they may perhaps be regarded as independent corroboration.

8. Arthur Långfors, ed., *Le Roman de Fauvel* (Paris: F. Didot et cie, 1914–19).

9. Elsewhere he writes, "Thagh I say soth, blamys not me— / I blustur forth as Bayard blynd" (*Epilogue* 380–81).

10. *Cleanness* has simply "blustered" (886); see Malcolm Andrew and Ronald Waldron, eds., *The Poems of the Pearl Manuscript*, 2nd ed. (Berkeley and Los Angeles: University of California Press, 1989), p. 148; and Chaucer has "blondreth forth" (*Canon's Yeoman's Tale* VIII 1413); see Larry D. Benson, ed., *The Riverside Chaucer*, 3rd ed. (Boston: Houghton Mifflin, 1987), p. 280. Where Whiting's other examples employ a verb at all, it is nonalliterating: *goes, trots, does*, etc.; see Bartlett Jere Whiting, with Helen Wescott Whiting, *Proverbs, Sentences, and Proverbial Phrases* (Cambridge, Mass.: Harvard University Press, 1968), p. 24 (B71).

11. See the prologue to *The Nun's Priest's Tale* VII 2820 (Benson, ed., *Riverside Chaucer*, p. 253); Rossell Hope Robbins, ed., *Secular Lyrics of the XIVth and XVth Centuries*, 2nd ed. (Oxford: Clarendon Press, 1955), pp. 19–21 (nos. 25, 26); Heywood's *Johan Johan*, in Richard Axton and Peter Happé, eds., *The Plays of John Heywood* (Cambridge: Brewer, 1991), pp. 75–92; and Edward Peacock, ed. *Instructions for Parish Priests by John Myrc*, EETS o.s. 31, 2nd ed., rev. F. J. Furnivall (1902; repr. New York: Greenwood, 1969), p. 48.

12. See *The Four Leaves of the Truelove* (also known as *The Quatrefoil of Love*), in Susanna Fein, ed., *Moral Love Songs and Laments* (Kalamazoo: Medieval Institute

Publications, 1998), pp. 180–96; *A Pistel of Susan* and *Somer Soneday*, in Thorlac Turville-Petre, ed., *Alliterative Poetry of the Later Middle Ages: An Anthology* (Washington, D.C.: Catholic University of America Press, 1989), pp. 123–39, 142–47, respectively; and Ralph Hanna, ed., *The Awntyrs off Arthure at the Terne Wathelyn* (Manchester: Manchester University Press, 1974).

13. See Ad Putter, "The Language and Metre of *Pater Noster* and *Three Dead Kings*," *Review of English Studies*, n.s. 55 (2004): 511–20.

14. Schmidt, *Piers Plowman*, pp. 506–8.

15. Cited from Whiting, *Poems*, pp. 18–19.

16. Eric G. Stanley, "*The True Counsel of Conscience* or *The Ladder of Heaven:* In Defence of John Audelay's Unlyrical Lyrics," in *Expedition nach der Wahrheit: Poems, Essays, and Papers in Honour of Theo Stemmler*, ed. Stefan Horlacher and Marion Islinger (Heidelberg: C. Winter, 1996), pp. 131–59 (pp. 155–59).

17. Cp. *friend or foe* and *murder and mayhem*, or *pretty as a picture* and *tall tales*.

18. Behold how good and how pleasant (Ps. 132:1).

19. It is that brothers always dwell in unity (Ps. 132:1).

20. (That) you love one another (John 13:34).

21. In the Acts of the Apostles.

22. The analogy was, however, conventional; see W. W. Skeat's note on C.20.168 (C.19.167, in Pearsall's edition) in his edition: *William Langland, The Vision of William Concerning Piers the Plowman in Three Parallel Texts Together with Richard the Redeless*, 2 vols. (Oxford: Clarendon Press, 1886), 2:245.

23. J. A. Burrow, "The Audience of *Piers Plowman*," *Anglia* 75 (1957): 373–84; repr. in J. A. Burrow, *Essays on Medieval Literature* (Oxford: Clarendon Press, 1984), pp. 102–16.

24. Susanna Fein, "Good Ends in the Audelay Manuscript." *Yearbook of English Studies* 33 (2003): 97–119 (p. 102).

25. Fein, "Good Ends," p. 104.

"CHOOSE YOURSELVES WHITHER TO GO"
JOHN AUDELAY'S *VISION OF SAINT PAUL*

Robert Easting

Audelay's collection of poems is, among other things, a program of priestly instruction on Christian living, with the goal of making a good end,[1] escaping hell by confession, shortening one's time in purgatory by penance in this life, and living in the hope of God's gracious mercy in such a way as ultimately to attain heaven. It is almost inevitable, therefore, that he should include an account of hell, of what a bad end entails. There was no shortage of homiletic accounts of hell pains that he might use as a model, and he chose one of the most widely known and long lived for his poem numbered 16 in Ella Keats Whiting's edition, a version of the Vision of Saint Paul (hereafter VSP).[2] VSP is the most influential of all the medieval accounts of journeys to the otherworld. It tells of Saint Paul's apocryphal tour of hell, led by the archangel Michael, during which Paul and Michael, moved by the appeals of the damned, make supplication to God and obtain respite for the souls in hell each Sunday. VSP exists in manifold forms and languages: the lost Greek prose Apocalypse of Paul of the third, or possibly of the late second, century, was translated as the Latin prose *Visio Sancti Pauli* in the fifth or sixth century; this survives in two long recensions and was modified into at least eleven further redactions and translated into a range of vernaculars in verse and prose especially from the twelfth century onward.[3] For instance, there survive three other independent verse versions and two prose versions in Middle English, and verse and prose versions in Anglo-Norman, continental French, German, and other languages.[4]

Audelay's poem is headed "Incipit narracio quo Michel duxit Paulum ad infernum" (Here begins the narration in which Michael led Paul into hell). As Whiting notes, it is "the longest and one of the most vivid of the narrative poems"[5] in Audelay's book, and the "story loses nothing in dramatic quality nor in interest"[6] in his telling. Though aware of a Latin source for the story, Whiting believed that Audelay's access to the tale of Paul's visit to hell was "through English metrical versions."[7] However, Audelay's poem is basically a translation of VSP Latin Redaction IV, as was established by Brandes.[8] Brandes's analyses were unfortunately not known by Whiting, who claimed, by comparing Audelay's version with that in the Vernon Manuscript, that Audelay added seven stanzas of his own, viz., lines 93–105, 223–35, 249–61, and 314–65; these constitute one-quarter of the poem. But, as we shall see, this demarcation is not entirely accurate: lines 314–26 are in fact nearly all dependent on the Latin, and Audelay is solely responsible for the introduction of many further lines. Eric Stanley says that in *The Vision of Saint Paul* Audelay "has simply retold the 'Visio Pauli,'"[9] but Audelay has in fact amplified his translation considerably, adding about 155 of the poem's 365 lines. Both in form (twenty-eight thirteen-line stanzas)[10] and content, Audelay's poem is more elaborate than the comparatively unadorned Latin prose.

Its heading introduces the narrative as explaining who first asked that souls in hell might have rest, to wit, Saint Paul and the archangel Michael, who led him through hell. Sunday, the Lord's Day, is the chosen day, on which, thanks to the prayers of Paul and Michael, souls in hell are allowed respite from their torments. In MS Douce 302 the poem follows another on the Observance of Sunday, *Our Lord's Epistle on Sunday*, and the sequence of the two poems is quite deliberate.

The poem is very much a priestly production in tones of voice and style, which Stanley has dubbed "sermonic."[11] Audelay stresses the failures of penance of those who "dyed in det and dedlé syn" (26) and hence went to hell, for "Satisfaccion in erth thai wold do non" (38). It is uncompromising about the torments of hell, spelling out Christ's Gospel injunction, "Bynd bundels togeder to be ibrent" (62), by pairing categories of sinners such as "spouse-brekers with awouters" (63) to be cast "in the fuyre without end" (66). It also castigates money counterfeiters and gluttons for not parting their goods with the "pore that were nedé" and the "pore nedy" (117, 156; in both cases these are Audelay's additions). The poem follows VSP Redaction IV closely in the repetitious structure of its tour of hell: as Paul and Michael move from one torment to the next—burning trees, furnace, flood, bridge, and so on—Paul sees the pains, laments, and asks Michael for an explanation, which is given. Some form of "Then (after) Paul . . ." or "There Paul . . ." introduces half the stanzas. Paul repeatedly weeps for the perpetrators of what might be the more parochial sins, the backbiters, usurerers, and unchaste (73, 106, 171), until Michael asks, "Why wepis thou soo?"

(172), as if to say, "you've seen nothing yet." He then takes Paul to see the pit, which emits a stench that Audelay says would kill all Christian men. Therein suffer those guilty of more fundamental errors of faithlessness, those who did not believe in the Virgin Mary and Christ's incarnation, those who were unchristened, and those who "never resayvyd Cristis body" (189). Audelay adds heretics and renegades: for them there is no redemption (186–96)[12]—the expression recalls the Response from the Office of the Dead, "In inferno nulla est redemptio."[13]

After witnessing the fates of two newly dead souls—one bad, one good—Michael and Paul are called upon by "al the soroufull soulus in hel" (262) to pray to God for them. The souls call on "the Sun of David" (273), and a voice from heaven asks why they deserve mercy. Paul, still weeping (288), and joined by all the angels of heaven, prays Christ to give the souls in hell "sum ryst" (291), and He grants them a Sunday respite as a "special grace" (295). The tour ends with Michael saying no tongue can tell the pains of hell, and the poem ends with Audelay's instructions on serving God.

A closer examination of the poem as translation will reveal the care and inventiveness with which Audelay Englished and versified his well-known visionary homily. The Latin heading ("Interogandum . . . electus") is taken from the opening of VSP Redaction IV (75/1–5).[14] The opening stanza adds lines 6–9 and line 13, the former opening up the "soroufull syght" (6) that is to ensue (cp. lines 17, 159), and the reason for Paul's tour of hell, "Because men nel not beleve" (9). No reason is given in the Latin for why God wishes Paul to see hell. Audelay's reason matches his own repeated anxiety about men's lack of faith, and by the fifteenth century it had long become one of the standard explanations for otherworld visions and soul journeys. It is found, for example, in the *Tractatus de purgatorio sancti Patricii*, where the explanation for the revelation of purgatory to Saint Patrick at Lough Derg is that, by entering the otherworld himself, Patrick might convert the unbelieving pagan Irish, who themselves could see the otherworld by entering the pit revealed by Christ.[15] Audelay's new line 13 makes a similar point, that Paul might prove for others the truth of hell's pains by witnessing them himself.

The first sorrowful sight, seen outside the gates of hell, is men and women suspended from fiery trees by various parts of their bodies: heads, tongues, feet, hands, and "Sum be the membirs of here body" (20). Latin manuscripts vary the list, and Audelay may well be following his exemplar, which would differ from the Vienna Manuscript printed by Brandes, which lists feet, hands, hair, ears, tongues, and arms. Tongues, hands, and feet are common to Brandes's text and Audelay, whose "hed" might derive from a text with "capillis" (hairs), and whose "membirs" might derive from "brachiis" (arms), if by it he intended "limbs," as glossed by Whiting. Possibly, by "membirs" Audelay meant "genitals," as these would fit appropriately with "lechory" (25); Dublin, Trinity College MS 519 adds "testiculos."[16] But then again, London, BL MS Harley 2851 adds "et sic per singula membra" (and thus by each limb), so Audelay's "membirs" may be a direct translation of a text with "membra." Audelay has, however, added lines 21–26 including Michael's explanatory commentary, listing the sins for which these souls were punished, "lechory, slouth, and glotoné" (25). Presumably, Audelay is being sufficiently careful here that we should also match up heads and tongues with gluttony, and hands and feet with sloth. One might now note that "the lymys of here body" (24) parallels "the membirs of here body" (20). The "det" (26) in which these sinners die in deadly sin must be their unpaid debt to God of confession and penance. Ever the preacher, Audelay thus supplies an initial explanation by Paul's guide (like those that Michael will provide later), which is missing at this point in the Latin.

Audelay *is* careful to take us inside the gates (27), a move ignored by the Latin, to where Michael and Paul next encounter souls in a furnace with four flames of diverse colors. Brandes's text has seven flames, but "quatuor" (four) occurs in London, BL MS Royal 11 B.iii. Around the furnace are seven sorrows (in Latin, seven *plage* 'torments'),[17] and again the lists are close: Audelay has snow, ice, cold, adders, stench, lightning, and fire; the Latin, snow, ice, fire, blood, serpents, lightning, and stench. In the Latin the torments are numbered; in Audelay each is insistently accompanied by the epithet "gret." Audelay loses "blood" and perhaps redundantly includes "cold" after "snow" and "yse," but again there may be warrant in his exemplar, as these lists also vary in order and content: for example, according to Silverstein, "sanguis" (blood) is omitted from Paris, BnF Cod. lat. 16246; London, BL MS Arundel 52 substitutes "angustus" (constriction) for "sanguis"; and London, BL MS Royal 8 C.vii has "frigus et sanguis" (cold and blood). Again, Audelay turns the Latin narratorial commentary into Michael's direct speech (36–51) and adds part of his explanation of the sins punished (35–37, 39) and Paul's response (52). One might note the "monslers" (manslayers) he adds at line 37; following Michael Bennett's lead, one might claim it is a significant (uncensored?) moment, given Audelay's involvement in his patron's fatal fracas in St. Dunstan's in the East on Easter Sunday 1417,[18] and these committers of manslaughter keep tough company, proud men, plunderers, extortioners, and robbers. That they "deseredyn treu ayrs unryghtfully" (39), presumably to inherit their stolen goods legally, might indeed be a point against the mafiosi-like family loyalties of the more rapacious of England's swashbucklers in the early fifteenth century.

The weeping of these punished souls and the whirling burning wheel closely match the Latin, except that Audelay has seemingly speeded up the wheel's revolutions from one thousand per day to one thousand per *hour* (49), a more dizzying spin, and he loses the Latin's idea that a thousand souls are punished at *each* turn, as well as the epithet "tartareo" (tartarean) for the angel (that is, devil) who "foresmytis" it (50).

Next Michael and Paul come to a horrible river, or "flood" as Audelay calls it, in which, he bizarrely says, are fishlike "develis bestis" (devilish beasts; 54: for "bestie dyabolicae"; 76/6) who devour souls "as hit chep were" (as if it [they] were sheep; 56). This demonic scene of sheep-eating fish is less surreal when the Latin shows that Audelay may have missed a crucial link: "quasi pisces in *medio* maris, que animas *peccatrices* devorant *sine ulla misericordia* quasi *lupi devorant* oves" (like fish in the middle of the sea, which devour the sinful souls without any mercy, as *wolves devour* sheep, 76/6–8; Audelay omits the Latin in italics).

Audelay follows the Latin text's unspecified spatial relationship between the bridge over the water and the mansions prepared for those bound in groups according to their sins, misquoting, shortening, and afterward translating Christ's (here faulty) Latin injunction, "'Lygate faceculus ad comburandum similis cum similibus'— / Bynd bundels togeder to be ibrent" (61–62), for "Ligate eos per fasciculos ad comburendum; id est similes cum similibus, adulteros cum adulteris, rapaces cum rapacibus, iniquos cum iniquis" (Bind them in bundles to be burnt; that is, like with like, adulterers with adulterers, robbers with robbers, the wicked with the wicked; 76/12–15, prompted by Matt. 13:30).[19] But he nicely varies the terms of likeness:

> spouse-brekers with awouters,
> And ranegates with raveners,
> And cursid levers with here cumpers.
> (63–65)

Audelay also simplifies this section, which in the Latin deals with (a) the bridge, which the just cross without hesitation: "pons, per quem transeunt anime *iuste sine ulla dubitacione*" (76/8–9); (b) sinful souls who are submerged in the river according to their merit: "*et multe peccatrices anime merguntur unaqueque* secundum meritum suum" (76/9–10); (c) the mansions and Christ's injunction "Ligate" (see above); and (d) how each could cross the bridge as far as they had merit: "*Tantum vero potest quisque per pontem illum ire* quantum habet meritum" (76/15–16). Audelay again omits those Latin passages I have given here in italics, conflates (a) and (d) as "That soulis passud over after here meryt" (58), and omits (b), though his "after here meryt" possibly owes more to "secundum meritum suum" than to "quantum habet meritum." It will be noted that in avoiding or losing the repetition of the merits of those submerged and the merits of those crossing the bridge, Audelay also ditches the echo of "sine ulla misericordia" (without any mercy; 76/7) and "sine ulla dubitacione" (without any hesitation; 76/9). If these are all conscious choices on Audelay's part, it suggests that he was careful to avoid potentially confusing reiterations in his source.

The souls are submerged in the river to four different parts of the body—in the Latin, to the knees, navel, lips, and eyebrows. Audelay substitutes "armes" for "umbilicum" (navel) and adds "a lytil layghere" and "moche deppere" (70, 71) to clarify the degrees of immersion. Audelay turns indirect speech, "qui essent dimersi usque ad genua" (76/20), into direct speech for Paul's question, "What soulis ben these, bene drownyd here?" (75), but then subsumes Paul's three subsequent questions about the different groups into Michael's reply (76–92). There is much elaboration here in lines 77–79, 83–89, and 91–92. Lines 83–88, on those immersed to the lips as punishment for jangling in church and other abuses, are much fuller than the Latin, "qui lites faciunt inter se in ecclesia non audientes verbum dei" (who make strife between themselves in church, not listening to the word of God; 76/24–26); these two faults become five in the poem, and, interestingly, given the general tone of address to parishioners, "non audientes verbum dei" yields both the personal failure to set store by the service of God and to reverence Christ's body, and the unneighborly prevention of others from hearing Mass by chattering. This last is a staple ingredient of late medieval injunctions to congregations, who were doubtless far less quiet than most modern churchgoers, and recurs as a topic in Audelay, as in his inclusion of the "japers and janglers" in *Over-Hippers and Skippers*, the alliterative verse lines he inserts into his excerpt on the sins of the heart from Rolle's prose *The Form of Living*.[20] In the same stanza (80–92) the last four lines are also an expansion:

> And tho that stod up to the elbow,
> At here neghtbors harmes thay low—

Yif thai ferd wel, her hertis hit slow,
   And of here losse, were glad and fayne.
                              (89–92)

They render "'Alii usque ad supercilia?' 'Hi sunt, qui gaudent de malitia proximi sui'" ("And those up to the eyebrows?" "They are those who joy in the misfortune of their neighbors"; 76/26–27). Line 90 most closely follows the Latin, "low" (laugh) being a benefit of the demands of rhyme, and lines 91–92 a paralleled elaboration. The appropriateness of "supercilia" (eyebrows) to facial indications of malicious glee perhaps outstrips whatever correlation one might imagine for Audelay's substitution of "elbow," which itself is presumably suggested by the "armes" of line 70, and required for the rhyme, but not previously mentioned. As noted, Audelay substitutes arms (70, 80) for "umbilicum" (navel), to which are submerged fornicators and adulterers; perhaps he bowdlerized here, thinking "navel" too suggestively appropriate for sexual misdoers, and replacing it with arms, fitting for lovers' embraces. These instances are typical of the mixed losses and gains in content, meaning, and suitability throughout the translation.

In the first of his additional stanzas (93–105), Audelay exhorts his audience—"A, synful mon! Hereof have mynd" (101)[21]—to pray well in church, the house of prayer, which is the gate of heaven; this is prompted by Michael's explanation to Paul that those immersed in the flood to the lips are so punished for saying their prayers undevoutly and preventing others from hearing Mass by their "changilyng" (jangling; 85–87).[22] But Audelay's addition also reinforces the bounty of God, who will grant what you ask if you are "in charet́e" (97) and serve him in love and dread. As with most accounts of hell or purgatory, Audelay's aim is to instill fear but not despair, and the counterpoint to the pains depicted is reassurance of the salvation available to those who repent while they have time: "Nolo mortem peccatoris" (I desire not the death of a sinner) is the refrain of the following poem, *God's Address to Sinful Men*.[23]

Audelay expands the Latin account of the merciless men and women, seekers of usury, who eat their tongues, adding, for instance, their use of false measures and their lack of pity to the poor as they hold fast to their ill-gotten gains. They "wettanly" (wittingly; 115) foreswear themselves; conscious of their own sin, they do nothing to avoid it. Audelay uses the word again at 337 of those who "wetyngly" anger God by not learning from the mistakes of others. It is one of the forms of faithlessness that most irks the preacher in

Audelay—you tell them and they still do it! It is a notable example of the false use of free choice.

Line endings tend to be more freely translated than line beginnings, not surprisingly: it is rare to find a rhyme deriving directly from the Latin, as with the "damselse *blake*" (120)—"puelle nigre" (77/3)—who have about their necks adders and "*snake*" (123)—"serpentes atque vipere" (77/4–5). Similarly, Audelay tends to start a new stanza with a new movement in the Latin, but then to elaborate in the later part of the stanza, perhaps when the demands of the rhyme scheme make it easier to invent freely than to translate faithfully.[24] At lines 139–44 Audelay elaborates on unchaste girls who slew their infants, and does so by showing them as the victims of the devil who blinded them with despair lest they repent, and made them afraid of the slander and penance they would suffer if they confessed. In the Latin the reader sees them as unchaste murderers, throwing their babies to pigs and dogs to eat, and then doing no penance; in Audelay, though they are certainly no less culpable, the condemnation is less one-sided—and he omits the pigs and "in escam" (for food; 77/11), while specifying "pittis" (138) for the vague "aliis perdicionibus" (other forms of destruction; 77/12). The poem thus again reinforces the efficacy of shrift and penance, for even these unchaste and murderous women would not have come "ta evyl endyng" (144) had they not been made to despair of doing penance. By many such shifts and pointed details, Audelay tends to make the stark moralism of the Latin a little more humanly apprehensible.

Audelay omits those in an icy place who injured widows and orphans, and they may have been absent from his exemplar; this episode (77/13–15) is not included in BnF Cod. lat. 16246. There follows another bizarre moment, called a "picturesque detail" by Whiting:[25] the tantalized men and women, who were fast-breakers, "on kamels rydyng" (146). Much fruit hangs before them, which they cannot reach. Brandes suggested that this odd image of the camel riders derives from a Latin text lacking "ampnis" in "super canelia ampnis" (above a broad stream of water; 77/16 [as Silverstein translates it]).[26] I take "super canalia amnis" (above channels of water) to be the original reading—the souls are seemingly suspended above the channels, presumably man-made sources of drinking water, and hence cannot drink, any more than they can reach the fruit hanging before them. Silverstein's evidence from a number of manuscripts shows that the expression caused scribes problems:[27] for example, "super carnalia ignis," "super alenantis aque," "super arenam," "super camena," and not only "super canalia/canelia," without "amnis," as Brandes supposed, but more importantly, "super camelos" in MS Arundel 52; Cambridge, St. John's College MS D.20 (95); Oxford, Balliol College MS 228; Oxford, Bodl. Lib. MS Laud misc. 527a and b;[28] and J.-P. Migne's unidentified source.[29] As Silverstein notes, the same reading is also found in the Middle English prose version in London, BL MS Addit. 10036, "wymmen aponn camayles & afore hem moche fruyt."[30] R. Priebsch, correctly pointing out that VSP was the source for Audelay's stanzas 1–25 (lines 1–326), noted that in London, BL MS Royal 8 F.vi, a text of VSP Redaction IV precedes the Latin text of "The Sunday [or Heavenly] Letter," which Audelay uses for *Our Lord's Epistle on Sunday* and which Priebsch published alongside the Latin from this manuscript.[31] But the variants at this point in the VSP show that the text of MS Royal 8 F.vi differs from Audelay's exemplar, for it here reads "uiros et mulieres superbos uolantes et morientes fame"[32] (proud men and women flying and dying of hunger [!]). It seems that Audelay was working from a Latin text that already had camels. "Moch froyt" also occurs in Audelay (147); unlike "fructus" in Brandes's text, several manuscripts have some variant of "*multus* fructus" (much fruit).[33] Audelay expands upon these fast-breakers in lines 152–57: he specifies their failure to fast on Good Friday for gluttony and fleshly lust—here, delight in gourmandizing not in sex—and observes that their hunger and thirst are punishment for not sharing their goods with the "pore nedy" (156).

The next "sorouful syght" (159, and cp. 6, 17) of "turmentré" (160, and cp. 178, 356) witnessed by Paul is an old man weeping between four devils. As Michael explains in Brandes's text, "Episcopus negligens fuit" (He was a negligent bishop; 77/20–21); Audelay turns him into a "neclygent mon" (165). Possibly this change occurs because Audelay, as a faithful servant of Holy Church, is cautious to preserve its honor, though elsewhere he is vocal in his castigation of negligent bishops who are blind to the lack of correction and example given by curates to those in their care.[34] More probably, therefore, his exemplar lacked the word "episcopus," as do the texts in MSS Balliol 228, Arundel 52, Laud misc. 527b, Munich, Bayerische Staatsbibliothek Cod. lat. 12728, and Migne, where Michael says, "Hic fuit negligens" (This man was negligent).[35] For the rest of this episode Audelay is close to the Latin, though he translates "dolosus" (deceitful; 77/23) as "ever out of charyté" (169), reusing the powerful New Testament word for love (cp. his addition at line 97, quoted above).

Michael asks why Paul weeps, "Thou sest not the gret payn that beth here! / Come, on with me now thou schal goo" (173–74). Line 174 is a colloquial addition. The context suggests that "*the* gret payn" of line 173 might be construed as an absolute or superlative. The Latin has the comparative: "Nondum vidisti maiores penas inferni" (Thou hast not yet seen the greater pains of hell; 77/25–26). There may be an error in line 173: it is not clearly a four-stress line;[36] *beþ* has been added in the margin; and the form *beþ* is frequently found in the manuscript for the plural as well as the singular, as in lines 188, 323. Perhaps *payn* is intended for *payn(e)s*. The pains of the "blak pit" (175), as Audelay dubs it, are certainly manifold, and he adds, "Therin was care, sorow, and wo, / Stenche, and al maner turmentry!" (177–78). And of the power of the stench, he adds that "Hit wold have slayn al Crystin men" (183). Michael's explanation of those suffering there, the unbelievers and the unchristened, is close to the Latin, and Audelay incorporates from an earlier speech the sentiment that "Of hem, schal never be memory" (191).[37] Again, the poet shows himself to be efficient at conflating and simplifying elements of the dialogue for ease of understanding. He also expands this account in lines 193–96, including heretics, false Christians, and renegades in Michael's catalogue of those in the pit, "Of hom is no redempcion" (196).[38] This matches Audelay's orthodox position on faithlessness and apostasy. "In a wonderful depe plase" (198)—"in alio loco" (in another place; 78/8)—distinct from the pit, souls are "couchid" upon each other (200). Audelay omits "quasi oves in ovili" (like sheep in a sheepfold), but he identifies them as those who had despised their parents (201).

Paul then sees the going-out from the body of a sinful soul and a righteous soul, and witnesses their Particular Judgments.[39] The sinful soul is borne howling between four fiends. There are seven fiends in most of the Latin texts, but again Audelay may have had four in his source text; Balliol MS 228, for example, reads "inter quatuor demones ululantes" (between four howling fiends), transferring the present participial adjective to the demons. Audelay specifies that this soul died "Without shrift, housil, contricion" (209); again the poem reinforces the necessity of the sacraments of the Church. There is some alteration in Audelay's handling of the presentation of evidence. In the Latin the angels cry out against the soul, "Ve, ve, misera anima, que operata es in terra?" (Woe, woe, wretched soul, what have you done on earth? 78/15–16). The angels then address each other:

> Dixerunt ad invicem: "Vide istam animam, quomodo contempsit in terra mandata dei."[40] Mox illa legit cartam suam, in qua erant peccata sua, et se ipsam iudicauit.

(They said to one another, "See this soul, how it despised on earth the commands of God." Presently the soul read [the tense of *legit* is the "historic" present] its chart, in which were its sins, and judged itself; 78/16–18.)

The equivalent passage in the poem (Whiting's edition) is as follows:

> "Alas! wrechid soule what hast þou done?"
> In erþ, þe fyndis þem verefyd,
>   Dispisid Godis laus euerechon;
> To-fore him þai red his dedis anon.
>   (W16.211–14)

First, I suggest, in the light of the Latin, that Whiting needs repunctuating:

> "Alas! wrechid soule, what hast þou done
> In erþ?" Þe fyndis . . .

though it is possible that Audelay intended "In erþ" to go with "Dispisid." The Latin has "in terra" twice (78/16, 17); Audelay has "In erþ" once. Second, the phrase "þe fyndis þem verefyd, / Dispisid Godis laus euerechon" is elliptical, presumably for "the fiends made known the truth to them [the angels, that he, the soul], despised every one of God's laws." Audelay replaces the angels addressing each other (direct speech), with fiends addressing the angels (indirect speech). But perhaps he understood the subject of "Dixerunt" to be seven/four *diaboli* of a previous sentence, in which case he could mean "the fiends confirmed among themselves." At any rate, Audelay then has the fiends read out the soul's sins, whereas in the Latin the soul reads its own sins from the chart and hence condemns itself. Variants in the Latin, however, suggest the possibility that Audelay was again being faithful to his source; in Balliol MS 228 the angels read the chart, "angeli . . . ipsam legerunt cartam."

Michael's question to Paul, "Credis et agnoscis, quia sicut homo fecerit sic accipiet?" (Do you believe and know that as each man does so shall he receive?; 78/21–22) becomes in Audelay the generalized hope or command, "Beleve uche mon, / As ye do . . ." ([May] each man believe, that as you do . . . ; 216–17). And Michael's one-line sentence in the Latin becomes twenty lines in the poem (216–35), the longest addition within the main body of the narrative. Basics of the faith are asserted: postmortem rewards match deeds on earth; mankind has free will to choose to do good or ill (218);[41]

good deeds are rewarded on earth and in heaven; cursed deeds are rewarded on earth, in purgatory, and in hell (219–22); the seven deadly sins—listed as "Pride, covetyse, wrat, envy / . . . / Lechoré, slouth, and glotery" (224, 226)[42]—are punished in hell; and above all is punished despair (cp. line 142), defined as the failure to seek grace and mercy, the sin against the Holy Ghost, mistrust of God's "mercy and grace" (233), and the sin of Judas. Thus again, unlike the Latin original, Audelay repeatedly calls attention to God's mercy and grace and the saving power of confession and penance.

The following stanza presents the contrary motion, the upward flight of a rightful soul to heaven, borne aloft by angels singing. Audelay omits the reading of good deeds, and, as the soul enters paradise, the sounds of acclamation as loud as if the heavens and earth were moved. But again he adds a stanza (249–61) to reinforce the unspeakable joys of the saved, reusing, as is his wont, lines appearing in some of his other poems.[43]

At this point the souls in hell cry out to Paul and Michael for aid in calling on the Lord, as they weep and cry to Christ the Judge, "Sun of David, in heven trone" (273), for mercy and pity. Christ's voice from heaven asks what good they have done, and in terms reminiscent of the Easter Reproaches, says that they crucified him, with Audelay adding the lines: "Ye did me to deth with passion and payn" (277), and "When I was on therst, hongyng on the rode" (282). Christ says, "I put myself to the deth fore yow, / That ye schul ever have levyd with me" (283–84). These lines derive from a Latin text reading "Ego pro vobis me ipsum in martirio dedi, ut viveretis mecum" (I gave myself for you in martyrdom, that you might live with me), as in BnF Cod. lat. 5266, as opposed to "ut vinceretis mecum" (that you might conquer with me), as in Brandes's text (79/12–13).[44]

Paul and the angels of heaven pray for rest for the souls in hell, and this Christ grants as what Audelay calls a "special grace" (295): pity and rest from noon on Saturday till the first hour of Monday, perpetually (288–300).[45] Audelay interposes, "And al the fest of the Sununday" (297), for this is the moment that the opening of the text foreshadowed.[46] The poem does not include the gatekeeper of hell and his dog Cerberus, found in Brandes's Vienna text (79/22–24), but again this was probably absent from Audelay's exemplar, as it is from MS Arundel 52, MS Laud misc. 527a, the incomplete Cambridge, St. John's College MS F.22 (159), and the late Middle English prose version.[47]

I have tried to show by reference to the variants in some of the Latin manuscripts that it is not wise to claim that Audelay definitely did or did not omit certain details, for we do not know the precise contents of the text(s) that he used for his translation. None of the manuscripts that I have examined matches up with all of the features that appear to have been in his exemplar.

The souls in hell cry out in thanks. Audelay's stanza at lines 301–13 is a loose rendering, ignoring the souls' claim that the Sunday respite means more to them than their whole life on earth (79/27–28), and instead reiterating Christ's grace, goodness, worthiness, grace and mercy (cp. line 233). Whiting's punctuation is again faulty: the souls' exclamation ends at the end of line 309, not the end of line 313, where Whiting places the closing quotation mark; it is the narrator who promises joy and bliss in heaven for whoever hallows Sunday (310–13).

When Paul asks how many pains there are in hell, Michael answers with curious precision that there are 4,140, which is contradicted by the end of his reply, "thai may not be noumbyrd, treuly" (322). The number is a corruption of 144,000, borrowed, as Paul Meyer suggests,[48] from the number of the sealed in Revelation 7:4. Again, Silverstein shows that the number "C.XL.IIII. milia" was variously garbled in transmission, yielding, for example, "111,000,000," "144," and "150,000."[49] But one hundred men with a hundred tongues each, speaking since the beginning of the world, could not "tel" (count; 321) them. Audelay here omits that these tongues are of iron, a detail VSP derived from Virgil, *Aeneid* 6.625–27.

The translation ends with the preacherly address to "dere breder that beth present" (323)—"karissimi fratres" (dearest brothers; 80/4)—who, hearing of these pains, should turn to God, that we might reign with him in heaven forever and ever. Thereafter, the final three stanzas are Audelay's addition, expanding this address to these "syrs" (339, 348, 361),[50] promising hell for those who serve the fiend (330, 341), and a "good end" for those who serve God (346–47). By forceful repetition he emphasizes the fate of sinners, who receive "schame and chenchip [perdition], confucion" (329), a "chamful end" (333), and are "eschend" (344), and "chamyd and schend" (363)—these being one of his favorite alliterative collocations.[51] The penultimate stanza is a variant of lines 13–25 of *True Living*, and the last stanza is also a variant of material Audelay uses elsewhere four times.[52] When he thanks God for "his gracious vesityng" (360), he is referring to his blindness and deafness, punishments in this life visited upon him by God, as in the *Finito libro* colophon on folio 22v following Audelay's *Epilogue*, "secus et surdus in sua visitacione" (blind and deaf in his [Christ's] visitation). But we are reminded, especially given the reiteration of "grace" throughout

Audelay's *Vision of Saint Paul*,[53] that this visitation is also gracious, a punishment which is also a gift.

The Vision of Saint Paul is carefully positioned toward the end of the surviving poems in Audelay's book called "*The Cownsel of Conseans* . . . / Or *The Ladder of Heven*" (*Epilogue* 417–18). It is one of the last things in that section of MS Douce 302 and also deals with one of the Last Things. It is itself very clearly a counsel of conscience, an invitation to repentance, and shows explicitly the fate of those who fail to make a good end and take the ladder to heaven.

An essential task of the priesthood and of curates, and one fulfilled by Audelay's book, is to tell their flocks how they might be saved:

> Fore treuly the pepul thai [the clergy] schuld tele,
> And warne ham of the payns of hele,
>   And mend that thai do mys.
>   (*Marcolf* 635–37)[54]

Audelay took this task in a serious and entirely orthodox fashion. He writes frequently of the threat of damnation in the pains of hell;[55] of the proximity of death and "Domysday . . . nygh cumyng" (*Epilogue* 59);[56] of the desire for a good ending and the assurance of entry into paradise;[57] and of the starkness of the choice available, of "Bale or blis" (*Visiting the Sick* 52), "Owther be saved, or ellus be schent" (*Remedy of Nine Virtues* 93, *Visiting the Sick* 394), like Lazarus or the rich man (*God's Address* 245–46):

> And thynk weder that thou wilt go—
> To hel or heven, on of tho—
>   Fore other joyse [choice] is ther non.
>   (*Epilogue* 219–21)[58]

To be sure, Audelay also counts the third place, purgatory, and emphatically repeats the need for penitence, but not too strict a penance, to gain access "to the mercé of God, to purgatoré" (*Marcolf* 928).[59] He exhorts his audience to quench the fire of purgatory by repentance here while there is time (*Visiting the Sick* 101–4, 152–56), and to assist those already in purgatory by prayers, masses, and alms deeds (*Visiting the Sick* 360–64). But admission to purgatory means you have already chosen right and are en route to heaven. The basic choice is twofold.[60]

The Vision of Saint Paul is, of course, the poem in which Audelay focuses on hell most forcefully. Audelay says that Saint Paul was granted the vision "Because men nel not beleve" (9), and he translates the story for the same reason:

> Fore men wil not beleven
> That heven nor hel ther is non,
>   Ne turmentré.
> And sekyr thou schalt have thet on—
> Joy or ellis dampnacion—
>   Perpetualy!
>   (*World's Folly* 49–54; W12.43–48)

Seeing is believing, even at secondhand, for "Non est verior probacio quam oculorum demonstracio" (There is no more truthful proof than the demonstration of the eyes; rubric following *Epilogue* 169).

Audelay's *Vision of Saint Paul* is preceded by *Our Lord's Epistle on Sunday*, the story of Christ's monitory letter on the proper observance of Sunday. This is a perfect preface to *Vision*, which begins "The Sononday is Godis oun chosyn day," telling of Paul's obtaining Sunday respite for the souls in hell after witnessing the separating judgments of a wretched and a rightful soul. It is succeeded, in *God's Address to Sinful Men*, by God as just judge—"Ego sum Deus judex et justus" (rubric following line 8)—addressing mankind, "Turn to me and you will be saved,"[61] and stressing the importance of penance and confession, shrift, contrition, and satisfaction, for "To heven ther is non other way" (111).[62] Audelay's *Epilogue*, the last poem in this section of the manuscript, is in the poet's own voice, or rather the Holy Ghost's speaking through Audelay,[63] as he sums up his fears of men's faithlessness, that is, their failure to take heed of "prechyng and techyng" (81) of the kind he has given, of some good word that he prayed Christ for, "To help mon soule, that hit may, / That hit heren in honé plase!" (51–52):

> Fore al that is nedful to bodé and soule
> Here in this boke then may ye se,
> And take record of the apostil Poule
> That Crist callid to grace and his mercé,
> Fore so I hope he hath done me
> And geven me wil, wit, tyme, and space,
> Throgh the Holé Gost, blynd, def to be,
> And say this wordis throgh his gret grace.
>   (*Epilogue* 14–21)

The injunction here to remember Paul works to align Blind Audelay's hope of salvation with Christ's calling of Paul via (blinding) conversion.[64] In the context of the manuscript, it cannot help but recall Paul's vision of hell, which the reader would have seen a little earlier in this book. *True Living*, the opening poem as we currently have it in the manuscript,[65] warns the reader to "Have mynd apon youre endyng, / Of the payns of helle" (158–59) and explains that without faith, hope, and charity, "the ground of thi beleve" (212), one may not be saved: "Thus Poul, in his pystyl, he doth preve" (215). And it is because men will not believe in the punishments reserved for sinners that God had Michael take Paul to see the pains, "The soth himselve he myght hit preve" (*Vision of St. Paul* 13). *Preve*, 'to declare' and 'to experience,' makes a common and fitting rhyme with *beleve*, both noun and verb. Audelay's book is intended to give his readers and hearers the opportunity to *preve*, that is test and prove, their belief. *The Vision of Saint Paul* is a crucial part of his counsel:

> Clyme up this ladder—then may ye se
> What joys in heven that ther be,
> And what payns in hel and turmentré.
> Then chese yourselve weder to go.
>   (*Epilogue* 426–29)

Notes

1. See Susanna Fein, "Good Ends in the Audelay Manuscript," *Yearbook of English Studies* 23 (2003): 97–119.

2. Ella Keats Whiting, ed., *The Poems of John Audelay*, EETS o.s. 184 (1931; repr. Oxford: Oxford University Press, 2006). Citations from MS Douce 302 are from John the Blind Audelay, *Poems and Carols (Oxford, Bodleian Library MS Douce 302)*, ed. Susanna Fein (Kalamazoo: Medieval Institute Publications, 2009).

3. On the dissemination of the text, see Peter Dinzelbacher, "Die Verbreitung der apokryphen 'Visio S. Pauli' im mittelalterlichen Europa," *Mittellateinisches Jahrbuch* 27 (1992): 77–90.

4. For an introductory bibliography and account of the ME versions, see Robert Easting, *Visions of the Other World in Middle English* (Woodbridge: Brewer, 1997), pp. 28–42, esp. pp. 37–39. For a fuller bibliography on the long Latin texts and vernacular versions, see Theodore Silverstein and Anthony Hilhorst, eds., *Apocalypse of Paul: A New Critical Edition of Three Long Latin Versions* (Geneva: Cramer, 1997). For AN and French versions, see Ruth Dean, with Maureen B. M. Boulton, *Anglo-Norman Literature:*

A Guide to Texts and Manuscripts, ANTS o.p.s. 3 (London: Anglo-Norman Text Society, 1999), nos. 553–55; and Uda Ebel, "Formes littéraires des visions d'outre-monde et des visions apocalyptiques," in *La literature didactique, allégorique et satirique*, ed. Hans Robert Jauss, 2 vols. (Heidelberg: C. Winter, 1968–70), 2:240–42. For German versions, see Nigel F. Palmer, "'Visio Sancti Pauli' I," and Volker Mertens, "'Visio Sancti Pauli' II," in *Die deutsche Literatur des Mittelalters Verfasserlexikon*, ed. Wolfgang Stammler et al., 11 vols. (Berlin: de Gruyter, 1977–), 10(2):418–23, 423–25, respectively. Most recently, Nigel Morgan relates the AN, French, and ME versions (with a brief mention of Audelay) to the contemporary iconography of hell; see Nigel Morgan, "The Torment of the Damned in Hell in Texts and Images in England in the Thirteenth and Fourteenth Centuries," in *Prophecy, Apocalypse and the Day of Doom: Proceedings of the 2000 Harlaxton Symposium*, ed. Nigel Morgan (Donington: Shaun Tyas, 2004), pp. 250–60.

5. The narrative poems also include saints' lives—*St. Winifred Carol* and *Salut. to St. Bridget*—and stories of the Annunciation and Passion—*Seven Bleedings*, *Prayer on Christ's Passion*, *O Deus qui voluisti*, *Seven Words*, *Pope John's Passion*, *Seven Hours*, and *Gabriel's Salut.*; see Whiting, *Poems*, p. xvii.

6. Whiting, *Poems*, p. xvii.

7. Whiting, *Poems*, p. xix.

8. Herman Brandes, "Über die Quellen der mittelenglischen Versionen der Paulus-Vision," *Englische Studien* 7 (1884): 34–65, esp. pp. 49–65. Brandes prints a text of Redaction IV, pp. 44–47, based on three fourteenth-century manuscripts: Vienna, Nationalbibliothek Cod. 876, with variants from London, BL MSS Addit. 26770 and Harley 2851. He reprinted his text in his subsequent study, Herman Brandes, *Visio S. Pauli, ein Beitrag zur Visionslitteratur, mit einem deutschen und zwei lateinischen Texten* (Halle: Niemeyer, 1885), pp. 75–80. On pp. 61–62, he takes brief notice of Audelay's poem (his version 4) and reiterates from his earlier article that it is, like the ME versions in Oxford, Bodl. Lib. MS Laud misc. 108 and the Vernon MS, directly dependent on VSP Redaction IV, and that the Vernon and Audelay poems remain closer to the Latin than does the Laud poem. For a preliminary list of Latin manuscripts, see Theodore Silverstein, *Visio Sancti Pauli: The History of the Apocalypse in Latin Together with Nine Texts* (London: Christophers, 1935), pp. 220–22. Unfortunately, I did not have access to the following important study until the final proof stage for this article, so I have not been able to make use of it here: Lenke Jiroušková, *Die Visio Pauli*, Mittellateinische Studien und Texte 34 (Leiden: Brill, 2006).

9. Eric G. Stanley, "*The True Counsel of Conscience*, or *The Ladder of Heaven*: In Defence of John Audelay's Unlyrical Lyrics," in *Expedition nach der Wahrheit: Poems, Essays, and Papers in Honour of Theo Stemmler*, ed. Stefan Horlacher and Marion Islinger (Heidelberg: C. Winter, 1996), pp. 131–59 (p. 135).

10. Audelay uses the same verse form, rhyming *ababbcbcdeeed*, in several poems: *True Living*, *Marcolf*, *Remedy of Nine Virtues*, *Visiting the Sick*, *Lord's Epistle*, *Epilogue*,

and *Conclusion*; see the tabulation of verse forms in J. Ernst Wülfing, "Der Dichter John Audelay und sein Werk," *Anglia* 18 (1896): 175–217 (p. 215).

11. Stanley, *"True Counsel,"* passim, and see pp. 158–59, his catalogue of "Sermonic assurances, words of counsel, corroborative statements, words of direct address"; and Eric G. Stanley, "The Verse Forms of Jon the Blynde Awdelay," in *The Long Fifteenth Century: Essays for Douglas Gray*, ed. Helen Cooper and Sally Mapstone (Oxford: Clarendon Press, 1997), pp. 99–121, where he contrasts Audelay's singable lyrics with his "more sermonic or expository poems" (p. 101).

12. Cp. *Visiting the Sick* 299.

13. "Peccantem me cotidie et non me penitentem, timor mortis conturbat me, quia in inferno nulla est redemptio. Miserere mei, Deus, et salva me" (Sinning as I am every day and not being penitent, the fear of death disturbs me, because in hell there is no redemption. God have mercy on me and save me). This is listed as R[esponsory] 68 in Knud Ottosen, *The Responsories and Versicles of the Latin Office of the Dead* (Aarhus, Den.: Aarhus University Press, 1993), p. 400. "Timor mortis conturbat me" is part of the burden of *Dread of Death Carol*.

14. I cite VSP Redaction IV from Brandes, *Visio S. Pauli*, pp. 75–80, in the form page/line number.

15. See Robert Easting, ed., *St Patrick's Purgatory*, EETS o.s. 298 (Oxford: Oxford University Press, 1991), p. 124 (lines 110–34).

16. Silverstein, *Visio Sancti Pauli*, p. 113, to whom I am indebted for some details of variants in some of the Latin manuscripts of Redaction IV. Silverstein, pp. 220–21, lists twenty-seven manuscripts in the following cities: Oxford, Cambridge, London, Dublin, Paris, Munich, and Vienna; of these I have myself checked the readings in the nineteen manuscripts located in England.

17. D. D. R. Owen questions the account of the origin of these torments given by Silverstein, *Visio Sancti Pauli*, pp. 72–75, and plausibly suggests that they derive from the *plagae* (scourges, plagues) meted out by the seven angels in Rev. 8–9, 15–16; see his "The Vision of Saint Paul: The French and Provençal Versions and Their Sources," *Romance Philology* 12 (1958): 33–51 (p. 34 n. 5).

18. Michael Bennett, "John Audley: Some New Evidence on His Life and Work," *Chaucer Review* 16 (1982): 344–55, and see Fein, "Good Ends," pp. 6–7, for further comment.

19. See Silverstein, *Visio Sancti Pauli*, pp. 78–79, for Redaction IV taking the assemblage of bridge, mansions, and binding of the souls from Gregory the Great's *Dialogues*. Silverstein refers to *Dialogues* 4.35–36 (*PL* 77:380–81, 385); the text of Gregory's *Dialogues* is now best read in the edition by Adalbert de Vogüé, *Grégoire le Grand, Dialogues*, 3 vols. (Paris: Cerf, 1978–80), 3:124, 130 (for 4.37.10 [bridge], 37.9, 13 [mansions], and 36.14 [binding of the souls]).

20. See Susanna Greer Fein, "A Thirteen-Line Alliterative Stanza on the Abuse of Prayer from the Audelay MS," *Medium Ævum* 63 (1994): 61–74, and nn. 13 and 18.

21. Cp. *Pope John's Passion* 81 and *Epilogue* 217.

22. Bennett alludes to this stanza ("John Audley," p. 355 n. 25) and notes that Audelay's "lengthy perorations on such topics as not disturbing divine service with chatter or discord and keeping the sabbath holy have a chilling appropriateness to a writer with his particular past (poems 9 and 15; *Virtues of Mass* and *Lord's Epistle*)" (p. 352).

23. Cp. too "And amendis betime ye make / Wile ye han space here specialy" (*Epilogue* 25–26), a sentiment commonly expressed in preacherly material by the formula "forsake sin, ere sin forsake you."

24. E.g., stanzas at lines 80–92, 106–18, 132–44, 145–57, 184–96, and 210–22.

25. Whiting, *Poems*, p. 242.

26. See Brandes, "Über die Quellen," p. 61; Silverstein, *Visio Sancti Pauli*, p. 53.

27. Silverstein, *Visio Sancti Pauli*, p. 114 n. 54.

28. This manuscript contains two copies of VSP: (a) fols. 191v–92v, and (b) fols. 263r–64v.

29. *PL* 94:501–2 (501D).

30. Silverstein, *Visio Sancti Pauli*, p. 114 n. 54, citing E. Kölbing, "Eine bisher unbekannte me. Version von Pauli höllenfahrt," *Englische Studien* 22 (1895): 134–39 (p. 135, lines 44–45).

31. R. Priebsch, "John Audelay's Poem on the Observance of Sunday and Its Source," in *An English Miscellany Presented to Dr. Furnivall in Honour of His Seventy-Fifth Birthday*, ed. W. P. Ker, A. S. Napier, and W. W. Skeat (Oxford: Clarendon Press, 1901; repr. New York: Blom, 1969), pp. 397–407 (p. 398 n. 2). It is noteworthy, as Whiting points out, that VSP and the Sunday Letter are juxtaposed in both Audelay and MS Royal 8 F.vi (*Poems*, p. 242), but the same, not unexpected juxtaposition occurs independently in London, BL MS Royal 11 B.x, and Oxford, Merton College MS 13.

32. A reading almost shared with Cambridge, Pembroke College MS 258, which substitutes "superba volentes."

33. Balliol MS 228; Cp., e.g., "multos fructus" (*PL* 94:501D), or "multos frutus [*sic*]" (MS Laud misc. 527b).

34. *Epilogue* 96; cp. *Marcolf* 715–23 and *Remedy of Nine Virtues* 60–61.

35. See Silverstein, who says, "The omission evidently arose through the abbreviation of 'episcopus' in many of the manuscripts" (*Visio Sancti Pauli*, p. 114 n. 56).

36. Though that in itself is not unusual in Audelay's verse. Stanley aptly notes that "within lines of varying syllabic count, the number of stresses is not fixed either, and is often difficult to determine" ("Verse Forms," p. 116).

37. This line translates "non fiet commemoracio eius " (78/3), and Audelay places it after the translation of "nec communicati corpore et sanguine Christi" (78/7–8) by "never resayvyd Cristis body" (189).

38. Whiting omits to punctuate for the end of this speech, which should come at the end of line 196.

39. On the postmortem Particular Judgment, see Robert Easting, "Personal Apocalypse: Judgement in Some Other-World Visions," in *Prophecy, Apocalypse and the Day of Doom: Proceedings of the 2000 Harlaxton Symposium*, ed. Nigel Morgan (Donington: Shaun Tyas, 2004), pp. 68–85.

40. Brandes erroneously ends the speech after "iudicauit." P. Meyer punctuates correctly in his edition, which is based on nonspecified manuscripts: "La Descente de saint Paul en enfer: poème français composé en Angleterre," *Romania* 24 (1895): 357–75 (p. 372).

41. Cp. *True Living*: "[Mon] has fre choys as we fynde, / Weder he wyl do good or ylle, / Owther ysavyd or ellys yschent. / Owther have heven or ellus have helle, / Thou hast fre choys!" (203–7).

42. "The order here used is basically Gregorian, although changed because of the exigencies of rime" (Morton W. Bloomfield, *The Seven Deadly Sins: An Introduction to the History of a Religious Concept, with Special Reference to Medieval English Literature* [East Lansing: Michigan State College Press, 1952], p. 434 n. 147).

43. Cp. *Visiting the Sick* 10–13, *Lord's Epistle* 174–75, 179–82, and *God's Address* 253–54.

44. See Silverstein, *Visio Sancti Pauli*, pp. 114–15 n. 58, for variants. The reading "viveretis" is found, e.g., in MSS Addit. 26770, Royal 8 C.vii, Royal 8 E.xvii, Royal 11 B.iii, Royal 11 B.x, Oxford, Merton College 13, Cambridge, Pembroke College 103, Cambridge, St. John's College F.22 (159), and *PL* 94:502C; and "vivetis" in MSS Arundel 52, Royal 8 F.vi, and Cambridge, Pembroke College 258, presumably via omission of the superscript abbreviation for *-er-*. Cambridge, St. John's College MS D.20 (95) reads "viuatis"! Silverstein notes that the Vernon/Simeon couplet version (*IMEV* 1898; see Easting, *Visions of the Other World*, 2.6.[C], pp. 36–37) follows "vinceretis": "I ȝaf my-self for ȝou to be, / For ȝe schulde *ouer-come* wiþ me."

45. This translates "ab hora nona sabbati usque in prima hora secunde ferie" (79/21–22), which matches the definition of the sabbath circulated in the Sunday Letter (cp. *Lord's Epistle* 93–94). See Priebsch, "John Audelay's Poem," p. 403; and Clare Lees, "The 'Sunday Letter' and the 'Sunday Lists,'" *Anglo-Saxon England* 14 (1985): 129–51 (p. 137).

46. See Silverstein, *Visio Sancti Pauli*, pp. 79–81, on the development of the Sunday respite and its inclusion in certain redactions of VSP, which became "not merely an account of the world to come and an exhortation to righteousness . . . [but] acquired the more special character of a homily on the *dominicus dies* [Lord's day]" (p. 81).

47. Easting, *Visions of the Other World*, p. 42 (2.9 [F]).

48. Meyer, "La Descente," p. 375.

49. Silverstein, *Visio Sancti Pauli*, p. 115 n, 60.

50. One of Audelay's standard forms of address to his audience; see Stanley, "*True Counsel*," p. 158.

51. Audelay uses variants of "schame and schend / chenship" at least twenty times, according to the lists provided by Stanley, "*True Counsel*," p. 157.

52. With some slight variation, lines 353–54 recur in *Remedy of Nine Virtues* 77–78, *Visiting the Sick* 378–79, *Lord's Epistle* 197–98, and *Epilogue* 495–96; lines 357–61 in *Remedy of Nine Virtues* 81–84, *Visiting the Sick* 382–86, *Lord's Epistle* 200–204, and *Epilogue* 499–503; lines 361–65 in *Conclusion* 35–39; and line 365 at *Remedy of Nine Virtues* 102, *Visiting the Sick* 390, *Lord's Epistle* 208, and *Epilogue* 507.

53. See also Stanley "*True Counsel*," p. 156, for the many reiterations of "grace and mercy" and "in grace to graunt mercy" in MS Douce 302.

54. Cp. *Epilogue* 310.

55. E.g., *True Living* 1, 13–14; *Marcolf* 367–77; *Remedy of Nine Virtues* 23, 58, 65; *Prayer on Christ's Passion* 30; *Anima Christi* 7–9 (W6.11–13); *Tu Domine*; *Virtues of the Mass* 203; and *God's Address* 119.

56. Cp. *Remedy of Nine Virtues* 75–76 and *God's Address* 3.

57. E.g., *Seven Words* 35–36, 91–96; *Virtues of the Mass* 123–25, 375–77, 411–13; *General Confession* 36–37 (W10.58–59); *Visiting the Sick* 7–13, 31–33, 283–86, 403; *Seven Hours* 87–90; *Epilogue* 1–13 (W55.18–21); and *Conclusion* 18–21.

58. Cp. *Remedy of Nine Virtues* 68–70, and *Epilogue* 397–99.

59. Cp. *Virtues of the Mass* 250–51, *Visiting the Sick* 137–43, and *God's Address* 142.

60. Takami Matsuda examines Audelay's presentation of purgatory in *Death and Purgatory in Middle English Didactic Poetry* (Woodbridge: Brewer, 1997), pp. 167–73, and rightly makes the point that "For Audelay, Purgatory is a condition of spiritual healing as much as it is a particular locale reserved for purgative punishment in the afterlife" (p. 170).

61. Heading: "Hec dicit Dominus Deus convertemini ad me et salui eritis."

62. Cp. *True Living* 120.

63. "This was the Holé Gost wercheng, / That sayd these wordis so faythfully" (*Epilogue* 497–98).

64. The incipit to the text of VSP in Oxford, Merton College MS 13, fol. 66ra, reads, "Incipit reuelatio sancti Pauli hiis tribus diebus quando conuersus et vocatus a Christo cecidit in terram nihil videns" (Here begins the revelation of Saint Paul during those three days when, converted and called by Christ, he fell to the earth seeing nothing).

65. *Marcolf* is numbered XI in MS Douce 302; see Whiting, *Poems*, p. vii. Probably "as many as nineteen leaves" containing nine full poems and part of the tenth are missing from the beginning of Audelay's collection (Fein, "Good Ends," p. 98).

JOHN AUDELAY AND THE BRIDGETTINES

Martha W. Driver

John Audelay's poem celebrating Saint Bridget of Sweden is Poem 23 in Ella Keats Whiting's edition of Audelay's modest "anthology of spiritual counsel," Oxford, Bodleian Library MS Douce 302, copied in or around 1426.[1] Like many of Audelay's compositions, the *Salutation to Saint Bridget* strikes the modern reader as simultaneously heartfelt, eccentric in form, and full of obscure historical allusion. Saint Bridget of Sweden was canonized in 1391, within Audelay's lifetime, and Audelay's poem describes the founding of the Bridgettine order by Bridget and later of "Bregit Sion" (138), or Syon Abbey, the Monastery of St. Saviour and St. Bridget of Syon, of the order of Saint Augustine, established by Henry V near his palace at Sheen, giving important witness to the royal founding of this influential order in England.[2]

In his depiction of Bridget, Audelay demonstrates his command of specific details of her biography, but he also notably describes Bridget, the mother of eight children, as a "maydyn" (1), or virgin, which seems rather ambiguously to reflect late medieval concerns about the purity and holiness of married women saints. Written, like the rest of the manuscript, in the Augustinian house of Haughmond Abbey, Audelay's poem provides insight into the daily practices of the Bridgettines, who were also governed by Augustinian rule. The *Salutation to Saint Bridget* is interesting to consider from a number of perspectives, among them the poetic, the miraculous, and the historical.

The Latin invocation to the verses of Audelay's *Salutation to Saint Bridget* opens with "Hic incipit salutacio Sancte Brigitte virginis" (Here begins the salutation to Saint Bridget, virgin) and ends "quod Awdelay." There are twenty-three rhymed stanzas, each with nine lines. The first eleven stanzas open with the word "Hail" and repeat the word persistently in each stanza. Stanzas 13 and 15 also begin with the word "Hail," after which we find it only once more, in stanza 16, which describes the founding of the Bridgettine convent by Henry V.

As one might expect, the formulaic repetition of "Hail" is most typically found in Middle English lyrics and songs directed to the Virgin Mary, echoing the opening words of the angel Gabriel in the Annunciation and also of Elizabeth's greeting to Mary at the Visitation. Karen Saupe, editor of *Middle English Marian Lyrics*, includes eleven poems that use the word "Hail," though none of these lyrics begins to approach the level of the repetition of this word as found in Audelay's *Salutation to Saint Bridget*.[3] Richard Leighton Greene's *The Early English Carols* includes eleven other examples of salutation poems, most of which, again, concern the Virgin Mary,[4] though Greene further presents a carol composed by James Ryman, a Franciscan writing about seventy years after Audelay, that also hails Queen Esther.[5] All of these contemporary examples use the word "Hail" in an opening line or sometimes at the start of several lines, but none can begin to match the emphatic usage by Audelay. In Audelay's *Salutation to Saint Bridget* the word "Hail" appears fifty-five times, repeated two to five times in each of the stanzas cited previously, except for stanza 16, where it occurs only once.

In the preface to her edition of Audelay's poetry, Whiting comments that the narrative of the salutation "proceeds awkwardly, being frequently interrupted by the word *hail*, for the poem is couched in the form of a salutation to the saint." She continues, "Audelay is more successful [elsewhere]."[6] While this may be, Audelay does employ anaphora, the device of repeating a word or phrase at the beginning of a line for emphasis or euphony, in several of his other poems. His better-known poem to Saint Winifred, for example, repeats the word "Hail," as do other poems in his manuscript that appear next to or close to the *Salutation to Saint Bridget*.[7]

For example, the *Salutation to Jesus*, a poem addressed to the Virgin and Jesus, opens each of the first sixteen lines with "Hayle!" The word "Hayle" then recurs at the start of sixty-nine of the 159 remaining lines of the poem, used for a grand total of eighty-six times. The *Salutation to Mary*, also called a prayer to Mary ("Alia oracio de Sancta Maria virgine"), repeats the word "Hayle" at the start of the majority of its 120 lines, with the refrain: "Haile, blessid froyt! Haile, swet floure!" In *Gabriel's Salutation to the Virgin*, a poem drawn from the greeting of angel Gabriel, Audelay shows some restraint: the word "Haile!" is repeated only twice in the first stanza. In *Song of the Magnificat*, the poem based on Luke 1:46–51, the word "Hail" does not appear. The next poem in this sequence is the Bridget poem. The *Saint Winifred Carol* that directly follows does not use the word "Hail," but the next poem, *Salutation to Saint Winifred* (prefaced by "Hic incipit salutacio Sancte Wenefrede virginis"), contains repetitions of the word "Hail" in the first three lines of each stanza. In the succeeding poem, *Salutation to Saint Anne*, each line opens with "Gaude!" Like the other poems in which the word "Hail" is repeated, this one has been titled a "salutation" by Audelay (or possibly by the scribe). The *Salutation to the Holy Face*, also described as a "salutation" in its rubric, opens the first line of each stanza with "Salve." In this cluster of poems (W19–W27), then, there is repetition of the word "Hail," with Latin captions describing them as salutation poems or prayers.[8]

Several scholars have attempted to group Audelay's poems or to make some sense of their order. Derek Pearsall has suggested, for example, that Audelay may not have written all of the poems in the manuscript himself: "After the first group of 18 poems, which Awdelay seems at one time to have regarded as his completed work (and which may well be the only poems that are entirely his own composition), there follow celebrations and salutation-poems."[9] Melissa Jones comments that "[n]os. 23 through 27 comprise a conspicuously hagiographic group." The last two poems in this group are salutations "directed at Sts Anne and Veronica respectively. . . . Each saint exemplifies a different model of feminine virtue, and the poems collectively create a miniature catalogue of Holy Women."[10]

In her essay "Good Ends in the Audelay Manuscript," Susanna Fein observes four groupings within Audelay's manuscript, which include as section 2 (fols. 22v–27v) Audelay's salutations and prayers. Then follows, according to Fein's division, section 3 (fols. 27v–32r), Audelay's carols.[11] These groupings make good sense, though the last salutary item on folio 27v (W27) may also describe itself as a carol. The inscription "I pray yow, syrus, boothe moore and las, / Syng these caroles in Cristemas" has been written by Scribe B in the upper margin of the leaf on which this poem appears. Generally interpreted as referring to the carol collection that follows, this inscription with its placement suggests perhaps a more ambiguous blending of genres. One of the Winifred poems (fol. 26r–v) is apparently described by Audelay himself as a carol:

> I pray youe al, pur charyté,
> Redis this carol reverently,
> Fore I hit mad with wepyng ye.
>   Mi name hit is the Blynd Awdlay.
>   (*St. Winifred Carol* 175–78; W24.117–20)[12]

Ideas about carols and about salutations do not seem fixed in this period, and poetry itself remained a loosely defined genre. Douglas Gray, for example, describes "verse prayer," which consists of lyrics "cast in the form of a prayer . . . meant for private devotional use." Such lyrics are often narrative or descriptive and are sometimes found as titles accompanying wall paintings or carvings.[13]

The form of iteration used by Audelay in his *Salutation to Saint Bridget* does not seem to appear in late medieval poetry more generally, to my knowledge, and I would suggest that it may be drawn from Augustinian prayer rather than from specifically poetic practice. As Fein has recently pointed out, not only are Audelay's salutations and prayers clustered in the manuscript, but their contents "are often sequenced for liturgical or private devotions."[14]

One also finds persistent, almost hypnotic iteration of the word "Hail" in another, much earlier work written in an Augustinian house, the *Ancrene Wisse*, in which the author "borrows from the Augustinian rule at several points," and "the religious schedule he outlines for the anchoresses . . . [has] many points in common with Augustinian practices."[15] The *Ancrene Wisse* contains several lengthy prayers, with each line beginning with "Hail," in the section on devotions. The women are instructed to prostrate themselves before the altar soon after rising, saying these salutations: "Hail, author of our creation! Hail, prince of our redemption! Hail, viaticum of our journeying! Hail, reward of our longing! Hail, comfort in our waiting!" This prayer then is repeated during the Mass after "the priest lifts up God's body." The anchoresses are instructed to "fall down with these greetings": "Hail, author of our creation!" Marian prayers follow, among them the "Hail Mary," which the anchoresses are instructed to say five times after each psalm and versicle. After the versicle beginning "The Holy Spirit shall overcome you, and the power of the most high shall overshadow you" follows this antiphon: "Hail, O queen of heaven; hail, Lady of the angels, hail, O holy source, from which light has dawned on the world; hail, most beautiful one, and pray to Christ always for us." After reciting one versicle and its antiphon, the anchoresses are further instructed to "Here sit for the *Hail Marys*, fifty or a hundred—more or less according to how much time one has."[16]

While the instructions for and explanations of the divine service in *The Myroure of Oure Ladye*, written for the Bridgettine nuns sometime after 1420, are not as emphatic as anchoritic practice, Middle English prayers that repeat the word "Hail" or that use the "Hail Mary" (in either Latin or Middle English) appear in other manuscripts associated with the Bridgettine order. Syon Abbey, South Brent MS 2, a Book of Hours copied about 1430 for use by a Bridgettine nun, for example, includes such prayers, as does London, Lambeth Palace Library MS 546, "a multiple volume of devotions with an invocation of Saint Bridget," copied in the early 1500s, in which the prayer texts further function as pardons or indulgences.[17] In form, Audelay's *Salutation to Saint Bridget* resembles a meditative prayer in which a word or phrase is regularly repeated.

Louis Althusser has discussed "the phenomenon of interpellation, or 'hailing,' as the means by which ideology 'recruits' or 'transforms' the individual into a subject."[18] Perhaps this, too, is part of the purpose of Audelay's poems that are placed at the center of his manuscript, transforming holy women—Bridget, Anne, and Veronica—into iconic subjects for celebration and prayer. It has been further pointed out that Winifred is "the only virgin in Audelay's catalogue of Holy Women," although (and this seems odd to the modern reader who knows her history) Audelay also makes this claim for Bridget.[19]

Bridget of Sweden was born ca. 1303 and died in 1373. After marrying and producing eight children, Bridget began at around the age of thirty to experience almost daily supernatural visions. The first stanza of Audelay's poem calls Bridget a maiden, a wife, and a widow ("mayden and wyfe, . . . wedow Brygytt"; 1), and Audelay then describes her (approvingly) as one who chose "to be chast and kepe charyté" and who persuaded her spouse "To be relegyous" (2–5), that is, to dwell with her in chaste marriage. The verse continues:

> Hayle, fore the love of Jhesus Crist,
> Ye foresake your fleschelé lust—
> Therfore be ye both eblest
>   In the name of swete Jhesus!
>   (6–9)

While the progression of Bridget from virgin to wife to widow seems natural enough, Audelay does not describe it as a progression. Instead, in this poem Bridget is simultaneously maid, wife, and widow. In the second stanza the Virgin appears to Bridget and tells her to thank Jesus, who has given her the power "To be wyfe, wedow, and may" (18), an inversion of the usual order.

The simultaneity of these roles is striking. A few stanzas on, Jesus appears to Bridget and favors her especially for her virginity: "he grownded thee in grace in thi vergeneté" (48). In Audelay's account Pope Urban also calls Bridget a "mervelus maide ful of mekenes" (82), which, given the history of their actual relationship (discussed below), seems fairly unlikely. In stanza 14 Bridget and her husband pledge to live in chastity:

> Hure husbond to his bredern con go,
> And to hure susteres heo whent him fro
>   To leve in chastité.
>   (124–26)

This is not quite historically accurate. Saint Bridget's Latin *Vita* specifies that the couple practiced chastity during the first year of their marriage, but not thereafter for some twenty years, until about one year before the death of Ulf, Bridget's husband. The Bridgettine order was then founded at Vadstena after Ulf died.[20]

The final stanza of the *Salutation to Saint Bridget* once more reiterates the virginity of Bridget, exhorting the reader to pray "to blisful Bregit, that merceful may" (200). As he does at the beginning of the poem, Audelay again identifies himself as its author, "That is both blynd and def, the synful Audelay," who "mad this with good entent, / In the reverens of this vergyn, verement" (out of reverence for Bridget, this "true virgin"; 202, 204–5). Audelay's description of Bridget as a widow becoming, as it were, re-virginized might strike a modern reader as odd, but the notion presented in Audelay's text reflects typical late medieval anxieties about married women saints, as well as those found in Bridget's own writings.

In several medieval texts virginity is represented as both a spiritual and a physical condition, and the boundary between these inward and the outward states was apparently seen as fluid. Citing Saint Augustine, the *Ancrene Wisse* author says this:

> For as Seint Austin seið, swa muchel is bitweonen—bituhhen Godes neoleachunge ant monnes to wummon—þet monnes neoleachunge makeð of meiden wif, ant Godd makeð of wif meiden. . . . Gode werkes ant treowe bileaue—þeose twa þinges beoð meiðhad i sawle.
>
> (For as Saint Augustine says, there is so much difference—that is, between God's advances to a woman and a man's—that a man's advances make a virgin into a woman, and God makes a woman into a virgin. . . . Good works and true faith—these two things are virginity in the soul.)[21]

Elsewhere in the *Ancrene Wisse* we are told, in a passage that has been discussed by Barbara Newman, Clarissa Atkinson, and Jocelyn Wogan-Browne, among others, that virginity is

> A deore licur. A deorewurðe wet as bas me is. In a feble uetles. Healewi ibruchel gles . . . for beo hit eanes tobroken; ibet no bið hit neauer. Ibet ne hal as hi was ear; namare þan gles. . . . ah þis manere bruche mei beon ibet eft ase hal allunge as hit wes eauer halest þurch medicine of schrift & bireowsunge.

> (a valuable liquid like balm, in a fragile vessel, an ointment in a brittle glass. Once broken it cannot be mended to the wholeness it had, any more than glass. . . . Yet this kind of breakage can be mended again, as entirely whole as it ever was, through the medicine of confession and true repentance.)[22]

The message remains ambiguous, as Wogan-Browne has pointed out: "[T]he passage both insists on the bodily absoluteness of virginity ('once it is broken, it may never be mended'), *and* asserts its applicability to more than the technically intact among its audience ('the balsam contained in it is virginity, or after the loss of virginity, chaste cleanness')."[23] Later medieval texts seem also to indicate that virginity is not a concept that is absolutely fixed in the physical body but may also refer to states of mind (and spirit). *The Mirroure of the Worlde*, translated by Stephen Scrope in the mid-fifteenth century, states that without a clean conscience, "ther is no chastite that plesith Godde," saying further that

> for al that in the state of marriage or in the state of wydowhoode men maye wel wynne the corone of blisse and haue more mede anenste [in the judgment of] Godde than many virgins hatthe. For ther be many of thoo that hatthe ben in marriage and in wydowhoode the whiche in paradis be nerer to Godde than many virginis.[24]

This Middle English text goes so far as to suggest that married or widowed persons with some experience of the world may be more valuable to God than virgins are. Similar arguments concerning the sanctity to which married women might aspire are made in a variety of late medieval stories, including narratives about Bridget, Elizabeth of Hungary, Elizabeth of Portugal, and Marie d'Oignies, and, of course, in the autobiography of Margery Kempe.

According to her *Vita* Bridget was betrothed at the age of thirteen to a wealthy young man, "a prudent and noble knight who was called Lord Ulf of Ulvåsa, . . . both spouses lived in virginity for one year, devoutly asking God that if they ought to come together he, the Creator of all, would from them create an offspring that would be at his service."[25] Bridget Morris, one of Saint Bridget's modern biographers, comments that there is no evidence that Bridget married unwillingly or that she wished to preserve her virginity. Instead, Saint Bridget herself says that she loved her husband dearly, in her words, "like her own heart." Morris says further: "Certainly her childhood visions do not suggest any opposition to marriage, but her daughter, Katarina Ulfsdotter, giving a predictably traditional and retrospective response, later testified that her mother repeatedly told her that she had entered into marriage reluctantly, that her family had 'compelled, coerced and forced her,' and that she would have preferred death to marriage."[26]

Many of the writings both by and about Bridget reveal a palpable anxiety about her status as wife, mother, and widow. As Atkinson has pointed out, "Birgitta had to be reassured frequently, by God or the Virgin, that all three states were virtuous. Once she heard a voice saying that 'virginity deserves a crown, widowhood comes close to God, marriage is not a bar to Heaven, but obedience leads all of these into glory.'"[27] In one section of Bridget's *Revelations*, titled "How oure blissid lady is redy to helpe alle, bothe wyues, widowes, and maydens," the Virgin tells Bridget that, as the Virgin is a mother, she helps all mothers who pray that their children may please God. And, as the Virgin is a widow, "in þat I hadde a sone in erthe that had no bodily fadre," she will aid widows. And, finally, the Virgin explains, "There is also no virgyn that desireth to kepe hir maydenhode to God vn-to hir deth, but þat I am redy to defende hir and to comforte hir." The Virgin then (rather unfortunately, in this reader's opinion) draws an analogy between these three female states and that of the polygamous King David, who desired Saul's virgin daughter and received her when she was a widow, and who "had also the wyf of Vyre, while hir husbonde lyued," that is, committed adultery with Bathsheba, wife of Uriah. And though in these matters, the text continues, David "was not with-oute synne," he was the kingly forebear of Jesus, who had no sin. Therefore, the Virgin instructs Bridget, "as these thre lyves, that is, maydenhod, widowhood, and wedlock, plesed Dauid bodily, so plese it my sone to haue hem in his moost chast delyt gostly."[28] Bridget's text suggests that Jesus willingly receives all three aspects of womanhood and that virginity is not particularly valued over motherhood or widowhood.

Atkinson has further pointed out that Bridget's early biographers "argued hotly for her equality with holy virgins, called her 'another Sara,' and reminded readers that chaste married people were pleasing to God and deserving of eternal blessedness. The passionate attention to this question displayed by Bridget and her biographer indicates the continuing ambiguity and unease surrounding the relationship of holiness and female sexuality."[29] Audelay, on the other hand, accepts Bridget's miraculous, simultaneously threefold status as wife, widow, and virgin, and celebrates her chaste marriage, which is traditionally found described in the lives of other married women saints, including those of the historical figures Marie d'Oignies and Elizabeth of Hungary as well as of the legendary Saint Cecilia.[30]

Can Bridgettine influence be seen more generally in Audelay's work? There are, in fact, several similarities between Bridget's work and Audelay's, though these may be commonplaces in the religious writing of the time. The stair or ladder, for example, is a central image in the works of both Bridget and Audelay. Michael Bennett, Eric Stanley, and Richard Firth Green, among others, have pointed out that Audelay himself regarded his volume "as an anthology of spiritual counsel to be entitled *Concilium conciencie* or *Scala celi*."[31] As Audelay writes in its last poem of section 1: "*The Cownsel of Conseans* this boke I calle, / Or *The Ladder of Heven*" (*Epilogue* 417–18), and he further explains that by climbing the ladder of conscience men may see heaven or hell, and then choose the proper path (423–29).

The ladder is also the central image in Bridget's *Revelations*, and it is typically illustrated both in manuscripts and early printed copies. In the fifth book of Bridget's *Revelations*, for example, the illustration in the German editions by Albrecht Dürer shows a man on a ladder wearing a cap and cowled gown (representing Magister Magnus, Bridget's confessor) and climbing from earth to heaven (Fig. 1).[32] In book 5, the central text of her *Revelations*, Bridget challenges Magnus and asks questions of God through him. According to Jungian interpretations, the monk represents "the *animus* of Birgitta; the doubts are but her own doubts projected upon the figure of the monk, who then takes over all the negative elements."[33] Tore Nyberg has pointed out that book 5 represents "the process of Birgitta's identification and purification of self by and through the concepts about God's action."[34]

In the works of both Bridget and Audelay, the ladder is viewed as crucial to salvation, but there is no guarantee that the person climbing it will reach heaven; in both cases, this goal can be attained only through informed choice. And in view of Audelay's own insistence on his blindness and deafness, it is further interesting to note the emphasis placed on the physical senses in book 5 of Bridget's *Revelations*, particularly on blindness, on spiritual illness, and on hearing and not hearing.[35]

Figure 1. The Ladder, book 5, *The Revelations of Saint Bridget*. London, British Library MS 489.i.1 (sig. C3v). Reproduced with permission.

Both Bridget and Audelay further share a lively interest in devils, Audelay most likely adding a stanza about Titivillus, "the devil of idle talk" to the Rolle prose extract, as Fein has argued (*Over-Hippers* 2, and cp. the story recounted in *Virtues of the Mass* 265–336). The demon "Tytyvyllus" also makes an appearance in *The Myroure of Oure Ladye*, the Bridgettine treatise on the divine service composed in the early fifteenth century. Here he collects bags of "faylynges, & of neglygences in syllables and wordes, that ar done . . . in redynge and in syngynge" by the sisters at the Mass.[36] Unlike Audelay, however, Bridget tends to racialize her demons, often describing them as "Ethiopians" (though she rejects slavery with great revulsion in her *Revelations* and is traditionally said to have been sent, as a gift from Queen Joanna of Naples, a black girl who was raised as a member of Bridget's household, became a nun at Vadstena, and died there in the odor of sanctity).[37]

Both writers describe powerful yet homely scenes of the Nativity. Audelay's *Joys of Mary Carol* describes the Incarnation, the birth of Jesus, and his suckling at the Virgin's breast (13–16), a scene also described by Bridget in her *Revelations*: "and wyth her pappe and her brest she made hym warme wyth full grete yoye and gladnes."[38] The *Revelations* of Bridget might also be a possible inspiration for Audelay's description of the sword that pierces the Virgin's heart in the *Salutation to Mary* ("Haile, hert that with a swerd was chorne"; 78) or perhaps for the image of the chaste sword of the spirit in the *Chastity Carol* (34), which Stanley cites as one of the "good phrases" in Audelay's verse. In a vision in the Church of St. Mary Major in Rome, Bridget saw the Virgin accompanied by an angel who "carried a long, very broad, and bloody sword which signified those very great sorrows which Mary suffered at the death of her most loving Son, which the just man Simeon prophesied would pierce her soul." At the presentation of Christ in the Temple, Simeon had said to Mary, "and a sword will pierce through your own soul also" (Luke 2:35), a prediction Bridget is more generally associating with the Virgin Mary in her vision.[39]

Some scholars have further surmised that Audelay shared with the Bridgettines an interest in the cult of the Holy Name, given his reference in the *Salutation to Saint Bridget* to "the name of swete Jhesus" (9). The cult of the Holy Name was among those that "saw significant developments in Henry's reign" and was associated with the Bridgettines.[40] Ann Hutchinson has pointed out that Syon Abbey "became influential in promoting this cult through particular devotions, such as its famous 'pardon beads.'" This was a string of five beads used to say a verse prayer, "Ih[es]u for thy holy name."[41]

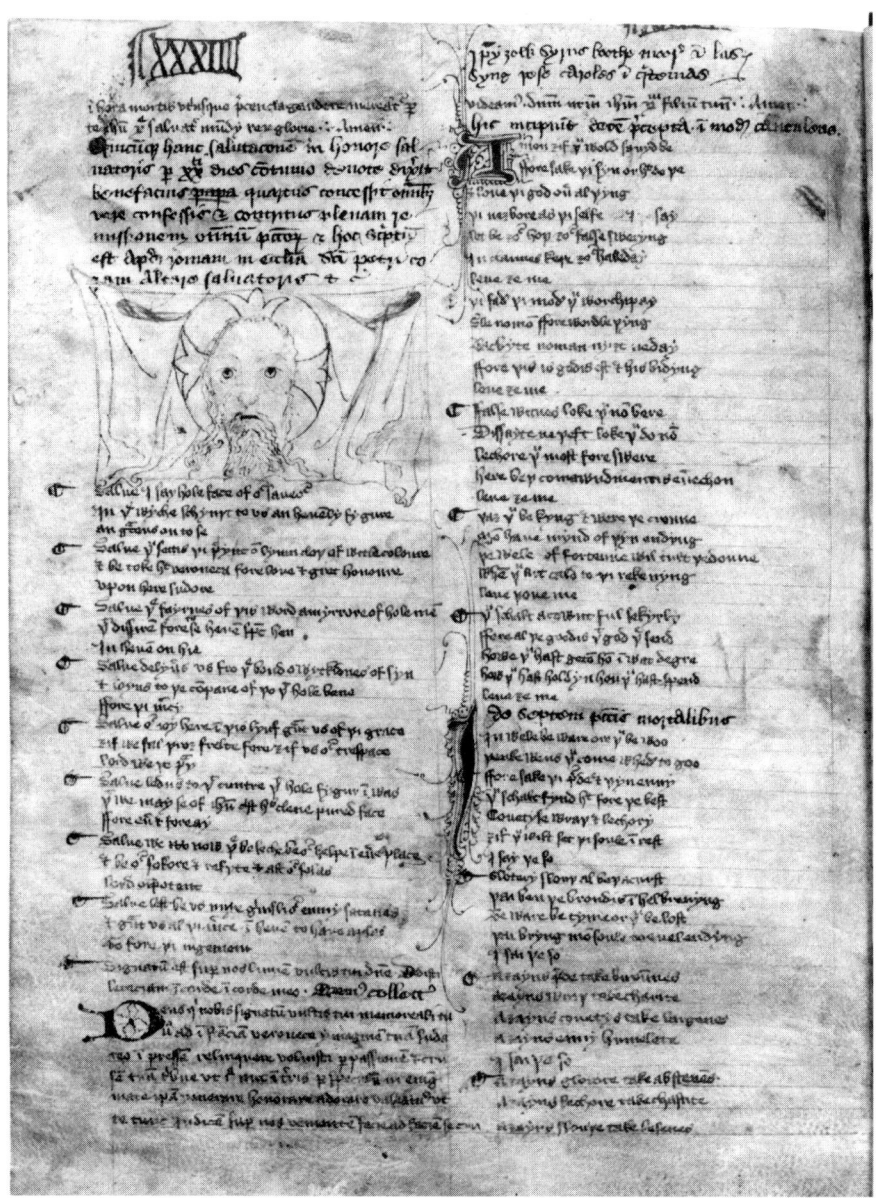

Figure 2. Drawing of the Vernicle, John Audelay Manuscript.
Oxford, Bodleian Library MS Douce 302 (fol. 27v). Reproduced
by permission of The Bodleian Library, University of Oxford.

Audelay may possibly be alluding to this popular cult in this line from his *Salutation to Saint Bridget*, but the word "name," part of the essential formula in prayers associated with the cult, actually occurs very seldom in Audelay's book.[42] Audelay's emphasis is placed instead on the Holy Face. References to it occur in six of Audelay's poems, including the sequenced *Meditation on the Holy Face* (W27), a prayer to the Vernicle accompanied by a drawing on fol. 27v of the head of Christ with a trefoil halo on the cloth (Fig. 2), the only illustration in the manuscript.[43] Given Audelay's self-proclaimed blindness, the visual emphasis of his poetry is particularly striking.

Indulgences and pardons are also central to both Bridgettine and Audelaian concerns. Saint Bridget has been described as "an eminent propagandist for indulgences," especially for pardons for the dead, and her order promoted the sale of indulgences both in England and on the Continent in the period of transition from manuscript to print.[44] Audelay's verses are full of references to remission of sins and pardon. *Seven Bleedings of Christ*, for example, concludes with an indulgence formula, the narrator asking for his "syns remyssion" through his saying "Fiftene Paternoster . . . / And fiftene Aves to our Lady" (112–13). This verse also promises other spiritual benefits, including the reward of heaven for those who teach the text to others: "He that techis another mon this, / He schal be sekyr of heven blis" (134–35). Audelay's *Devotions at the Levation of Christ's Body* (W8) promises that he who says a verse prayer after the elevation of the Host will have remission of sins (*Instr. for Prayer 4* 1–8; W8.63–67). *Virtues of the Mass* also offers a pardon:

> Alle that han herd this sermon,
> A hundred days of pardon,
> >   Saynt Gregoré grauntis you this.
> >   (409–11)

Saints with the power of granting pardon who are invoked in Audelay's verses are Gregory (*Virtues of the Mass* 411, *St. Gregory's Indulgence* 5–6), Anne (*Salut. to St. Anne* 24), Stephen (*St. Stephen Carol* 26–28; W34.21–22), and John the Evangelist (*St. John Carol* 58; W35.42).[45] But the prayer that contains the most mention of pardons is the *Salutation to Saint Bridget*, which specifically uses the word "remission" five times.[46]

Audelay's emphatic interest in the remission of his own sins, as well as those of others, has been tied to his role as chantry priest for the household of Lord Richard Lestrange of Knockin (d. 1449), who was associated with a notorious murder case that occurred in London. Audelay himself was an "active participant . . . in aiding and abetting the assault," which took place in church on Easter Sunday in 1417.[47] According to the court record, Audelay had spent time in London, and the *Salutation to Saint Bridget* suggests further that he knew exactly where the Bridgettine house of Syon was located: "Beside the Chene, sothly, seven myle fro Lundun" (136). Audelay particularly notes the famous indulgence supplied by the Bridgettines to pilgrims who visited their house, along with a lesser-known pardon. While his description of the origins of the Syon indulgence is again not entirely accurate in historical terms, Audelay does cite several points directly relevant to Bridgettine practice that reflect Syon's influence on the larger community outside its walls.

In Audelay's version Jesus appears to Bridget and tells her to go to Urban in Rome:

> "to Pope Urban, to Rome, thou schalt goon,
> . . .
> To have the same pardon
> That is in Peters Cherche at Rome,
> To al the pilgrems that to thee cum,
> That vesid [visited] thee in Cristis name,
> To have playn remyssion."
> (57, 59–63)

This indulgence granted pilgrims remission from purgatorial punishment for visiting a holy place, in this case the Bridgettine foundation of Vadstena and, later, its sister convents elsewhere, including Syon. In Audelay's ahistorical version of this story, Pope Urban then immediately grants Bridget the papal indulgence for Vadstena, modeled on that which Saint Francis had requested for the Church of St. Peter ad Vincula in Rome.[48] According to Audelay, the pope tells Bridget: "I grawnt to al remyssioun / That chryven [shriven] hem clene with contrichon, / . . . / . . . to al that worthely vesetyn the holé place" (87–88, 91). But this is not what actually happened. Neither Urban V, Urban VI, nor Gregory XI, all of whom Bridget approached about granting the indulgence to her order, would allow it. In 1347 Innocent rejected the Bridgettine order out of hand. Later, Pope Urban V issued a bull that required every new monastic order to accept the rules of an existing order. The Bridgettine rule could not then be approved in its own right but was ultimately allowed as a supplement to the Augustinian rule.[49] The rosy relationship between Pope Urban and Bridget that Audelay paints in his poem is contradicted by the report of Bridget's biographers. When her order was not given the indulgence by the pope, Bridget immediately had a vision in which the Virgin Mary severely chided Urban. Later, Bridget had visions in which the Virgin predicted that Urban would have an attack of illness in which "his teeth will chatter and fall out. His sight will grow dim, all his limbs will shake and the glow of the Holy Spirit will die out in him."[50] (Urban, in fact, died soon after this.) The disputed indulgence, which was the same as that for the Church of the Chains of St. Peter in Rome, was finally granted to Vadstena, however, after Bridget's death in 1391. The Syon Pardon, or Vincula Indulgence, was given in 1425 by Pope Martin V to the Bridgettines at Syon.[51]

Audelay seems to know more about the true history of the Vincula Indulgence than he fully reveals in his text. According to her biographers, Bridget was determined to attain the Vincula Indulgence for her order from the pope without the monetary payment customary in such cases. In the *Salutation to Saint Bridget* Jesus speaks to Bridget and cautions her that

> "Yif that pope wil grawnt thee no grace
> Without moné or mede, becawse of covetys,
> Haile, the Fader of Heven schal prevelege thi place."
> (64–66)

That is, if the pope will not give Bridget the indulgence for her order without money or reward, then God will still privilege it. As described in her *Revelaciones extravagantes* (which consists of texts excluded from the main text of Bridget's *Revelations*), Bridget, like Saint Francis, directly receives the indulgence from Jesus, who tells her: "'If you cannot get the pope's letter, favor, and seal for the concession of [this indulgence], let my blessing suffice. . . . I will approve and confirm My word, and all the saints shall be My witnesses. Let My Mother be your seal, My Father a surety, and the Holy Ghost the comforter of those who come to your convent.'"[52] Audelay echoes the same language in his *Salutation to Saint Bridget*. Jesus tells Bridget:

> "Haile, I schal conferme thi bul that above him is,
>   . . .
>   Haile, my moder my sele schal be,
>   My witnes al the sayntis of heven on hye,
>   My blessyng the Holé Gost I betake to thee.
>   The pope schal lout ful low."
> (67, 69–72)

Even if the pope will not grant the Vincula Indulgence, Jesus has still given it directly to Bridget; His mother is the seal, and the witnesses are all the saints in heaven. Audelay further hints that the pope will be forced to bow down ("lout ful low") before Bridget's demands, which did eventually happen, though several popes later and not during Bridget's lifetime. It is not entirely clear to me how Audelay knew this passage so well. Johannes Jørgensen, the modern Bridget biographer, says that Christ's words to Bridget, directly giving her the Vincula Indulgence, as endorsed by the Virgin, God the Father, and God the Holy Ghost, are chiseled in Swedish upon a stone set into the wall by the gate of Vadstena's Blue Church. It is possible that a similar engraved stone, now lost, might have been seen at Syon, which modeled itself directly on Vadstena.[53] By repeating these phrases in the *Salutation to Saint Bridget*, Audelay is showing familiarity with a fairly obscure Bridgettine tradition.

The Vincula Indulgence was given on Lammas Day, or August 1, to commemorate Saint Peter's freedom from prison (literally "from chains"), which symbolically represented the freeing of humanity from sin. In England this was a festival day also associated with harvest and the collection of rents. The Vincula Indulgence is mentioned, along with another pardon for "Myd-Lentyn Sunday," by Audelay in a subsequent stanza in which he describes the pope confirming these special indulgences by papal bull:

> In the worchip of Saint Bregit,
> To al here pilgrems an Lammes Day,
> And also Myd-Lentyn Sunday,
> This pardon to last foreyever and ay.
> (140–43)

The Lammas Day pardon given by the Bridgettines to pilgrims to Syon is known to modern scholars mainly because Margery Kempe famously visited Sheen in about 1434, "three days before Lammas Day to purchase her pardon through the mercy of the Lord." Margery further describes Lammas Day as "the principal day of pardon." While in church during the festival, Margery describes herself collapsing with one of her "weepings," but she is then aided by one of the many attentive young men who support her throughout her book. Earlier, in 1414, while on her continental travels, Margery had also collected the Portiuncula Indulgence at Assisi on Lammas Day.[54]

The Syon Pardon is further described at some length, along with other Bridgettine indulgences, in several extant manuscripts. In Oxford, Bodl. Lib. MS Ashmole 750, and London, BL MS Harley 955, for example, we are told that all who visit the Monastery of Syon from the beginning of the first evensong of the feast of Peter for an eight-day period (or "utas") will be granted "plenary remission of al synnes."[55] In MS Ashmole 750 the text is titled "The indulgences of the monstarie of Syon" (fol. 140r) and is directed "to all verraie contrite and shryuen that devoutely visiten this cherche frome the begynnynge of the firste euensonge of the feste of Saynt petre Aduincula vnto the ende of the euensonge in the last daie of the vtas" (fols. 140v–41r). It grants penitents remission of all of their sins ("plenerie remission of al synnes"). Perhaps the most significant part of the indulgence for Audelay, the pardon is further extended to all Augustinian houses: "Also ther is all the pardon that is graunted to any places of saynt Austyns ordre through all the worlde" (fol. 141r).

The Lenten pardon appears in London, BL MS Harley 4012, along with several other Syon indulgences. There is one for the feast of Saint John the Baptist, for example, that offers two hundred days of pardon to anyone coming to Syon who says "a Pater noster, and an Aue, before the image of Sent Briget and Sent John," yet another example among many of the power of images in promoting lay devotion in this period. If the pilgrim appears "on Mydlent Sonday, from Saturday none till Monday euensong," she will receive "clene remission of all synne." Given Audelay's insistence on Bridget's miraculous virginal widowhood, it is interesting to note that pilgrims arriving at Syon for the feast of Saint Bridget, "deuotely ther visiting the Holie Virgen Sent Brigit [and] geuyng sum almes to the sustentacion of the same monastery, shall haue pardon, and clene remyssion in all casis reserued and unreserued." This description of Bridget, in the indulgence for her feast, seems to indicate that her miraculously restored virginity was more generally known and promoted by Syon, and not just by Audelay. Finally, pilgrims visiting Syon "in the fest of Sent Peter, whiche is callid Lammas or Advincula, . . . shall haue playne remission in all casis reserued and unreserued," except for those who have violently killed a priest.[56] Indulgences like these may have been very appealing to Audelay, particularly in view of his affiliation with the murderous Lord Lestrange.

As poetry, Audelay's *Salutation to Saint Bridget* is not altogether successful. Rather than appreciating its evocative imagery or powerful command of language, the reader feels distracted by its unwieldy construction and compelled to count verbal repetitions, make lists, and create groupings of similar texts within the manuscript, as many scholars have done previously.[57] As history, however, Audelay's *Salutation to Saint Bridget* is quite compelling. It refers to topical events in the author's own lifetime, and the stanzas reveal much about Bridgettine rule and associated ideas, most specifically about the promotion and circulation of indulgences. In fact, and in closing, I would suggest that Audelay intended the salutation to Bridget not as a poem at all, but as an indulgence and a prayer. In the final stanza, Audelay refers to the verse itself as an indulgence to be read by readers who will then pray for "sinful Audelay":

> Al that redis reverenly this remyssioune,
> Prays to blisful Bregit, that merceful may,
> Fore hom that mad this mater with dewocion,
> That is both blynd and def, the synful Audelay.
> (199–202)

The language of pardon and the references to remission of sins that run throughout Audelay's collection have here become self-reflexive: the poem is the indulgence, and readers are encouraged to pray through its text to Saint Bridget for Audelay's salvation. The act of reading the text, with its verbal repetitions, becomes religious practice, redeeming the life of the author on his ladder heavenward.

Notes

1. Michael Bennett, "John Audley: Some New Evidence on His Life and Work," *Chaucer Review* 16 (1982): 344–55 (p. 345); and Ella Keats Whiting, ed., *The Poems of John Audelay*, EETS o.s. 184 (1931; repr. Oxford: Oxford University Press, 2006), pp. 164–71. Citations of MS Douce 302 in this essay are from John the Blind Audelay, *Poems and Carols (Oxford, Bodleian Library MS Douce 302)*, ed. Susanna Fein (Kalamazoo: Medieval Institute Publications, 2009). I use the English spelling of the name of Saint Bridget of Sweden.

2. George James Aungier, *The History and Antiquities of Syon Monastery, the Parish of Isleworth, and the Chapelry of Hounslow* (London: Nichols and Son, 1840), p. 27. This is the name of the foundation in Henry V's royal charter: "And we will and decree that it shall be called '*The Monastery of St. Saviour and St. Bridget of Syon, of the order of St. Augustine,*' through all successive ages." For Audelay's value as a contemporary witness to the founding of Syon, see Whiting, *Poems*, p. 247 n. 138; Bennett, "John Audley," p. 346; Neil Beckett, "St. Bridget, Henry V and Syon Abbey," in *Studies*

in St. Birgitta and the Brigittine Order, ed. James Hogg (Salzburg: Institut für Anglistik und Americanistik, 1993), pp. 125–50 (p. 140); Ann M. Hutchison, "Reflections on Aspects of the Spiritual Impact of St. Birgitta, the Revelations and the Bridgettine Order in Late Medieval England," in *The Medieval Mystical Tradition in England*, ed. E. A. Jones (Cambridge: Brewer, 2004), pp. 69–82 (pp. 72–73).

 3. For comparisons, see Karen Saupe, ed., *Middle English Marian Lyrics* (Kalamazoo: Medieval Institute Publications, 1998), nos. 9, 11, 12, 51, 53, 66, 69, 73, 74, 75, 91.

 4. Richard Leighton Greene, ed., *The Early English Carols*, 2nd ed. (Oxford: Clarendon Press, 1977), cites several carols dedicated to or concerning the Virgin, e.g.:

(1) No. 179.1, London, BL MS Egerton 3307, fol. 67r (fifteenth century), a song to the Virgin, which repeats "Hail" in the first line of the first three stanzas. Mary is described in stanza 2: "Hayle be thou, madyn, modir, and wyff" (p. 119; *IMEV Suppl.* 1030.5).

(2) No. 201, Cambridge, CUL MS Ee.1.12, fol. 21v, composed by James Ryman (ca. 1492), includes four stanzas devoted to Mary and the last stanza addressed to Esther ("quene Hester"), thus comprising five four-line stanzas plus refrain. The first line of each stanza opens with "Haile," stanza 2 also repeats "Haile" at the start of the second line, and stanza 3 repeats "Haile" at the start of the first three lines (p. 131; *IMEV* 1042).

(3) No. 245, CUL MS Ee.1.12, fol. 12v, by James Ryman, a song to the Virgin (ca. 1492), uses "Hayle" only once as the first word of the first line of the first stanza (ten four-line stanzas plus refrain) (pp. 155–56; *IMEV* 1043).

(4) No. 182, Oxford, Bodl. Lib. MS Arch. Selden. B.26, fol. 24r (fifteenth century), opens "Hayl, Godys Sone in Trinite," the sole use of "Hail" in this carol of five four-line stanzas (no refrain) (p. 121; *IMEV* 1931).

(5) No. 235, MS Arch. Selden. B.26, fol. 23r (fifteenth century), a song to the Virgin; the first line of the refrain is "Hayl, Mary, ful of grace," and the word does not appear elsewhere in the poem (pp. 148–49; *IMEV* 3385).

(6) No. 239, Oxford, Bodl. Lib. MS Eng. poet. e.1, fol. 51v (fifteenth century), a Christmas carol celebrating the Annunciation; the word "Hayle" is repeated at the start of three consecutive lines in the third verse (p. 152; *IMEV* 3736).

(7) No. 250, CUL MS Ee.1.12, fol. 82r, by James Ryman (ca. 1492), the refrain opens "Heyle, Mary, meyden meke and mylde," and the carol consists of nine four-line stanzas (pp. 158–59; *IMEV* 283).

(8) No. 125.1, London, BL MS Egerton 3307, fol. 55v (fifteenth century), is one stanza with a burden (refrain), an Epiphany carol in which "Hail" is repeated in the first two lines of the stanza: "Hayl, most myghty in thi werkyng, / Hail, thou lord of all thing" (p. 76; *IMEV Suppl.* 1070.5).

(9) No. 207, CUL MS Ee.1.12, fol. 77v, by James Ryman (ca. 1492), a song to the Virgin; the first three lines of the first three stanzas begin "Hayle" (twelve four-line stanzas), and the third stanza says: "Hayle, quene of blisse, emperesse of

hell; Hayle, doughter Syon full of beautie; Hayle, closed gate of Ezechiell, *Mater misericordie*" (p. 135; *IMEV* 1072).

(10) No. 194, CUL MS.Ee.1.12, fol. 16r, James Ryman (ca. 1492), a song to the Virgin (12 stanzas); stanza one repeats "Haile" at the start of the first three lines (pp. 127–28; *IMEV* 1074).

(11) No. 202, CUL MS Ee.1.12, fol. 22r–v, by James Ryman (ca. 1492), a song to the Virgin with six four-line stanzas, the last line is in Latin ("Super omnes speciosa") in each stanza; the word "Haile" is used fourteen times (p. 132; *IMEV* 1080).

5. Greene, *Early English Carols*, p. 131 (no. 201). For more on Ryman, see Greene, ibid., pp. cliv, 321.

6. Whiting, *Poems*, p. xvii.

7. Incidences of the word "Hail" in MS Douce 302 are: *Salut. to Jesus* (86 times); *Salut. to Mary* (91 times); *Gabriel's Salut.* (2 times); *Salut. to St. Bridget* (55 times); *Salut. to St. Winifred* (26 times); *Salut. to St. Anne* ("*Gaude,*" 24 times); *Salut. to Holy Face*, an indulgence verse to the Vernicle ("*Salve,*" 8 times); *Mary Flower Carol* (4 times).

8. The salutations are presented with Latin prefaces that seem further to indicate their specific genre: "Hic incipiunt salutaciones beate Marie virginis" (for *Salut. to Jesus*); "Hec salutacio composuit angelus Gabrielus" (for *Gabriel's Salut.*); "Hic incipit salutacio Sancte Brigitte virginis . . . quod Awdelay" (for *Salut. to St. Bridget*); "Hic incipit salutacio Sancte Wenefrede virginis" (for *Salut. to St. Winifred*); "Quicumque hanc salutacionem in honore Sancte Anne matris Marie . . ." (for *Salut. to St. Anne*); "Quicumque hanc salutacionem in honore Salvatoris per xx dies continuo devote dixerit . . ." (for *Salut. to Holy Face*).

9. Derek Pearsall, *Old English and Middle English Poetry* (London: Routledge and Kegan Paul, 1977), p. 250. See also A. I. Doyle, "The Shaping of the Vernon and Simeon Manuscripts," in *Studies in the Vernon Manuscript*, ed. Derek Pearsall (Cambridge: Brewer, 1990), pp. 1–13 (p. 9 n. 31): "Not all the contents of Douce 302 are Audelay's own work." I am, however, treating the entire volume as Audelay's, following Richard Firth Green, who suggests that while *Epilogue* (W18) may indeed indicate the death of the poet, the poems that follow in the manuscript "probably represent a miscellany of Audelay's other work, collected together . . . by his literary executor" ("Marcolf the Fool and Blind John Audelay," in *Speaking Images: Essays in Honor of V. A. Kolve*, ed. R. F. Yeager and Charlotte C. Morse [Asheville, N.C.: Pegasus, 2001], pp. 559–76 [p. 565]).

10. Melissa Jones, "'Swete May, Soulis Leche': The Winifred Carol of John Audelay," *Essays in Medieval Studies* 14 (1997): 1–7 (p. 1) (available online at http://www.luc.edu/publications/medieval).

11. Susanna Fein, "Good Ends in the Audelay Manuscript," *Yearbook of English Studies* 33 (2003): 97–119 (p. 99).

12. Greene, *Early English Carols*, p. 317, notes two ownership inscriptions recovered by N. R. Ker, one from an Augustinian canon in the Priory of St. John the

Baptist, Launde, Leicestershire, and the other written by a minstrel. Greene comments, "This is the only note of ownership by a minstrel in all the carol MSS.—and the minstrel gives the volume to a religious." In the fifteenth century MS Douce 302 was given by William Vyott (or Wyatt), a minstrel of Coventry, to John Barker, a canon of the Priory of Launde in Leicestershire.

13. Douglas Gray, *Themes and Images in Medieval English Religious Lyric* (London: Routledge and Kegan Paul, 1972), pp. 154–55. Gray is rather dismissive of salutation poetry: "The verse prayers addressed to various saints are hardly ever of much literary value" (p. 156). Very few images of Bridget survive in English wall painting or church furniture, though woodcuts of Bridget proliferate, preserved in early printed books. See David Griffith, "The Reception of Continental Women Mystics in Fifteenth- and Sixteenth-Century England: Some Artistic Evidence," in Jones, *The Medieval Mystical Tradition in England*, pp. 97–117 (pp. 109–16, plates 4, 5).

14. Fein, "Good Ends," p. 104.

15. Anne Savage and Nicholas Watson, trans., *Anchoritic Spirituality: Ancrene Wisse and Associated Works* (New York: Paulist, 1991), pp. 9–10.

16. Savage and Watson, *Anchoritic Spirituality*, p. 63; see also pp. 53 (part 1, "Devotions"), 58–59, 61–62. A possibly related version of this text has been published in Alexandra Barratt, ed., *Women's Writing in Middle English* (New York: Longman, 1992) under the title "An Anchoress's Hymn to the Virgin," pp. 277–79. This poem (*IMEV* 1046) is ascribed by its copyist John Shirley to "an holy Ankaresse of Maunsffeld" (Oxford, Bodl. Lib. MS Ashmole 59, fol. 68r-v). Barratt explains that the poem, consisting of five eight-line stanzas, and opening "Heille, glorious Virgyne, grounde of al oure grace," survives as well in London, BL MS Cotton Caligula A.ii, where it is unattributed, and in London, BL Addit. MS 29729, a manuscript compiled by John Stow in 1558. For more on Addit. MS 29729, see Ian Gadd and Alexandra Gillespie, eds., *John Stow (1525–1605) and the Making of the English Past: Studies in Early Modern Culture and the History of the Book* (London: British Library, 2004), pp. 114–16, 118, 128, 129, fig. 19.

17. Christopher de Hamel, *Syon Abbey: The Library of the Bridgettine Nuns and Their Peregrinations after the Reformation* (Otley, Eng.: Roxburghe Club, 1991), pp. 65, 98.

18. Saupe, *Middle English Marian Lyrics*, p. 19, quoting Louis Althusser, "Ideology and Ideological State Apparatuses," in *Lenin and Philosophy and Other Essays*, trans. Ben Brewster (London: New Left Books, 1971), pp. 127–93 (pp. 173–75). Althusser comments that "all ideology hails or interpellates concrete individuals as concrete subjects, by the functioning of the category of the subject" (p. 173) and follows with a brief discussion of the use of interpolation in Christian religious ideology (pp. 177–83).

19. Jones, "Swete May," p. 2.

20. Saint Bridget's Latin *Vita* was produced soon after her death by her two Swedish confessors, Peter Olafsson of Alvastra and Peter Olafsson of Skänninge, but this was probably not accessible to Audelay, though he clearly knows the basic outline of her story. Standard modern biographies of Bridget include Johannes Jørgensen,

Saint Bridget of Sweden, trans. Ingeborg Lund, 2 vols. (New York: Longmans, Green, 1954); and Bridget Morris, *St. Birgitta of Sweden* (Woodbridge: Boydell, 1999).

21. Bella Millett and Jocelyn Wogan-Browne, eds., *Medieval English Prose for Women: Selections from the Katherine Group and "Ancrene Wisse"* (Oxford: Clarendon Press, 1992), pp. 118–19.

22. Savage and Watson, *Anchoritic Spirituality*, p. 109. The ME quotation is taken from J. R. R. Tolkien, ed., *The English Text of the Ancrene Riwle: Ancrene Wisse, Edited from MS Corpus Christi College Cambridge 402*, intro. N. R. Ker, EETS o.s. 249 (London: Oxford University Press, 1962), pp. 85–86 (fol. 44v, lines 8–9, 14–15, 19–21). For another English translation of the passage, see M. B. Salu, trans., *The Ancrene Riwle (The Corpus MS: Ancrene Wisse)*, intro Gerard Sitwell, pref. J. R. R. Tolkien (London: Burns & Oates, 1955), pp. 72–73. See Clarissa W. Atkinson, "'Precious Balsam in a Fragile Glass': The Ideology of Virginity in the Later Middle Ages," *Journal of Family History* 8 (1983): 131–43 (p. 137); Barbara Newman, "Flaws in the Golden Bowl: Gender and Spiritual Formation in the Twelfth Century," *Traditio* 45 (1989–90): 111–46 (p. 115); and Jocelyn Wogan-Browne, "Chaste Bodies: Frames and Experiences," in *Framing Medieval Bodies*, ed. Sarah Kay and Miri Rubin (Manchester: Manchester University Press, 1994), pp. 24–42 (pp. 25–26). For more on ambiguities of attitude toward virginity in the Middle Ages, see John Bugge, *Virginitas: An Essay in the History of a Medieval Ideal* (The Hague: Nijhoff, 1975); Cindy L. Carlson and Angela Jane Weisl, *Constructions of Widowhood and Virginity in the Middle Ages* (New York: St. Martin's, 1999); Elizabeth Castelli, "Virginity and Its Meaning for Women's Sexuality in Early Christianity," *Journal of Feminist Studies in Religion* 2 (1986): 61–88; Monica H. Green, "Female Sexuality in the Medieval West," *Trends in History* 4 (1990): 127–58; Kathleen Coyne Kelly, *Performing Virginity and Testing Chastity in the Middle Ages* (London: Routledge, 2000); and Sarah Salih, *Versions of Virginity in Late Medieval England* (Woodbridge: Brewer, 2001).

23. Wogan-Browne, "Chaste Bodies," p. 26.

24. Robert R. Raymo and Elaine E. Whitaker, eds., with Ruth E. Sternglantz, *The Mirroure of the Worlde: A Middle English Translation of Le Miroir du Monde* (Toronto: University of Toronto Press, 2003), pp. 359–60.

25. Marguerite Tjader Harris, ed., *Birgitta of Sweden, Life and Selected Revelations*, intro. Tore Nyberg, trans. Albert Ryle Kezel (New York: Paulist, 1990), p. 74.

26. Morris, *St. Birgitta of Sweden*, pp. 44–45, 41, citing accounts in Isak Collijn, ed., *Acta et processus canonizacionis beate Birgitte*, issued in 10 parts (Uppsala: Almqvist & Wiksell, 1924–31), pp. 305, 479.

27. Atkinson, "Precious Balsam," pp. 140–41.

28. William Patterson Cumming, ed., *The Revelations of Saint Birgitta*, EETS o.s. 178 (1929; repr. New York: Kraus Reprint, 1971), pp. 99–100. Rosalynn Voaden, *God's Words, Women's Voices: The Discernment of Spirits in the Writing of Late-Medieval Women Visionaries* (Woodbridge: York Medieval Press, 1999), cites another passage from Bridget's *Revelations* in which Christ "tells Bridget that maidenhood, wifehood

and widowhood are immaterial to him, as long as the desire of the woman is for him alone" (pp. 105–6).

29. Atkinson, "Precious Balsam," p. 141.

30. For a brief history of chaste marriage in the early Middle Ages, see Jo Ann McNamara, "Chaste Marriage and Clerical Celibacy," in *Sexual Practices and the Medieval Church*, ed. Vern L. Bullough and James Brundage (Buffalo, N.Y.: Prometheus, 1982), pp. 22–33. For an overview of chaste marriage in the later Middle Ages, see Clarissa W. Atkinson, *Mystic and Pilgrim: The Book and the World of Margery Kempe* (Ithaca: Cornell University Press, 1983), esp. pp. 159–61, 168–79, 190–94. See also Elizabeth M. Makowski, "The Conjugal Debt and Medieval Canon Law," *Journal of Medieval History* 3 (1977): 99–114; and James A. Brundage, *Law, Sex, and Christian Society in Medieval Europe* (Chicago: University of Chicago Press, 1987).

31. Bennett, "John Audley," p. 345. See also Eric G. Stanley, "*The True Counsel of Conscience*, or *The Ladder of Heaven*: In Defence of John Audelay's Unlyrical Lyrics," in *Expedition nach der Wahrheit: Poems, Essays, and Papers in Honour of Theo Stemmler*, ed. Stefan Horlacher and Marion Islinger (Heidelberg: C. Winter, 1996), pp. 131–59 (p. 154); and Green, "Marcolf the Fool," p. 565.

32. The editions of the *Revelationes Sancte Birgitte* with illustrations usually attributed to Dürer are: 1st ed., ptd. A. Koberger, with Latin text (Nuremberg, 21 September 1500); 2nd ed., ptd. A. Koberger, with German text (Nuremberg, 12 July 1502); 3rd ed., ptd. Peypus, with Latin text (Nuremberg, 1517). The book has fifty-eight woodcuts on eighteen pages, which have been produced from thirty blocks (some blocks have been designed to work with others in a variety of combinations). An older edition, produced in Lübeck (1492), was Dürer's model. The picture of the ladder appears on leaf 12, captioned "St. Bridget while riding to her castle of Vadstena with retinue and multitude of people, has a vision of Magister Magnus ascending to Heaven," reproduced in Willi Kurth, ed., *The Complete Woodcuts of Albrecht Dürer*, trans. Silvia M. Welsh (1936; repr. New York: Arden, 1963), p. 23. The woodcut of the man on the ladder from the Lübeck edition is reproduced in Harris, *Birgitta of Sweden*, p. 100. For manuscript illuminations, see Carl Nordenfalk, "Saint Bridget of Sweden as Represented in Illuminated Manuscripts," in *De artibus opuscula XL: Essays in Honor of Erwin Panofsky*, ed. Millard Meiss, 2 vols. (New York: New York University Press, 1961), 1:371–93, plates 122–27; and Isak Collijn, *Handskrifter, urkunder och böcker rörande Birgitta och Vadstena* (Uppsala: Almquist & Wiksell, 1918).

33. Tore Nyberg, "Introduction," in Harris, *Birgitta of Sweden*, pp. 13–51 (p. 26).

34. Nyberg, "Introduction," p. 27.

35. Harris, *Birgitta of Sweden*, pp. 101–2, 113, 114–16.

36. Susanna Greer Fein, "A Thirteen-Line Alliterative Stanza on the Abuse of Prayer from the Audelay MS," *Medium Ævum* 63 (1994): 61–74 (pp. 63–64); John Henry Blunt, ed., *The Myroure of Oure Ladye*, EETS e.s. 19 (1873; repr. Millwood, N.Y.: Kraus Reprint, 1975), pp. 54, 342. For analysis of the *Myroure* passage and

comparison with the roles of Titivillus in medieval drama, see Rebecca Krug, *Reading Families: Women's Literate Practice in Late Medieval England* (Ithaca: Cornell University Press, 2002), pp. 171–72.

37. Bridget's comments about slavery are recorded in her *Revelations* 7.28.9–17. The story of the black girl raised in Bridget's household is recounted in Harris, *Birgitta of Sweden*, p. 246 n. 84 (written by Kezel). In the version told by Jørgensen, Bridget's exhortations against slavery led Queen Giovanna to ransom "a Turkish woman," who was sent "as a gift of friendship to the Swedish saint. . . . Later the Turkish woman came to Vadstena and died there as Sister Caterina Magnus' daughter" (*Saint Bridget of Sweden*, 2:287).

38. Cp. *Gabriel's Salut.*, *Nativity Carol*, *Holy Innocents Carol*, *Circumcision Carol*, *Epiphany Carol*, and *Tree of Jesse Carol* with Bridget's account of her vision of the Nativity (ed. from Oxford, Bodl. Lib. MS Rawlinson C.41, fols. 12v–16r, in Barratt, *Women's Writing*, pp. 86–89).

39. Stanley, " *True Counsel*," p. 154; Harris, *Birgitta of Sweden*, p. 160. Gray comments: "One of the favourite ideas of late medieval devotion is that the Virgin suffers a passion which is parallel to that of her son. She says to St. Bridget in her Revelations, 'the sorrows of Jesus were my sorrows, because his heart was my heart'" (*Themes and Images*, p. 135). This language echoes Bridget's expression of love for her husband (see above).

40. Beckett, "St. Bridget," p. 130. For more on the Cult of the Holy Name in England, see Eamon Duffy, *The Stripping of the Altars: Traditional Religion in England, c.1400–c.1580* (New Haven: Yale University Press, 1992), pp. 45, 113–16, 236; R. W. Pfaff, *New Liturgical Feasts in Late Medieval England* (Oxford: Clarendon Press, 1970); Denis Renevey, "Name Above Names: The Devotion to the Name of Jesus from Richard Rolle to Walter Hilton's *Scale of Perfection* I," in *The Medieval Mystical Tradition: England, Ireland and Wales. Exeter Symposium VI*, ed. Marion Glasscoe (Cambridge: Brewer, 1999), pp. 103–21; Sue Powell, "Syon, Caxton and the *Festial*," *Birgittiana* 2 (1996): 187–207 (pp. 196–99); and Sue Powell, "What Caxton Did to the *Festial*," *Journal of the Early Book Society* 1 (1997): 48–77 (pp. 54–55).

41. Hutchison, "Reflections," p. 77; see also Aungier, who cites "'The pardon of the beads at Syon," and a letter written in 1486 by Edward Plumpton to Sir Robert Plumpton that mentions a gift given by "my lady of Syon [Elizabeth Gybbes that] . . . was a par [*sic*] of Jeneper beads *pardonet*" (*History and Antiquities*, p. 426). For an alternate text of the Holy Name prayer, see London, BL MS Harley 494 (currently being edited for publication in *Anne Bulkeley and Her Book: Fashioning Female Piety in Early Tudor England; A Study of London, British Library MS Harley 494*, by Alexandra Barratt [Turnhout: Brepols, forthcoming]), fol. 105r–v, beginning "Here folow þe bedis of pardon in englyshe of saynt gregorys pyte, . . . O swete blessyd Jhu."

42. In a discussion of baptism, Audelay describes the godfathers and godmothers answering "In the name of Jhesus" (*Marcolf* 24). Other poems, *Seven Bleedings* and

Salut. to Jesus, directly call on Jesus, but the word "name" is not used. In *Virtues of the Mass* the names of the seven deadly sins are listed, and the reader then told that "Yif any of these that ye in falle, / Anon on Crist loke that ye calle / With contricion" (151–53), though, again, there is no specific reference to "name." In *Magnificat* Mary says that all might is in God, "And his holé name, when I him bere / To bryng his pepul unto his blis" (27–28). *Dread of Death Carol*, among the best known of Audelay's poems (with the refrain "Timor mortis conturbat me"), states that God gives and takes away, blessed be his name ("His name be blessid both nyght and daye"; 21), an echo of the passage familiar from funerals. I thank the Reverend John Douglas Ousley, Church of the Incarnation, New York, for identifying this text as partially derived from 1 Tim. 6:7. *Paternoster* is a discussion of the Lord's Prayer in which "halouyd be thi name" makes an appearance (11). Audelay's *Conclusion* describes the names of the righteous recorded in the "bok of lyfe" (18–19).

43. The poems referring to the Holy Face are *Seven Bleedings* 66–70, *Salut. to Christ's Body* 35–36 (W8.41–42), *Visiting the Sick* 182, *Lord's Epistle* 27, *Epilogue* 273, and *Salut. to Holy Face* 16–17. There is also a possible misreading in *Salut. to Jesus* 46–47 (see Whiting, *Poems*, p. 236). MS Douce 302 also has some marginal drawings, several of which may have been supplied by a later reader. These are: fol. 4r, rough drawing in red in right margin of index [pointing finger] with acanthus leaves; fol. 5r, index in red; fol. 6r, drawing of a horn (?), in upper margin, horn with belt (?); fol. 15v, face in initial O, flower in initial C; fol. 35v, grotesque heads in initial with cadels. A pastedown of "The Three Living" has been pasted into the back cover of MS Douce 302. It is a very close copy of the woodcut of "The Three Living" that appears in the *Danse Macabre* edition published in Paris by Guy Marchant in 1491. This edition is described by Arthur M. Hind, *An Introduction to a History of a Woodcut*, 2 vols. (1935; repr. New York: Dover, 1963), 2:644–46. The Marchant woodcut has been reproduced (though misdated) in Fritz Eichenberg, *Dance of Death: A Graphic Commentary on The Danse Macabre through the Centuries* (New York: Abbeville, 1983), p. 15. The woodcut and its relevance to Audelay's book have recently been discussed by Susanna Greer Fein, "Life and Death, Reader and Page: Mirrors of Mortality in English Manuscripts," *Mosaic* 35 (2002): 69–94 (pp. 87–91) (and reproduced on p. 90).

44. Barbara Obrist, "The Swedish Visionary: Saint Bridget," in *Medieval Women Writers*, ed. Katharina M. Wilson (Athens: University of Georgia Press, 1984), pp. 227–51 (p. 234). See also my discussion in Martha W. Driver, *The Image in Print: Book Illustration in Late Medieval England and Its Sources* (London: British Library, 2004), pp. 8–12, 115–22.

45. In addition, *Visiting the Sick* advises the sinful man to serve God and forsake the Fiend in order to get "remyssion" (65); *Pope John's Passion* mentions a pardon given by the pope at Avignon ("Avyon") for "Thre hundred days of remyssion" (1, 5) and ends with instructions to the reader to pray five Paternosters and five Aves and to say the Creed, so "That Crist graunt thee remission" (119); *Seven Hours* again prescribes a formula for salvation, including confession to a priest through which

God will grant "him, of his grace, ful remyssion / Of al his trespace" (85–86); and *God's Address* cites the remission given those who follow God's laws (251).

46. *Salut. to St. Bridget* 63, 87, 94, 152, 199.

47. Bennett, "John Audley," p. 348; see also Fein, "Good Ends," pp. 99–100.

48. For a description of the feast of Saint Peter in Chains (*festum sancti Petri ad vincula*), see Jacobus de Voragine, *The Golden Legend: Readings on the Saints*, trans. William Granger Ryan, 2 vols. (Princeton: Princeton University Press, 1993), 2:34–39.

49. Obrist explains: "Bridget's first demand to Pope Innocent for approbation in 1347 was blankly rejected on the grounds that since the Lateran Council of 1215, founding new orders was forbidden. Then, Pope Urban V issued a bull with the decisions of the Council of Lyons, which required that every new monastical order had to accept the rules of an existing order. Thus the Brigittine rules were declared to be a supplement to the Augustinian rules" ("The Swedish Visionary," p. 235). Jo Ann Kay McNamara, *Sisters in Arms: Catholic Nuns through Two Millennia* (Cambridge, Mass.: Harvard University Press, 1996), pp. 317–21, cites Bridget's frustration with the pope's refusal to allow her to follow her "direct orders from Christ to reform the church by means of a new order of women" (p. 317), and the problems peculiar to its being a double order of women and men. In the sixteenth century a version of the Augustinian rule was produced for the Bridgettine nuns at Syon by Richard Whitforde, the self-proclaimed "wretch of Syon" and "bedeman." Whitforde produced two editions of Augustine's Rule in English for the nuns (*Saynt Augustyns Rule*; *STC* 922.3, 922.4).

50. Urban died soon after being told of Bridget's vision (Harris, *Birgitta of Sweden*, p. 11; see also Jørgensen, *Saint Bridget of Sweden*, 2:221).

51. Powell, "Syon," p. 199. See also her discussion of the Lammas Day sermon of the Syon brother Simon Wynter (pp. 199–201); she cites an edition of Wynter's sermon (p. 200 n. 43) by M. A. Hughes, "The Syon 'Pardon' Sermon Edited from MS Harley 2321 with Introduction, Notes and Glossary" (master's diss., University of Liverpool, 1959).

52. According to Morris, *St. Birgitta of Sweden*, p. 7, the *Revelaciones extravagantes* consists of some 116 revelations that were excluded from the main text of Bridget's *Revelations*. This work apparently did not have wide circulation; Morris cites Lennart Hollman, ed., *Den heliga Birgittas Reuelaciones extrauagantes* (Uppsala: Almqvist & Wiksell, 1956). See also Obrist, "The Swedish Visionary," pp. 245–46, and Jørgensen, *Saint Bridget of Sweden*, 2:208, both quoting *Rev. extravag.* 44.

53. Jørgensen, *Saint Bridget of Sweden*, 2:208. See also Julia Bolton Holloway, trans., *Saint Bride and Her Book: Birgitta of Sweden's Revelations, Translated from Middle English* (Newburyport, Mass.: Focus Information Group, 1992), pp. 16–17.

54. Lynn Staley, trans. and ed., *The Book of Margery Kempe* (New York: Norton, 2001), pp. 179, 68. See also Hutchison, "Reflections," pp. 75–76. On Bridget as a model for Margery, see Janet Wilson, "Communities of Dissent: The Secular and Ecclesiastical Communities of Margery Kempe's Book," in *Medieval Women in Their*

Communities, ed. Diane Watt (Toronto: University of Toronto Press, 1997), pp. 155–85 (p. 161).

55. Oxford, Bodl. Lib. MS Ashmole 750, and London, BL MSS Harley 955 and Harley 4012, art. 9, are reproduced in Aungier, *History and Antiquities*, pp. 421–26.

56. Aungier, *History and Antiquities*, pp. 422–25.

57. Pearsall, *Old English and Middle English Poetry*, p. 250; Jones, "Swete May," p. 1; Fein, "Good Ends," pp. 99, 112–19; Fein, "Stanza," pp. 68–70, 74 n. 31 (a–h); Stanley, "*True Counsel*," pp. 155–59.

Audelay's Carol Collection

Julia Boffey

The sequence of twenty-five Middle English carols occupying folios 27v–32r of Oxford, Bodleian Library MS Douce 302 is among the most numerically significant bodies of such texts to survive in a single manuscript.[1] Only a few of the carol manuscripts described in the "Original Sources" section of Richard Leighton Greene's *Early English Carols* contain more carols than the manuscript associated with Audelay's name, and the majority of these seem to have been collections that served dedicated choral purposes in chapels or major religious houses.[2] Apart from being an unusually large collection, the carol sequence of MS Douce 302 is also a relatively early one: most of the other significant surviving carol collections date from the second rather than the first half of the fifteenth century, and some from the early sixteenth. This section of MS Douce 302, numbered XXXV in the system that marks off different items and groups of items in the manuscript as a whole, is furthermore curious in terms of the formal homogeneity of its contents. Rough groupings of certain kinds are discernible throughout the manuscript—the salutations and devotions that make up the items numbered XXVII to XXXIIII are a case in point—but the carol sequence, with its own single number, and its own heading, seems clearly to have been conceived as a small anthology of linked items. In the context of other late Middle English manuscripts, it stands out as an especially unusual instance of the amassing of a selection of short poems, texts much more often relegated to positions as fillers or flyleaf jottings. Very few other late medieval manuscripts group Middle English lyrics (whether carols or other kinds) in very comprehensible ways, and only very small numbers collect them together according to discernible principles such as shared subject matter or common authorship.[3]

The carol collection in MS Douce 302 announces itself with a couplet suggesting that the texts were copied as a written record of materials that were for communal oral use: "I pray yow, syrus, boothe moore and las, / Syng these caroles in Cristemas" (fol. 27v). Exhortations to communal acts of worship or prayer recur in several of the carols that follow (e.g., the burdens of *Holy Innocents Carol* and *Saint Thomas Carol*; carols 9 and 10), and reinforce the possibility that the sequence is in some respects an *aide-mémoire* to support the declaiming or singing of the poems. But the conclusion of the last carol, *Saint Francis Carol*, moves with easy fluidity into a mode suggestive of written circulation ("I pray youe, seris, pur charyté, / Redis this caral reverently"; 73–74; W52.52–53), and the likelihood of oral performance is not to be pushed too hard.[4] As Greene has shown, while in the earlier medieval period the Middle English word *carole* often suggested a song to accompany dancing (and by association singing), by the fifteenth century its accepted meaning, relating to the formal properties of poems rather than to their performative functions, seems to have denoted those that were constructed in regular stanzas accompanied by a burden or chorus.[5] The recommendation that the carols of MS Douce 302 are for "Cristemas"—oddly specific, when the content of many of them is completely unrelated to this festival—seems to derive from a general late medieval reflex to associate these sorts of song with this particular season, a "loose usage" (in Greene's term)[6] noticeable especially in the titles of early printed carol collections.[7]

Some of the carols certainly are relevant to the Christmas season. The sixth celebrates the Nativity (its burden is "Welcum, Yole, in good aray, / In worchip of the holeday"), and the following five carols (carols 7–11) are appropriate to the feasts that follow Christmas: of Saint Stephen (December 26), Saint John the Evangelist (December 27), the Holy Innocents (December 28), Saint Thomas of Canterbury (December 29), and the Lord's Circumcision (January 1). But overall the sequence does not seem to follow the liturgical calendar in any very marked way. Carols on Henry VI, on the four estates, and on childhood (carols 12–14) interrupt the post-Nativity sequence before a brief return to it in the form of a carol for Epiphany (carol 15). Elsewhere, the sequence seems to consist of carols on related subjects, roughly grouped together rather than marking any calendarial progression. Carols at the start (carols 1–5) deal with Christian essentials: the Ten Commandments, the seven deadly sins, the seven works of mercy, the five senses, and the seven gifts of the Holy Ghost, respectively; a later group (carols 16–19) focuses on the Holy Family; and there is a trio of carols on virginity and chastity (carols 20–22). The connections between the carols in some of the groups consist not just of shared themes but also of occasional repeated phrases. Jesus's descent from the line of Jesse is identically expressed in both the *Saint Anne Carol* ("Then God hem grawntid graciously / Betwene youe two a floure schul spryng, / The rote therof is clepid Jesse"; 29–31; W43.23–25) and in each stanza of the following *Tree of Jesse Carol*, for example: "There is a Floure sprung of a tre, / The rote therof is called Jesse" (7–8, from the four-line burden; W44.1–2).

Although there is no evident overarching shape to the sequence beyond these rough groupings, there is nonetheless a clear attempt to supply some kind of closure. The final three carols (carols 23–25) deal first with the love of God, then the fear of approaching death (with a burden that includes the phrase "Timor mortis conturbat me" [Fear of death disturbs me]), and finally a prayer to Saint Francis, recalling that he, at his own death, had prayed for the souls of his brothers.[8] The two final carols in the sequence are furthermore carefully particularized, as if to establish some parallel between poetic closure and approaching death. The *Dread of Death Carol* details the sickness and failing senses that portend the ending of the speaker's life ("Here is a cause of gret mornyng— / Of myselfe nothyng I se, / Save filth, unclennes, vile stynkyng"; 25–27; W51.19–21). In the final *Saint Francis Carol* the actions of the dying Saint Francis are elided with those of the dying "broder Jon":

> His last prayer to Crist this was,
> Fore al that sustens this holé place:
> "Gracious God, grawnt ham thi grace,
> Tofore thi Jugement at Domysday."
>   Saynt Frances, to thee I say,
>   Save thi breder both nyght and day!
>   (61–66; W52.44–47 plus burden)

Instances of arranged lyric sequences in Middle English are rare, but there are just a few other collections that afford comparison with the sequence of carols in MS Douce 302. The translation into Middle English by John Quixley of the French poems that make up Gower's *Traitié pour essampler les amantz marietz*, surviving only in London, BL MS Stowe 951 is one example.[9] Another is the short sequence of love lyrics, formerly attributed to the duke of Suffolk, in Oxford, Bodl. Lib. MS Fairfax 16.[10] The "Book of Love," a large number of Middle English poems attributed to Charles d'Orléans in London, BL MS Harley 682, is made up of lyrics in a variety of forms, organized so that they construct a developing narrative.[11]

Other substantial collections, like the fourteenth-century religious lyrics of Friar William Herebert in London, BL MS Addit. 46919 or the later fifteenth-century carols of James Ryman in Cambridge, CUL MS Ee.1.12, bundle together poems related by the fact of single authorship, but make no attempt to organize them in formally or thematically significant ways.[12]

In the carol section of MS Douce 302, the only gestures toward spinning a narrative thread—and a thin one, at that—are supplied by the details in the final poems that chronicle a physical decline, and in the sporadic mention of Audelay's name (the latter a feature that the carol section of the manuscript shares with other of its parts). The first occurrence of his name in this section comes in the *Henry VI Carol* ("Thus prophecis the Blynd Awdlay"; 94; W39.66), perhaps regarded as an especially auspicious location. He is then named again in the last two carols: as the "Blynd Awdlay" who offers the lesson to be learned (*Dread of Death Carol* 61; W51.43); and as the speaker of the address to Saint Francis, whose own concluding prayer is organized to lead up to a naming that forms the last word of the last line:

> I praye youe, seris, pur charyté,
> Redis this caral reverently,
> Fore I mad hit with wepyng eye,
> Your broder Jon the Blynd Awdlay.
>   (*St. Francis Carol* 73–76; W52.52–55).

The question of Audelay's claim to authorship of the carols has received less attention than it might warrant. The title of Ella Keats Whiting's edition of the contents of MS Douce 302, *The Poems of John Audelay*, like the general tenor of her introductory discussion, suggests implicitly that she regarded the manuscript as a collection of Audelay's "works" (even though she notes that he "does not show much originality" and demonstrates "a lack of inventiveness").[13] Greene presents the carols as poems "by John Audelay,"[14] and the attribution has not been much questioned elsewhere.[15] Leaving aside larger questions concerning Audelay's claims to be author of works in other sections of the manuscript,[16] it would be possible to argue that his association with the carols might have taken a wider variety of forms than is usually allowed. "Authorship" in relation to lyrics, perhaps more than to any other medieval genre, is a concept of some fluidity, sufficiently elastic to accommodate situations in which citing or using a poem can constitute ownership and thus virtual authorship of it: John Shirley's copy of the poem known as "A Gentlewoman's Lament" (*NIMEV* 154) in Cambridge, TCC MS

R.3.20 notes that it was "sayde by a gentilwomman whiche loued a man of gret estate," but gives it the running title "A wommans compleynte made by Lidegate." The commonest form of attribution in Middle English manuscripts—a phrase in which a name is preceded by the word *quod* (= 'quoth, said')—deftly preserves this ambiguity (and can sometimes anyway be demonstrated to refer to a scribe rather than a putative author).[17] Among the possible kinds of circumstance in which Audelay's relationship to the carols in MS Douce 302 might be that of author, we have, at one end of the spectrum, a situation in which he actually conceived and "authored" each poem; at the other, a situation in which the sequence was compiled by or even for him from carols in existing circulation, with minor adjustments at certain points to include mention of his name. In the middle of these, another set of circumstances would allow for a mixture of "authoring," as it is generally conceived, and activities closer to adaptation (to unrecoverable degrees) of existing material. It remains a likely hypothesis that this section of the manuscript contains copies of carols that were collected from a variety of sources and kept by Audelay, and thus "Audelay's" in the sense that he made them available to others for copying and embellishment.

The survival in other carol repertories of variant texts of some of the carols in MS Douce 302 lends some support to the possibility that we should think of them as adaptations or redactions. Six of the twenty-five carols occur in witnesses other than MS Douce 302,[18] and although the extent of variation between the texts is quite high, the similarities are sufficiently striking to suggest that Greene's view of the *Nativity Carol*—"probably [Audelay's] version was made with more or less revision from a prototype"[19]—might apply to others of the sequence. The manuscripts that share carols with MS Douce 302 are mostly significant carol repertories, collections which in the case of London, BL Sloane 2593 (probably from Bury St. Edmunds) and Oxford, Bodl. Lib. MS Arch. Selden. B.26 (probably from Worcester) seem to have been associated with large religious houses and to have gathered up for communal use a number of widely circulating lyrics.[20] The carols in the rather different and later Oxford, Balliol College MS 354, an anthology compiled by the London grocer Richard Hill, seem to be old favorites, copied by Hill in some instances from printed exemplars.[21] It may be significant that the carols MS Douce 302 shares with this manuscript (*Epiphany Carol*, *Tree of Jesse Carol*, and *Joys of Mary Carol*) all occur on the same few leaves of Balliol MS 354 (fols 219r–21v), as if perhaps available to Hill (as maybe also to the compiler or compilers of MS Douce 302) in a small group.

The assortment of carols in MS Douce 302 is conventional in a number of aspects. Their subject matter is mostly not unusual: Greene's edition includes numerous analogues to the carols of religious counsel (carols 1–5),[22] and to the groups of Nativity, post-Nativity, and Marian pieces (carols 6–11, 15, and 16–18, respectively),[23] many occurring in the major carol collections that share contents with MS Douce 302. Even the *Henry VI Carol* has an analogue of a kind, in the lyric (not in carol form) in praise of this king by James Ryman.[24] Carols to saints are rarer, and no other surviving carols make reference to the particular saints addressed in the carols in MS Douce 302.[25] Audelay's carols to Saint Francis and Saint Anne are unusual and may reflect the preoccupations of a specific personal, community, or other local piety, or the concern of whoever shaped the contents of this particular section of the manuscript. Local concerns clearly must have determined the inclusion of a carol to Saint Winifred (the subject of a cult in Shrewsbury and the surrounding area)[26] in the portion of the manuscript devoted to salutations and devotions, where Winifred figures alongside Mary and Saint Anne.

In terms of their phrasing and burdens, however, even some of the carols that appear unique to MS Douce 302 echo, or are echoed by, parts of texts surviving in other witnesses. The "welcome" anaphora that is a feature of Audelay's *Nativity Carol* is duplicated in a carol in MS Sloane 2593;[27] the phrase "Moder and maydon was never non mo" used in the refrain to the *Joys of Mary Carol* (W45) seems to echo "mother and maiden was never non but she" in the penultimate line of "I syng of a mayden þat is makeles," also in MS Sloane 2593.[28] The "I praye youe" opening of the introductory couplet ("I pray yow, syrus, boothe moore and las") has a number of analogues elsewhere[29] and reappears several times within the carol sequence: in the burdens of three pieces (*St. John Carol*, *St. Thomas Carol*, and *Virginity Carol*; W35, W37, W48), and again, in the context of more extended repetition, in parts of the *Henry VI Carol* (85–86; W39.59–60) and the final *Saint Francis Carol* (73–74; W52.52–53). These internal echoes are matched by further correspondences between the carols and poems in other sections of the manuscript).[30]

A collection such as this bears comparison with major repertories that include large numbers of carols: MS Arch. Selden. B.26; MS Sloane 2593; Oxford, Bodl. Lib. MS Eng. poet. e.1; and London BL MSS Addit. 5465, Addit. 5665, and Egerton 3307. All of these except the last have musical settings with some or all of their carol texts,[31] and, in terms of provenance, most have been fairly convincingly associated with large religious houses or chapels of some kind. MS Egerton 3307 has been connected variously with the Chapel Royal, the College of St. George's Windsor, or the Cistercian abbey of Meaux, near Beverley;[32] while Beverley Minster seems likely to have been the original home of MS Eng. poet. e.1.[33] Dr. Robert Fayrfax of the Chapel Royal (d. 1529) probably owned MS Addit. 5465,[34] and John Alcock, bishop of Worcester, has been plausibly associated with MS Arch. Selden. B.26.[35] MS Sloane 2593 may have originated in the Benedictine abbey of Bury St. Edmunds,[36] and MS Addit. 5665 at Exeter Cathedral.[37] Even though it was a humbler institution than most of these, Haughmond Abbey presumably needed carols for some of the same extra-liturgical and convivial purposes, and the collection organized around Audelay's name in MS Douce 302 could be seen as a smaller but not essentially dissimilar repertory (an analogy supported by the material it has in common with MS Sloane 2593).

The absence of music from MS Douce 302, while not necessarily setting it apart from these larger semi-institutional collections (MS Sloane 2593, after all, has no musical notation), might be argued to imply that they were intended to be read (not sung) as a coherent group, a possibility also reflected in the care with which the carols have been organized in one section of the manuscript and personalized with references to Audelay's name. But it remains hard to find significant similarities with any other sorts of carol manuscript. Apart from the large institutional repertories just listed, manuscripts that contain more than one or two carols tend on the whole to be informal compilations put together by students or clerics, or anthologies of material for domestic use.[38] The extent to which carols are grouped together in these categories of manuscript is variable. The five carols in Aberystwyth, NLW MS Brogyntyn II. 1 (Porkington 10) all occur in one single gathering,[39] admittedly copied by two different hands, but nonetheless clearly components in what was conceived as a "lyric" section in this very comprehensive, seemingly coherently planned miscellany. In the collection of rather similar material which is now Edinburgh, NLS MS Advocates 19.3.1, however, the carols (three in number), occur at widely separated points, each supplied by a different scribe, and in some cases perhaps filling what would otherwise have remained blank space.[40] The reasons that prompted the copying of carols into both these manuscripts—whether to record songs for singing or poems for reading—are irrecoverable.

In the end, the all-purpose usefulness of carols in a wide range of social situations, and thus in a correspondingly large variety of manuscript contexts (where their appearance may also be determined by pragmatic considerations to do with filling space or trying out writing implements), tends to stand in the way of analysis of the forms of their transmission and survival. The sequence of carols in MS Douce 302, even though in some respects shaped as a semiautobiographical part of the oeuvre that the manuscript attributes to Audelay, constitute a small anthology of useful pieces. The opening addresses of some of the carols, directing them variously at "syrus" (*St. Thomas Carol, Henry VI Carol*), "lord and lady" (*Nativity Carol*), and "mon" (*Ten Commandments Carol*), give some indication of their social inclusiveness. Even though a few are more specifically targeted—whether at "breder everychone" (*St. John Carol*), or at "maydyns" (*Virginity Carol*) and "women" (*Chastity of Wives Carol*)—their overall range suggests a collection designed for audiences who would include laypeople as well as religious, and women as well as men, across a social spectrum. They seem entirely appropriate to the repertoire of a chaplain-turned-brother such as Audelay, someone well placed to learn or acquire carols from various sources, and ready to turn his hand to adaptations for local occasions and needs.

As Andrew Taylor has pointed out,[41] the later history of MS Douce 302 exactly confirms the usefulness of such a collection in contexts of different kinds. Faded (or possibly partially erased) notes on folio 35 indicate that the manuscript came into the hands of "Wi*lliam* Vyott . . . A [min]sstrale / In Coventry" before reaching "Ihon Barkre," a canon of the Augustinian Priory of St. John the Baptist at Launde, in Leicestershire. While it is easy enough to comprehend the appeal of a collection we might like to think of as part of "Audelay's works" to an Augustinian canon of Launde, it is salutary to know that it seems to have reached him through an intermediary for whom carols were much more likely to have been tools of the performer's trade.

Notes

1. To this total can be added the *St. Winifred Carol* ("Wenefrede thou swete may": W24; *NIMEV* 413) on fol. 26r–v of MS Douce 302, which terms itself a "carol" (118). Individual carols in MS Douce 302 are cited from John Audelay, *Poems and Carols (Oxford, Bodleian Library MS Douce 302)*, ed. Susanna Fein (Kalamazoo: Medieval Institute Publications, 2009), accompanied by references (poem and line numbers prefixed by "W") to Ella Keats Whiting, ed., *The Poems of John Audelay*, EETS o.s. 181 (1931; repr. Oxford: Oxford University Press, 2006). Line numbers in these editions differ because Fein prints the repeated refrains after each stanza, while Whiting prints them only at the head of each carol.

2. Richard Leighton Greene, ed., *The Early English Carols*, 2nd ed. (Oxford: Clarendon Press, 1977), pp. 296–341; see also Karl Reichl, "The Middle English Carol," in *A Companion to the Middle English Lyric*, ed. Thomas G. Duncan (Cambridge: Cambridge University Press, 2005), pp. 150–70, and the notes accompanying editions of surviving musical settings in John Stevens, ed., *Mediaeval Carols*, 2nd ed. (London: Stainer and Bell, 1958).

3. For an attempt at an overall view of lyric manuscripts, see Julia Boffey, "Middle English Lyrics and Manuscripts," in *A Companion to Middle English Lyrics*, ed. Thomas Duncan (Cambridge: Cambridge University Press, 2005), pp. 1–18; and on single-author collections, see A. S. G. Edwards, "Fifteenth-Century Middle English Verse Author Collections," in *The English Medieval Book: Studies in Memory of Jeremy Griffiths*, ed. A. S. G. Edwards, Vincent Gillespie, and Ralph Hanna (London: British Library, 2000), pp. 101–12.

4. The functions of MS Douce 302 as book are emphasized in other sections: see, e.g., the lines in the overall conclusion (fol. 35): "No mon this book he take away, / Ny kutt owte noo leef" (*Conclusion* 40–41).

5. Greene, *Early English Carols*, pp. xxi–xxxiii.

6. Greene, *Early English Carols*, p. xxix.

7. For instance, *Christemasse carolles, newely enprinted*, by de Worde in 1521 (*STC* 5204) and the several collections following this, which kept the same title (*STC* 5204.3, 5204.5, 5205).

8. See Susanna Fein, "Good Ends in the Audelay Manuscript," *Yearbook of English Studies* 33 (2003): 97–119.

9. Henry Noble MacCracken, "Quixley's Ballades Royal (?1402)," *Yorkshire Archaeological Journal* 20 (1908): 33–50.

10. Julia Boffey, "'Cy ensuent trois chaunceons': Groups and Sequences of Middle English Lyrics," forthcoming.

11. Mary-Jo Arn, ed., *Fortunes Stabilnes: Charles of Orléans's English Book of Love* (Binghamton, N.Y.: Medieval & Renaissance Texts & Studies 1994).

12. Stephen R. Reimer, ed., *The Works of William Herebert, OFM* (Toronto: Pontifical Institute of Mediaeval Studies, 1987); and J. Zupitza, "Die Gedichte des Franziskaners Jakob Ryman," *Archiv für das Studium der neueren Sprachen* 89 (1892): 167–338.

13. Whiting, *Poems*, pp. xix, xx.

14. Greene, *Early English Carols*, p. 317; also Richard Leighton Greene, "Carols," in *MWME* 6:1743–52, 1940–2018: "Most of the fourteenth- and fifteenth-century carols . . . are anonymous, though there are 26 by John Audelay" (p. 1744).

15. Audelay's claims to be author of the poems are perpetuated in the relevant entries in *NIMEV*. A note of caution is sounded by Derek Pearsall, *Old English and Middle English Poetry* (London: Routledge and Kegan Paul, 1977), p. 250, with the suggestion that only the first eighteen poems in the manuscript are likely to be Audelay's own compositions.

16. The "signing" of Audelay's name in a variety of contexts and at a number of points throughout the different sections of the manuscript implies some claim to authorship, although at least one item in the contents (*Sins of the Heart*, numbered as XXXVI) is actually an extract from Rolle's *Form of Living*.

17. The addition of the name "Halle" ("Quod Hallis," fol. 37; "Amen quod Hall," fol. 13v) to items in the former Hopton Hall Manuscript, now in Keio University Library, is an instance of one such case; see the description in Takami Matsuda, ed., *Mostly British: Manuscripts and Early Printed Materials from Classical Rome to Renaissance England in the Collection of Keio University Library* (Tokyo: Keio University Press, 2001), pp. 56–63, and for further discussion, A. S. G. Edwards, "The Hopton Hall Manuscript at Keio University," in *Codices Keionenses: Essays on Western Manuscripts and Early Printed Books in Keio University Library*, ed. Takami Matsuda (Tokyo: Keio University Press, 2005), pp. 69–86. The attribution to Chaucer of "Deuise prowe and eke humylitee" (*NIMEV* 679)—"Quod Chaucer quhen he was richt avisit"—is another instance; see Julia Boffey and A. S. G. Edwards, introduction to *The Works of Geoffrey Chaucer and "The Kingis Quair": A Facsimile of Bodleian Library, Oxford, MS Arch. Selden. B. 24.* (Cambridge: Brewer, 1997), fols. 119v–20r.

18. *Nativity Carol* occurs in London, BL MS Sloane 2593; *Circumcision Carol* in Cambridge, TCC MS O.3.58 and Oxford, Bodl. Lib. MS Arch. Selden. B.26; *Epiphany Carol* in MS Sloane 2593 and Oxford, Balliol College MS 354; and *Tree of Jesse Carol* and *Joys of Mary Carol* in Balliol MS 354. Greene, *Early English Carols*, prints variant texts or full collations of all of these. A further, previously unnoticed correspondence concerns *Seven Deadly Sins Carol*, which appears also in Aberystwyth, NLW MS 334A, copied on an endleaf.

19. Greene, *Early English Carols*, p. 344, note to no. 7. It is worth noting that the other witnesses of *Nativity Carol* preserve it with music.

20. For descriptions, see Thomas Wright, ed., *Songs and Carols, Now First Printed, from a Manuscript of the Fifteenth Century*, Percy Society 23 (London: Richards, 1847); Bernhard Fehr, "Die Lieder der Hs. Sloane 2593," *Archiv für das Studium der neueren Sprachen* 109 (1902): 33–72; Stevens, *Mediaeval Carols*, p. 125; Greene, *Early English Carols*, pp. 306–7, 314–15.

21. Roman Dyboski , ed., *Songs, Carols and Other Miscellaneous Poems from the Balliol MS 354: Richard Hill's Commonplace Book*, EETS e.s. 101 (London: Kegan Paul, Trench, Trübner, 1907), pp. xiii–lix; R. A. B. Mynors, *Catalogue of the Manuscripts of Balliol College, Oxford* (Oxford: Clarendon Press, 1963), pp. 352–54.

22. Greene, *Early English Carols*, pp. 197–205.

23. Greene, *Early English Carols*, pp. 4–79, 115–44.

24. *NIMEV* 2745.

25. Greene, *Early English Carols*, pp. 184–92.

26. *NIMEV* 413 (W25); for bibliography concerning ME lives of Saint Winifred, see Charlotte D'Evelyn and Frances A. Foster, "Saints' Legends," in *MWME* 2:410–29, 553–644 (pp. 633–34).

27. Greene, *Early English Carols*, 7B (*NIMEV* 3877).
28. *NIMEV* 1367; cp. also the earlier lyric *NIMEV* 2366.
29. *NIMEV* 1341.5–1344.5.
30. *St. Winifred Carol* concludes with a stanza identical to the last one of *St. Francis Carol*. Other correspondences include: *Ten Commandments Carol* 29–32 with *Epilogue* 110–13; *Seven Works of Mercy Carol* 15–18 with *True Living* 238–41 and *God's Address* 197–200; *Seven Works of Mercy Carol* 22–28 with *True Living* 251–58 and *God's Address* 213–20; and *Seven Gifts Carol* 36 with *True Living* 218, 229. The *Gaude* opening of *Joys of Mary Carol* reflects the opening of some of the salutations (W19–W27).
31. Stevens, *Mediaeval Carols*, edits the music.
32. See Greene, *Early English Carols*, pp. 299–301, for a bibliography and account of the various arguments.
33. Greene, *Early English Carols*, pp. 317–18.
34. Greene, *Early English Carols*, p. 307; see also John Stevens, ed., *Early Tudor Songs and Carols* (London: Stainer and Bell, 1975).
35. Greene, *Early English Carols*, pp. 314–15.
36. Greene, *Early English Carols*, pp. 306–7.
37. Greene, *Early English Carols*, pp. 307–8; and Stevens, ed., *Early Tudor Songs and Carols*, pp. xviii–xix.
38. See details of the following manuscripts in Greene, *Early English Carols*, pp. 323–37: CUL MS Addit. 5943 (four carols); Cambridge, Gonville and Caius College MS 383 (nine carols); Edinburgh, NLS MS Advocates 18.7.21, compiled by John Grimestone (four carols), and MS Advocates 19.3.1 (3 carols); Aberystwyth, NLW MS Brogyntyn II. 1 (also known as Porkington 10) (five carols). The only other manuscripts with significant numbers of carols are TCC MS O.3.58, a vellum roll of carols, with musical settings, and Cambridge, St. John's College MS S.54, a single gathering in a vellum wrapper (see Greene, ibid., pp. 325–27).
39. See Daniel Huws, "MS Porkington 10 and Its Scribes," in *Romance Reading on the Book: Essays on Medieval Narrative Presented to Maldwyn Mills*, ed. Jennifer Fellows, Rosalind Field, Gillian Rogers, and Judith Weiss (Cardiff: University of Wales Press, 1996), pp. 189–207. The gathering is item 25 in Huws's collation and contains the following carols: fol. 198r, "By a chapel as I came" (a carol of the Mass; *NIMEV* 298); fol. 198v, "Jhesu whas borne in Bedlem Jude" (Epiphany carol; *NIMEV* 1785); fol. 200r, "Whan nothing whas but God alone" (*Veritas verbi domini*; *NIMEV* 4001); fols. 201r–2r, "A babe is born to blis vs brynge" (lullaby carol; *NIMEV* 22); fol. 202r, "The boris hede in hond I bryng" (convivial carol; *NIMEV* 3314), along with *NIMEV* 3743 and 674.
40. See Phillipa Hardman, introduction to *The Heege Manuscript: A Facsimile of National Library of Scotland MS Advocates 19. 3. 1* (Leeds: University of Leeds, School of English, 2000). The carols are: item 10, fol. 59r–v, "Ihesu almyghty kyng of blys" (Nativity carol; *NIMEV* 340); item 33, fols. 95v–96r, "Man in þi mynd loket þis behest'" (satirical carol; *NIMEV* 358); and item 48, fols. 210v–11r, "This endurs nyȝt I see a sight" (lullaby carol; *NIMEV* 3627).

41. Andrew Taylor, "The Myth of the Minstrel Manuscript," *Speculum* 66 (1991): 43–73. On minstrel use of carols (specifically with reference to MS Sloane 2593), see also Karin Boklund-Lagopoulou, *"I have a yong suster": Popular Song and the Middle English Lyric* (Dublin: Four Courts, 2002).

"Wo and Werres . . . Rest and Pese"
John Audelay's Politics of Peace

John C. Hirsh

For all of his evident fascination with the power of divine love to inform and to transform humankind, John Audelay is rarely thought of as a socially engaged poet, and he has never been considered "political," at least not as the word is generally understood. The reasons for this circumstance are not hard to find: as a poet, Audelay is sometimes compared to the seventeenth-century courtier and cleric George Herbert (1593–1633), the metaphysical poet some of whose powerful and felt religious values he seems to echo, even without the latter poet's often ingenious attention to biblical and devout allusion, and to compressed and witty wordplay. His attachment, in his role as chaplain, to the nobility, and to the notorious Lord Richard Lestrange in particular, seems to preclude any but the most perfunctory social criticism, and his putative involvement with the sacrilege commited by Lestrange on Easter Sunday 1417, together with his own subsequent apprehension and public penance, further distance him from representing meaningful political attitudes, or so runs the critique.[1]

But no writer, and particularly no poet, is ever entirely indifferent to the age in which he or she lives, and in certain important ways the same holds true of Audelay. In what follows, I am going to examine some of the literary and social implications in one of Audelay's most familiar poems, his carol in honor of King Henry VI (1421–71, reigned 1422–61 and 1470–71). In doing so, I will briefly discuss some of the ways in which Henry VI was perceived, paying particular attention to his contemporary reputation for religious devotion, and note the extent to which that reputation contrasts with his father's, before turning to a reading of Audelay's poem and to its religious and secular implications.

Because Audelay's *Henry VI Carol* is influenced, as we shall see, not only by a long Middle English poem which John Lydgate wrote in connection with the very young king's coronation in 1429, but also by the complex mood of celebration that attended upon his father's glorious past, I want to begin by considering what is in some ways the most important poem to come down to us concerning Henry V's victory at Agincourt, the anonymous text now usually known as "The Agincourt Carol" (*IMEV*, *NIMEV* 822). Since the poem is important for the reading of Audelay I am developing, I am going to quote it here:[2]

Deo gracias Anglia
Redde pro victoria.

Owre kynge went forth to Normandy,
With grace and might of chyualry,
Ther God for hym wrought mervelusy,
Wherfore Englond may calle and cry,

Deo gracias . . .

He sette a sege, the sothe for to say,
To Harflu, tovne with ryal aray.
That tovne he wan and made a fray,
That Fraunce shal rywe tyl domesday.

Deo gracias . . .

Than went oure kynge, with alle his oste,
Thorwe Fraunce, for alle the Frenshe boste.
He spared no drede of lest ne moste,
Tyl he come to Agincourt coste.

Deo gracias . . .

Than, forsoth, that knyght comely,
In Agincourt feld he faught manly,
Thorw grace of God most myghty,
He had bothe the felde and the victory.

Deo gracias . . .

There dukys and erlys, lorde and barone,
Were take and slayne, and that wel sone,

And summe were ladde into Lundone,
With joye and merthe and grete renone.

Deo gracias . . .

Now gracious God, he saue oure kynge,
His peple, and alle his wel-wyllynge,
Yef hym gode lyfe and gode endynge,
That we with merth mowe sauely synge,

Deo gracias . . .

 Because of the repeated reference to "oure kynge" and the liberal use of the third-person pronoun referring to Henry, the poem is sometimes read simply as a celebration of Henry himself, though one in which the Almighty is invited to join, and even offered an important supporting role, in the Agincourt victory. Yet it is quite true, as Wolfgang Müller remarks, that the construction of the poem is "largely genre-conditioned," and Müller points out as well that a sense of an alluded to, but suppressed, narrative concerning the battle informs the lines.[3] So read, the poem stands at some distance from purely historical accounts, literary and historical both, like the anonymous Middle English poem Rossell Hope Robbins has called "The Battle of Agincourt" (*IMEV* 3213), which attends not only to the circumstances of the battle, but also to the behavior of individual lords who took part in it, so as to celebrate their courage and their feats of arms. "God omnipotent" is cited in the last line of that poem, but only as a witness to the truth of what has come before, and the poem as a whole differs markedly from the more subtle religiousness of "The Agincourt Carol."[4] Changes having been made, the same is largely true of the late Percy Folio Manuscript ballad which John W. Hales and Frederick J. Furnivall named "Agincourt Battell," and which, like "The Battle of Agincourt," places emphasis on the details of the battle—the way the English employed pointed stakes and archers to bring down the tightly-packed French knights—and also avoids any but the most perfunctory religious allusion, while investing its narrative in the deeds of the day.[5] Against these celebratory and historical poems, "The Agincourt Carol" stands in sharp contrast. Like them, it offers a theme of joy and celebration, a theme appropriate to its genre, but it avoids dwelling on the circumstances and details of the battle, which circulated so widely in chronicles, ballads, and (to contemporaries at least) accounts of returned veterans. These details, however, would have been altogether familiar to its first audience and are indirectly encoded in the song.

In his edition of the carol, Richard Leighton Greene notes the religious resonances of the poem and suggests that they may indicate clerical authorship, not only because of the evident religious allusions, but also because of the careful rhetoric within which Henry's victory is cast. So understood, the poem, unlike the other texts I have been examining, shifts the center of the action away from powerful Henry to Almighty God instead. In this reading of the poem, Henry's own actions lessen in significance, so that the focus of the interest finally lies elsewhere. "*Our* kyng" (emphasis added) goes forth with "grace and myght of chivalry." It is God, not Harry, who "wrought mervelusy," so that England's celebration, its "calle and cry" (the words imply a third party who will answer), responds to God's intervention, not simply to Henry's success. Henry's victory at Harfleur is briefly noted, but only as a way station to "Agincourt coste," where "thorw grace of God most mighty" he wins our great victory. The song, with its repeated "Deo gracias," does not lose its spirit of celebration, but closes with a prayer to "gracious God" to "saue oure kynge, / His peple, and all his wel-wyllynge," and concludes by petitioning God to give Henry "gode lyfe and gode endynge," a devout and prescient conclusion, particularly if, as seems probable, the carol was composed before Henry's relatively early death in 1422.

Following his victory, Henry attributed his clearly unlikely success at Agincourt to God alone, and he directed that "credit" for the battle's outcome be given only to him. But, in that joy and celebration, "The Agincourt Carol" does not omit reference to the "fray" at Harfleur, nor to the French nobles who were "take and slayne" at Argencourt itself. Its joy goes beyond Henry's somewhat self-serving declaration that the victory was God's, to imply that the entire weight of the expedition was as well, and that that circumstance informs all of human life too—hence the important but otherwise irrelevant reference to Henry's future death at the end. The effect of this representation is at once to de-emphasize the manifestly military nature of Henry's conquest, a conquest accompanied, however, as virtually all the contemporary sources attest, by a loss of life large even by contemporary standards. One of the most compelling and best-known examples of that violence—apart from the general massacre of the French, which the battle became—appears in Henry's order, issued when he believed (thanks to the late arrival of a group of French knights freshly arrived) that the French were about to return to the attack, for all prisoners (except the noblest and most valuable) to be put to the sword. This order was resisted by some of those in his company, either for moral and chivalric reasons or because they stood to lose their ransoms, so that the king had to order his archers to carry it out. The killing, however, was consonant with the established norms of medieval warfare, and neither English nor French contemporary sources regard it as a violation of chivalry, though as one modern commentator has recently written, the fact that in the earliest commentary the king's role was "obfuscated" serves to suggest "that there was a fear that Henry might be deemed culpable for killing men who had surrendered, especially as it was in anticipation of an attack that never came."[6] Though not publicly discussed at the time, Henry's actions were part of the contemporary historical record and could have been taken as mitigating the splendor of the victory, however necessary or at least understandable they may have appeared to contemporaries.[7]

But it was thus against these actions and others that the poem's evident celebration is set. Henry's actions in ordering the execution of the prisoners could be apologized for—more easily in the French account as the result of the actions of certain knights—but they still needed to be explained, or at least taken into account. Celebrations like "The Agincourt Carol" did so implicitly, turning from the battle's well-known carnage to the joyful national celebration that followed, recording, however, that the joy followed a battle that was won as the direct result of God's intervention. This theme of joy after woe has evident theological (and also Chaucerian) resonances and was frequently present in Middle English lyrics and songs, almost always involving a religious context. Indeed medieval literary joy is almost always conditional, particularly when it appears in a secular context. Christmas carols frequently allude both to Christ's Passion and to the reasons for it at the time of the Nativity, and the carol "A child is boren amonges man" (*IMEV, NIMEV* 29) engages it directly, repeatedly sounding the familiar Christmas sentiment of joy, now seen as springing from Adam's *felix culpa*: "Senful man, be blithe and glad." In another context, the extraordinary Middle English philosophical poem "I wolde witen of sum wys wiht" (*IMEV, NIMEV* 1402) turns upon itself to advise that, following philosophical reflection, "make we murie and sle care," a counsel that does not deny the troubling reflections that have come before, but places them in the theological context of our lives, a treatment present in "The Agincourt Carol" too.[8] The use of "joye and merthe" in medieval English lyrics does not negate the brute realities of sin and war, nor the troubling reflections that attend upon Christian philosophy, but it can set them in a larger context, one in which God is necessarily present to endow human life with a complex, contingent, but finally joyful meaning, if only we can perceive it. Read from this perspective, life is a battle too, and its reward is joy eternal. "The Agincourt Carol" is not at all an allegory, but it does encode Christian teaching in the course of its celebration. And the echoes of that celebration sound elsewhere.

In this tradition, it would be a mistake to read "The Agincourt Carol" simply as jingoistic, or to see it as innocent of any larger purpose. When placed against the circumstances of the battle itself, the evident religious dimension of the carol takes on a different meaning. No longer does it simply reflect Henry's own position, that the victory was God's own, but it remains a celebration, albeit a conditional one, that acknowledges the grace of "God most mighty" as the joyful reason for the battle's outcome. The king who led the troops will himself die (as in relatively short order he did), but even then his people will thank God for his life. What emerges in the tone and substance of the poem is thus less an encomium than a clerical reaction both to Henry's victory and to the wave of patriotic sentiment that accompanied it. In this way, "The Agincourt Carol" may be said to negotiate between the circumstances of victory in war and an ecclesiastical preference for peace. It represents, when all is said and done, one of the more considered, even inflected, representations of the English victory, and so contributes to a far more complex understanding of the popular reaction than is sometimes assigned to it. But both aspects of that reaction—both the popular joy and the religious sense of divine approval—inform John Audelay's carol on Henry VI. And thus an examination of the literary tradition created around the victory, such as I have offered here, constitutes a necessary prologomia to any serious study of Audelay's own poem.

If it was against a background of popular enthusiasm, and modified ecclesiastical approval, that celebration of Henry V's military prowess progressed, it was against it too that, in the course of time, the reputation of his son Henry VI developed. That reputation, however, took on quite a different character. Acknowledging in particular Henry's religiousness, it gradually developed into a popular devotional cult of some significance, and one that grew apace after his death in 1471.[9] The cult generated a following among both clerics and educated laypersons, so that many of the texts written for it are in Latin. But as the cult grew, lyrics circulated in Middle English too, and these took quite a different form from those connected with Henry *pere*. Probably the most important poems associated with Henry VI's monarchy and reputation are those John Lydgate inscribed, which moved from his "pedigree" through his coronation and his coronation banquet, to his triumphal entry into London in 1432, to the presentation to him of the gift of an eagle. In general, these poems—the first of which almost certainly informed Audelay's carol—represent Henry in a largely, but not entirely traditional role: of noble birth; born to love and fear God; triumphant in adversity (the description of the civic pageantry which attended upon Henry's 1432 entry into London is particularly impressive); and in some ways like the eagle itself, the king of birds, with which he is presented as a New Year's gift.[10] This early reputation, powerful if conventional in its way, would in time give way to another, one that instead privileged Henry's religious values. This emphasis on the monarch's piety also was a tradition on which Audelay drew and to which he contributed. A good example appears in the "Pudsay Lyric" (*IMEV Suppl.*, *NIMEV* 333.5) so called for its association with the Pudsay family of Barford, with whom Henry probably had a passing association. It follows:[11]

> As far as hope will [ ] yn length,
> On the, Kyng Henry, I fix my mynde.
> That be my prayour: I may have strenkith
> In vertuous lyfe my warkes to bynde.
> Though I to the haue ben vnkynde,
> Off wilfulnesse long tyme and space,
> Off forgeuenesse I aske the grace:
> Hop hathe me meuyde to seke this place.
> In trust off socore by thyn olde properte.
> Was neuer man cam beforene thi face,
> Rebellion or other yn aduersite,
> Off thyn compassion commaundid them goo free.
> Now, for thi pety to Hym that all schall deme,
> Pray for me thy seruaunt and pilgreme.

The differences between this lyric and the tradition that attached itself to Henry V's victory are immediately apparent, and both register in Audelay's carol. This text is as much a prayer as a poem, one that involves a repentant and meditative Christian, a servant and pilgrim, who seems to be addressing a saint as much as a monarch. S/he seeks now to live a virtuous life, and so repents past wrongs, seeking from Henry both forgiveness and a monarch's "grace." S/he turns to Henry because, as s/he insists, never did a man come before him, even in "rebellion," but Henry, for his compassion, granted the man freedom.[12] There is nothing—*pace moderni*—in Henry VI's saintly life that requires apology, and it is the evident holiness of that life that is honored and esteemed. The personal, military, and civil disasters that attended upon Henry in later life are kept at a discreet distance, as were his father's military depredations in "The Agincourt Carol," but they are somehow present still in the poem's tone of studied repentance for past mistakes. Even as the king's weaknesses are tacitly acknowledged, his reputation is carefully burnished.

The association of the poem and its manuscript with Bolton Hall is also interesting, as is the family story associated with it, that Henry took refuge with the Pudsay family after his defeat in the Battle of Hexham on 15 May 1464, and left behind—either from haste or as (somewhat curious) mementoes of his visit—a glove, a boot, and a spoon, which the family thereafter treasured. The narrative accords easily with what became Henry's posthumous reputation of "a man who has lost an earthly kingdom but gained a heavenly one," according to Simon Walker.[13] His reputation is developed further in a forty-eight-line Middle English lyric (*IMEV, NIMEV* 2393) which, in the course of much praise, thus hails Henry:

> O crownyd kyng with sceptur in hand,
> Most nobyll conqueror I may the call,
> For thou hast conqueryd, I undyrstand,
> A hevynly kyngdome most imperyall
> Hwar joye abundeth and grace perpetuell
> In presens of the holy Trenite,
> Off wych grace thou make me parcyall—
> Now, swet Kyng Henre, praye for me.
>   . . .
> Thy trowbulas lyf and grett vexacion
> With pacyens that thou had therein,
> And thi constans in contemplacion
> Has mad the hevyn for to wyne.
>   (9–16, 33–36)[14]

In death, Henry thus preserved some at least of his nobility, and though identified lastingly as having endured a "trowbulas lyf and grett vexacion," became as well one who might be turned to "in trust of socore" when it was time to seek "forgeuenesse" for past wrongs. These were not petitions that would have been directed to his more military father, and though they were not broadly circulated until after his death, they were present, if muted, as well, in an earlier tradition, such as the one that informed Audelay's now-familiar carol.

It is against these Henrican poetic traditions of felt but not entirely uncritical adulation, tempered with hints of both respect and apology, that we must read Audelay's carol. On the one hand, it is informed by the monarchs' respective and popular reputations, and invested in celebrating (with modifications) their respective persons, but, on the other hand, it also seeks to recognize and account for the considerable differences between them:

De rege nostro Henrico Sexto

> A, perles Pryns, to thee we pray,
> Save our kyng both nyght and day!

Fore he is ful yong, tender of age,
Semelé to se, o bold corage,
Lovelé and lofté of his lenage,
Both perles prince and kyng veray!
                    (1–4)

His gracious granseres and his grawndame,
His fader and moder, of kyngis thay came;
Was never a worthear prynce of name,
So exelent in al our day.
                    (7–10)

His fader fore love of mayd Kateryn,
In Fraunce he wroght turment and tene;
His love, hee sayd, hit schuld not ben,
And send him ballis him with to play.
                    (13–16)

Then was he wyse in wars withalle,
And taght Franchemen to plai at the balle—
With tenés hold, he ferd ham halle!—
To castelles and setis thi floyn away.
                    (19–22)

To Harflete a sege he layd anon,
And cast a bal unto the towne;
The Frenchemen swere be se and sun,
Hit was the Fynd that made that fray.
                    (25–28)

Anon thai toke ham to cownsele;
Oure gracious kyng thai wold asayle;
At Agyncowrt, at that patayle,
The floure of Frawnce he fel that day.
                    (31–34)

The kyng of Frawns then was agast—
Mesagers to him send in hast—
Fore wele he west hit was bot wast
Hem to witstond in honé way.
                    (37–40)

And prayd hym to sese of his outrage,
And take Kateryn to mareage;
Al Frawnce to him schuld do homage,
And croune him kyng afftyr his day.
                    (43–46)

Of Frawnce he mad him anon regent,
And wedid Kateren in his present;
Into Englond anon he went,
And cround our quene in ryal aray.
                    (49–52)

Of Quen Kateryn our kyng was borne,
To save our ryght that was forelorne,
Oure faders in Frawns had won beforne;
Thai han hit hold moné a day.
                    (55–58)

Thus was his fader a conqueroure,
And wan his moder with gret onoure;
Now may the kyng bere the floure
Of kyngis and kyngdams in uche cuntré.
                    (61–64)

> On him schal fal the prophecé,
> That hath ben sayd of Kyng Herré,
> The holé cros wyn or he dye,
> That Crist halud on Good Fryday.
> (67–70)
>
> Al wo and werres he schal acese,
> And set alle reams in rest and pese,
> And turne to Cristyndam al hethynes—
> Now grawnt him hit so be may!
> (73–76)
>
> Pray we that Lord is Lord of alle
> To save our kyng his reme ryal,
> And let never myschip uppon him falle,
> Ne false traytoure him to betray.
> (79–82)
>
> I pray youe, seris, of your gentré,
> Syng this carol reverently,
> For hit is mad of Kyng Herré—
> Gret ned fore him we han to pray!
> (85–88)
>
> Yif he fare wele, wele schul we be,
> Or ellis we may be ful soré,
> Fore him schal wepe moné an e—
> Thus prophecis the Blynd Awdlay.
> (91–94)[15]

    Given what we have observed concerning the reputation of both Henrys, it is possible to say with some confidence that the poem was written relatively early in the reign of Henry VI, though exactly when is hard to say. It is clearly not necessary to follow Robbins's date of 1429, since it is finally unlikely that the poem was written for Henry's coronation, as he believed.[16] It evidently was influenced deeply by Lydgate's poem on Henry's pedigree, which was indeed connected to that coronation, and may well have derived both its general argument, and some of its details—like the tennis balls—from that source.[17] But it also reacts against that poem, and the references to the young king imply only that it was probably written some time after Lydgate's encomium. It could in fact have been written anytime in the 1430s, after Lydgate's poem had been circulated but when it still would have been appropriate to invoke the father in a song dedicated to so young a king. In any case, it was probably because of Lydgate's example that Audelay chose the somewhat unusual strategy of treating two monarchs in the same poem, though Audelay is as much concerned to contrast the two as to suggest the kind of continuation that Lydgate, in his coronation poem, was disposed to imply—further evidence that the carol is not connected directly to Henry's coronation. Indeed, part of the reason for Audelay's inclusion of the two monarchs in the same poem seems to be to recontextualize, even to delimit, the father's reputation, and to suggest that there are other possibilities available to his son.

The representation of Henry V in Audelay's carol initially follows the traditional representation of a powerful and victorious monarch, one whose victory at Agincourt helped to generate and sustain the idea of an English nation, and so bring joy to his people. In this somewhat limited sense it bears out Christopher Cannon's description of the carol as "a Lancastrian *apologia* worthy of Lydgate, endorsing dynastic claims by justifying the 'wars' of Henry V 'conqueroure.'"[18] And yet, unlike Lydgate, Audelay trumpets Henry's amorousness more than his military prowess, emphasizing his love for the woman who became his queen, and all but suggesting that it was her father's refusal to permit the suit that precipitated the war: "His love, hee sayd, hit schuld not ben" (15). Even more surprisingly, Audelay does not avail himself of the traditional religious justification for Henry's war, as was present in "The Agincourt Carol," a justification that Henry himself had approved, and that sought to temper any charge of aggressiveness and conquest by referring the outcome to God's provenance. On the contrary, Audelay does not hesitate to emphasize what was only just present in the earlier poem, the aggressive nature of war itself. At Harfleur, the French swear "be se and sun, / Hit was the Fynd that mad that fray" (27–28). After Agincourt, Henry's own active participation is emphasized ("The floure of Frawnce he fel that day"; 34), so that the French king is made "agast" (37) and begs him "to sese of his outrage, / And take Kateryn to mareage" (43–44).

This treatment has the effect of acknowledging and celebrating Henry's greatness (and popularity), but it focuses as well on the nature and effectiveness of his victory, and it does so in a way that had specifically been avoided in "The Agincourt Carol." Gone is the ascription of Henry's victory to God's intervention; gone too is the repeated injunction to praise God for the victory. True enough, by the time Audelay was writing, Agincourt was no longer a recent victory. Yet it is Henry's popular military success that Audelay has chosen to emphasize. This very human prince fought hard.

The same cannot be said of his son. Contrary to the practices of his day, later in life Henry VI would repeatedly absent himself from battle, defer the responsibility of actually leading his troops into battle to more experienced and able captains, and as a general policy, seek peace rather than war. In spite of the civil war that raged about him, his interests and pursuits were a good deal less martial than his father's. Many English monarchs established monastic, educational, and other foundations. Henry V founded the twin monasteries of Syon and Sheen, while Henry VI's careful and financially generous establishment of Eton College Windsor and King's College Cambridge, equally twinned, showed great attention to detail and demonstrated much about his attitudes toward kingship. Even a critical modern biographer is constrained to acknowledge both "Henry's devotion to his new foundations" and "the compassionate, humane and sensitive trait in Henry's character."[19] Changes having been made, the distinctions between father and son that Audelay's carol both records and approves reflect those that are present in the historical record too.

The celebration of two monarchs in one carol, which made perfect sense in Lydgate's coronation poem of a young king, thus takes on a different focus in Audelay's somewhat later carol. It was clearly Audelay's intention now to contrast the two monarchs and to imply that although the son has not his father's list of admirable military accomplishments, he also lacks his somewhat more ambiguous attitudes. The first reference as the poem turns from Henry V to Henry VI is thus to predict that the new king shall "wyn," that commonplace of devotional literature and devout meditation, the "holé cros . . . / That Crist halud on Good Fryday" (69–70). Hallowed by its intimate and sacred association with Christ's Passion, the Cross remained the single most important relic available to the medieval imagination, and its connection to kingship would be sounded again in an extraordinary analogue to these lines at the end of Sir Thomas Malory's *Morte Darthur* when, following Arthur's death, the narrator insists that "som . . . men say that he shall com agayne, and he shall wynn the Holy Cross."[20] To associate a king, young or old, with the holiness necessary to seek out, and the power to "wyn," Christ's Cross was effectively to identify him with the highest of Christian enterprises, and to testify to his own sacred worthiness as one selected by God to undertake it. The following stanza makes explicit what Audelay desires for the new king: hopes that accord with what was to become his reputation and that may have been associated with him because of his youth, and also because his religious character was beginning to become known. Unlike his father, Audelay all but says, "Al wo and werrres he schal acese, / And set all reams in rest and pese" (73–74). In line with this pacific purpose, Audelay records his hope that Henry will "turne to Cristyndam al hethynes" (75), going to the Holy Land not as a crusader in arms (the implication seems to be: "as his father would have done"), but, like Saint Francis of Assisi centuries earlier, to convert the heathen.[21] What is involved here is at once more and less than the usual encomium on a prince, involving as it does not only that tradition, but also a barely muted prayer for peace.

Here too Lydgate, but not only Lydgate, seems to have served as Audelay's source, since the carol clearly reflects the desire for peace present in other Middle English lyrics, and indeed in a poetic tradition that begins in antiquity and flourished in the Renaissance as well. Medieval examples are less frequent, though especially after the twelfth century there are poems that allude to it, particularly among those that lament the devastation of war.[22] Thus in "Praise of Peace" (*IMEV, NIMEV* 2156; the title is his modern editor's), John Lydgate writes at length about allegorical, religious, and historical figures who sought peace, boldly insisting that "Al werre is dreedful, vertuous pees is good." And while praising Henry V, who "Sparyd nat to pursue his riht," Lydgate does not fail to point out in this lyric that he "Deyed in his conquest."[23] Writing without the protection that fame and clerical status might afford, Thomas Hoccleve represented a like position, and though attentive as ever to his own person and voice, developed a position that, *inter alia*, represents virtue as both the "cause and effect" of peace. Though mindful of his status, he, like Audelay, also could inscribe what one perceptive critic has called "occasional hearty endorsements of chivalric prowess."[24] The theme and concern for peace is thus variously but unmistakably inscribed by three of the best and most familiar Middle English poets of the fifteenth-century, Audelay, Hoccleve, and perhaps most vigorously, Lydgate. Taken together, their treatments represent an important if delicate meeting of poetry and policy.

But the theme of peace was exploited by less familiar poets as well. An anonymous Middle English poem, which Robbins has called "Peace May Stand" (*IMEV, NIMEV* 1772), is explicitly religious throughout, powerfully introducing a persona who wonders, "I haue mych mervel . . . how mony a gud mon has ben slene."[25] The poem, like others in this section of Robbins's anthology, is formally and explicitly about peace and, by its focus and direction, is so in a way that Audelay's carol is not. It is for this reason, among others, that I have called Audelay's poem, which is clearly concerned with peace as a princely virtue, "political," even though its politics, rooted in Christian teaching, is finally both sacred and even ecclesiastical, and involves not only the king but also the people. If the purpose of the carol is at least in part to delimit the unqualified praise which had grown up around the young king's father, it is also to suggest another avenue of accomplishment that is available to young Henry "our kyng." The only truly "perles Pryns," the poet reminds, is neither Henry V nor Henry VI, but rather the Prince of Peace (the burden may well carry an echo of the *principes pacis* from Isaiah 9:6): Christ himself. And yet unlike "The Agincourt Carol," Audelay's carol does not place all of human effort within God's providence. His Henrys—both of them—act in the world, for better or for worse. They retain the ability to do both right and wrong, and it is the poem's implication that one did and the other shall do both. For Audelay, Henry *fils* will be known for less martial exploits. "Hit so be may" that, besides bringing a lasting peace, he will "turne to Crystyndam al hethynes," so long, the blind Audelay seems almost to offer prophecy, that no "false traytoure" will betray him (75–82). And yet Audelay's final lines seem almost to predict the thirty-year-long civil war that attended upon Henry's finally difficult reign, and finally disastrous ending in the Tower.

In Audelay's carol the contrast between father and son is detailed and explicit. For all the poem's praise, both apparent and real, of Henry V, it israther with Henry VI, and with a different approach to kingship, that Audelay is concerned. Gone is Lydgate's celebration of the son by his father's deeds alone; gone too is the careful justification of Henry VI's monarchy, which now is rather assumed. Praising, with apparent confidence, the values of peace, it is with these, rather than with war, that the poem is finally concerned. Choosing his words carefully, Audelay in this rare religious and political poem calls upon his fellow Englishmen to respond to the grace that God has offered each of them through their new monarch.

At the beginning of this chapter I noted that, at least in modern literary discourse, John Audelay is rarely thought of as either socially engaged or as political, and I could have said too that his poems are rarely considered nuanced. But these attitudes will not stand scrutiny. Audelay must be read attentively, not only in himself, but also against the literary traditions with which he was in dialogue. His knowledge not only of John Lydgate but also of the larger literary traditions on which he and Lydgate both drew is so clear that I found myself wondering, as I was writing this study, exactly how completely and for how long John Audelay was actually blind. He may of course have had literary assistants, but blindness in the fifteenth century, as in the twenty-first, could be a relative designation, and we certainly should not use it as a reason to separate our poet from contemporary literary traditions or contemporary authors—if only because it is both in connection and also in reaction to these that Audelay's originality often will present itself. Perhaps, as with another blind poet of even greater distinction, John Milton (1608–74), there were reasons concerning Audelay's own vulnerability that led him to remind his reader as often as he did about his blindness. In any case, negotiating as he did between the social presuppositions of those who would hear or read his poems, and the different, sometimes very different, social and religious attitudes that he sought both to reveal and encode, he often achieved an inflected, felt, and even socially responsive poetic, political in its way, but inclined rather to sacred than to secular significance. Like the great majority of his contemporaries, he does not hesitate to see God's hand in war and in victory, but he is further inclined to believe that its greater manifestation is in rest and peace, and that even the best ruler will require God's freely given grace in order to succeed. The comparison with George Herbert to which I have already alluded is both meaningful and revealing, for John Audelay shared not only Herbert's secular past and sacred poetic present, but also the Anglican poet's sense of human contingency and divine love, finally liberating categories that applied as equally to king as to commoner.

Notes

1. For a summary of Audelay's connections to Lestrange, see Susanna Fein, "Good Ends in the Audelay Manuscript," *Yearbook of English Studies* 33 (2003): 97–119, esp. pp. 99–101.

2. I cite "The Agincourt Carol" (*IMEV, NIMEV* 2716), from the text printed in John C. Hirsh, ed., *Medieval Lyric: Middle English Lyrics, Ballads and Carols* (Oxford: Blackwell, 2005), pp. 165–66 (no. 49). It is also printed in Richard L. Greene, ed. *The Early English Carols*, 2nd ed. (Oxford: Clarendon Press, 1977), pp. 257–58 (no. 426). For a rich collection of translated and modernized English and French texts concerning the battle at Agincourt, see Anne Curry, ed. and trans., *The Battle of Agincourt: Sources and Interpretations* (Woodbridge: Boydell, 2000).

3. Wolfgang G. Müller, "The Battle of Agincourt in Carol and Battle," *Fifteenth-Century Studies* 8 (1983): 159–78, esp. pp. 162–63.

4. Rossell Hope Robbins, ed., *Historical Poems of the XIVth and XVth Centuries* (New York: Columbia University Press, 1959), pp. 74–77 (no. 27).

5. John W. Hales and Frederick J. Furnivall, eds., *Bishop Percy's Folio Manuscript: Ballads and Romances*, 3 vols. (London: Trübner, 1867–68), 2:158–73. Müller perceptively contrasts this "chronicle ballad" with the ballad "King Henry Fifth's Conquest of France," in Francis J. Child, ed., *The English and Scottish Popular Ballad*, 5 vols. (1882–98; repr. New York: Cooper Square, 1965), 3:158, which equally lacks a religious dimension (and circulated in America).

6. Anne Curry, *Agincourt: A New History* (Stroud: Tempus, 2005), p. 250. Curry calls her epilogue "Battle or Murder?" (pp. 246–51), and while allowing for the "military necessity" of Henry's actions (p. 250), suggests that their contemporary reception may not have been unambiguous.

7. Anne Curry, *Battle of Agincourt*, passim. The battle is described, and its consequences considered, in Christopher Allmand, *Henry V* (Berkeley and Los Angeles: University of California Press, 1992), pp. 83–101, and in Curry, *Agincourt*, pp. 193–224. It is now sometimes thought that Henry's actions were further justified because the French had unfurled the Oriflamme, the war banner proclaiming that no mercy would be shown, nor quarter given. See, among other places, Michael Prestwich, *Armies and Warfare in the Middle Ages: The English Experience* (New Haven: Yale University Press, 1996), p. 240. Allmand notes the circumstances that attended upon Henry's execution of his prisoners, but remarks that the reasons "are not clear" (p. 94).

8. Both cited from Hirsh, *Medieval Lyric*, pp. 89–90, 64–69 (nos. 25, 19), at pp. 89, 65, 68.

9. See Paul Grosjean, *Henrici VI Angliae Regis miracula postuma. ex codice Musei Britannici Regio 13. C. VIII* (Brussels: Société des Bollandistes, 1935), esp. chap. 8, "De cultu Henrici VI," p. 234, superceding the prayers and poems concerning Henry preserved in a Trevalyan family manuscript prayer roll and printed by J. Payne Collier, ed., *Trevelyan Papers, Prior to A.D.1558*, 3 vols., Camden Society, ser. 3, 67, 84, 105 (London: Camden Society, 1857–72), 1:53–60.

10. All the poems cited are printed in Henry Noble MacCracken, ed., with Merriam Sherwood, *The Minor Poems of John Lydgate*, 2 parts, EETS o.s. 107, 192 (1911, 1934; repr. London: Oxford University Press, 1961, 1962), 2:613–51 (nos. 28–33).

11. Cited from Hirsh, *Medieval Lyric*, p. 195. On the Pudsay family, see James Raine, "The Pudsays of Barford," *Archaeologia Aeliana* (Society of Antiquaries of Newcastle-upon-Tyne), n.s. 2 (1858): 173–190. The poem is preserved in Oxford, Bodl. Lib. MS Don. e. 120, fol. 4r (the "Pudsay MS").

12. The last characteristic was widely understood and praised by contemporaries, though modern historians have accounted it a sign of weakness that contributed to civil war. See John Watts, *Henry VI and the Politics of Kingship* (Cambridge: Cambridge

University Press, 1996), passim. On Henry's reputation, see M. R. James, ed., *Henry the Sixth, a Reprint of John Blacman's Memoir* (1919; repr. Cambridge: Cambridge University Press, 1955); Ronald Knox and Shane Leslie, eds. and trans., *The Miracles of King Henry VI* (Cambridge: Cambridge University Press, 1923); and a popular account by Cardinal [Francis Aidan] Gasquet, *The Religious Life of King Henry VI by Cardinal Gasquet* (London: Bell and Sons, 1923), which contains a list of contemporary examples relevant to the *cultus* of Henry VI (pp. 119–34).

13. Simon Walker, "Political Saints in Later Medieval England," in *The McFarlane Legacy: Studies in Late Medieval Politics and Society*, ed. R. H. Britnell and A. J. Pollard (New York: St. Martin's, 1995), pp. 77–106 (p. 95). The details relating to Henry's stay at Bolton Hall are in Raine, "The Pudsays of Barford," p. 177. Henry may indeed have taken refuge there. Ralph A. Griffiths, *The Reign of King Henry VI: The Exercise of Royal Authority, 1422–1461* (Berkeley and Los Angeles: University of California Press, 1981), notes that Henry took refuge during the Battle of Hexham at nearby Bywell Hall, and "spent the following year on the run in northern England, where he could keep beyond the arm of Edward IV and rely on sympathizers to give him shelter and protection" (p. 888).

14. Qtd. from Douglas Gray, ed., *A Selection of Religious Lyrics* (Oxford: Clarendon Press, 1975), pp. 74–76 (no. 69), lines 9–16, 33–36.

15. Cited from John the Blind Audelay, *Poems and Carols (Oxford, Bodleian Library MS Douce 302)*, ed. Susanna Fein (Kalamazoo: Medieval Institute Publications, 2009), where the burden is printed at the end of each stanza. See also the edition in Hirsh, *Medieval Lyric*, pp. 195–99 (no. B9).

16. Robbins, *Historical Poems*, pp. 108–110 (no. 41). Robbins entitles Audelay's carol "A Recollection of Henry V (1429)," but notes that it was written "about the time of the coronation" when Henry was but ten years old (p. 305).

17. MacCracken and Sherwood, *Minor Poems*, 2:613–22 (no. 28). At 328 lines Lydgate's poem is much longer than Audelay's carol, but some of the compression present in Audelay's seems to assume some knowledge of Lydgate, or at any rate of the events it describes, which would have been familiar to most contemporaries.

18. Christopher Cannon, "Monastic Productions," in *The Cambridge History of Medieval English Literature*, ed. David Wallace (Cambridge: Cambridge University Press, 1999), pp. 316–48 (p. 344).

19. Griffiths, *Reign*, chapters "Education and Foundations," pp. 242–48 (p. 243), and "The King's Character," pp. 248–54 (p. 249). For a survey of modern historical attitudes toward Henry, including Griffiths's, see Watts, *Henry VI*, pp. 103–8.

20. Eugéne Vinaver, ed., *The Works of Sir Thomas Malory*, 3rd edn., rev. P. J. C. Field, 3 vols. (Oxford: Clarendon Press, 1990), 3:1242.

21. And yet the reference to "hethynes" is not in Lydgate and seems oddly to refer to a crusade of some sort, if only as a reaction to it. Possibly it may encode either an allusion or a memory of Bishop Henry Beaufort's participation in the crusade against the Hussites in Bohemia, a crusade that was encouraged by Pope

Martin V. Audelay prefers conversion. On the crusade against the Hussites, see Griffiths, *Reign*, pp. 82, 158.

22. See James Hutton, *Themes of Peace in Renaissance Poetry*, ed. Rita Guerlac (Ithaca: Cornell University Press, 1984), esp. pp. 44–49, 60–72. Hutton remarks that in the medieval period, "Lamentations over the ravages of war are not infrequent, but a positive celebration of peace would be hard to find" (p. 60). The medieval tradition of writing about peace is indeed complex, and as Hutton's relatively few remarks about Alain de Lille and Jean de Meun suggest, is often rooted in an understanding of Nature that supports a sometimes conflicted view of human action. Audelay's own complex treatment of the subject acknowledges the morally contingent attitudes that informed martial celebration, but reads them against his larger religious purpose.

23. MacCracken and Sherwood, *Minor Poems*, 2:785–91 (no. 64) (p. 791).

24. Hoccleve's position is detailed in Andrew Lynch, "'Manly Cowardyse': Thomas Hoccleve's Peace Strategy," *Medium Ævum* 73 (2004): 306–23 (pp. 313, 317.)

25. Robbins, *Historical Poems*, pp. 239–42 (no. 99). In a section Robbins calls "Will for Peace," he also prints Lydgate's "A Prayer for England" (pp. 235–39 [no. 98]; *IMEV, NIMEV* 2218; see also MacCracken and Sherwood, *Minor Poems*, 1:212–16 [no. 41: "A Prayer for King, Queen and People, 1429"]) and "Send Us Peace" (p. 242 [no. 100]; *IMEV* 1710).

THE ALLITERATIVE *THREE DEAD KINGS* IN JOHN AUDELAY'S MS DOUCE 302

Eric Gerald Stanley

Audelay's "Metrical Divinity"

Dr. Johnson begins his essay on criticism with this lofty sentence: "CRITICISM, though dignified from the earliest Ages by the Labours of Men eminent for Knowledge and Sagacity, and since the Revival of polite Literature, the favourite Study of *European* Scholars, has not yet attained the Certainty and Stability of Science."[1] I like to think of James Simpson as one, among English scholars, in the forefront of "men eminent for knowledge and sagacity," and so I was delighted to find that he too has a high opinion of at least some of Audelay's poetry. He calls the poem that appears as the second in Audelay's manuscript, Oxford, Bodleian Library MS Douce 302, folios 2r–8v, *Marcol and Solomon*, names mentioned significantly in the stanza headed "Vox populi vox Dei " (W2.66–78), and says of the poem, "John Audelay's almost unnoticed yet brilliant poem *Marcol and Solomon* (1,013 lines) is all the more remarkable for its discursive fluidity."[2] In Simpson's book the adjective *brilliant* is not used of many poems; I should not wish to detract from this supreme praise, though I should have chosen a less enthusiastic epithet for Audelay's "metrical divinity," as Joseph Ritson termed this area of Audelay's verse a little over two hundred years ago.[3] Simpson says that for a significant part of Audelay's oeuvre (presumably for at least the first eighteen poems that have come down to us in MS Douce 302)[4] the poet himself provides the title: "Audelay seems to entitle the whole collection *The Council of Consience*."[5] I agree with that, though I wish to read *Counsel* rather than *Council*, and I give the whole title as *The True Counsel of Conscience, Or the Ladder of Heaven*.[6] This title agrees with Audelay's *Epilogue*:

> Þe cownsel of conseans þis boke I calle,
>   Or þe ladder of heuen. I say fore-wy:
> Þer is no mon may clym vp a walle
>   Without a ladder sekyrly,
> No more may we to heuven on hye
>   Without treu cownsel of consians.
>   (W18.417–22)[7]

The poem, entitled in the manuscript *De tribus regibus mortuis* (Concerning Three Dead Kings), accords with Ritson's "metrical divinity." Its poet is praised—"he was so remarkably skilled"—by Angus McIntosh in a paper on the poem of which I have made frequent use in this paper.[8] That it is not thought to be an item of Audelay's oeuvre is in large measure attributable to philological localization, insufficiently informed with the literary likelihood, ultimately undemonstrable, that when a poet turns to heavily alliterative versified narration, away from verse less narrative and less heavily alliterative, he may look westwards for his differently winged words, as, for example, does Chaucer in London when writing alliterative verse in his account of the Battle of Actium in *The Legend of Good Women*, where at line 638 he introduces the word *heterly*; or he may look northwards, if, like Audelay, he is from the northwest Midlands.[9] The main hand (as also the second hand) of the manuscript is assigned in *LALME* to Staffordshire.[10] What little is known of Audelay's life associates him with residence in Shropshire, but of course his scribes may have been from Staffordshire. The evidence on which *LALME* bases its localizations of scribes is cumulative; no attempt is made to localize the author's own written language, and in the case of Audelay it may never have been available for a scribe to copy because, being blind, Audelay is not thought to have been able to write.

The Art of Rhyming and Alliterating

Of Audelay's poetry it has been said that his rhymes are very inexact, so that nothing can be safely deduced from them about how the authorial dialect may be at variance with the scribal dialect, deduced not even by those who have faith in rhymes as evidence of provenance, a faith I do not share.[11] Chaucer rhymed accurately, and he is a great poet, but, as I have said elsewhere, "it is not necessary for a poet to rhyme accurately to be a good poet," and there is the possibility always that in order to achieve a rhyme a poet may go beyond the borders of his own dialect to haul in a word or form of a word; he may even make up a grammatical form such as *miste* for *misse*, infinitive 'to fail'.[12]

Certain variation of stem vowels given in the *LALME* "Linguistic Profile" may be significant for rhyming: MS Douce 302 uses the following variants: *ane ~ eny ~ ony*; *ben ~ bun*; *came ~ come* pl.; *fyrth ~ forth* 'fourth'; *haþ ~ has*; *-ing ~ -and* pres. p.; *-ys ~ -yþ* pres. 3 sg.; *myȝt ~ maȝt* vb.; *moche ~ meche*; *ore ~ ere* 'ere'; *schul ~ schal ~ schil*; *seche ~ suche*; *syȝ ~ se ~ saw ~ sey* 'to see, saw' vb; *syn ~ sun*; *two ~ twey*; *þroȝ ~ þoroȝ*; *was ~ wes*. In alliterative verse—and, of course, *Three Dead Kings* alliterates regularly—rhyme may be regarded as a further ornament, so that Audelay may in such verse be even less exact in his use of rhyme than elsewhere. On the other hand, in this poem (as in the poem preceding it in the manuscript, headed "Pater noster qui es in celis," also regarded by some as not by Audelay), he seems to take a special delight alternating near-sounding rhyme words, that is, delight in pararhyme or half-rhyme. Thus, in the first stanza and similarly the sixth, the rhyme words (for which bold is used by me to indicate alliterative agreement, and a, b, c, and d refer to the pattern *ababababcdccd* of the thirteen-line stanza)[13] are as follows: lines 1–13, **bry**ȝt a, **bro**ȝt b, *a-ry*ȝt a, *þo*ȝt b, **se**ȝt[14] a, **so**ȝt b, **ny**ȝt a, **no**ȝt b, **þrow** c, **þrew** d, *blow* c, **how** c, **hew** d; and lines 66–78: **my**ȝt a, **my**ȝt (perhaps better emended to **ma**ȝt)[15] b, **sy**ȝt a, **sa**ȝt b, *ly*ȝt a, *la*ȝt b, *ty*ȝt a, *ta*ȝt b, **trow** c, **trew** d, *how* c, *row* c, *rew* d. It is by no means farfetched to seek and find further alliterative linking in these rhyme words, every one of which shares in the alliteration of its line.[16]

"Unfortunately Audelay's fondness for elaborate stanzaic forms was not matched by unusual skill in the making of rhymes," says Ella Keats Whiting, and then she spends several pages to demonstrate how inferior his art is.[17] It is true that occasionally he avails himself of what etymologists recognize as doublets to supply rhymes for his intricate scheme; thus, among examples given by Whiting: *coldis*, the form of the denominal verb derived from *cold* and collocated with heart, 'to shock the heart' (line 81); and *knoc kelddus*, perhaps 'chills the knuckle' (line 82).[18] In the body of the line, he resorts to *fold* (line 93) for *old*, in *faders of fold*, to provide an alliterative form.[19]

Exploiting the Resources of the Language for the Sake of Poetry

Audelay is not the only poet who exploits the linguistic resources of the language to show with what skill he pursues the craft of poetry. One thinks of the *Pearl* poet, who also combines alliterative ornamentation, less heavy than that in *Three Dead Kings*, with a rhyming stanzaic structure, though one less complex and therefore less technically demanding than in *Three Dead Kings*. He uses the doublets *lombe* also spelled *lomp(e* in wordplay with *lompe*, strikingly so in lines 1045–48, and Whiting and McIntosh have stressed that *Three Dead Kings* has much in common with the work of the poet who wrote *Sir Gawain and the Green Knight* and *Pearl*:[20]

> Of sunne ne mone had þay no nede:
>   Þe Self God watz her lombe-lyȝt,
> Þe Lombe her lantyrne withouten drede,
>   Þurȝ Hym blysned þe borȝ al bryȝt.

> (They had no need of sun or moon: God's Own Person was their lamp-light/Lamb-light, the Lamb their Lantern without doubt, the [Heavenly] City all brightly shone through Him.)

More extreme in doing violence to the language in order to fit the wording into a difficult poetic form is the *Pearl* poet's use of tmesis, *of- lyȝtly leme* for *lyȝtly of-fleme*, in lines 357–60:[21]

> Hys comforte may þy langour lyþe,
>   & þy lurez of- lyȝtly leme:
> For, marre oþer madde, morne & myþe,
>   Al lys in Hym to dyȝt & deme.

> (His solace can alleviate your misery, and can quickly drive away your sorrows: for [whether you] lament or rave, grieve or restrain yourself, it all lies in His power to dispose and ordain.)

That the prosodic scheme of *Three Dead Kings* was too difficult for the poet, or even that it would have been too difficult for any poet, is the judgment of Thorlac Turville-Petre: "[T]he author of 'De Tribus Regibus Mortuis' has at times to admit defeat. It is not that he is lacking in skill, but rather that he overloads his stanza with more complicating features than any poet could control with entire success. The poem can claim to be the most ornate in the language."[22] The recognition of technical difficulties as challenging artistic skill leads to a fuller understanding of medieval (and Renaissance) art, poetic and visual: the greater the self-imposed complexities, the greater the artist's triumph. For the scribe of MS Douce 302, however, the difficulties of the poem meant that he found it a more troublesome exemplar than usual. As McIntosh says:

It is clear from the number of obvious errors in it, considerably above the average for the manuscript as a whole, that no. 54 gave the scribe special difficulty. Evidently the highly complex form and the unusual diction were in places too much for him; besides, we do not know what errors may already have marred the text from which he made his own version. His task was not made easier by the fact that the original, if not the very text he copied, was almost certainly in a dialect distinctly more northerly than his own.[23]

The poet himself demonstrated how "the highly complex form" may have been felt to be "in places too much for him," for after concatenating the first and second stanzas—thus, line 13 "In holtes herde I neuer soche hew" (I never heard such din in the woods), echoed in line 14 "Soche a hew in a holt were hele to beholde" (It would be happiness to perceive such a din in a wood)—he did not use concatenation regularly, but only in seven of the eleven stanzas of the poem,[24] unlike the *Pearl* poet, who triumphed regularly over such self-imposed prosodic difficulties.

McIntosh attaches a footnote to the last sentence quoted above, to express his limited agreement with Bruce Dickins's view, later seconded by Turville-Petre, who summarized it thus: "*Kings* is however not by Audelay, for the poet's dialect is from further to the north; see Dickins (1932)."[25]

Stanzaic Art in MS Douce 302

There is good reason for thinking that *Three Dead Kings* is by Audelay, though the prevailing opinion, not shared by Norman Davis,[26] is that the poem is not by Audelay. The onus of proof is on those who think that it is not by him, for it is included in MS Douce 302 together with the poems by Audelay,[27] some (beginning with *True Living*, the acephalous first poem in the book) written in stanzas thirteen lines long. In some of them alliteration plays a significant prosodic role; for example, in the intellectually distinguished second poem, headed "De concordia inter rectores fratres et rectores ecclesie" (Simpson's *Marcol and Solomon*), which is also in thirteen-line stanzas, seventy-eight of them, that is, $13 \times 13 \times 6$.[28] As we have seen, in *Three Dead Kings*, however, the poet has set himself the task of producing thirteen-line stanzas of greater complexity than in any other poem in the manuscript, probably, as Turville-Petre has said, of greater complexity than in any poem in the English language: rhyming verse with alliteration, often involving not just a single initial consonant but often with initial double consonants providing a kind of heightened alliteration, and a further prosodic feature that involves final consonants.[29]

The Complex Rhyme Scheme Invites Emendation

The editors of the poem and commentators on it have rightly felt that they had to resort to emendation for some rhyme words, most often in the edition by Storck and Jordan.[30] In that edition as in Whiting's, the full complexity of the alliterative rhyme-scheme had not yet been recognized. Thus at line 42 a rhyme word is needed that alliterates on <s(c)h> and rhymes on <ew(e)>; the rhyme words are *fewe*, *lew* 'weak', *bewe* 'bend'.[31] Dickins uses the guidance provided by the complex prosodic scheme of the poem, involving both the initial consonant or consonants of the rhyme word as well as rhyme itself, when emendation seems to be called for: "It is a scheme that would tax the skill of the most ingenious rhymer. . . . Actually it enables one to postulate what the poet wrote with unwonted plausibility."[32] When the poet is driven by rhyme to use an unusual form of a word or of words, unfamiliar perhaps to the scribe, the scribe may have substituted a form more familiar to him. Thus Dickins suggests plausibly that somehow MS *at ens* has taken the place of an original *at s(c)heue* 'in view' as the rhyme word of line 42, though I prefer *at on scheue*, for that might better explain the manuscript reading:[33]

> Where þai not forþ gone fotis bot a fewe
>   Þai fondon feldus ful fayre & fogus ful fow.
> Schokyn out of a schawe þre schal[k]ys at [o]n s[ch]e[ue],
>   Schadows vnshene were chapid to ch[o]w
> With lymes long & lene & legges ful lew,
>   Hadyn lost þe lyp & þe lyuer seþyn þai were layd loue.
> Ther was no beryn þat þer was dorst bec nor bewe,
>   Bot braydyn here brydilys agayne, hor blongis can bl[ow].
>   (W54.40–47)

(They had hardly gone forth a few feet when they came upon very excellent fields and very brightly coloured meadows. Three men proceeded out of a grove in one showing, ugly ghosts were bodied forth to be seen with their long spindly limbs and very weak legs, they had lost lip and liver from the time they were buried. There was not a man there who dared either to nod or bow, but they jerked up their bridles again, and their horses did snort.)

Much of this translation is dependent on Whiting's, Dickins's, McIntosh's, and Turville-Petre's glossaries and notes, yet in some respects it remains contextual and doubtful.[34] My extension of Dickins's emendation, *at on scheue*, means 'in one showing', and that is not far in sense from the MS reading *at ens* 'at one and the same time', which may have replaced the authorial reading.[35] McIntosh thinks that lines with only two words alliterating could be improved by emendation (thus lines 4, 18, 66, 110, 137). He suggests emendation for some of them: for line 4 he accepts Turville-Petre's convincing emendation that *roʒt* be substituted for *poʒt*;[36] for line 18 McIntosh suggests reading *tome toke(n)* 'were enjoying their leisure' for *come trewle*, though scribal *trewle* for authorial *toke(n)* is not readily explicable; and for line 66 he suggests for *bes[po]ke þe ij kyng* that we might read *meled* (or *melte*) *þe middel* (or *midmest*) *kyng*. McIntosh has no improvements for lines 110 and 137. Since five of the eleven stanzas contain a line with only two alliterating syllables, and the ingenious emendators of the poem have not come up with even an unpersuasive emendation for two of the lines, I am content to accept the emendation of line 4 but to let the four other lines stand, alliterating less strongly than is usual in this poem, rather than try to fit in *fulle so fayre* in line 110 and rather than try to provide line 137 with an alliterating word such as a feeble *permyd* (with short vowel, and so not even rhyming perfectly with *glyde*, *ryde*, and *hyde*) for *þat tyde*. In each case we are dealing with two or more lines alliterating on the same sound, and in such a succession of lines one single line with only two words alliterating would be less obviously audible than in poems in which the norm is that the alliterative letter is confined to one line.

A Midlands Poet Northernizes When Writing Heavily Alliterative Narrative Verse

Philological analysis, such as Whiting and Dickins as well as McIntosh look to, and in which Turville-Petre and Putter seek support, is insufficient to determine if *Three Dead Kings* is or is not by Audelay and not in his dialect. Its inclusion in MS Douce 302, written by the main hand, weighs heavily in favor of Audelay's authorship. Its vocabulary is not identical with the lexis of the other poems, nor is that surprising. A poet of the early fifteenth century has a choice of modes: various rhyme schemes, various stanzaic forms, various degrees of alliteration are available, and if heavy alliteration is combined with narrative, the special vocabulary of alliterative narration is to be used. Of course, that makes the poet's language look superficially more northerly than the dialect of Shropshire or Staffordshire.

Nicholas Grimald, born in Huntingdonshire in 1519,[37] contributed alliterating blank verse to *Tottel's Miscellany*, and used, in "The death of Zoroas, an Egiptian Astronomer, in the first fight, that Alexander had with the Persians," the dialectal ending *-and* for the present participle, though more northerly than the Midlands; and he used *beurn* 'man, warrior' (< OE *beorn*) as well as *seg* (< OE *secg*) with a similar meaning, though both by his time archaic poeticisms.[38] His phrases *the shinand swoord*, *The boldest beurn*, and *the silly seg* are to be seen as far removed in word-geography from the language of Huntingdonshire and, more generally, from the southeast because, redolent of derring-do, they are placeless and timeless. Some morphemes, much lexis, and some syntax have, according to philological record, passed into desuetude, yet it lies within a poet's power to breathe into them new life, however Spenserian or even Romantic that may sound, and however feeble that life may seem in the case of a feeble practitioner of poetic art. It is at the poet's choice to seek language outside the geographical area circumscribed by birth and upbringing, yet made memorable by poets long dead. Whiting has diligently assembled words *Three Dead Kings* shares with *Sir Gawain and the Green Knight*, in order to demonstrate that it is not by Audelay.[39] As we have seen, some of those who followed her have been content to accept her verdict. The lexis of the *Pearl* poet and that of *Piers Plowman* are now readily accessible through concordances; we are no longer dependent on Rolf Kaiser's contribution to word-geography, a diligent doctoral thesis, but with more Middle English source material and especially place-name material available, Kaiser now provides only a rough guide.[40] The *MED* is now complete, and we can see whether the poet of *Three Dead Kings* has drawn, as if with modern partiality, on *Sir Gawain*, or whether he has, with late medieval literary self-consciousness made his deliberate choice, allying himself as a narrative poet with the poets of alliterative verse, more northern in their choice of words.

Notes on Some Words in Three Dead Kings

Some of the words used in *Three Dead Kings* deserve further consideration, not only because of their association with the language of other alliterative verse, but because of a variety of difficulties or other points of interest. A little over a quarter of a century ago McIntosh said that in his paper he had "not hesitated to call attention to difficulties that have hitherto been glossed over," and he expressed a hope "that this may lead to the poem being given fuller and closer attention than it has hitherto received." (p. 386). McIntosh's hope is my excuse for discussing some of the difficult and interesting words in the poem. I list them in alphabetical order: <c>

and <k> and similarly <i> and <y> are taken together, yogh is ranged between <g> and <h>.

amys (103) 'wrongly' < Scandinavian, cp. Icelandic *amys*. The adverb *amis* is used in this manuscript as a convenient rhyme word, at the same time supplying alliteration on *m*; thus *Marcolf* W2.450, but more usually in standard phrases with such verbs as *don* or *faren*. It does not occur in the *Pearl* MS (London, BL Cotton Nero A.x); it is common in southern texts, and is found in *Piers Plowman*.

arne (1) 'are' < Anglian *aron*. Whiting, p. xxxvii, mentions *arne* as a rare form found in *Gabriel's Salut*. W21.38, where it rhymes with *barne*. *OED* s.v. *be*, v., A. I. 1. d. *β*., records *arne* as late as 1528. Forms with /n/ (more usually without final <e>) occur in the *Pearl* MS and in manuscripts of *Piers Plowman*.

bedon (96) emended to *byndon* 'bind' < OE *bindan*. Jordan proposes the emendation, which has been accepted by all because it fits the rhyme and the sense; cp. s.v. *beton*, below.

beryn (46), **barns** (49) 'man' < OE *beorn*, a noun confined to alliterative verse and in frequent use. The form *barn* is rare and late, and may be influenced by ME *barn* < OE *bearn* 'child, youth', which is recorded in ME with the sense 'young warrior', and, when the reflexes of *beorn* and *bearn* had become indistinguishable, *barn*, whatever its etymon, can mean 'man' more generally. See *MED* s.v. *barn* n., 4., and *bern* n. (1). Jordan toys with the emendation *bales* 'misdeeds', but that gives no easier reading and is not accepted either into his edition nor into Whiting's, nor by Turville-Petre, who translates *Siche* [sic] *barns þai can hom bede* 'These men (the Dead) summoned them (the Kings)' (p. 153), and that seems preferable to McIntosh's suggestion; see *byde*, below.

besopke, the manuscript reading obviously for *bespoke* (66) 'spoke' < OE *sp(r)æc*.

beton (96) 'beat' < OE *beatan*, **beton** (97) 'atone for, make amends' < OE *betan*. There is wordplay, as Turville-Petre, p. 155, suggests, and so is there play on 'to bind', the rhyme words of lines 96–97: 'as you beat and bind those who disobey you, so you will be bound in torment unless you atone for that wrong', for which the editors emend *bedon* (the rhyme word of line 96) to *byndon*.

be tyme (130) 'in good time', prepositional phrase (often printed as one word by editors) < OE *bi, tima*. OE prepositional phrases with *tima* are *on* (*þam*, rarely *þone*) *timan* 'at (the) time', *ær* (. . .) *timan* 'before the appropriate or appointed time', *æfter timan* 'following the time', *fram (or of) þam timan* 'from the time', *ofer (his) timan* 'after (his) time', *oð (þone) timan* 'up to the time of . . .', *to . . . timan* 'to (the) time', *to timan* 'immediately', *foran to (or to foran) þam timan* 'before the time', *ymb(e) þone timan* 'at the time'; *to rihtes timan* means 'at the proper time'.[41] When in OE *be* occurs with a statement of time, it does not mean 'betimes' but 'with reference to' some specified time.[42] ME *betime(s* is common; however, it occurs only in one line in *Piers Plowman*[43] and does not occur at all in that sense in the *Pearl* MS, for in *Sir Gawain and the Green Knight* 41 *by tymez* is rightly glossed by Andrew and Waldron 'on occasions'.[44] It is noteworthy that *by tyme* 'betimes' occurs at *St. Erkenwald* 112.[45]

bewe (46) 'bend, change direction' < OE *bugan, biegan*. The verb is very common, though *MED*'s entry *bouen* v. (1) indicates that forms with <eu, ew> are rare.[46]

byde (49) emended to *bede* 'summon, ?advise' < OE *beodan, biddan*. Both Dickins, p. 518, and McIntosh, p. 388, have notes on the sense. The latter suggests the word might mean 'took thought' here, comparing reflexive uses of *avisen*, from OF usage;[47] but see *beryn, barns*, above.

byrchyn (1) 'birchen, covered with birch-trees' < OE *birc(e + -en*. Surprisingly, since *OED* refers to the occurrence in the Scottish poem *Golagros and Gawane* 31, *Birkin bewis about*, the use of 'birchen' with 'boughs' in this stanzaic alliterative poem, as in *Three Dead Kings*, has not been commented on.[48]

breme adverb (17), **brym** adjective (105) 'loud(ly' < OE *breme*. The alliterative phrase *brym bere* 'loud din' occurs in *The Wars of Alexander*. For the form *brym*, influence of *grim* has been suggested (thus *MED* s.v. *brim*), but s.v. *greme* adj. *MED* suggests that perhaps *breme* be read); the adjective *greme* occurs once only, in *Castleford's Chronicle*.[49]

cappid (127) 'wearing a fool's cap' < OE *cæppe* (noun). The sense here is well explained by McIntosh, p. 290, as 'off his head' with reference to Scottish *cappit*, and is accepted by Turville-Petre, p. 157; that seems more likely than the alternative 'wearing a cope or coif': line 127, 'unless he is a madman or a fool' rather than 'unless he is a cleric or a fool' (*kymyd* is discussed below).[50]

care (35) 'care, sorrow' < OE *c(e)aru*, emended for the rhyme to *chist* < OE *ceast* 'trouble, tribulation'. As McIntosh says, "*care*: the rhyme is defective and the word required is *chist*. The more normal form of this would be *chest(e)*, see *MED cheste* n. sense 2 'trouble, tribulation'. The emendation does not affect the sense" (p. 387). The unemended line is much like line

89, *Can Y no cownsel bot care*, and reminiscent of *Marcolf* W2.287, *Thus haue I cumford ȝou . . . & counsel ȝou fro care . . .* It is a likely speculation that the scribe came to write line 35 as he did—though that does not explain *mo no*, discussed below—because he knew that Audelay's habitual line of presenting his afflictions by such thoughts as, "I have no comfort but care," that is, "My only comfort is that my hope of joy in the next world is the recognition that in this world I had nothing but sorrows." The word *chist* is rare, and so the scribe substituted the more usual *care* for it. That the scribe's eye skipped forward to line 89 (or sideways because, as Putter, p. 515, hazards, his exemplar was in double-column format) requires some convincing parallel error in MS Douce 302 or evidence about the scribe's exemplar. The rare word *chist* is used in *Piers Plowman* in that sense, *cheste and meschaunce*, where the second noun means 'a state of unhappiness', and the first has the significant modernizing variant *sorov* or *sorowe*.[51] Rasmussen, §§ 97–101, has no example of <i> for long /ē/ < OE /ēa/; at line 56 the rhyme requires short /i/ in *fest* (see s.v. below), and the editors emend to *fyst*. whereas the MS form is unshortened with /ē/.

care me be cryst (58) with <c> twice for /g/ < Scandinavian cp. Icelandic *gøra* 'prepare, make someone + infinitive' and < OE *(a-)grisen* 'terrify'. McIntosh, p. 388, was the first to read the manuscript as *care* (not *cace*); he solved the crux as having arisen as a result of occasional <c> for /g/ in this manuscript (see Rasmussen, § 165). The usual spelling of *geren* in *Piers Plowman* is *garen*, perhaps <a> in this verb is due to the influence of the cognate *ȝaren* (cp. *MED* s.v. *yaren*) < OE *gierwan, gearwian* (and many variant forms) similar in meaning.[52] ME *grisen* is a strong verb not recorded with a past participle *grist*, but weak past forms are recorded (as also for the verb *agrisen*) with the ending *-ede*, etc., so that *grist* might have been produced for the rhyme here, or it may have been an available variant.

karpyng (52) 'saying' < Scandinavian, cp. Icelandic *karpa*. ME *carpen* is frequently used in alliterative verse, including that of the *Pearl* poet, especially for alliteration. It is common in *Piers Plowman*; for example, *Thus Conscience of Crist and of þe cros carpede*.[53]

kelddus (82) 'chills', cp. OE *cealdian*;[54] <dd> is explicable from *kelden*, and *MED* s.v. *colden* has a quotation with *keldeþ*, "Le regret de Maximian" from Oxford, Bodl. Lib. MS Digby 86.[55]

kymyd (127) to be emended to *kyme* 'simpleton, fool' (etymology obscure) to rhyme with *be tyme*. Dickins, p. 518, suggested the rhyme word is *kyme*, given in *OED* s.v. *kime*, with one quotation only, from *The Plowman's Tale* II.695, *the sely kyme* 'the innocent (or silly) wretch', according to its editor, but perhaps better translated 'wretched fool'.[56]

knaue (125) < OE *cnafa* 'child, male child, servant'. The sense of the word here is uncertain: Turville-Petre's edition provides no gloss for *knaue*, but cp. Whiting's glossary, 'one of low condition', and *MED* s.v. *knave*, 4. (a) 'A wastrel, good-for-nothing; rogue, knave, villain'. The word occurs in *Cleanness*, once meaning 'servant' and once meaning 'knave'; it is common in various senses in *Piers Plowman*, and in many other texts.

coyntons (124) 'acquaintance, ?entourage' < OF *cointance*. Jordan's somewhat obscurely worded note attached to *coyntons*, but referring to *poȝt me*, apparently suggesting that he would interpret *poȝt me* as 'considered myself', and the line therefore perhaps 'but I considered myself as ever so faultless a king of (his) entourage'.[57] The two ME verbs *thinken* might allow a reflexive construction with the sense 'to consider oneself', though that appears to be unusual. Slightly unusual too would be the function of *of*; it seems more than a mere prepositional equivalent of a genitival relationship of the type 'England's king' = 'king of England', meaning rather 'a king in relation to his entourage'. It is preferable to translate the line, 'but never did a king with his entourage seem to me so faultless (as I am)'.

comys (132) the alliteration on /g/ and the relative frequency with which <c> is written for /g/ in this manuscript make it likely that the word is *gomys* 'men' < OE *guma*. See Rasmussen, § 165; therefore McIntosh, p. 390, suggests <g> should be read for <c>; he rightly rejects *MED* s.v. *come*, n. (2), 'guest, stranger', which accepts Whiting's glossary entry, "comys, *sb. pl.* strangers 54.132. OE. cuma" (p. 270), an interpretation that finds support only in uses of OE *cuma* in very late copies of OE texts. Whiting's explanation is based on Jordan's note.

kouþyn (134) 'got to know, recognized' < OE *cunnan*, preterite plural *cuþon*. It is unlikely that *kouþyn* governs, as an auxiliary verb, an infinitive *rade*. If, as suggested by McIntosh, p. 390, it does so govern *rade*, and that is a verb, *kouþyn* must be a lexical verb, 'knew how to *rade*'. The explanation given by Turville-Petre, p. 157, is preferable: he translates the verb as 'recognized'. Instead, the sense given in *MED* s.v. *connen* 5. (a) 'come to know' may be better. Cp. *rade*, below.

kraft (34) 'skill' < OE *cræft*. As McIntosh, p. 387, says, ME *craft connen* means 'be master of a skill, be resourceful', and the half-line *fore kraft þat I can*, with intercalated *I* (as in Turville-Petre, p. 152), means 'for all the skill of which I am capable'. At *Pearl* 890 the poet uses *craftez . . . þay knewe* 'the skills, or arts, they were good at';[58] that locution comes quite often in *Piers Plowman*. It alliterates, but is not confined to alliterative discourse.

donyng (19) 'din, confused noise' < OE *dynian*. Turville-Petre emends to *tonyng* 'making musical notes'; and he similarly emends at line 64 *connyg* 'expertise (of hunting)' to *tounyng* (though two alliterating syllables only are not infrequent in the short lines of the wheel); he does so on the grounds that "[i]n this ms. voiced and voiceless initial consonants (/d/ and /t/, /g/ and /k/ are sometimes interchanged; see Whiting (1931: xxxiii)" (p. 151). She, however, tells us significantly that there is only one instance of /d/ written <t>, none of /t/ written <d>, while he compares *comys* for *gomys* line 132, discussed above. He thinks the poet of this poem (and, I presume, in his view also Audelay, whom he regards as not the poet of this poem) distinguished voiced from voiceless, unlike the scribe of MS Douce 302. If however, the poet (or poets), like the scribe, thought them near enough for alliteration there is no need to emend. There is in the alliteratively less strict *Marcolf* W2.342, perhaps alliteration of /t/ with /d/ as well as alliteration on /s/: **S**aynt **T**homas **s**oferd **d**eþ; and note initial /t/ and /d/ chiming in the alliteration of *Marcolf* W2.937–38:

> ȝe most haue **t**reuþ & ryȝtwysnes in ȝour **d**emyng:
> Þen let **t**reuþ **d**ele to hym boþ merce and grace.

After all, poets may not be as prosodically strict as are philologists, especially philologists brought up on the metrically exact *Beowulf*.

dore (91) 'door' < OE *dor, duru*. The phrase *ditten dor* is well recorded in alliterative verse; cp. *MED* s.v. *ditten*, 1b., 'block (a doorway)': *dor* is used in a sense wider than just 'door, gate'. In "The Man in the Moon" 14 the word is used of gaps in a hedge. Here it may mean, as Turville-Petre, p. 155, suggests, something like 'escape route'; the word is also used in Old English and Transitional English of the gate of heaven, that is, of entry to a place one wishes to enter rather than escape out of; thus several times in the Blickling Homilies, and once in Oxford, Bodl. Lib. MS Bodley 343.[59]

dred (128) 'fear' < OE *-drædan*. McIntosh, p. 390, suggests that for *dred* the original reading may have been *dre* 'suffer' (< OE *dreogan*), and he would then translate the line, 'act in such a way that you do not suffer the ultimate penalty'. That verb, written *dryȝe*, etc., occurs several times in the

Pearl MS. Yet 'dread' goes habitually with doomsday; thus in the Kildare MS version of "Earth upon Earth" 76, *And dred þe of þe dome lest sin þe schend*; in *Piers Plowman*, A.8.171, *At þe dredful dom whanne dede shal risen*; and the burden of the doomsday carol in MS Sloane 2593, merrily jingling, but not quite so jolly as it ends in *drydful domisday*. Doomsday is to be dreaded in this world, long before it has to be endured; and an original reading *dre*, though not impossible, seems unlikely, unless it is thought that in transmission an easier reading was substituted for a harder reading.[60]

feldus (85) emended to *foldus* (to improve the rhyme) 'bends' < OE *ge-)fieldan* (weak), *fealdan*, Anglian *faldan* (strong). The manuscript has *feldus* as the rhyme word of both lines 85 and 86; at line 85 the sense is 'bends' with reference to *flagge* 'reed'; at line 86 the sense is 'clutches', that is, of the fingers of the hand, clutching convulsively for *ferdchip* 'fear'.

ferdchip (86) 'fear' < ME *ferd(e*, cp. *fered, afered* < OE *afæred* + *scip*. The suffixed noun is rare according to *MED* s.v. *ferdship*, occurring in alliterative verse in *The Wars of Alexander*, where Dublin, Trinity College MS 213 [*olim* MS D.4.12] has, wrongly, *frendshipys*, a less unfamiliar word, for *ferdschip* in Oxford, Bodl. Lib. MS Ashmole 44.[61]

ferys (109) 'companions' emended to *fere* 'group of companions' to improve the rhyme < OE *gefer*. Dickins, p. 518, proposed the emendation, as also of *lerys* line 111 to *lere* 'learn, study', second person plural with loss of final /n/.

ferle (109) 'marvel' < Scandinavian, cp. Icelandic *ferligr*. The ME word is used frequently in *Piers Plowman* and the *Pearl* MS. The use here is close to uses in *Piers Plowman*, thus *ferly me þynkeþ*, and to the negative use in *Sir Gawain and the Green Knight* 2414, *hit is no ferly*.[62]

fest (56) 'fist' emended to *fyst* for the sake of the rhyme < OE *fyst*. Spellings with <i> or <y> (as in the emendation, first by Jordan) show normal shortening before final /st/; the change is sporadic, and <e> is probably not the result of <i> and <e> confusion in this manuscript.[63]

fogus ful fow (41) 'very brightly colored meadows' < a Scandinavian word + OE *ful* + *fah*. The words are well explained by McIntosh, p. 387. The word *fogge* occurs in *Cleanness* 1683, where it means 'grass'; it is rare.[64]

fore (32) 'on account of', (34) 'despite, for all' < OE *for*. McIntosh, p. 387, invokes for both lines 32 and 34 the sense 'despite' recorded in ME. The sense 'on account of' is preferable at line 32. Turville-Petre, p. 152, having forced the sense 'earth' on *lare*, interprets the line to fit in with that sense, with *fore* as 'in consequence of'.

fotis (40) 'feet' < OE *fotas*. ME *fotes* is not uncommon. In OE verse, where the meter requires disyllabic *fotas*, it is used several times instead of monosyllabic *fet*.[65]

frayns (109) 'ask!' < OE (Anglian) *frægnan*. McIntosh, p. 389, explains *frayns* < OE *gefrægnan* as 'find out', but that is far from certain: both 'ask, inquire' and 'find out, learn (by asking)' are quite common in ME, though the former is more common, and I have found no example of the sense 'learn' with *at* 'from'.

gar (15) quasi-auxiliary verb 'cause something to be done'. The word is among long-recognized northernisms, and any ME northernizing poet might well use it, as does Chaucer when he makes the northern scholar John use it in *The Reeve's Tale* I(A) 4132:[66] "Gar vs haue mete and drynk & make vs chere."

glydyn (131) 'glide, proceed' < OE *glidan*. The rhyme with *tyde* requires *glyde* with omission of final <n>; see Dickins, p. 518. Rasmussen, §§ 208, 210, shows that present indicative plural forms are found both with and without final <n>.

grayþ (131) 'ready', **grayþle** (132) 'readily' < Scandinavian, cp. Icelandic *greiðr* + OE *-lice*. The quotations in *MED* show that these ME words and the verb *greithen* (and derivatives) occur frequently, and not only in *Piers Plowman* and the *Pearl* MS; specialized senses are used in the Wycliffite Bible versions.

gre (57) '?shudder'. In MS Douce 302 /ē/ spelled <e> is found occasionally where <ye> might be expected; thus *dee* 'die' in *Visiting the Sick* W11.355 in rhyme with *be* and *charite*. The verb *gre* may be compared with *gryed*, probably a doublet but spelled with <ye>, occurring only in *Sir Gawain and the Green Knight* 2370, *So agreued for greme he gryed withinne* 'so overcome with mortification he shuddered within himself'. This phonaesthetic word is probably a doublet of ME *gruen*, with cognates in the closely related West Germanic languages.[67] The verb is common in northern dialects.[68] McIntosh, p. 388, rightly rejects the emendation to *grede* proposed by the earlier editors, and suggests emendation to *gru(e)* or *grise* 'shudder'.

hede þenke (122) 'capital thing', probably in origin an attributive use of the noun *hede* < OE *heafod* 'head' + *þing*. *MED* has an entry for *hed* as an adjective; it is better regarded as the first element of a compound, as it is in *A Dictionary of the Older Scottish Tongue* s.v. *Hede*, n.[1], 12.c. That use does not occur in the *Pearl* MS nor in *Piers Plowman*, but is found in alliterative verse in *Mum and the Sothsegger* 117, *heed dere* 'chief deer', and *The Destruction of Troy* 1925, *hede rewmes* 'chief countries', 2213, *hede shame* 'great cause for shame', and 10902, *hed maidons* 'highly honoured maidons'.[69]

heme & . . . hyne (123) 'villagers and rustics' < OE *-hæme, higan (hiwan)*. The meaning of the phrase has been much discussed, most recently by Neil Cartlidge.[70]

hene (122) 'treat with contempt' < OE *hynan*. According to *MED* s.v. *henen*, this is the last occurrence of the verb; *henen at* occurs nowhere else. McIntosh, p. 390, thinks it possible that *at* may be an error for *al*.[71]

hengyr (136) emended by the editors (first by Jordan) to *hen[d]yr* 'more gracious, kinder' < OE *gehende*. The meaning of ME *hende* embraces a wide range of favorable qualities, and may well have become so hackneyed as to be used ironically, as by Chaucer when he refers to *hende Nicholas* in *The Miller's Tale*.[72] In the use of the comparative here, qualifying *hert* 'heart', there is no irony; Putter, p. 526, translates it 'humbler'; see s.v. *hew* (135), below. Perhaps 'kindlier' is better.

hew (13) 'noise', ***how!*** (13) < AN and OF *hu!, hou!* The dictionaries provide well to explain the various meanings of this interjection and noun, and its derivatives.[73] The phonology of ME *hew* and *how* is to be accounted for by the two Romance forms with different vowel, *hu* with /ȳ/ and *hou* with /ū/; in a West Midland area in which /ȳ/ is retained in native words *hu* > *hew*: it has not suffered unrounding to /ī/ nor, as further north, merged with /ū/. Romance *hou* is not much changed in vocalic quality and quantity, and the word is usually written *how*, as here.[74]

hew (135) 'color, complexion' < OE *hiew, heow. MED*, s.v. *heu* n. 2.(b) supported by *hide* n. (1) 1. (b), is probably not right to regard *be hew ne be hyde* and *of hyd and hew* as set phrases, in this single instance generalized to 'entirely, in every way', or, in the rendering of McIntosh, p. 390, 'in any way at all'. Putter, pp. 525–26, is right to point out that in other "attestations . . . the literal sense of the words remains operative," and his expansion of contracted *p's* to *pris*, not *pres*, is persuasive. The phrase *holden pris* is well attested. At the end of the poem the kings reform (in Putter's translation), 'they never attached preeminent value to complexion or skin, but had a humbler heart forever after'; cp. *hengyr*, above.

-hyʒtus (115) 'highest' < OE *heah* and *hiehðu* + superlative ending. Cp *MED* s.v. *height* adj. for the form of the stem. The reduction to <us> of the superlative ending *-est*, in this manuscript written <ust, ist, est> (see

Rasmussen, § 185), is difficult seeing that final /t/ appears to be stable; perhaps all that is involved is that the scribe got confused by the rhymes in this stanza (see *hyust*, below) and so blundered within the line as well as at the end.[75]

hyust (115) the rhyme requires *hyus*, 'dost hie, dost hasten' < OE *higian*. Cp. *wryust*, below. The word was understood by the editors and commentators as 'highest', and they introduce a mark of punctuation at the end of the line (Putter a comma, Whiting a semicolon, Turville-Petre a full stop), instead of running on, 'and you hasten away from this world'. The verb is common in ME, common in the *Pearl* MS, and it occurs in *Piers Plowman*.

hope (verb) (32) 'assume; believe, think' < OE *hopian*. Cp. McIntosh, p. 387, for the sense here, very common elsewhere in ME, beside the sense 'hope'.

husbondus (122) 'villein, rustic' < late OE *husbonda*. The sense was well understood by Jordan, who glosses the noun 'kleine bauern', and then renders it more freely 'arme leute'.

lagmon (114) remains obscure; the explanations by Robert J. Menner and McIntosh, however, are attractive, and that by Menner underlies *MED*'s sense 'last or hindmost person' given s.v. *lag-mon*.[76] Nothing has more intensely led to connecting *Three Dead Kings* with *Sir Gawain and the Green Knight* than the coincident occurrence of this word in these two poems and nowhere else.

layþe (70, 118) 'loathsome, foul, putrid' < Scandinavian, cp. Icelandic *leiðr*. Audelay uses the adjective at *Marcolf* W2.536 of the beggar Lazarus (Luke 16:19–24), traditionally identified with Lazarus of Bethanie, brother of Martha and Mary (John 11:1–44), described as stinking because dead for four days (John 11:39). *MED* s.vv. *lōth*, n. and adj., does not distinguish the word of Scandinavian origin from the native word < OE *lað*: the forms are similar, and the senses overlap. The alliterative formula *ljúfr ok leiðr* has its parallel in English both in alliterative verse and outside it.[77] The native and the Scandinavian word occur together as *leiðe & lo[dl]ike* (MS *loldike*) in the alliterative "Spider" passage of *The Middle English Physiologus*, line 314.[78]

lare (112) 'teaching' < OE *lar* (> *lore* line 111). Turville Petre, p. 156, suggests that at line 112 the word has the figurative sense of 'earth, filth'; cp. *MED* s.v. *leir* n. (2), < Scandinavian, cp. Icelandic *leir(r)* 'mire (of sin)', which occurs (spelled *laire*) twice in *The Wars of Alexander*, in literal senses, 'earth, clay'.[79] Probably *þat lare* refers to the teaching of the flesh, and presumably *hit* in line 113 (twice) refers back to it. Whether paronomasia is likely or even possible depends on the acceptability of the spelling *lare*, found in very late spellings of place-names; see *MED* s.v. *leir* n. (2). It is to be regarded as a graphemic development in late northern ME, with which Scottish spellings, with <ar> alternate with <air> may be compared.[80] The subtle use of rhyme in this poem raises other aspects involving the form *lare*. In MS Douce 302 /ā/ is found in rhyme, against the usual graphemic practice of writing long <o>; thus (the vowel involved is printed bold) *Marcolf* W2.201–3[81] c**a**re / l**a**re; *Marcolf* W2.859–64 decl**a**re / **a**re / f**a**re / s**a**re; *Virtues of the Mass* W9.46–47 g**a**se 'goest' / f**a**ce; *Holy Innocents Carol* 1–3 (W36.3–5) b**a**ba / w**a** w**a** / ag**a**. It is a matter of opinion whether we regard the occasional use of /ā/ as a dialectal phenomenon, that is, that the poet was near an isoglossic border operative at his time and place, or whether the need to find a rhyme has driven him to go further north than his own area of operation, or whether, most probably, both these factors are at play in MS Douce 302. To provide a rhyme, the poet uses *lare* instead of *lore*; *lare* for *laire* is unlikely. See further the discussion of *(ham) lykyd . . . lare*, below.

lede (26) 'man' < OE *leod*. The word, variously spelled, is common in all alliterative verse including that of the *Gawain* poet, *Piers Plowman*, and *The Wars of Alexander*.

leke (119) 'leek' < OE *leac*. As Whiting says, "The legs of the ghost wound in linen cloth are likened to the leek with its many layers of skin" (p. 259); more revolting still, the leek is white except insofar as it has grown discolored, reminiscent of gangrene.

lele (39) 'truly' < OF *lëal*, AN *leel* + adverbial ending < OE *-lice*. The adverb and the adjective *lel* are common in the *Pearl* MS and in *Piers Plowman*, but in Audelay the adverb is often—perhaps also here—little more than a stock asseveration introduced mainly for the sake of the alliteration.[82]

(ham) lykyd . . . lare (25) 'liked . . . teaching' < OE *lician, lar*. The reflexive verb *lykyd* is so common as to be of little interest, and so is the noun *lare*, except that Turville-Petre, p. 152, has an unnecessary emendation and a note that forces a strained meaning on an easy line: *lare* is taken to be from ME *leir(r)* 'earth' of Scandinavian origin, discussed above, in connection with *lare* at line 112. (He uses that interpretation of *lare* again to make sense of *honor of erþ* at line 32.) Lines 25–26 mean, 'Being lorded over did not please them in teaching any man who wants to listen and learn', or, as Whiting says, 'they liked no guidance in teaching' (p. 256).

lykyr (94) 'more likely to' < OE *ge)lic(c)ra*, and Scandinavian, cp. Icelandic *g-likare*. Turville-Petre, p. 155, emends to *lytyr*, in which, regardless of the absence of yogh, he sees a pun on 'lighter' (one among several puns in his interpretation), because he wishes to associate it with the proverbial *as light as lef on linde* (MED s.v. *lind(e* 1b.). The half-line *Now ȝe beþ lykyr to leue*, however, means 'now you are more likely to leave', and the second half-line *þen leues on þe lynde* means 'than leaves on the lime-tree'. Here the proverbial lightness of the leaves of the lime-tree in autumn, when they are very ready to fall, may be played with, but not punningly.[83] McIntosh, p. 389, thinks *beþ lykyr to leue* means 'have more lust for life': *to leue* is taken to mean 'to live', but whether *beþ lykyr* can really mean 'have more lust for' is questionable, and whether the lords from every habitation from Argyllshire to London have some particular lust for life seems questionable too (see n. 85, below).

lynde (94) 'lime-tree' < OE *lind(e* + Scandinavian, cp. Icelandic *lind*. I fail to understand the emendation of *lynde* to *lynde[n]* (thus Whiting's text, followed by Turville-Petre). Modern English *linden* is not recorded as a noun till the sixteenth century according to OED s.v. Admittedly, the rhyme is imperfect, monosyllabic *lynde* with silent final <e> does not rhyme exactly with disyllabic *fynden* and *wyndon*; but, though the noun was weak in OE, no ME weak forms are recorded, and if it is desired to improve the rhyme, it would be better to leave off the <n> and write *fynde* and *wynde*, for final <n> is left off from verbal endings very frequently in this manuscript.[84]

lyus (113, 114), at line 113 the verb 'lies (speaks in falsehoods)' < OE *leogan*; at line 114 the noun 'lies, falsehoods' (< OE *lyge*), perhaps to be emended to *leus* to rhyme with *wreus* line 117, since <us> is in this manuscript a common spelling for the plural ending (see Rasmussen, § 176). Forms with /e+ȝ/ > /ē/ are found in rhyme, thus in *Visiting the Sick* W11.141 (cp. the discussion of *ne* 'nigh', below), and the poet often plays with complicated doublets in the rhymes of *Three Dead Kings*. It is fairly certain that *be lyus* (read *be leus*) here means 'by falsehoods', as Whiting's glossary says; her translation is convincing: 'why should you believe it . . . , since it lies; it leads you astray by lies . . .' (p. 258). Turville-Petre, p. 156, however, takes *lyus* (he emends to *leus* for the rhyme) to be 'over the fields', which he extends to mean 'all over the place', for which MED s.v. *lei(e* n. (3) gives no warrant.

Loron (95) 'Lorne'. It seems odd that Lorne in Argyllshire should have been singled out for a comment, unless it were for some topical allusion involving the nobles of the Campbell family in the early fifteenth century. Were the lords of Lorne in the north as keen to leave their ancestral estates as were lords of London in the south? There is a danger, whenever topical allusions are to be substantiated, that stray items of information are too readily seized on.[85]

losse (143) 'perdition' < OE and Scandinavian *los*. It appears, from *MED* s.v. *los* n. (1) 3. (b), that the sense 'perdition, damnation' is particularly Wycliffite; in *Piers Plowman* the word is used only of 'loss of possessions'. In the *Pearl* MS the word is used of 'damage, injury' with reference to one's possessions (the primary meaning of the word) or to having drawn a losing lot; it is never used of the soul's 'perdition' as in the concluding word of the prayer ending this poem.

lost past participle (39) 'lost' < OE *losian*; cp. *leosan*; the two verbs have merged in ME. The rhyme requires the past participle form *lest*, and the editors emend it accordingly.

masse (139) 'mass' < OE *mæsse*. I fail to understand why McIntosh regards *masse* 'mass' as a sense that "would scarcely fit here" (p. 390). The phrase *here . . . masse* is used also in *Marcolf* W2.33. Would they not have celebrated the completion of a minster church with a mass? His attempt to read the word as a form of *MED*'s *mes* n. (3) 'dwelling house, messuage' is unpersuasive.

masse (140) the rhyme requires *mos(se* 'bog, moor' < OE *mos*. Dickins, p. 518, was the first to suggest the emendation, which has been further explained by McIntosh, p. 390. The manuscript reads *þen men on þe masse*, and *þen* is emended to *þe* by all. The word *mos* occurs at *Sir Gawain and the Green Knight* 745, not as a toponym, but as the plant-name, 'moss, lichen'. In the verse quotations given in *MED* s.v. *mos* n. (1), 2., the toponym is always combined with a synonym: *The mosse and þe marrasse; for myre ne mos; through marris, mosse, & myre*. It stands alone only here and in topographical records. McIntosh would wish for an identifiable place, presumably 'the Moss', but successful identification is unlikely in view of the wide geographical distribution of the term: what McIntosh is looking for is a "topographically eligible church which has or had appropriate murals . . . in the north west Midlands."[86]

men (30) 'fellowship', cp. OE *gemæne*. Thus McIntosh, p. 387.

mete (30) '(table-)companions' < OE *gemetta*, cp. MLG *māt*. McIntosh, p. 387, dismisses too lightly as unconvincing Whiting's solution that *mete* is derived from OE *gemetta*. The spelling with a single <t> may be due to the influence of MLG *māt* > ME *māte* n.[87] The word occurs twice in the same passage in the B and C Texts of *Piers Plowman*, and, as often, the textual variants give us some insight into late Middle English understanding and misunderstanding.[88] McIntosh's solution (followed by Turville-Petre, p. 152), draws on Scandinavian parallels to suggest an otherwise unrecorded ME borrowing: *mete* 'party', here 'hunting party'. The *Piers Plowman* variants indicate that the word was well understood as 'mate, fellow', and emendation of *mete* to *metes* is an easier solution. I agree with McIntosh that a weak plural from earlier weak -*n*, < OE *gemettan*, is unlikely.

myȝt, emend to **maȝt** n. (67) 'might' < OE *meaht*. The editors agree in emending to *maȝt* in order to improve the rhyme, and to match the rhyme words *syȝt* and *saȝt* and *lyȝt* and *laȝt* of the next four lines, as well as to avoid what looks like *rime très riche* (if the rhyme pattern is ignored), with *of myȝt* as the rhyme in these two lines. That might not be a sufficient reason for rejecting the MS reading since rich rhyme was used by Middle English versifiers, but perhaps not in MS Douce 302. The emended form *maȝt* would be exceptional in this manuscript; cp. *Marcolf* W2.310, *Salut. to Christ's Body* 19 (W8.25), *Visiting the Sick* W11.57, etc. I do not know what the dialectal distribution of the noun *maȝt* is. The form does not occur in the *Pearl* MS and would be aberrant if it were to occur in any *Piers Plowman* manuscript.[89]

mynn (29, 104) 'remind, remember' < Scandinavian, cp. Icelandic *minna*. The collocation of *mynn* and *mas* (104) is not very common in ME; both the verb and the noun occur in *Piers Plowman*, but they are not collocated. It is therefore worthy of note that the version in this manuscript of *De meritis misse*, *Virtues of the Mass*, also has the collocation at W9.197, and, less close, W9.164–65, 337–38.[90]

myschip (137) 'trouble' < OF *meschief*. *MED* regards the spelling *mischip* as an error; but *myschip* occurs also in Audelay's *Henry VI Carol* 81 (W39.57), and the native suffix *-ship* has replaced the French ending.

mo adv. (35) 'more' < OE *ma*, preceding *no* is unusual, *no mo . . . bot* 'no greater . . . other than' would be normal and would give good sense.

mon (78) 'must, shall', < Scandinavian, cp. Icelandic *munu*. Putter, p. 505, has noted that the verb comes only here in MS Douce 302. Following *MED* s.v. *mannen* v., 2., he accepts a suggestion made by Robert J. Menner to Whiting, who records it in her note on *Marcolf* 344 (p. 230), but does not make use of it. Menner based his interpretation on eighteenth-century quotations in *OED* s.v. *boothall* 'town hall' in Gloucester; there were no earlier uses readily available then, but they are since 1997.[91]

Kaiser, *Zur Geographie*, lists *mon* as a "Nordwort," but where does "North" begin? The Thornton *Alliterative Morte Arthure* is a northernized text from further south; Kaiser lists it in support, without revealing the distribution of *mon* and *mot, most* in that text: according to Kiyokazu Mizobata's *Concordance*, the "Nordwort" comes only five times whereas *mot(t), mote, moste* comes 23 times.[92] One swallow does not make a summer, and one use of *mon* does not make a northern text.

morþis (121) 'murders, heinous crimes' < OE *morþ*, and Scandinavian, cp. Icelandic *morð*.[93] The word does not occur in the *Pearl* MS, nor in *Piers Plowman*; it occurs in other alliterative verse and is common in Laʒamon's *Brut*. That the Otho MS more than once reads *morþre* where Caligula has *morðe* may indicate that *morþ* was obsolescent.[94] However, *morþ* is used several times in *The Destruction of Troy* (spelled *murthe*), and it occurs in *The Wars of Alexander*, so that too much should not be made of the difference between Caligula's *morðe* and Otho's *morþre*.

ne (7) 'nearly' < OE *neah, neh*. Whiting avers boldly, "*Ne* is a northern and West Midland form of *nigh*" (p. 256). The development of OE /ǣᵃx/ to ME /ɛ̄/, ME /ē/, /nī/ is not confined to this word in MS Douce 302: thus *Visiting the Sick* W11.141 *heuen on he* in rhyme with *shal be* and *truly*, *St. Stephen Carol* 13 (W34.11) in rhyme with *maieste* and *to þe*, but 'high' is more usually spelled *on hye*, as in *Visiting the Sick* W11.246 in rhyme with *mercy* and *Mare* ('Mary'); *LALME* 3:454 (Linguistic Profile 189), lists *ne* as a form of 'nigh' for this manuscript.[95] In fact, *ne*, *ny*, and *nye* are not uncommon in manuscripts roughly contemporary with MS Douce 302. In *Piers Plowman* manuscripts they occur among variants often rejected by the editors.[96]

[*no*] (125). A negative is required, and the editors, first Jordan, have inserted *no*. Turville-Petre, p. 157, emends *is* to *nis*. That by itself is hardly sufficient, and perhaps we should read *Now [n]is þer [no] knaue*, or *Now [n]is þer [neu*er*] knaue* (with -*er* suspended).

of fold (93) '?earthly' < OE *?of folde*. The usual ME prepositional phrase is *(up)on folde* 'on earth'; the much rarer *of folde*, as used in *Pearl* line 334, means 'away from the world'. McIntosh, p. 389, says that the phrase *of fold* here means 'earthly'; if so, the preposition has to be emended to *on*, or has to be understood as *o fold* for *on fold* miswritten *of fold*. Jordan emended *of fold* to the common phrase *of old*; but that would reduce the alliteration of the line. Whiting's note may well be right: the unemended phrase stands for *of old* by metanalysis (cp. n. 19, above): "*old* is spelled *fold* for the sake of the alliteration" (p. 258).

pres (135). See *hew* (135), above.

rade (134), ***rad(de)le*** (78, 133) 'quickly, readily, immediately' < OE *hræþe, hrædlice*. McIntosh discusses the use of the word in lines 78 and 133, and gives the sense as 'immediately, forthwith' (p 389). In MS Douce 302 the word is found with the sense 'readily' rather than 'immediately', thus *Marcolf* W2.8 (*redle*), 212 (*redely*), 262 (*redele*); it occurs in *Sir Gawain and the Green Knight* (five times), and (as an asseveration) in *Piers Plowman*. The most that can be said is that, as so often, the distinction, either 'readily' or 'immediately', is too absolute for Middle English; in Modern English we may prefer to use for some occurrences the one sense rather than the other. The use at line 134 is disputed: McIntosh, p. 390, takes *rade* to be derived from OE *rædan* (preterite *radde*), and takes it to be a present form of ME *reden* (with the /a/ perhaps the result of Scandinavian influence, cp. Icelandic *ráða*); and he provides it with a contextual meaning 'guide', rejecting Whiting's (I think preferable) interpretation, p. 259, 'to discern, or perceive' with the same etymology; similarly Jordan, with the gloss 'erkennen'. The adverb is common in MS Douce 302, and in this poem Turville-Petre, p. 157, has 'immediately' in his translation of the line, 'The men immediately (*rade*) recognised the red rays of daylight'. Cp. *kouþyn*, above.

rede (84) 'ready' < OE *ge)ræde* + *-i(g*; final <e> of *rede* = /i/ or /ī/. The phrase 'ready way' is well documented in *MED* s.v. *rēdī* adj. (3), 3. McIntosh, p. 389, draws attention to the fact that the phrase comes also in *Marcolf* W2.596. It occurs frequently in ME carols.[97] It is not a characteristic locution of alliterative verse, and occurs in neither the *Pearl* MS nor *Piers Plowman*.

redyn (133) 'agree together on, decide' < OE *rædan*. *MED reden* v. (1) demonstrates how polysemous this verb is; Whiting's glossary s.v. *rede*, v.[2], gives 'advise, agree' for the sense here, and 'to agree' is *MED*'s sense 10. (b), whereas sense 10. (a) is 'to decide', the sense favored by Turville-Petre in his glossary.

rerde (3) 'noise, sound, voice' < OE *reord*. The word occurs often in ME verse, and is common in the *Pearl* MS, spelled *rurd(e*, but does not occur in *Piers Plowman*.

rydyn (133) 'ride, move, go' < OE *ridan*. The rhyme with *tyde* requires *ryde* with omission of final <n>; see Dickins, p. 518. Rasmussen, § 210, shows that present indicative plural forms with and without final <n> occur in this manuscript. Cp. the discussion of the emendation of *lynde* under *lykyr*, above.

rynkkys (134) 'knight, man' < OE *rinc*, cp. Scandinavian **renk-* > Icelandic *rekkr*. The word is common in alliterative verse, including *Piers Plowman* and the poems in the *Pearl* MS, as well as in nonalliterative verse and prose. The northern form, as used in the *Pearl* MS and in *Piers Plowman*, is *renk* from Scandinavian, unlike the form here, the only occurrence of the word in the manuscript.

row (4) 'peace' < OE *row*. It is spelled *rou* at *Vision of St. Paul* W16.300, where it is also collocated with *rest*.

row (77) 'group or row (of people)', ***rowys*** (134) 'ray, beam of light' < OE *raw*, cp. ME *rew* < OE *ræw*. This polysemous word, variously spelled, is very common; see *MED* s.v. *reue* n. (2), and the phrase *bi rowe* is also given s.v. *bi*, prep. 8a. (a), and cp. McIntosh, p. 389. The sense 'ray, beam of light' is recorded in *MED* s.v. *reue* n. (2), 2. (c). Lydgate uses it often, sometimes collocated with 'red', or in the combination *þe rowes and þe raies rede*.[98] This sense appears not to be found elsewhere in alliterative verse.

saȝt (69), the sense is disputed, < OE *seht*. The OE etymon means 'reconciliation, reconciled'. The twelfth-century Peterborough Chronicle has adjectival *sæhte* several times (not clearly distinguishable from the noun, more usually written *sehte*), and ME /a/ may be traced back to that form.[99] The sense 'reconciled' does not fit, as McIntosh points out, pp. 388–89, but his suggested meaning 'accepted, faced up to' is difficult to parallel, as is that suggested by Turville-Petre, p. 154, 'afflicted', a sense that would do well for *soȝt*, the past participle of *sechen* (cp. *MED* s.v. *sēchen*, 8. (d)), and he found that word in that sense earlier in his anthology, that is, in *Somer Soneday*, line 109 (p. 146). Semantic history and context make some meaning based on 'at peace' likely; cp. *MED* s.v. *saughten* sense 2. If so, the line means 'that ever a man saw on earth and felt at peace'.

selquoþ (68) 'rare, wondrous' < OE *sel(d)cuþ*. The word occurs once in the *Pearl* MS, at *Cleanness* 1274, and quite frequently in *Piers Plowman*.

telde (19) 'ridiculed, reviled' < OE *tælan*. Thus Dickins, p. 517, not accepted by Turville-Petre, p. 256, s.v. *told* (*telde* 'spoke'), presumably misled because Dickins had suggested that "*Telde* is perhaps a bye-form of *tolde*," as if from *tellan*.

tene (72) 'go' < OE *teon*. The word is common in ME, including alliterative verse. It does not occur in *Piers Plowman*. The distribution is not clear to me; the verb occurs in a rhyme in the verse of Adam Davy.[100]

þrew (10) 'moved about (with great agitation)' < OE *þrawan, þreow*. The verb is common, though unusual in this sense; cp. *MED* s.v. *throuen* v. (1).

þrobyt (10) 'shuddered, twisted violently', etymology obscure. Whiting bids the reader, "Note the Northern ending *yt*" (p. 256), but that is to be contrasted with what she has found more generally in the manuscript: "The ending *-ed* of the preterite and of the past participle sometimes becomes *-et*, or *-it*: *chaunget* 2.395, *comawndit* 9.337" (p. xxxiii, § 12 (c)). And one might add *bakbidit* (*Vision of St. Paul* W16.77, with <t ⇌ d> switch), *cordit* (*Marcolf* W2.700), *pynchit* (*Marcolf* W2.558), and *wepit* (*Salut. to St. Bridget* W23.12); *-yt* for *-it* is probably not significant since both *-id* and *-yd* are common preterite endings.[101] Whiting draws attention to *þrobbant* in *Piers Plowman* A-text, and to the use in alliterative verse of the frequentative, *MED* s.v. *thrublen* 'to jostle, crash together, press', including *Cleanness* 504 and 879, *þrublande* and *þrobled*. The verb *þrobben* is rare in ME, and the connection with Modern English *to throb* is likely but not certain. If, as seems likely, phonaesthesis involves these verbs, exactitude of sense is not to be expected: the sound helps to convey the meaning.

tytle (65) 'title, just reason' < OF *title*. McIntosh is too absolute when he asserts that "no attested ME. meaning of *title* 'title' readily suggests itself" (p. 388). Turville-Petre, p. 154, suggests attractively that *fore tytle* means 'as of right, with due claim'. *MED* part T.6 appeared as recently as 1995, so that the full range of senses was not available to McIntosh or Turville-Petre: the nearest to the use here (which is not in the entry) appears to be *bi title of*, perhaps calqued on OF *par titre de* 'on the basis of'.[102] Putter, p. 508, suggests unpersuasively that *tytle* is the adverb *tytli* 'soon' (with *-le* for the adverbial ending as elsewhere); that adverb appears, however, not to occur with verbs of thinking or believing.

tome (129) 'sufficient time' < Scandinavian, cp. Icelandic *tom*. Though of Scandinavian origin, *tom(e* is used in southern as well as northern areas, and in nonalliterative as well as in alliterative verse including the *Pearl* MS and once in *Piers Plowman* (all three versions). In ME, *tome* is often collocated with *time*; cp. *be-tyme* at the end of the next line.[103]

tryffylyng (19) 'jollity', cp. OF *truf(l)er*; ***tryuyls*** (130) 'things of no value or moment', cp. OF *truff(l)e*. The verbal noun is less common than the noun *tryfel*, which occurs, variously spelled, in both *Sir Gawain and the Green Knight* and *Piers Plowman*.

vpo last (118) 'at last', cp. OE *latost*. The phrase 'upon last', instead of such more usual phrases as 'at last', is difficult to parallel. *MED* s.v. *upo* 6. has

'During the course of (a space of time)', and s.v. *upon* prep. 18. 'In temporal uses' lists several prepositional phrases, the nearest to the use here is *upon longe (lengthe)*, 'after a long time, after a while; at length, finally'. *OED* s.v. *upon*, prep., 6. and 7., has various temporal uses, but none near to the use here.

wallon & wyndon (98) 'swarm and enshroud' < OE *ge)weallan, windan*. According to *MED* s.v. *wallen* v. (1) 3., the sense 'to swarm (of worms)' is rare, and it is even rarer, presumably a nonce-use to provide a rhyme, to use 'to wind' in a hyperbole: worms so numerous, they enshroud the corpse.

waltyn (21, 22) 'command, prevail' < OE *wealdan*, Anglian *waldan*. Confusion of medial /d/ and /t/ is unusual in MS Douce 302 (see the discussion s.v. *donyng*, above); Rasmussen lists no examples. Presumably, Whiting's glossarial entry, s.v., with the meaning 'chose', is also from OE *wealdan*, Anglian *waldan*, though the semantic development is not clear to me. The lines are difficult:

> Þese wodis & þese wastis þai waltyn al to w[e]lde,
>   Þai waltyn at here wil to ware
>   Þese wodis & þe wastus þat þer were.
>   (W54.21–23)

A possible meaning may be: 'These woods and these wastelands they commanded to govern [*wylde* emended to *welde* for the rhyme] entirely, they prevailed to watch over (*ware*) these woods and the wastelands that there were'.[104] The sense of *ware* is uncertain; see s.v., below.

wanne (28) 'dark' < OE *wann, wonn*. The editors emend the rhyme words of lines 28–34 in various ways; but there is no need, unless to make them look more exactly rhyming: *wanne / mon / on / can*. In this text <on> has merged with <an> in sound, and <nne> is pronounced as if written <n>. The word *wonne* occurs quite frequently in ME, but only once in the *Pearl* MS (*Patience* 141) and once in *Piers Plowman*.

ware (22, 108) 'guard, watch over' < OE *warian*. The sense of the word *ware* is not clear. Whiting's note on lines 21–23 and her glossary have 'employ' for line 22, and her glossary has 'possess' for line 108. Some such sense as 'to take possession of', a semantic extension of 'to guard' appears to be found in OE verse for the etymon *warian*.[105] The semantic history of the verb may be influenced in ME by the specialized senses of the imperative *ware*, probably influenced, as *MED* s.v. *waren* v. (1)

says—following *OED* s.v. *ware*, v.¹—by AN *ware!*, and cp. the related history of the ME adjectives *ware*, *aware*, and (probably later) *beware*. These developments contributed to the demise of such senses as 'to occupy, make use of, take possession of', which go back to OE. *MED* has the subsense 'to possess or enjoy (goods, property)' s.v. *waren* v. (2), subsense (d), quoting both these occurrences. *MED* derives the verb "Prob. from O[ld] N[orse]." In view of the OE poetic uses, that derivation is improbable. It is more likely that forest laws are involved, leading to royal hunting rights.

warlaws (83) 'devils' < OE *wǣrloga*. The word occurs also in the preceding poem, *Paternoster* W53.30 (*warlouys*) and 63 (*warlawys*). It occurs twice in the *Pearl* MS, but not in *Piers Plowman*. The semantic development of the word is well explained in *OED*, s.v. *warlock*, sb.¹, as is its phonology.[106]

wylde (21) 'to govern', **wildus** (84) 'rules' < OE *wieldan* (weak), cp. *wealdan* (strong). At line 21 MS *wylde* is emended by the editors to *welde*, to rhyme with *helde* / *telde* (and *b[e]ld[e]* emended from MS *bild* for the rhyme); and at line 84 MS *wildus* is emended to *weldus* to rhyme with *heldis* / *kelddus* / *feldus*. The existence of the weak and strong verbal doublets resulted in ME *wilden* (whence the MS forms) and *welden*, whence the emended forms for the rhyme.

woȝe (141) 'wall' < OE *wag*. For such inscribed church walls see the reference given in n. 30. It is not clear whether *þis* refers to the whole story, the subject of this poem, or to the foundation story of the church on the 'moss', or only to the words that constitute the next line, *To lyte will leue þis allas* 'alas, too few will believe this!'

wondon (107) '(we) dwelt' < OE *wunian*. Scribal reduction of the sequence <e we w> to <e w> in *wyle we wondon* is likely, as McIntosh suggests, p. 389. Though omission of the subject pronoun is common in ME, it is, however, unusual to omit it when the subject is not obvious from what precedes.[107]

worchip (107) 'honour, esteem' < OE *weorþscipe*. The entries in *MED* and *OED* do not include *at worship*.[108]

wrase (99) 'band (for tying a winding-sheet)' < OE *wrasen* 'band, tie'; thus Whiting's glossary, ignored in Turville-Petre's glossary, who gives 'bundle', which, I think, fits less well. *MED* shows that the word is very rare, and does not decide firmly which of the two senses is better for the occurrence here.

wreus (117) 'reveals' < OE *wreg(i)an* 'to accuse'. The verb has several senses according to the entries in *MED* s.v. *wreien* and *OED* s.v. *wray*, v.¹ There are points of contact between them, and often it is difficult to decide whether the declaratory element weighs more heavily than the accusatory. *MED* has the use here: s.v. *wreien* 3. (c) 'to make accusation of or against (a fault, misdeed, etc.); denounce; also in *fig.* context'. Whiting's glossary has 'betrays'; Turville-Petre's glossary s.v. *wryeth* has 'reveals'. The object of the verb is *wild werkys*, here perhaps 'sinful deeds', and where several senses seem to be applicable to a use, it is usually best to treat them not as alternatives, but as supporting each other. However, when translating, a choice has to be made, 'reveal' or 'accuse', because 'to reveal by accusing' or 'to accuse by revealing' would be too clumsy. The verb, though common in ME, is rare in alliterative verse; it does not occur in *Piers Plowman*, and in the *Pearl* MS it occurs only once, in *Sir Gawain and the Green Knight* 1706.

wryust (116) the rhyme requires omission of final <t> (as does *hyust* in the preceding line) 'dost deviate (from the straight and narrow)' < OE *wrigian*. Both Whiting s.v. *wry* and Turville-Petre s.v. *wryus* in their glossaries give only 'turn', and by their punctuation seem to take it as 'dost turn away from this world', whereas I think lines 114–17 mean (cp. *hyust*, above), 'By lies it leads you *be lagmon* (?to your disadvantage). When you are highest of all and hasten away from this world, whenever you deviate (from the straight and narrow), it (Christ's teaching [line 111, as Jordan says]) accuses you by revealing all your wicked deeds (*or*, it [Christ's teaching] reveals all your wicked deeds)'. The verb occurs several times in MS Douce 302, but is rare in alliterative verse, occurring never in *Piers Plowman* nor in the *Pearl* MS.

Conclusion

This is a long list of lexical, textual, phonemic, and graphemic difficulties and oddities. Audelay's authorship of *Three Dead Kings* has been doubted in the last three-quarters of a century. Some words or rare meanings of words are not in either *Piers Plowman* or the *Pearl* MS; thus *wreus* 'reveals, accuses'. Some words the poem shares with other poems generally accepted as by Audelay; thus *lele* 'truly', common enough in Middle English verse including *Piers Plowman* and the *Pearl* MS, but used with special frequency in Audelay's verse; and *wryust*, here perhaps 'deviate from the straight and narrow', used four times in *Marcolf and Solomon* in more than one sense.[109] *Three Dead Kings* shares some words with *Piers Plowman*, words that are not in the *Pearl* MS: thus, *amys* 'wrongly'; *be tyme* 'in good time'; *chist* 'care, sorrow' (emended from MS *care*); *cappid* 'wearing a . . . cap'; *mete(s)* 'table-companion(s)'; *mynn* 'remind, remember'; *probyt* 'shuddered, twisted violently'. It shares some words with poems in the *Pearl* MS, especially with *Sir Gawain and the Green Knight*, but not in *Piers Plowman*: thus: *gre* 'shudder' (cp. *gryed*); *lagmon* '?last or hindmost person'; *masse* emend to *mosse* 'moor' (different sense, 'lichen'); *warlaws* 'demons'.

When it comes to conclusions, one is too easily inclined to make too much of too little; deliberately or by self-delusion, one is inclined to interpret malleable evidence in the direction in which one wishes to go. Editors and commentators have made much of *lagmon* because they gladly follow a trail, blazed by Whiting in her introduction, that leads to *Sir Gawain and the Green Knight*. In my reading, I make much of the connection with *Marcolf and Solomon*, and with *Piers Plowman*, and I acknowledge the frequency with which the vocabulary of this poem has significant items that occur in *The Wars of Alexander* too. The last two are long texts containing many words. Probably such shared lexical items between *Three Dead Kings* and other alliterative poems of the fourteenth and fifteenth centuries signify no more than that, when narrative poets are in alliterative "mode," they rummage around in what in British English might be described as the bran-tub of obsolete or strangely dialectal lexis, and which we, when in a different but comparably traditional "mode," might call the wordhoard of ancient poetic dainties. Such an alliterative poet shows himself to be a bookman, unlike poor Dull of whom Sir Nathaniel says in *Love's Labour's Lost*:[110]

> [Sir] Nath[aniel]. Sir hee hath neuer fed of the dainties that are
>   bred in a booke.
> He hath not eate paper as it were:
> He hath not drunke inke.

Poetry is an artful game. It plays with language. When we look outside Audelay's manuscript, we find *losse* meaning 'perdition', a sense found in the writings of the followers of Wycliffe. Because this narrative poem is heavily alliterative, the unusual in it is not infrequently to be contrasted with the diction in some of the rest of the manuscript, more lightly alliterative when alliterative at all. But there are also locutions in *Three Dead Kings* that are among Audelay's favorites. Some collocations are so common in Middle English that that agreement may signify nothing; for example, line 18 *treule itolde*, comparable with *Marcolf* W2.498 *þis tale treule . . . is told* and, similarly, with *Marcolf* W2.761, *Epilogue* W18.170 *treule me tolde*, is not enough to establish common authorship. Yet I believe that there are no grounds for doubting that John Audelay wrote *Three Dead Kings*. The alliterative poems in MS Douce 302 include the long *Marcolf and Solomon* and the short *Paternoster* (for which Audelay's authorship has also been denied), philosophical and contemplative, as well as the narrative *Three Dead Kings*, also religious of course, and much nearer to the literary kind to which alliterative romances belong, *Sir Gawain and the Green Knight* preeminent among them. The greater density of linguistic features that *Three Dead Kings* shares with *Sir Gawain*, features uncommon elsewhere in MS Douce 302, is to be explained by that literary recognition. The demands of alliteration at times lead the poet to introduce what look like locutions from other genres: in *Marcolf*, for example, *Syr Sathanas* (W2.16), as when in the York "Harrowing of Hell" Belsabub addresses Sattan; or in *Paternoster* W53.18, heaven referred to as *þat courte*, as when in *Cursor Mundi* Lucifer is excluded from heaven as unclean.[111] An assemblage of linguistic details is insufficient for conclusions of authorship, and is not attempted by Rasmussen. Whiting, in her edition, uses selectively what she trusts will substantiate her view that *Three Dead Kings* goes with *Sir Gawain and the Green Knight*, and Putter, finding himself in the same hole with Whiting and Dickins, digs deeper and with a broader shovel. Philology is deaf to the essential divergency of the various literary kinds to which the poems in MS Douce 302 belong. Audelay showed his mastery of the craft of versifying in the poems of MS Douce 302, responding with linguistic and poetic skill to the varied demands made by each verse form and literary kind.

NOTES

Different versions of short parts of this paper were read at the Thirty-Ninth International Congress on Medieval Studies at Kalamazoo in May 2004, and at the Second International Conference on Lexicography and Lexicology at Gargnano (Brescia) in June 2004. I am grateful to the Faculty of English, University of Oxford, for contributing toward expenses incurred in attending these conferences.

    1. Samuel Johnson, *The Rambler*, 3 vols. (London: Payne and Bouquet, 1750–52), 941–42, no. 158, 21 September 1751; see W. J. Bate and Albrecht B. Strauss, eds., *Samuel Johnson, The Rambler*, 3 vols. (New Haven: Yale University Press, 1969), 3:75–76.

    2. James Simpson, *The Oxford English Literary History*, vol. 2, *1350–1547: Reform and Cultural Revolution* (Oxford: Oxford University Press, 2002), p. 379.

3. [Joseph Ritson, ed.] *Bibliographia Poetica: A Catalogue of Engleish Poets, of the Twelfth, Thirteenth, Fourteenth, Fifteenth, and Sixteenth, Centurys* (London: G. and W. Nicol, 1802), pp. 43–44.

4. Eighteen as numbered in Ella Keats Whiting, ed., *The Poems of John Audelay*, EETS o.s. 184 (1931; repr. Oxford: Oxford University Press, 2006) (hereafter cited as "Whiting"). In this paper the poems in MS Douce 302 are quoted from Whiting's edition, which preserves the MS letter forms, but not all editorial details, emendations, punctuation, etc., have been followed. References to items in MS Douce 302 follow the short titles used throughout this volume (see the table on pp. xv– xix) accompanied by the numbers used in Whiting's edition; thus "*Epilogue* W18.417–22" = Audelay's epilogue to *The Counsel of Conscience*, Whiting's poem 18, lines 417–22. A more recent edition of *Three Dead Kings* W54 (*De tribus regibus mortuis*) is that by Thorlac Turville-Petre, ed., *Alliterative Poetry of the Later Middle Ages: An Anthology* (Washington, D.C.: Catholic University of America Press, 1989), pp. 148–57 (hereafter cited as "Turville-Petre"). [Editor's note: Where line numbers differ from those found in John the Blind Audelay, *Poems and Carols (Oxford, Bodleian Library MS Douce 302)*, ed. Susanna Fein (Kalamazoo: Medieval Institute Publications, 2009)—as does occur with the carols in particular—the Whiting line numbers appear in parentheses.]

5. Simpson, *Reform*, p. 379 n. 114.

6. Cp. Eric Gerald Stanley, "*The True Counsel of Conscience*, or *The Ladder of Heaven*: In Defence of John Audelay's Unlyrical Lyrics," in *Expedition nach der Wahrheit: Poems, Essays, and Papers in Honour of Theo Stemmler*, ed. Stefan Horlacher and Marion Eslinger (Heidelberg: C. Winter, 1996), pp. 131–59 (pp. 154–55).

7. *Concilium* and *consilium* are often confused, and the details provided by the *Finito libro* colophon at the end of the *Epilogue* enhance that confusion: "Finito libro: sit laus et gloria. Christo liber vocatur: *Concilium conciencie,* sic nominatur aut *Scala celi* et vita salutis eterni. Iste liber fuit compositus per Johannem Awdelay capellanum qui fuit secus [i.e., *caecus*, with <s> for <c>] et surdus in sua visitacione.Ad honorem Domini Nostri Jhesu Christi, et ad exemplum aliorum in monasterio de Haghmon. Anno Domini millesimo cccc visecimo vj" (The book being finished, praise be and glory. The book is called in Christ, "The Counsel of Conscience," or it is named thus, "The Scale of Heaven eternal and the life of salvation." This book was devised by John Audelay the chaplain, who was blind and deaf in his affliction. To the honor of Our Lord Jesus Christ, and as an example of others in the Monastery of Haughmond, in the year of the Lord 1426).

8. Angus McIntosh, "Some Notes on the Text of the Middle English Poem *De tribus regibus mortuis*," *Review of English Studies*, n.s. 28 (1977): 385–92 (p. 385); hereafter cited as "McIntosh."

9. For Chaucer, see J. R. R. Tolkien, "Chaucer as a Philologist: *The Reeve's Tale*," *Transactions of the Philological Society* (1934): 1–70 (p. 47) (and cp. further below, s.v. *gar*). For the view that Audelay is not the author of *Three Dead Kings* W54, see Bruce Dickins, "The Rhyme-Schemes in MS. Douce 302, 53 and 54," *Proceedings of the Leeds*

Philosophical and Literary Society, 2 (1932), 516–18 (hereafter cited as "Dickins"); accepted by McIntosh, p. 385; by Turville-Petre, p. 148; and by Ad Putter, "The Language and Metre of *Pater Noster* and *Three Dead Kings*," *Review of English Studies*, n.s. 55 (2004): 498–526 (hereafter cited as "Putter"). For a contrary view, see E. G. Stanley, "The Verse Forms of Jon the Blynde Awdelay," in *The Long Fifteenth Century: Essays for Douglas Gray*, ed. Helen Cooper and Sally Mapstone (Oxford: Clarendon Press, 1997), pp. 99–121 (pp. 108–11). The poem discussed in this paper is more complex than *Paternoster* W53, in a different stanzaic form, and different in form from *Marcolf and Solomon* W2, though nearer to it in content. *Three Dead Kings* shares some linguistic features with *Marcolf*; cp., e.g., the discussion below of *amys*, *care*, *laype*, *masse*, *rade* and *rad(de)le*, *rede*.

10. *LALME* 1:148, 3:454 (Linguistic Profile 189).

11. Cp. E. G. Stanley, "Rhymes in English Medieval Verse: From Old English to Middle English," in *Medieval English Studies Presented to George Kane*, ed. Edward Donald Kennedy, Ronald Waldron, and Joseph S. Wittig (Woodbridge: Brewer, 1988), pp. 19–54; I do not discuss verse later than Chaucer.

12. Stanley, "Rhymes in English Medieval Verse," p. 54; *miste* in The Owl and the Nightingale 764 is discussed at p. 51. In his note on the line, Neil Cartlidge, ed., *The Owl and the Nightingale: Text and Translation* (Exeter: University of Exeter Press, 2001), gives other examples of anomalous forms "presumably invented for the sake of the rhyme" (pp. 122–23).

13. As Turville-Petre, p. 148, has stated: "The rhyme-scheme complements and contrasts with the alliterative scheme as follows:

rhyme-scheme: a b a b a b a b c d c c d
alliteration: a a b b c c d d d d x f f."

Thorlac Turville-Petre has also given a good account of the complexities of the stanza form in his article "'Summer Sunday', 'De Tribus Regibus Mortuis', and 'The Awntyrs off Arthure': Three Poems in the Thirteen-Line Stanza," *Review of English Studies*, n.s. 25 (1974): 1–14, esp. p. 6. Cp. Dickins, p. 516.

14. Whiting emends to *s[i]ȝt*, but ME may not have clearly distinguished in pronunciation the vowel written variously <i> or <e> before <ȝt>; cp. Karl Luick (completed by Friedrich Wild and Herbert Koziol), *Historische Grammatik der englischen Sprache*, 2 vols. (Stuttgart, 1914–40; repr. Oxford: Blackwell, 1964), §§ 270–77 (hereafter cited as "Luick" by section number). Richard M. Hogg, *A Grammar of Old English*, vol. 1, *Phonology* (Oxford: Blackwell, 1992), 5.94 and 5.95, dismisses the <e> variants as "of no significance," presumably meaning that they are graphemic or allophonic rather than phonemic, and his book is a phonology in which allophones play no major role.

15. See the discussion of *myȝt* below and at n. 89.

16. In two stanzas only (1 and 6), the rhyme words of lines 4 and 11 do not share in the alliteration. The alliteration of line 66 involves only the rhyme word

and the stressed word sharing in the same phrase, *mekil . . . of myȝt*, but that phrase leads in the alliteration of the line that follows (and similarly, e.g., line 18, *trewle itolde*, in stanza 2). In analyzing Audelay's stanzaic pattern in this poem, Whiting gives the pattern as *aabbccddddeff* (in fact, the alliterative scheme), and says of it, "The scheme was too difficult to be carried out with absolute consistency, but in six stanzas it is followed almost perfectly" (p. xxvi). A footnote lists the almost perfect stanzas as 2, 6, 7, 8, 9, and 10, and she quotes stanza 7 in full to demonstrate her faulty pattern.

17. Whiting, p. xxiii. Cp. n. 16, above, for her faulty understanding of the stanza form.

18. See Whiting, p. xxvii. Cp. *MED* s.v. *colden* (variant spelling *kelden*) where these two lines are, however, not quoted; they are given s.v. *knok(ke* 'blow' b. figurative. Dickins, p. 518, translates *kelddus* as 'chills'. McIntosh, p. 389, suggests *knoc* means 'knuckle', and Turville-Petre, p. 154, emends MS *knoc* to *þe knoc*; cp. *MED* s.v. *kēlen*.

19. Metanalysis is here used to provide alliteration. Other examples of metanalysis include *attese* (= **at tese* or **a tese*) < *at ese*; see *Piers Plowman* C.1.19, in George Russell and George Kane, eds., *Piers Plowman: The C Version* (London: Athlone, 1997), p. 213. The adverbial phrase *at home* is occasionally spelled *atom(e*. This is related to the development of *nuncle* and *naunt* as in *Sir Gawain and the Green Knight*, line 2467 (= fol. 124r, line 6) *com to þy naunt*; see the facsimile: I. Gollancz, introduction to *Pearl, Cleanness, Patience and Sir Gawain, Reproduced in Facsimile from the Unique MS. Cotton Nero A.x in the British Museum*, EETS o.s. 162 (1923; repr. Oxford: Oxford University Press, 2007), and in Audelay's *no noþer Lord* (*True Living* W1.221), *my nenmys* (*Seven Bleedings* W4.77), and *þi ne* 'thy eye' (*Visiting the Sick* W11.153).

20. Gollancz, intro., *Pearl, Cleanness, Patience and Sir Gawain*, fol. 53v, lines 1–4. Audelay did not shrink from using the tag *withouten drede* to help his rhyme in this stanza. Cp. Whiting, pp. xxiv–xxv n. 3; and McIntosh, p. 386 and n. 4.

21. Gollancz, intro., *Pearl Cleanness, Patience and Sir Gawain*, fol. 43v. See E. G. Stanley, "*Pearl*, 358, *And þy lurez of lyȝtly leme*: Metanalysed Tmesis for the Sake of Alliteration," *Notes & Queries* 235 (1990): 158–60. The verb **of-flemen* is not otherwise recorded in ME.

22. Turville-Petre, "Summer Sunday," p. 6.

23. McIntosh, pp. 385–86.

24. The repetition in lines 73–74, condemned by McIntosh, p. 389, and attributed by him to haplography, may be regarded as concatenating the "wheel" to the body of the stanza, and similarly lines 8–9, 47–48, 125–26, 138–39, and probably 99–100. This is not a regular prosodic feature of the other poems in thirteen-line stanzas in this manuscript. Audelay similarly abandoned a prosodic feature in *Salut to St. Anne* W26.9–12, namely half-rhyme, which he may have found too difficult for regular use in the rest of the poem. Putter, p. 514, pronounces on this abandonment

of a prosodic difficulty in *Salut. to St. Anne* and fails to relate it to abandonment of such difficulties elsewhere in MS Douce 302.

25. Turville-Petre, p. 148, referring to Dickins, p. 516: "They [*Paternoster* and *Three Dead Kings*] are to be assigned to an area a good deal further north than Audelay's Shropshire and, in fact, belong to the alliterative school of which *Sir Gawain and the Green Knight* is the most splendid product." McIntosh, p. 386 n. 1, extends Dickins's localization of the poem to the scribe, giving as his only example that OE *hw-* is commonly represented in MS Douce 302 by <hw>, but that spelling is not found in *Paternoster* and *Three Dead Kings*. In *Paternoster* <wh> occurs at W53.45 and 63, and <hw> does not occur. In *Three Dead Kings* <wh> occurs at W54.27, 40, 76, 115; there is, as McIntosh says, no <hw>. Written in Hand 2, <hw> occurs in Audelay's *Conclusion* W55.1, 2, 8, 33, <wh> at W55.41. That distribution is not significant for *Paternoster* and *Three Dead Kings*. In *Seven Bleedings* (of about the same length as *Three Dead Kings*), <wh> occurs at W4.27, 32, 45, 48, 72, 122; <hw> does not occur; <w> occurs at W4.50 and 78. *God's Address* has <w> and <hw> (W17.100–101), and that confused the scribe who, if Whiting's emendation is right (as seems likely), wrote *Hwom* (with <H> corrected) for *Hwen*, and for the second *hwom* inserted <h> (p. xxxiii, § 14). J[ulius] K[arl] Rasmussen, *Die Sprache John Audelay's (Laut- und Flexionslehre)* (PhD diss., Bonn University, 1914) (hereafter cited as "Rasmussen," by section number), concentrates on rhyme words and does not comment on these spellings.

26. Norman Davis's second edition (Oxford: Clarendon Press, 1967) of J. R. R. Tolkien and E. V. Gordon, eds., *Sir Gawain and the Green Knight* (1925, several times reprinted with corrections), contains a note on line 1729: "*lad hem bi lagmon*. The only known parallel is 'Hit [*sc*. lust] ledys ȝou be lagmon' in the fifteenth-century Shropshire poet Audelay (ed. E. K. Whiting, E.E.T.S. 184 (1931), p. 232 [*sic* for p. 222], line 114). *Lagman* was used in western dialects for the last of a line of reapers" (p. 120). In the notes of later reprints of the first edition (1925), the editors state: "this obscure phrase is also used by the Shropshire poet Audelay (p. 222, line 114 in the E.E.T.S. edition)." It may be inferred that Tolkien was not impressed by Whiting's argument that *Three Dead Kings* was not by Audelay.

27. Inclusion in MS Douce 302 is, of course, not in itself proof of Audelay's authorship; thus *Virtues of the Mass* W9 is to be seen in relation to the versions in the Vernon MS and London, BL MS Harley 3954; see A. I. Doyle, introduction to *The Vernon Manuscript: A Facsimile of Bodleian Library, Oxford, MS. Eng. Poet. a. 1* (Cambridge: Brewer, 1987), fols. 302va–3vc; and F. J. Furnivall, ed., *The Minor Poems of the Vernon MS.*, part 2, EETS o.s. 117 (1901; repr. Oxford: Oxford University Press, 2006), pp. 493–511. Extracts of the version in MS Harley 3954 have been edited; for details, see Whiting, pp. 235–37. Cp. Stanley, "*True Counsel*," pp. 137–38, 144–48.

28. I do not wish to make too much of Audelay's numerical sophistication in poems that include some of his most intellectual compositions: I doubt if, e.g., in *Visiting the Sick* it is significant that he has thirty-one thirteen-line stanzas: chiastically $13 \times 31 = 403$ lines. I note that *Epilogue* has thirty-nine thirteen-line stanzas, that

is, 13 × 13 × 3 = 507 lines. I leave it to others to speculate numerologically: such things may not be chance, but it is hard to see how a totally blind poet could have counted a great number of stanzas, unless he asked the scribe, who took down what he composed, how far he had got in his multiples of thirteen.

29. Sometimes Audelay's final consonants look medial because followed by a final <e> that would not have been pronounced; cp. Rasmussen, § 15.

30. Willy F. Storck and Richard Jordan, eds., "John Awdelays gedicht 'De tribus regibus mortuis': Eine englische fassung der legende von den drei lebenden und den drei toten," *Englische Studien* 43 (1911): 177–88. Storck transcribed the poem and wrote the introduction in which it is placed within the history of late medieval literature, with some mention of pictorial representations. Jordan provided glossarial annotations and apparently exercised philological control. (For this reason, the Storck-Jordan edition of *Three Dead Kings* is hereafter cited as "Jordan.") Jordan was very ready to emend, and that without reference to the rhyme-scheme that would have guided him better, as Dickins showed some twenty years later. Jordan was, however, a great help to Whiting, a more conservative editor. Storck wrote "Aspects of Death in English Art and Poetry," *Burlington Magazine* 21 (1912): 249–56, 314–19, with a brief mention of *Three Dead Kings* at p. 255, and a substantial *catalogue raisonné* of pictorial representations, on which E. Carleton Williams based her study, "Mural Paintings of the Three Living and the Three Dead Kings in England," *Journal of the British Archaeological Association*, ser. 3, 7 (1942): 31–40. See also Susanna Greer Fein, "Life and Death, Reader and Page: Mirrors of Mortality in English Manuscripts," *Mosaic* 35 (2002): 69–94.

31. See *MED* s.v. *leu(e* adj. (3), and s.v. *bŏuen* v. (1).

32. Dickins, p. 516.

33. Dickins, p. 517.

34. The closely similar rhyme words on *-ew* alternating with *-ow* exploit an alternation available in ME; thus *prow / prew / blow / how / hew* (lines 9–13), the rhyme words of lines 40–47 quoted above, and *trow / trew / how / row / rew* (lines 74–78). If Dickins's suggestion *at [sch]e[ue]* is right, the alternation depends on two ME developments of the OE diphthong *ēa* after *sc*, either *ēa > ā* (as a result of Akzentumsprung) *> ō* (*schow-*) or *ēa > ɛ̄* spelled <e> (*schew-*); cp. Luick, §§ 265, 279, 373e. Both <e> and <o> spellings are to be found in MS Douce 303; thus *Marcolf* W2.798, *schowe*; *True Living* W1.187, *schewe* in rhyme with *know*; *Virtues of the Mass* W9.145, *schew* in rhyme with *know*; *Visiting the Sick* W11.172 and *Epilogue* W18.159, *chewe* in rhyme with *loue* (or *lowe*) 'to humble (oneself)'; *Visiting the Sick* W11.189, *shew* in rhyme with *crowe, low, know*. McIntosh, p. 387, suggests emending to *to schewe* 'into view' (cp. *to sight* 'so as to be seen'), but that is further from the MS reading than *at schewe*.

35. See *MED* s.v. *at* prep. 4b (d), *at ene(s*.

36. Turville-Petre, "Summer Sunday," pp. 6–7.

37. See Michael G. Brennan's entry for "Grimald, Nicholas," in *Oxford Dictionary of National Biography*, ed. H. C. G. Matthew and Brian Harrison, 60 vols. (Oxford: Oxford University Press, 2004), 24:12–15.

38. Hyder Edward Rollins, ed., *Tottel's Miscellany*, 2nd ed., 2 vols. (Cambridge, Mass.: Harvard University Press, 1965), 1:115 (line 34), 116 (line 30), and 117 (line 32). Evidence that his contemporaries may have thought *shin*and archaic or dialectal is provided by the 2nd ed. (1557, the same year as the 1st ed.), where the reading is *shining* (Rollins, 2:252), as also in subsequent editions. Cp. Karl Brunner, *Die englische Sprache: ihre geschichtliche Entwicklung*, 2 vols. (Tübingen: Niemeyer, 1962), 2:191, 193–94.

39. Whiting, pp. xxiv–xxv n. 3.

40. Barnet Kottler and Alan M. Markman, eds., *A Concordance to Five Middle English Poems: Cleanness, St. Erkenwald, Sir Gawain and the Green Knight, Patience, Pearl* (Pittsburgh: University of Pittsburgh Press, 1966); and Joseph S. Wittig, ed., *Will's Visions of Piers Plowman, Do-Well, Do-Better and Do-Best: Piers Plowman Concordance* (London: Athlone, 2001). Rolf Kaiser, *Zur Geographie des mittelenglischen Wortschatzes* (1937; repr. New York: Johnson Reprint, 1970), first published in part as "Zur geographischen Verteilung des mittelenglischen Wortschatzes" (PhD diss., Berlin University, 1936); cp. Richard Mummendey, *Language and Literature of the Anglo-Saxon Nations as Presented in German Doctoral Dissertations 1885–1950: A Bibliography* (Charlottesville: University of Virginia Press, 1954), p. 24 (no. 412). Kaiser's prefaces acknowledge the imperfection of what he recognizes as merely a first attempt at a comprehensive ME word-geography.

41. Felix Liebermann, ed., *Die Gesetze der Angelsachsen*, 3 vols. (Halle: Niemeyer, 1898–1916; repr. Aalen: Scientia, 1960), 1:380, Northumbrisches Priestergesetz, line 9.

42. Thus Dorothy Bethurum, ed., *The Homilies of Wulfstan* (Oxford: Clarendon Press, 1957), p. 125 (III.56); Hans Hecht, ed., *Bischof Wærferths von Worcester Übersetzung der Dialoge Gregors des Grossen*, 2 vols. (Leipzig, 1900; Hamburg, 1907; repr. as 1 vol., Darmstadt: Wissenschaftliche Buchgesellschaft, 1965), 1:67 (line 25).

43. George Kane, ed., *Piers Plowman: The A Version*, 2nd ed. (London: Athlone, 1988) p. 312, A.6.123 = George Kane and E. Talbot Donaldson, eds., *Piers Plowman: The B Version*, 2nd ed. (London: Athlone, 1988), p. 347, B.5.638 = Russell and Kane, eds., *Piers Plowman: The C Version*, p. 345, C.7.291.

44. Malcolm Andrew and Ronald Waldron, eds., *The Poems of the Pearl Manuscript* (London, 1978; 2nd ed. Berkeley and Los Angeles: University of California Press, 1989), p. 354 s.v. *tyme*.

45. Israel Gollancz, ed., *St. Erkenwald (Bishop of London 675–693): An Alliterative Poem* (London: Milford, Oxford University Press, 1922), p. 5. Gollancz is among those who believe that the poem is a work by the *Pearl* poet, or by "some disciple who very cleverly caught the style of his master" (p. lvii). Henry L. Savage, ed., *St. Erkenwald, a Middle English Poem* (New Haven: Yale University Press, 1926), is

cautious: "the test of vocabulary indicates an unusually close connection between the five poems" (p. lv). The use of *by tyme*, though in itself not sufficient for so weighty a conclusion, may be added to the reasons given by Larry D. Benson, "The Authorship of *St. Erkenwald*," *Journal of English and Germanic Philology* 64 (1963): 393–405, for doubting that proposition; cp. Turville-Petre, p. 102. The proposition that *St. Erkenwald* is by the *Gawain* poet has been accepted, by, e.g., Marie Borroff, *Sir Gawain and the Green Knight: A Stylistic and Metrical Study* (New Haven: Yale University Press, 1962), pp. 59, 232–33.

46. Jordan draws attention to the verb *bew* in Joseph Wright, ed., *The English Dialect Dictionary*, 6 vols. (London: Frowde, 1898–1905).

47. See Adolf Tobler and Erhard Lommatzsch, eds., *Altfranzösisches Wörterbuch*, 11 vols. (Berlin: Weidmann; Stuttgart: Steiner, 1925–2002), 1:cols. 742–43, s.v. *aviser*.

48. F. J. Amours, ed., *Scottish Alliterative Poems in Riming Stanza*, STS 27, 38 (1892, 1897; repr. New York: Johnson Reprint, 1966), p. 2 (line 31). Turville-Petre, "Summer Sunday," p. 14, lists *Golagros and Gawane* in his appendix of all works in this stanza form, but does not consider it further. *MED* ignores the text, presumably because it is Scottish and survives only in the Chepman and Myllar print of 1508 (*STC* 11984). *A Dictionary of the Older Scottish Tongue* dates it "*c*1475" (1:vi) and "*a*1500" (12:ccx) (William A. Craigie et al., eds., *A Dictionary of the Older Scottish Tongue*, 12 vols. [Chicago: University of Chicago Press; Aberdeen: Aberdeen University Press; Oxford: Oxford University Press, 1931–2002]). The adjective *birchen*, more northerly, is not uncommon in place-names; see David Parsons and Tania Styles, with Carole Hough, eds., *The Vocabulary of English Place-Names*, 3 fascicles to date (Nottingham: Centre for English Name Studies, 1997, 2000, 2004), 1(Á–Box):104.

49. See Walter W. Skeat, ed., *The Wars of Alexander, an Alliterative Romance*, EETS e.s. 47 (1886; repr. Millwood, N.Y.: Kraus Reprint, 1975), p. 16 (line 496) = Hoyt N. Duggan and Thorlac Turville-Petre, eds., *The Wars of Alexander*, EETS s.s. 10 (Oxford: Oxford University Press, 1989), p. 14 (line 496); Caroline D. Eckhardt, ed., *Castleford's Chronicle, or, The Boke of Brut*, 2 vols., EETS o.s. 305, 306 (Oxford: Oxford University Press, 1996), 2:643 (line 23811).

50. Turville-Petre, p. 36, applies that sense to "Thomas of Erceldoune's Prophecy," *a capped man* (line 1), and in that poem the sense 'madman' is plausible. *MED* s.v. *cappen* (c) had taken the sense of *cappid* here as 'wearing a clergyman's cap, priestly'; cp. R. E. Latham and D. R. Howlett, eds., *Dictionary of Medieval Latin from British Sources*, 9 fascicules to date (Oxford: Oxford University Press, 1975–), s.v. *cappare*, only the past participle 'wearing a cape (esp. mon[astic])'; *cappid* might refer not to the cope, but to the coif that covers the tonsure. *MED* does not quote the prophecy poem; the only occurrence in *Piers Plowman* is quoted under sense (c). W. W. Skeat, ed., *The Vision of William Concerning Piers Plowman*, part 4, sect. 1, notes to texts A, B, and C, EETS o.s. 67 (1877; repr. Oxford: Oxford University Press, 2000), had given the sense as 'capped with learning', and had suggested further that "The word 'capped' refers to the caps worn by masters of divinity, as a mark of their degree" (p. 239).

51. Russell and Kane, *The C Version*, p. 203, C.Prol.105; the apparatus gives the variant readings in Oxford, Bodl. Lib. MS Douce 104 and London, BL MS Addit. 34779.

52. Cp. Olof Arngart, ed., *The Middle English Genesis and Exodus* (Lund: Gleerup, 1968), pp. 230–31 s.v. *garen*.

53. Kane and Donaldson, *The B Version*, p. 643, B.19.199, and similarly Russell and Kane, *The C Version*, p. 655, C.21.199.

54. In *The Riming Poem* (George Philip Krapp and Elliott Van Kirk Dobbie, eds., *The Exeter Book*, ASPR 3 [New York: Columbia University Press, 1936], p. 168), the MS reading *colað* (line 69) is emended by the editors to *cealdað* to rhyme with *ealdað* (though two editors emend both rhyme words to unbroken Anglian forms resulting in initial /k/). See O. D. Macrae-Gibson, ed., *The Old English Riming Poem* (Cambridge: Brewer, 1983), pp. 34–35. Dickins, p. 518, seeks to derive *kelddus* from OE *cēlan* with initial /k/, but <dd> makes that unlikely. See further n. 18, above.

55. See Carleton Brown, ed., *English Lyrics of the XIIIth Century* (Oxford: Clarendon Press, 1932), p. 94 (no. 51, line 64).

56. W. W. Skeat, ed., *The Complete Works of Geoffrey Chaucer*, vol. 7, *Chaucerian and Other Pieces* (Oxford: Clarendon Press, 1897), pp. 169, 489. *MED* does not include *kime*: The *Plowman's Tale* cannot be traced further back than to William Thynne's 2nd ed. of *The Workes of Geffray Chaucer* (London: Wyllyam Bonham, 1542) (*STC* 5069), though Skeat gives its date of composition as around 1395 or 1396 (p. xxxiv and note), a date that seems too early. *MED* has entries for *akimed* (a word to which Jordan had drawn attention), *bikimet*, and the variant reading *ikimet*. A copious discussion of the word, with an etymology dependent on acceptance of an unlikely semantic development, is given, without mention of the use in MS Douce 302 or its entry in *MED* s.v. *kimid* (published in 1969), in S. R. T. O. d'Ardenne and E. J. Dobson, eds., *Seinte Katerine*, EETS s.s. 7 (Oxford: Oxford University Press, 1981), pp. 242–43 (the first of two notes on line 473), and p. 300, s.v. *bikimet* 'struck silly, stunned, dumbfounded'.

57. Turville-Petre, p. 157, suggests that *neuer* might be emended to *euer*, disregarding the historical note in *OED* s.v. *ever*, 9. b. *ever so*.

58. Andrew and Waldron, eds., *Poems of the Pearl MS*, p. 96, and note on lines 889–94.

59. See G. L. Brook, ed., *The Harley Lyrics: The Middle English Lyrics of MS. Harley 2253*, 4th ed. (Manchester: Manchester University Press, 1968), p. 70; and cp. Turville-Petre, p. 32; Richard Morris, ed., *The Blickling Homilies of the Tenth Century*, EETS o.s. 58, 63, 73 (1874–80; repr. as 1 vol., Oxford: Oxford University Press, 1997), pp. 9 (line 1, *heofonrices duru*), 61 (lines 8–9, *seo duru þæs heofonlican rices*, etc.); and A. G. Belfour, ed., *Twelfth-Century Homilies in MS. Bodley 343*, EETS o.s., 137 (1909; repr. Oxford: Oxford Unviersity Press, 1997), p. 44 (line 30).

60. See Hilda M. R. Murray, ed., *The Middle English Poem, Erthe upon Erthe*, EETS o.s. 141 (1911; repr. London: Oxford University Press, 1964), p. 4; Kane, *The A*

Version, p. 364, and similarly Kane and Donaldson, *The B Version*, p. 381, B.7.193, and Russell and Kane, *The C Version*, p. 388, C.9.339; and Richard Leighton Greene, *The Early English Carols*, 2nd ed. (Oxford: Clarendon Press, 1977), pp. 199, 430 (no. 329 and notes).

61. See Skeat, *The Wars of Alexander*, pp. 48–49, line 988 = Duggan and Turville-Petre's edition, p. 33, (line 1112), and see their note, p. 204, giving the source.

62. Tolkien and Gordon, *Sir Gawain*, rev. Davis, p. 66.

63. See Luick, § 409.3. Chaucer's form appears to have been *fest*; cp. Friedrich Wild, *Die sprachlichen Eigentümlichkeiten der wichtigeren Chaucer-Handschriften und die Sprache Chaucers*, Weiner Beiträge zur englischen Philologie 44 (Vienna: Braumüller, 1915), p. 130.

64. Andrew and Waldron, *Poems of the Pearl MS*, p. 179.

65. Thus in the following four half-lines: *fealwe fotas* (*Phoenix* 311a), and three times in the Paris Psalter, *fotas mine* 121.2.1b, *þær his fotas ær* 131.7.3a, *woldan mine fotas* 139.5.5a. See Krapp and Dobbie, *Exeter Book*, p. 102; and George Philip Krapp, ed., *The Paris Psalter and the Meters of Boethius*, ASPR 5 (New York: Columbia University Press, 1932), pp. 119, 126, 136. A use in London, BL MS Addit. 23211 of the late ninth century appears to be unique in OE prose, according to Richard L. Venezky and Antonette diPaolo Healey, *A Microfiche Concordance to Old English* (Toronto: Pontifical Institute of Mediaeval Studies, 1980), s.v.: *ðonne he hof his hond upp to hiofonum ðonne hofon ða deor heora fotas upp;* see Henry Sweet, ed., *The Oldest English Texts*, EETS o.s. 83 (1885; repr. London: Oxford University Press, 1966), p. 178 (lines 22–23).

66. See F. J. Furnivall, ed., *The Cambridge MS. Dd. 4. 24. of Chaucer's Canterbury Tales*, Chaucer Society, ser. 1, 95–96 (London: Kegan Paul, Trench, Trübner, 1901–02), p. 118. This manuscript is among those used by Thomas Tyrwhitt, ed., *The Canterbury Tales of Chaucer*, 5 vols. (London: Payne, 1775–78), 1:xxii; he well understood that Chaucer had northernized the language of the northern scholars (4:250–51). Tyrwhitt used the line with *Gar* in his edition (1:161, his line 4130) and mentions '*gar* for *make*, or *let*' (4:250). His use of the line with *Gar* follows the editorial principles he had praised (1:xx–xxi), "the only rational plan of publishing Chaucer, by collating the best Mss. and collecting from them the genuine readings." Skeat, in his edition, does not use the line, but refers to Tyrwhitt's use in his discussion of northernisms (W. W. Skeat, *The Complete Works of Geoffrey Chaucer*, 6 vols. [Oxford: Clarendon Press, 1894], 5:121). Tolkien follows the information from Tyrwhitt as provided by Skeat ("Chaucer as Philologist," pp. 12 n. 2, 43). Putter, pp. 505, 511, refers to *gar* as a northernism, but has nothing on Chaucer's northernizing use.

67. Andrew and Waldron, *Poems of the Pearl MS*, p. 294. Cp. Wolfgang Pfeifer, ed., *Etymologisches Wörterbuch des Deutschen*, 3 vols. (Berlin: Akademie, 1989), s.v. ^{2}*grauen*. Many phonaesthetic words have doublets, and to aver that the word was "corrupted by the scribe," as does Putter, p. 509, is misconceived.

68. Wright, *English Dialect Dictionary*, s.v. *grue*.

69. Mabel Day and Robert Steele, eds., *Mum and the Sothsegger*, EETS o.s. 199 (1936; repr. Oxford: Oxford University Press, 2001), p. 10; George A. Panton and David Donaldson, eds., *The "Gest Hystoriale" of the Destruction of Troy*, EETS o.s. 39, 56 (1869, 1874; repr. London: Oxford University Press, 1968, 1976), pp. 63, 73, 355.

70. Cartlidge, *The Owl and the Nightingale*, pp. 127–28 (note on line 1115).

71. The verbal noun *hening* is used in the fourteenth century, in Una O'Farrell-Tate, ed., *The Abridged English Metrical Brut* (Heidelberg: C. Winter, 2002), p. 98 (line 1031).

72. Cp. E. Talbot Donaldson, "Idiom of Popular Poetry in the *Miller's Tale*," in his *Speaking of Chaucer* (London: Athlone, 1970), pp. 13–29 (pp. 17–18).

73. Cp. *MED* s.vv. *heu(e* n. (2), *hou* interj. (1)—and cp. *hou* interj. (2), said to come from OE *hū* interj. (one may wonder how the two etymologies are kept apart so definitely)—and *heuen* v. (3); Tobler and Lommatzsch, *Altfranzösisches Wörterbuch*, s.vv. *hu!*, *hua*, *hüer*, and derivatives; and Walther von Wartburg, ed., *Französisches Etymologisches Wörterbuch*, 25 vols. or parts of vols. to date (Bonn: Fritz Klopp; Leipzig: Teubner; Basel: Helbing & Lichtenhahn; Tübingen: Mohr [Paul Siebeck]; Heidelberg: C. Winter; Basel, more recently St. Alban-Vorstadt: [R. G.] Zbinden, 1922–), vol. 4, s.v. *hū-*.

74. Cp. Luick, §§ 411–12, Richard Jordan, *Handbook of Middle English Grammar: Phonology*, trans. and rev. Eugene Joseph Crook (The Hague: Mouton, 1974), §§ 229–30.

75. It is unlikely that the rare addition of final /t/ inorganically, as in *lordist* (emended to *lordis* at *Epilogue* W18.491), might have led, inversely, to the omission of final /t/ in *aldyr-hyʒtus*. On the other hand, in the second person singular present indicative of verbs either /es/ or /est/ is not uncommon in the fifteenth century, especially in the north (cp. Brunner, *Die englische Sprache*, 2:190), so that the forms—required for the rhymes, with *lyus* for *leus* 'lies, tells falsehoods' and *wreus* 'betrays, reveals'—at lines 115 (*hyus* 'dost hie' [see s.v. *hyust*, below]), 116 (*wryus* 'dost turn (away)') are readily explicable in this MS; see Rasmussen, § 204.

76. Robert J. Menner, "Middle English 'Lagman' (*Gawain* 1729) and Modern English 'Lag,'" *Philological Quarterly* 10 (1931): 163–68, together with the spirited explanation by McIntosh, pp. 390–92. There is no connection with the name of the poet Laʒamon (or Laweman in London, BL MS Cotton Otho C.xiii), for that is a surname of occupation. See G. L. Brook and R. F. Leslie, eds., *Laʒamon: Brut*, 2 vols., EETS 250, 277 (London: Oxford University Press, 1963, 1978), 1:2–3; cp. Bertil Thuresson, ed., *Middle English Occupational Terms* (Lund: Gleerup, 1950), p. 143, s.v. *Laweman*. The occupation is explained in Latham and Howlett, *Dictionary of Medieval Latin*, s.v. *lagemannus*.

77. Thus *Beowulf* 511a, *ne leof ne lað* (Fr. Klaeber, ed., *Beowulf and the Fight at Finnsburg*, 3rd ed. [Boston: Heath, 1950], p. 20); and *Genesis and Exodus* 340, *lef or loðt*

(Arngart, *ME Genesis and Exodus*, p. 62). And cp. Rossell Hope Robbins, ed., *Secular Lyrics of the XIVth and XVth Centuries* (Oxford: Clarendon Press, 1952), pp. 134–35 (no. 134, refrain, "That (w)ons was lefe let neuer be lothe"); and Gower, *Confessio Amantis* 4.669, *lief ne loth* (G. C. Macaulay, ed., *The English Works of John Gower*, 2 vols., EETS e.s. 81, 82 [1900, 1901; repr. London: Oxford University Press, 1963], 1:319).

78. Hanneke Wirtjes, ed., *The Middle English Physiologus*, EETS o.s. 299 (Oxford: Oxford University Press, 1991), p. 12.

79. See Skeat, *Wars of Alexander*, pp. 237 (line 4445), 257 (line 5088) = Duggan and Turville-Petre, *Wars of Alexander*, pp. 145 (line 4574), 163 (line 5214).

80. See A. Jack Aitken, "Variation and Variety in Written Middle Scots," in *Edinburgh Studies in English and Scots*, ed. A. J. Aitken, Angus McIntosh, and Hermann Pálsson, (London: Longman, 1971), pp. 177–209, esp. pp. 182–92, 207 n. 32. The Lancashire place-name Larbrick is earlier Lair- and Leyr- (see Eilert Ekwall, *The Place-Names of Lancashire* [Manchester: Manchester University Press, 1922], p. 154; and cp. Henry Cecil Wyld, with T. Oakes Hirst, *The Place Names of Lancashire, Their Origin and History* [London: Constable, 1911], p. 170).

81. Cp. Whiting: "The rhymes show $\bar{a}$-forms: *care: lare* 2.201:203; and also $\bar{o}$-forms: *more: restore* 2.83:85" (p. xxxi).

82. See Stanley, "*True Counsel*," p. 159.

83. Cp. Bartlett Jere Whiting with Helen Wescott Whiting, eds., *Proverbs, Sentences, and Proverbial Phrases* (Cambridge, Mass.: Harvard University Press, 1968), L139, and esp. L142 *Swifte so lefe on lynde*, as well as L144 *and alle we fellen doun as a leef, and our wickidnessis as wynd han take awei vs*, the second Wycliffite version of Isa. 64:6 (Josiah Forshall and Frederic Madden, eds., *The Holy Bible . . . by John Wycliffe and His Followers*, 4 vols. [Oxford: Oxford University Press, 1850], 3:336, rendering *Biblia Sacra iuxta Latinam Vulgatam Versionem*, 18 vols. [Rome: Typis Polyglottis Vaticanus, 1926–95], 13:226, "et cecidimus quasi folium universi et iniquitates nostrae quasi ventus abstulerunt nos").

84. Cp. Rasmussen, §§ 199–216, and Whiting, p. xxxvi, § 34. Dickins, p. 518, comments on the imperfect rhymes of lines 131, 133, 135, 137 (*glydyn/rydyn,/hyde/tyde*), saying that to improve them we should emend lines 131 and 133 to *glyde* and *ryde*. These emendations are accepted by Turville-Petre, p. 157.

85. One such stray item of information is provided by John MacGregor who tells us ("Campbell, Earl and Marquess of Breadalbane," in *The Scots Peerage*, ed. James Balfour Paul, 9 vols. [Edinburgh: D. Douglas, 1904–14], 2:174) that Sir Colin Campbell, whose father gave him the lands of Glenurchy in Lorne in 1432, went three times to Rome. The founder of the great family of Argyll was as ready to leave the ancestral estates as any lord in Scotland or England. But would the poet have known? It seems doubtful that line 95—meaning 'and you hold sway over every town from Lorne to London' (thus McIntosh, p. 389)—refers back to *ʒe beþ* (line 94) and carries that sense, instead of referring, as I believe, to *lykyr to leue*, however that may

be interpreted. Turville-Petre asks if *Loron* might be 'Lorraine' (*Alliterative Poetry*, p. 155); the spelling <-on> makes that unlikely.

86. For the use in *Sir Gawain*, see Andrew and Waldron, *Poems of the Pearl MS*, p. 236. McIntosh refers to Williams, "Mural Paintings," from which, however, the church he is looking for does not emerge. Fein, "Life and Death," discusses the manuscript iconography. See n. 30, above.

87. Intervocalic single <t> for etymological /tt/ seems not to occur in MS Douce 302; but note such verbal forms as *wyttyng* 'knowing' (*True Living* W1.44), *wetyng* (*Marcolf* W2.482), *wytyng* (*Marcolf* W2.826), *wittyng* (*Epilogue* W18.240), *wettyng* (*St. Anne Carol* 37 [W43.29]), *wyttyngly* (*Marcolf* W2.158), *wettanly* (*Vision of St. Paul* W16.115, marked "?error" in *MED* s.v. *witingli*), *wetyngly* (*Vision of St. Paul* W16.337); and the etymologically obscure verb 'to put' occurs with *potyn* and *pottyn* in the same poem (*Marcolf* W2.519, 634). For the MLG word, see Agathe Lasch et al., eds., *Mittelniederdeutsches Handwörterbuch*, in progress (Hamburg, later Neumünster: Wachholtz, 1928–), 2:col. 923, s.v. ³*māt*, and Jan de Vries, ed., *Nederlands etymologisch Woordenboek* (Leiden: Brill, 1971), p. 421 s.v. *maat* 2. This word may have led Jordan to emend *mete* to *mates*.

88. See the relevant variants in Kane and Donaldson, *The B Version*, and Russell and Kane, *The C Version*: B.13.35 (*mettes, macches*) = C.15.40 (*mettes, metes, mates, macches*); B.13.48 (*mete, macche*) = C.15.54 (violent emendation in text; *mete, mate, mache, felow*).

89. See Kottler and Markman, *Concordance*, s.v. *might*; and Wittig, *Piers Plowman Concordance*, s.v. *myȝt*; see also Luick, §§ 148, 194/2 Anm. 3, 199/2, 276. The form of the second singular present indicative of *may* is, in MS Douce 302, either *maȝt* (*True Living* W1.214) or *myȝt* (*Remedy of Nine Virtues* W3.16); that, however, may be irrelevant.

90. Cp. the parallel version from the Vernon MS edited by Thomas Frederick Simmons, *The Lay Folks Mass Book*, EETS o.s. 71 (1879; repr. London: Oxford University Press, 1968), pp. 128–47 (line 193 and, less close, lines 390–91); another version in London, BL MS Harley 3954 has the words as the rhyme words; see the extract edited by Wright, in Thomas Wright and James Orchard Halliwell, eds., *Reliquiæ Antiquæ*, 2 vols. (1840–43; repr. New York: AMS, 1966), 2:59–63 (p. 60) (lines 31–32).

91. See Parsons and Styles, *Vocabulary of English Place-Names*, s.v. *both-hall*. Putter criticizes *OED* and *MED* for not including *boþ-halle* ("Language and Metre," p. 505 n. 28), when in fact these dictionaries produced the entry for the first element of the compound in 1887 and 1958, 110 and 39 years before the validating evidence became available. Comment on *Marcolf* W2.344 requires reference to that evidence; Putter's comment lacks it.

92. Kiyokazu Mizobata, ed., *A Concordance to the Alliterative 'Morte Arthure'* (Tokyo: Shohakusha, 2001), pp. 396, 398.

93. For the meaning of the OE word, cp. E. G. Stanley, "Words for the *Dictionary of Old English*," in *The Dictionary of Old English: Retrospects and Prospects*, ed.

M. J. Toswell, Old English Newsletter: Subsidia 26 (Kalamazoo: Medieval Institute Publications, 1998), pp. 33–56 (pp. 48–51, 55–56).

94. See Frederic Madden, ed., *Laȝamons Brut, or Chronicle of Britain*, 3 vols. (1847; repr. Osnabrück: Zeller, 1967), 2:405 (line 19739), 2:456 (line 20964), 3:36 (line 26095) = Brook and Leslie, eds., *Laȝamon*, 2:512–13 (line 9849), 2:544–45 (line 10460), 2:682–83 (line 13024; morþre second <r> no longer clearly legible).

95. See Rasmussen, § 101, Whiting, p. xxxii, § 9, Jordan, *Handbook*, trans. Crook, § 98, § 198 b. "On high" is a favorite phrase of Audelay's; cp. Stanley, *"True Counsel,"* p. 156.

96. I do not know to what extent Kane, Kane and Donaldson, and Russell and Kane list such variants in *Piers Plowman* MSS; they may have regarded them as insignificant for their purposes; at C.3.183, *ny* is in Russell–Kane's text. The word *nigh* is taken by me in all its functions.

97. See Greene, ed., *Early English Carols*, pp. 20–21 (no. 37, 4.10), 24 (no. 44 , 5.3), 116 (no. 174 , 6.3), and 213–14 (no. 357, 8.4).

98. See Henry Bergen, ed., *Lydgate's Troy Book*, 4 pts. in 3 vols., EETS e.s. 97, 103, 106, 126 (1906–35; repr. Millwood, N.Y.: Kraus Reprint, 2003), 1:103 (line 3093).

99. E.g., Susan Irvine, ed., *The Anglo-Saxon Chronicle*, VII MS. E (Cambridge: Brewer, 2004), annals 1077 (p. 91, bottom line), 1091 (p. 102, line 18), 1135 (p. 134, line 2).

100. F. J. Furnivall, ed., *Adam Davy's 5 Dreams about Edward II: The Life of St. Alexius, Solomon's Book of Wisdom, St. Jeremie's 15 Tokens before Doomsday, The Lamentation of Souls*, EETS o.s. 69 (1878; repr. Millwood, N.Y.: Kraus Reprint, 1999), p. 16 (line 162, *tee* in rhyme with *be*). In the lines that follow, we are told by Davy, "Adam þe marchal / In stretforþe-bowe he is yknowe." Ernst Dölle, *Zur Sprache Londons vor Chaucer*, Studien zur englischen Philologie 32 (1913; repr. Halle: Niemeyer, 1973) takes the rhymes in Davy's *Dreams* as part of his documentary evidence for the language of London before Chaucer (pp. 2–3); he discusses this rhyme at p. 38, § 23 C. However, R. W. Chambers and Marjorie Daunt, eds., *A Book of London English, 1384–1425* (Oxford: Clarendon Press, 1931), approach Davy's language more cautiously: "although the author wrote at Stratford-at-Bow before Chaucer was born, we have his *Dreams* extant only as copied by a scribe [of Oxford, Bodl. Lib. MS Laud misc. 622], whose speech need not have been that of London at all, and whose period was certainly Chaucerian rather than pre-Chaucerian" (p. 5).

101. Cp. Rasmussen, §§ 221, 222 (referred to by Whiting), and Jordan, *Handbook*, trans. Crook (replacing Jordan's original German edition, referred to by Whiting), pp. 182–84, § 200.

102. See Tobler and Lommatzsch, *Altfranzösisches Wörterbuch*, vol. 10, col. 336 s.v. *title* (this fascicle published in 1974).

103. It was used in sixteenth-century Scottish when it was no longer in use south of the border; see *A Dictionary of the Older Scottish Tongue*, 11:122 s.v. *tume*, n.[1].

104. Turville-Petre, p. 152, derives the form from *walden* 'wished', preterite plural, found in the early southwest Midlands language of *Ancrene Wisse* and Oxford, Bodl. Lib. MS Bodley 34, but quite unlikely in the dialect of this poem or this manuscript, even if it were not for the unusual confusion of /d/ and /t/ which it shares with the derivation from *waldan*.

105. *The Wanderer* 32, and the *Riddles* 31.21 and 93.28 (in both, obscurely, *hord* is the object; at 93.28 a hostile person takes possession), 83.4 (where an enemy appears to take possession of the subject of the riddle); see Krapp and Dobbie, *Exeter Book*, pp. 134, 196 (and note, p. 339), 242. The editions of the *Riddles* give alternative explanations.

106. Kaiser, *Zur Geographie*, p. 272, lists *warlagh* among his *Nordwörter*, and Putter is content to follow him. But though more common in northern texts, the word is not confined to them; cp. the use in alliterative prose from MS Bodley 34. See Frances M. Mack, ed., *Seinte Marherete þe Meiden ant Martyr*, EETS o.s. 193 (London: Oxford University Press, 1934), p. 12 (lines 17–19): "Þa awariede werlahen leiden se luðerliche on hire leofliche lich, þet hit brec ou*er*al & liðerede o blode" (The accursed evil ones assailed her lovely body so wickedly that it broke all over and lathered in blood). London, BL Royal MS 17 A.xxvii has *wiðerlahen* 'persecutors, thugs', and Mack believes that this rare word was replaced in MS Bodley 34 by the more common word (p. 13 [line 20], and see her note, p. 63). For references to discussion of the dialect of these two West Midlands manuscripts, see Margaret Laing, *Catalogue of Sources for a Linguistic Atlas of Early Medieval English* (Cambridge: Brewer, 1993), pp. 124, 105.

107. Cp. Ludwig Gebhardt, *Das unausgedrückte Subjekt im Mittelenglischen* (Giessen: Selbstverlag des englischen Seminars der Universität Giessen, 1922); Herbert Koziol, *Grundzüge der Syntax der mittelenglischen Stabreimdichtungen*, Weiner Beiträge zur englischen Philologie 58 (Vienna: Braumüller, 1932), pp. 155–56.

108. In the badly disorganized pagination (vol. 12, between pp. 286 and 319) involving the entry *Worschip*, *A Dictionary of the Older Scottish Tongue* does not give the preposition *at* with the noun.

109. *Marcolf* W2.202 (*þai wryn fro me away* 'they turn away from me'); *Marcolf* W2.564 (a difficult line, *Þis makys þe worchip of clerkys wrong fore to wry*, perhaps to be translated 'this makes it wrong to wrest honorable recognition away from those in holy orders'); *Marcolf* W2.916 (*Bot wrys away fro Godys word to his wyckydnes* 'but turns away from God's word to his sinfulness'); and *Marcolf* W2.995 (*wry not fro Godis word* 'do not turn away from God's word').

110. *Loue's Labour's Lost*, IV.ii; quoted from Charlton Hinman, ed., *The First Folio of Shakespeare* (New York: Norton, 1968), p. 149 (lines 1174–77).

111. Cp. Lucy Toulmin Smith, ed., *York Plays* (1885; repr. New York: Russell and Russell, 1963), p. 382 (line 169), qtd. in *MED* s.v. *sir(e* 1. (c); or Richard Morris, ed., *Cursor Mundi (The Cursur o the World)*, EETS o.s. 57, 59, 62, 66, 68, 99, 101 (1874–93; repr. London: Oxford University Press, 1963), i.e.: EETS o.s. 57, p. 72

(line 1127), when God politely addresses Cain as *sir cayn* (the variant reading avoids that act of divine courtesy). To *Paternoster* W53.18, cp. *Cursor Mundi*, EETS o.s. 57, p. 34 (line 467), qtd. in *MED* s.v. *court*, n. (1), 3; and *Cursor Mundi*, EETS o.s. 66, p. 1180, *Al heuen court* (line 20619), where service as at court is the subject.

Death and the Colophon
in the Audelay Manuscript

Susanna Fein

Who was John Audelay? The name attaches to a chantry priest said to be, in the year 1426, blind and deaf and living in his retirement from a secular chaplaincy at Haughmond Abbey, an Augustinian house in Shropshire—a site that is now a medieval ruin open to tourists. Until a reference to Audelay's earlier life—a criminal event in 1417—was discovered in London by Michael Bennett, the only records of the man were the eighteen instances of his name in a single manuscript that appears to have been copied in that same abbey during Audelay's lifetime.[1] Although my focus here will be on the manuscript, the earlier event is of some interest. John Audelay was chaplain to Lord Richard Lestrange of Knockin and he was in Lestrange's entourage in London when his patron got involved in a violent altercation with Sir John Trussell at the London parish church St. Dunstan's in the East on Easter Sunday. A sword was drawn, Trussell wounded, and an innocent parishioner killed. Punishment for this crime fell upon the hot-headed Lestrange and his company, which included Audelay the chaplain. Lestrange and his wife had to lead, barefoot and in plain shifts, a procession of public penance and humiliation from St. Paul's to St. Dunstan's. It was an infamous event—according to Bennett, one of the biggest reported scandals of the day. Though several accounts survive, Audelay's name occurs only once in them.[2]

It does appear certain, though, that John Audelay was a participant in the act of public penance, and as he was Lestrange's own chaplain—responsible for his lord's soul and his own, and thus bearing the moral weight of his patron's reckless breach of a commandment, committed in a holy place on a holy day—Audelay must have been traumatized with shame and fear before God. Or so it may seem when we read the Audelay Manuscript, with its many fervent calls for repentance by others, for reform of the clergy, and for prayers on behalf of the soul of the poet-chaplain whose name appears so many times in the book. Before anyone knew of the London event, there had been speculation that Audelay's persistent tone of dire repentance meant that he had had a licentious, goliardic youth that needed serious atonement. Such hypotheses were offered by James Orchard Halliwell, E. K. Chambers, and Audelay's EETS editor, Ella Keats Whiting.[3] Our present knowledge of his accessory involvement in high public scandal appears to solve that mystery. Audelay had a past that no chaplain in the early decades of the fifteenth century would have envied.

The book Douce 302 serves, it seems, as part of an ongoing atonement before God and man. In reading it, with its many poems signed "John the Blind Audelay," one cannot help but suspect that the public nature of the crime led Audelay to live out the latter portion of his life as a "public penitent," at least within a local setting, even as he remained in service to Richard, praying for the souls of family members in the abbey chantry recently endowed by Lestrange. Audelay's verse tells us that he was the first priest appointed to tend to this duty in the Lestrange chantry. The appointment was probably granted as a way to permit the chaplain to live out his old age in a cloistered environment. My interest here lies in how the life story and penitential consciousness of a shamed chaplain conjoin with the make-up—especially the drawn-out endings—of Audelay's book.

The last poem in MS Douce 302, a farewell from Audelay, includes an important statement on authorial intentionality. The poet explains that what one finds in the book is exactly what he *intends* to be there, for he admonishes a reader to "Loke in this book; here may ye se / Hwatt ys my wyl and my wrytyng" (*Conclusion* 32–33).[4] His authorial purpose has been fulfilled. The admonition pertains, as well, to the book's material integrity: no one should deface the manuscript because doing so would mar Audelay's creation and intent.[5] So states the last stanza of Audelay's farewell, written on the last folio copied by Audelay's second scribe, his correcting scribe:

> *Cuius finis bonum, ipsum totum bonum. Finito libro. Sit laus et gloria Christo.*[6]
>   No mon this book he take away,
>   Ny kutt owte noo leef, Y say forwhy,
>   For hit ys sacrelege, sirus, Y yow say!
>   Beth acursed in the dede truly!
>   Yef ye wil have any copi,
>   Askus leeve and ye shul have,

> To pray for hym specialy
> That hyt made your soules to save,
>   Jon the Blynde Awdelay.
> The furst prest to the Lord Strange he was,
> Of thys chauntré, here in this place,
> That made this bok by Goddus grace,
>   Deeff, sick, blynd, as he lay.
>   (*Conclusion* 40–52)
>
> *Cuius anime propicietur Deus.*[7]

Audelay states that his motive for preserving his *wrytyng* in this book is to save the souls of readers, but an ancillary intent is also put forth: prayers in perpetuity for the named author. Thus it is crucial that John the Blind Audelay be named for each future reader, and that his identity and profession be known: priest of the Lestrange chantry; maker of *this* very book; infirm old man languishing upon his deathbed in the lingering last image with which we are left. What is quite arresting about this image is how the poet writes as though his action—the completing of the book—is an action taken in dying. He closes the book upon a portrait of himself on his deathbed, so that we are left with that lingering picture and a sense that somehow Audelay composed what we have just read while in that very state, and, even more, that we are listening to the spoken words of a man as he dies. At the same time, there is something of perpetual stasis in this image of dying-but-not-yet-being-dead. And yet when the final phrase is intoned in Latin, the poet seems now to have departed, for the scribe (or is it Audelay?) pronounces a benediction: *Cuius anime propicietur Deus*, "On whose soul may God be propitious."

Finding this phrase at another point in the book, on folio 22v, Richard Firth Green speculates that Audelay was already dead when the phrase was written there and then again here, on the final folio.[8] While it is plausible that a personal scribe would insert a benediction when an author has recently died, I do not think that is the case here, because for Audelay to have orchestrated his own departure from the book, *in the manner of a death*, fits perfectly with his conception of the book as being coextensive with his own life and deeds. Furthermore, Audelay's book is emblematic of eternal life in general. It is made the physical medium by which a faithful reader can strive to have his own name inscribed in "the bok of lyfe in hevun blys" (*Conclusion* 19). As such, it stands for that magnificent book in which God sets the names of the saved to be read on the Day of Doom. Every Christian wants his name in that book, and so, likewise, will every faithful reader note Audelay's name—and Lord LeStrange's too—in *this* book, and offer a prayer for Audelay's soul. As Robert Meyer-Lee has astutely observed, the book of John Audelay fulfills a memorial function similar to the office of a chantry priest. It serves as a chantry of perpetual prayer on behalf of departed souls—Audelay's in particular—so long as there are readers to read it and regard its injunctions.[9] I would add that it also emblematizes the spiritual Book of Life in Heaven's Bliss, the ultimate record of saved souls from the beginning to the end of time. And just as Audelay sets his name forever in the Audelay Manuscript, eighteen times (see the appendix, below), he intends for his own name to be safely inscribed in the Book of Eternal Life.

Two scribes worked on MS Douce 302, and they performed their duties in anonymity, as scribes generally do. Enacting the *wyl* of the book's maker, John the Blind Audelay, they filled the book with his name, voice, and personality. An ever-fervent "I" speaks admonitions and pious instructions to the reader and often, it seems, to an assembled listening body, whom Audelay usually addresses as "sirs." The first scribe (Scribe A) followed a plan of copying out the poet's compositions in three generic parts—moral texts, salutations, carols—with an added, fourth section devoted to a meditation that progressively moves to last things. As I have shown previously, the work of this scribe evinces a program—undoubtedly Audelay's—to organize each section and end it well, usually upon subjects of dying or the beatific vision to be beheld on the apocalyptic Last Day.[10] This plan accords with Audelay's own insistence that "alle ys good that hath good ende" (*Conclusion* 38). His context for this assertion is generally that of a preacher: living souls must strive to have good ends, properly full of contrition, well confessed, set to penance, and absolved by a priest. But, very clearly, ending well was the habit of Audelay's moral and daily existence, one that extended, where he was able, to *all* his actions—not just to the professional business of saving souls, but also to the acts of composing verse and shaping an anthology.

The manuscript has a structure that reveals the preoccupations of its author. The two scribes were presumably resident Augustinian canons in Haughmond Abbey, recruited to serve the blind chaplain so that he might create the book he planned. Scribe A copied out virtually all of sections 1 to 3, omitting incipits and explicits.[11] He also copied most of the material in section 4, everything but the last two items, the Latin moral poem and Audelay's *Conclusion*. Sometime after Scribe A finished his work, Scribe B added his hand to the book, and Scribe A's hand then disappears. Scribe A's work appears to have followed a plan to assemble the collected works of John Audelay. Although some bits are missing now, I believe that Audelay's intention and original execution of it were comprehensive, as his phrase "my wyl and my wrytyng" implies.

Section 1 closes almost as strongly as does section 4. Its last elements are Saint Paul's vision of hell's torments, a stern appeal from God to humankind, and then the important final poem, Audelay's *Epilogue*. Here Audelay explains his vocation as a blind poet of prophecy, which began as a visitation from God—a divine, apocalyptic dream—following some human calamities: earthquake and famine. Audelay read these signs as tokens that he was to warn the people of God's impending doom (*Epilogue* 27–65). Audelay now provides a retrospective dual-title for all of section 1: *The Counsel of Conscience, or the Ladder of Heaven* (*Epilogue* 417–18). There are moments in this poem where Audelay's apocalyptic admonitions are reminiscent of William Langland, while another piece in section 1, the alliterative *Marcolf and Solomon*, has been frequently cited as evidence of Audelay's imaginative indebtedness to *Piers Plowman*.[12] Historical importance attaches then to Audelay's evidently deep background knowledge of alliterative verse traditions, which he must have imbibed when he was a young man. His book displays his capacity both to rework the style in various ways, and to preserve older specimens, as he does in section 4.

In pursuing his duties, Scribe A also redacted all the salutations of section 2 and the carols of section 3. These sequences likewise are arranged to save souls and end well: section 2 culminates in a vision of the Savior's Face, and section 3 consists of twenty-five carols in formal sequence. The penultimate carol meditates on the dread of death. The final one offers pious devotion to Saint Francis, recounting the legend of the saint's life, death, and place in heaven, where he now has the capacity to intercede on behalf of his brethren, among whom Audelay seems to place himself.[13]

As Scribe A carried out his work, he anticipated the work of Scribe B, who later joined the operation as planned, after what must have been a short interval. The typical pattern of copying items, then, is: incipit in red (Scribe B), text in black (Scribe A), and explicit in red (Scribe B). This is the pattern throughout the manuscript, *except* for section 4, which carries forth an interesting program of multiple endings. Before turning to the process for that section, I wish to note one more detail about the copying of section 1, *The Counsel of Conscience*. When Scribe A reached the end of that section, he left a large gap to prepare for an unusually long colophon in Latin, which Scribe B supplied later. This colophon represents another key spot at which detailed biographical information about John Audelay is recorded. After repeating the title, the colophon explains that Audelay has composed this *liber* to the honor of Christ and for the example of others in Haughmond Abbey, in the year 1426. Thus the colophon locates the manuscript in year and place, while also naming Audelay as a chaplain, the book's composer, and a resident of Haughmond, blind and deaf in his afflictions from God. It provides the same benediction, "Cuius anime propicietur Deus," found after the autobiographical passage at the end of the manuscript. The opening words of the colophon, "Finito libro," misled many earlier scholars into thinking that the manuscript once stopped here and was later resumed.[14] The work of Scribe A surrounds this colophon, however; his hand is continuous, moving from section 1 to section 2 without interruption. Thus the physical evidence confirms that a compiler's initial conceptual plan for the book of John Audelay was to sequence all four sections just as we find them here, just as Scribe A copied them.

Now we can turn to section 4 to look specifically at its eccentric process of ending three times. Here the manuscript shifts from the lyric appeal of carols to the *moralitee* of religious prose. Scribe A left eight lines blank before the prose (fol. 32r), indicating a juncture of some weight. Scribe B later filled in the last four lines with the compiler's rhyming injunction to

> Rede thys offt, butt rede hit sofft,
> And whatt thou redust, forgeete hit noght,
> For here the soth thou maght se
> What fruyte cometh of thy body.
> (*Instr. for Reading 4* 1–4)

This portion of Audelay's book deals in matters pertaining to death: the body's decay, the bodily sins that account for it, and the soul's ecstasy. Somewhat like the Parson with his prose meditation in *The Canterbury Tales*, the chaplain Audelay seems now to counsel a distinct thinking upon last things.[15]

The first item of prose, an extract from Richard Rolle's *Form of Living*, summarizes the sins of the heart, the mouth, and the hand, and it contains an interesting interpolated stanza of alliterative verse, an aphorism on the abuse of prayer, neatly embedded in Rolle's prose.[16] The stanza seems to erupt spontaneously from Audelay's own preaching practice, triggered by the word *rabuld* in Rolle. The second prose item, an allegory of the soul's purification, follows upon Rolle's enumeration of sins with sequential logic. This haunting meditational exercise, to which Ian Doyle has given the title *Bonum lectum*, likens the cleansing of the soul to the preparation of a bed for Christ.[17] It is a figurative readying for death and the mystical Bridegroom, with the bedchamber's four walls signifying the four ages, that is, "childehode, youeth, parfite age, and the last age whan thou art an old mon ore womon" (*Honest Bed*). The bed straw, the mattress, the pillows, the curtains, the cords, the tester, and every other part of a splendid bed—the bed of a lord, not an ascetic—each represents a segment of the private penitential process by which the soul is cleansed:

> Thus be the bedde that our Lord wil have lykyng to ly in. And when he is in this bed, angelys wil syng about him this song of prophesé: *Exulta et lauda habitacio Syon, quia magnus in medio tui sanctus Israel*,[18] "thoue Syon, mon soule, the dwellyng place of Jhesu, be joyful and glad for the gret Holé God of Israel is now within thee, the wyche is Jhesus." (*Honest Bed* 70–75)

In the spiritual process reflected in Audelay's concluding fourth section, the soul—of poet, of reader—is now readied for death and receptive to Christ.

After the meditative prose Audelay selected two anonymous alliterative poems.[19] A more northern cleric than was Chaucer's Parson, the Shropshire chaplain has elsewhere demonstrated intimate knowledge of "'rum, ram, ruf,' be lettre."[20] These two poems, *Paternoster* and *Three Dead Kings*, are the last poems inscribed by Scribe A, and they mark the first ending of the Audelay Manuscript. Their position of honor suggests that Audelay respected the alliterative mode as a medium for lofty, serious matter. For all his seeming indebtedness to *Piers Plowman*, it is *stanzaic* alliterative forms, and especially the thirteen-line type, that Audelay reveres and emulates in his manuscript.[21] These last poems establish an aura of stately, sacramental formality. The penultimate poem expounds the Paternoster in eleven-line stanzas. This prayer, Audelay tells us elsewhere, has the power to protect a soul from damnation, so here its utterance is a sign of preparation for dying well.[22] The final poem is the densely ornate *Three Dead Kings*, the most accomplished literary piece in the book, an admonitive narrative of three kings who encounter the animated corpses of their fathers, receive warnings from them, and use these mirrors of what they will become to reform their ways in the world.

The book written by the first hand ends here. The positioning of *Three Dead Kings* at the end of the Audelay Manuscript invites a reader to look upon the book as if in a mirror in which dead author and living reader occupy reciprocal positions: the living should pray for the dead and think upon their own dying.[23] If we understand this point as the first ending of the Audelay Manuscript, as it is where Scribe A's work ends, we have here a sense of closure that relies upon an unspoken understanding of the penitential, monitive purpose implicit in the Three Living and the Three Dead motif. It bears the aesthetic authenticity of a vernacular icon—austere, wise, and magnificent in its simple, stark appeal. Scribe A's final four works—*Sins of the Heart*, *Honest Bed*, *Paternoster*, and *Three Dead Kings*—create an ending that captures the mystery and dread of death. If indeed it was Audelay who compiled this first ending, as probably it was, we must see this sequence as one of his better accomplishments.

But though the book in its initial conception seems to end here, it does not stop here. A second ending takes the book into Latin, as if the language of the Church will solemnize and sanctify the process toward death. In a formal hand seldom seen elsewhere,[24] Scribe B inscribed a commonplace poem on the vanity of life, a poem probably learned by most every medieval English schoolboy. For a modern reader, this ending dilutes the first one, but for Audelay, who apparently needed to add more to his book as he lived on, the change to Latin provides an appropriate coda. It proceeds from the clerical logic by which several of his other works conclude with Latin prayers. *Cur mundus militat sub vana gloria* moralizes upon the world's transitoriness in the professional manner of Audelay as chaplain.[25]

Finally, at the very last phase in the book's production, Audelay apparently authorized Scribe B's further finalization of the manuscript, as he added *yet another* last poem. This piece, Audelay's *Conclusion*, signed by Audelay in the familiar manner, possesses the chaplain's distinctively earnest voice. The presence of this poem provides one of our strongest bits of evidence that the poet oversaw the manuscript's copying to its completion. This third ending is telling, for it seems that Audelay was himself unable to finish his book without adding a last word—one that articulates his own death as an example for others. This poem treads very close to the line; if there is a way to speak convincingly as if already dead, Audelay is able to find it. His goal is to address sinning mankind from the perspective of the admonitory dead who can warn us from the other side of the divide:

> Here may ye here now hwat ye be.
> Here may ye cnow hwat ys this worlde.
> Here may ye boothe *here and se*

Only in God ys all comforde.
. . .
Herfore Y have dyspysed this worlde,
And have overcomen alle erthely thyng.
My ryches in heven with dede and worde
I have ypurchest in my levyng.
          (*Conclusion* 1–4, 27–30; my italics)

He talks of his life in the past tense, and thus speaks virtually as if he were one of the Dead in *Three Dead Kings*. I do not think Audelay planned this move in advance. The work of the two scribes suggests that it happened as an afterthought, because Audelay *lived on* in his state of dying well, and he incorporated the prior first ending into his own stance as author-preacher. Indeed, this third and final ending exhibits Audelay achieving his goal: by an imaginative fulfillment of his last desire, he receives in his afterlife the benefits of his readers' prayers.

    To conclude, the codicological evidence in section 4 suggests that Audelay planned to close an anthology of his works with devotional vernacular writings chosen from among his best models: an instructional meditation by Richard Rolle, an allegorical prose treatise on the mystical Bridegroom, a versified Paternoster, and stark alliterative stanzas on confronting one's own mortality. He arranged these texts to inspire good dying, as the best way to cap his own compositions, arranged into generic groups that ended well. If my hypothesis is correct, when Audelay first conceived of the anthology, he had not yet written the "last poem," his *Conclusion*. The concept of the book—his own material one reflecting the spiritual one of heaven—grew within him as the compilation came to fruition.

    By his act of constructing an anthology of his own verse upon an apparently deliberate meditational design suggestive of the progress of the soul toward death and God, John Audelay gives scholars an interesting reason not to neglect him. The section 4 arrangement of prose, alliterative verse, and Latin reflection occurred because Audelay continually sought appropriate endings, and he continually ruminated upon his own. And in ruminating, he developed, over time, a book with a long and lingering farewell.

Appendix

The Eighteen Signatures and Three Endings of the Audelay Manuscript

SECTION 1. THE COUNSEL OF CONSCIENCE

[X]	TRUE LIVING
XI	MARCOLF AND SOLOMON **(signed)**
	. . .
[XV]	THE REMEDY OF NINE VIRTUES **(signed)**
XVI	SEVEN BLEEDINGS OF CHRIST
XVII	PRAYER ON CHRIST'S PASSION
XVIII	THE PSALTER OF THE PASSION (sequence)
XIX	SEVEN WORDS OF CHRIST ON THE CROSS
XX	DEVOTIONS AT THE LEVATION OF CHRIST'S BODY (sequence)
XXI	VIRTUES OF THE MASS
XXII	FOR REMISSION OF SINS (sequence)
XXIII	VISITING THE SICK AND CONSOLING THE NEEDY **(signed)**
XXIIII	BLIND AUDELAY'S ENGLISH PASSION (sequence) **(signed twice)**
XXV	OUR LORD'S EPISTLE ON SUNDAY **(signed)**
XXVI	THE VISION OF SAINT PAUL **(signed)**
XXVII	THE LORD'S MERCY (sequence)

    1. God's Address to Sinful Men
    2. Audelay's *Epilogue* **(signed twice)**
    3. Latin Colophon to *The Counsel of Conscience* (fol. 22v) **(signed)**

SECTION 2. SALUTATIONS

XXVII	DEVOTIONS TO JESUS AND MARY HIS MOTHER (sequence)
XXIX	OTHER DEVOTIONS TO MARY (two salutations)
XXX	SONG OF THE MAGNIFICAT
XXXI	SALUTATION TO SAINT BRIDGET **(signed twice)**

XXXII	Devotions to Saint Winifred (sequence) **(signed)**	
XXXIII	Devotions to Saint Anne (sequence)	
XXXIIII	Meditation on the Holy Face (sequence)	

Section 3. Carols

XXXV	Carol Sequence (25 carols) (**signed thrice:** Carol 12. King Henry VI; Carol 24. Dread of Death; Carol 25. Saint Francis)	

Section 4. Meditative Close

XXXVI	Devotional Prose (penitential meditation) 1. The Sins of the Heart (extract from Rolle's *Form of Living*) 2. An Honest Bed	
XXXVII	Paternoster	
XXXVIII	Three Dead Kings	← Ending 1 (Scribe A)
	Latin Poem *Cur mundus*	← Ending 2 (Scribe B)
	Audelay's *Conclusion* (**signed twice**)	← Ending 3 (Scribe B)

Notes

1. See Michael J. Bennett, "John Audley: Some New Evidence on His Life and Work," *Chaucer Review* 16 (1982): 344–55, and his essay in the present volume, "John Audelay: Life Records and Heaven's Ladder," pp. 30–53. On the signatures in MS Douce 302, see the appendix, above.

2. Bennett, "John Audelay: Life Records," p. 50 n. 29.

3. James Orchard Halliwell, ed., *The Poems of John Audelay: A Specimen of the Shropshire Dialect in the Fifteenth Century*, Percy Society 47 (London: Richards, 1844), p. vii; E. K. Chambers, *English Literature at the Close of the Middle Ages* (Oxford: Oxford University Press, 1945), p. 93; and Ella Keats Whiting, ed., *The Poems of John Audelay*, EETS o.s. 184 (1931; repr. Oxford: Oxford University Press, 2006), pp. xv–xx.

4. All citations from the Audelay Manuscript are from my edition: John the Blind Audelay, *Poems and Carols (Oxford, Bodleian Library MS Douce 302)*, ed. Susanna Fein (Kalamazoo: Medieval Institute Publications, 2009).

5. The opening of this admonition (lines 40–43) borrows from the scribal tradition of the book curse, a long-standing trope discussed by Glending Olson, "Author, Scribe, and Curse: The Genre of *Adam Scriveyn*," *Chaucer Review* 42 (2008): 284–97. A milder plea to the reader ("Huyde hyt not in hodymoke, / Lete other mo rede þys boke") appears at the end of John Mirk's *Instructions for Parish Priests* (ed. Edward Peacock, EETS o.s. 31, 2nd ed., rev. F. J. Furnivall [1902; repr. New York: Greenwood, 1969], p. 59 [lines 1919–20]).

6. "[He] whose end is good is entire[ly] good itself. The book is finished. Praise and glory be to Christ." Cp. fol. 22v: "Finito libro. Sit laus et gloria Christo," the opening words of the colophon that concludes *The Counsel of Conscience*.

7. "May God be propitious to his soul." Cp. fol. 22v: "Cuius anime propicietur Deus," the closing words of the *Finito libro* colophon.

8. Richard Firth Green, "Marcolf the Fool and Blind John Audelay," in *Speaking Images: Essays in Honor of Essays in Honor of V. A. Kolve*, ed. R. F. Yeager and Charlotte C. Morse (Asheville, N.C.: Pegasus, 2001), pp. 559–76 (p. 565).

9. Robert J. Meyer-Lee, "The Vatic Penitent: Audelay's Self-Representation," in the present volume, pp. 54–85 (p. 67). It should also be noted that making a book as a public "counsel of conscience" and as a site from which the author may petition for a reader's prayers has good Augustinian precedence. See R. S. Pine-Coffin, trans., *Saint Augustine, Confessions* (London: Penguin, 1961), p. 207 (X.1: "I wish to act in truth, making my confession both in my heart before you [i.e., God] and in this book before the many who will see it.") and also pp. 203 (IX.13: Augustine petitioning prayers for his deceased mother), 209 (X.4: Augustine petitioning prayers for himself). The gesture also occurs at the end of Mirk's *Instructions for Parish Priests* (ed. Peacock), pp. 59–60; like Audelay, Mirk dwelled in an Augustinian monastery. See also Simon Roffey, *The Medieval Chantry Chapel: An Archaeology* (Woodbridge: Boydell & Brewer, 2007), pp. 12, 21, 23.

10. Susanna Fein, "Good Ends in the Audelay Manuscript," *Yearbook of English Studies* 33 (2003): 97–119.

11. The texts of one carol (*Circumcision Carol*) and one salutation (*Gabriel's Salutation to Mary*) are begun by Scribe A but largely supplied by Scribe B. These are the only substantial exceptions to the usual copying pattern, and even here it is clear that Scribe A knew what items to insert where, even if he did not have ready access to the full texts.

12. See especially Green, "Marcolf the Fool, pp. 559–76, and his essay printed in the present volume, "Langland and Audelay," pp. 153–69; James Simpson, "Saving Satire after Arundel's Constitutions: John Audelay's 'Marcol and Solomon,'" in *Text and Controversy from Wyclif to Bale: Essays in Honour of Anne Hudson*, ed. Helen Barr and Ann M. Hutchison, Medieval Church Studies 4 (Turnhout: Brepols, 2004), pp. 387–404; and Mishtooni Bose, "Religious Authority and Dissent," in Peter Brown, ed., *A Companion to Medieval English Literature and Culture c. 1350–c. 1500* (Oxford: Blackwell, 2007), pp. 40–55 (pp. 50–51). Derek Pearsall, *Old English and Middle English Poetry* (London: Routledge and Kegan Paul, 1977), p. 249, first noted the verbal and metrical

likeness, though he refines his position in the essay printed in the present volume, pp. 138–152.

13. The background for Audelay's interest in Saint Francis is unknown. Nothing in his life records indicates that he had Franciscan associations, and he evidently spent the end of his life in an Augustinian house. As Whiting notes, it is "unusual that Audelay should glorify St. Francis, the founder of one of the rival orders" (*Poems*, p. 255), yet the carol evinces sincere admiration of the saint's piety. For further discussion, see the explanatory notes to this carol in Audelay, *Poems and Carols*, pp. 313–15.

14. See Fein, "Good Ends," p. 104 n. 16.

15. Cp. *Parson's Prologue* X 46–51 *and Parson's Tale* X 75 (Larry D. Benson, ed., *The Riverside Chaucer*, 3rd ed. (Boston: Houghton Mifflin, 1987), pp. 287–88.

16. Susanna Greer Fein, "A Thirteen-Line Stanza on the Abuse of Prayer from the Audelay MS," *Medium Ævum* 63 (1994): 61–74.

17. A. I. Doyle, "'Lectulus noster floridus': An Allegory of the Penitent Soul," in *Literature and Religion in the Later Middle Ages: Philological Studies in Honor of Siegfried Wenzel*, ed. Richard G. Newhauser and John A. Alford (Binghamton, N.Y.: Medieval & Renaissance Texts & Studies, 1994), pp. 179–90.

18. "Rejoice, and praise, habitation [of] Sion, for great is he that is in the midst of thee, the holy one of Israel" (Isaiah 12:6).

19. The matter of their authorship remains open, however; see my essay "John Audelay and His Book: Critical Overview and Major Issues," in the present volume, pp. 3–29 (p. 14).

20. *Parson's Prologue* X 43 (Benson, *Riverside Chaucer*, p. 287).

21. Susanna Greer Fein, "The Early Thirteen-Line Stanza: Style and Metrics Reconsidered," *Parergon* 18 (2000): 97–126; and Thorlac Turville-Petre, "'Summer Sunday', 'De Tribus Regibus Mortuis', and 'The Awntyrs off Arthure': Three Poems in the Thirteen-Line Stanza," *Review of English Studies*, n.s. 25 (1974): 1–14.

22. See *Marcolf* 927–28, and cp. *Virtues of the Mass* 124. For further discussion, see the explanatory note to *Paternoster* in Audelay, *Poems and Carols*, pp. 317–18, and Fein, "Good Ends," p. 108 n. 21.

23. Susanna Greer Fein, "Life and Death, Reader and Page: Mirrors of Mortality in English Manuscripts," *Mosaic* 35 (2002): 69–94.

24. This hand was once thought to be that of a third scribe (Whiting, *Poems*, p. viii), but Doyle believes it to be "probably a more formal mode (bastard anglicana) of the second [scribe]; cf. 'Quicumque inspexerit' on fol. 32v" ("Lectulus noster floribus," pp. 181–82 n. 15).

25. For *Cur mundus*, see F. J. E. Raby, ed., *The Oxford Book of Medieval Latin Verse* (Oxford: Clarendon Press, 1961), pp. 433–34, 501 (no. 284), and the references cited in Audelay, *Poems and Carols*, pp. 333–34.

WORKS CITED

Aitken, A. Jack. "Variation and Variety in Written Middle Scots." In *Edinburgh Studies in English and Scots*, ed. A. J. Aitken, Angus McIntosh, and Hermann Pálsson, pp. 177–209. London: Longman, 1971.

Allmand, Christopher. *Henry V.* Berkeley and Los Angeles: University of California Press, 1992.

Althusser, Louis. "Ideology and Ideological State Apparatuses." In *Lenin and Philosophy and Other Essays*, trans. Ben Brewster, pp. 127–93. London: New Left Books, 1971.

Amours, F. J., ed. *Scottish Alliterative Poems in Riming Stanza*. STS 27, 38. 1892–97; repr. New York: Johnson Reprint, 1966.

Andrew, Malcolm, and Ronald Waldron, eds. *The Poems of the Pearl Manuscript*. London: Arnold, 1978. 2nd ed. Berkeley and Los Angeles: University of California Press, 1989.

Arn, Mary-Jo, ed. *Fortunes Stabilnes: Charles of Orleans's English Book of Love*; Binghamton, N.Y.: Medieval & Renaissance Texts & Studies, 1994.

Arngart, Olof, ed. *The Middle English Genesis and Exodus*. Lund: Gleerup, 1968.

Ashley, Kathleen. "Historicizing Margery: The Book of Margery Kempe as Social Text." *Journal of Medieval and Early Modern Studies* 28 (1998): 371–88.

Atkinson, Clarissa W. *Mystic and Pilgrim: The Book and the World of Margery Kempe*. Ithaca: Cornell University Press, 1983.

——. "'Precious Balsam in a Fragile Glass': The Ideology of Virginity in the Later Middle Ages." *Journal of Family History* 8 (1983): 131–43.

Audelay, John the Blind. *Poems and Carols (Oxford, Bodleian Library MS Douce 302)*. Ed. Susanna Fein. Kalamazoo: Medieval Institute Publications, 2009.

Aungier, George James. *The History and Antiquities of Syon Monastery, the Parish of Isleworth, and the Chapelry of Hounslow*. London: Nichols and Son, 1840.

Axton, Richard, and Peter Happé, eds. *The Plays of John Heywood*. Cambridge: Brewer, 1991.

Barratt, Alexandra, *Anne Bulkeley and Her Book: Fashioning Female Piety in Early Tudor England; A Study of London, British Library Harley 494*. Turnhout: Brepols, forthcoming.

——. "The Prymer and Its Influence on Fifteenth-Century English Passion Lyrics." *Medium Ævum* 55 (1975): 264–79.

———, ed. *Women's Writing in Middle English*. New York: Longman, 1992.
Barron, Caroline D. *London in the Later Middle Ages: Government and People, 1200–1500*. Oxford: Oxford University Press, 2004.
Bate, W. J., and Albrecht B. Strauss, eds. *Samuel Johnson, The Rambler*. 3 vols. New Haven: Yale University Press, 1969.
Baugh, G. C., and D. C. Cox. *Monastic Shropshire*. Shewsbury: Shropshire Libraries, 1988.
Beaty, Nancy Lee. *The Craft of Dying: A Study in the Literary Tradition of the Ars Moriendi in England*. New Haven: Yale University Press, 1970.
Beckett, Neil. "St. Bridget, Henry V and Syon Abbey." In *Studies in St. Birgitta and the Brigittine Order*, ed. James Hogg, pp. 125–50. Salzburg: Institut für Anglistik und Americanistik, 1993.
Belfour, A. O., ed. *Twelfth-Century Homilies in MS. Bodley 343*. EET o.s. 137. 1909; repr. Oxford: Oxford University Press, 1997.
Bennett, Michael J. "John Audley: Some New Evidence on His Life and Work." *Chaucer Review* 16 (1982): 344–55.
———. *Richard II and the Revolution of 1399*. Stroud: Sutton, 1999.
———. "Richard II and the Wider Realm." In *Richard II: The Art of Kingship*, ed. Anthony Goodman and James Gillespie, pp. 187–204. Oxford: Clarendon Press, 1999.
Benson, Larry D. "The Authorship of *St. Erkenwald*." *Journal of English and Germanic Philology* 64 (1963): 393–405.
———, ed. *The Riverside Chaucer*. 3rd ed. Boston, Houghton Mifflin, 1987.
Bergen, Henry, ed. *Lydgate's Troy Book*. 4 pts. in 3 vols. EETS e.s. 97, 103, 106, 126. 1906–35; repr. Millwood, N.Y.: Kraus Reprint, 2003.
Bethurum, Dorothy, ed. *The Homilies of Wulfstan*. Oxford: Clarendon Press, 1957.
Biblia Sacra iuxta Latinam Vulgatam Versionem. 18 vols. Rome: Typis Polyglottis Vaticanus, 1926–95.
Blake, N. F. "Vernon Manuscript: Contents and Organisation." In *Studies in the Vernon Manuscript*, ed. Pearsall, pp. 45–59.
Bloomfield, Morton W. *The Seven Deadly Sins: An Introduction to the History of a Religious Concept, with Special Reference to Medieval English Literature*. East Lansing: Michigan State College Press, 1952.
Blunt, John Henry, ed. *The Myroure of Oure Ladye*. EETS e.s. 19. 1873; repr. Millwood, N.Y.: Kraus Reprint, 1975.
Boffey, Julia. "'Cy ensuent trois chaunceons': Groups and Sequences of Middle English Lyrics." Forthcoming.
———. "Middle English Lyrics and Manuscripts." In *A Companion to Middle English Lyrics*, ed. Duncan, pp. 1–18.
Boffey, Julia, and A. S. G. Edwards. *A New Index of Middle English Verse*. London: British Library, 2005.

———. Introduction to *The Works of Geoffrey Chaucer and "The Kingis Quair": A Facsimile of Bodleian Library, Oxford, MS Arch. Selden. B. 24.* Cambridge: Brewer, 1997.

Boklund-Lagopoulou, Karin. *"I have a yong suster": Popular Song and the Middle English Lyric.* Dublin: Four Courts, 2002.

Borroff, Marie, *Sir Gawain and the Green Knight: A Stylistic and Metrical Study.* New Haven: Yale University Press, 1962.

Bose, Mishtooni. "Religious Authority and Dissent." In *A Companion to Medieval English Literature and Culture c. 1350–c. 1500,* ed. Peter Brown, pp. 40–55. Oxford: Blackwell, 2007.

Bowers, John M. "John Lydgate." In *The Oxford Encyclopedia,* ed. Kastan, 2:340–43.

———. "Thomas Hoccleve." In *The Oxford Encyclopedia,* ed. Kastan, 2:62-65.

Boyle, Leonard E. *Pastoral Care, Clerical Education and Canon Law, 1200–1400.* London: Variorum Reprints, 1981.

Brandes, Herman. "Über die Quellen der mittelenglischen Versionen der Paulus-Vision." *Englische Studien* 7 (1884): 34–65.

———, ed. *Visio S. Pauli, ein Beitrag zur Visionslitteratur, mit einem deutschen und zwei lateinischen Texten.* Halle: Niemeyer, 1885.

Braswell, Laurel. *The Index of Middle English Prose. Handlist IV: A Handlist of Douce Manuscripts Containing Middle English Prose in the Bodleian Library, Oxford.* Woodbridge: Brewer, 1987.

Brennen, Michael G. "Grimald, Nicholas." In *Oxford Dictionary of National Biography,* ed. H. C. G. Matthew and Brian Howard Harrison. 60 vols., 24:12–15. Oxford: Oxford University Press, 2004.

Breuer, Joseph, and Sigmund Freud. *Studies in Hysteria.* Trans. A. A. Brill. Boston: Beacon, 1950.

Brie, Friedrich W. D., ed. *The Brut, or the Chronicles of England, Part II.* EETS o.s. 136. London: Kegan Paul, Trench, Trübner, 1908.

Brock, Edmund, ed. *Morte Arthure.* EETS o.s. 8. London: Trübner, 1865.

Brook, G. L., ed. *The Harley Lyrics: The Middle English Lyrics of MS. Harley 2253.* 4th ed. Manchester: Manchester University Press, 1968.

Brook, G. L., and R. F. Leslie, eds. *Laʒamon: Brut.* 2 vols. EETS 250, 277. London: Oxford University Press, 1963, 1978.

Brown, Carleton, ed. *English Lyrics of the XIIIth Century.* Oxford: Clarendon Press, 1932.

———, ed. *Religious Lyrics of the XVth Century.* Oxford: Clarendon Press, 1939.

———, ed. *Religious Lyrics of the XIVth Century.* 2nd ed. G. V. Smithers. Oxford: Clarendon Press, 1957.

Brown, Carleton, and Rossell Hope Robbins. *The Index of Middle English Verse.* New York: Columbia University Press, 1943.

Brundage, James A. *Law, Sex, and Christian Society in Medieval Europe.* Chicago: University of Chicago Press, 1987.

Brunner, Karl, *Die englische Sprache: ihre geschichtliche Entwicklung*. 2 vols. Tübingen: Niemeyer, 1962.
Bugge, John. *Virginitas: An Essay in the History of a Medieval Ideal*. The Hague: Nijhoff, 1975.
Burrow, J. A. "The Audience of *Piers Plowman*." *Anglia* 75 (1957): 373–84. Repr. in J. A. Burrow. *Essays on Medieval Literature*, pp. 102–16. Oxford: Clarendon Press.
———. "Autobiographical Poetry in the Middle Ages: The Case of Thomas Hoccleve." *Proceedings of the British Academy* 68 (1982): 389–412.
Burrow, J.A., and A. I. Doyle. Introduction to *Thomas Hoccleve: A Facsimile of the Autograph Verse Manuscripts*. EETS s.s. 19. Oxford: Oxford University Press, 2002.
Calendar of the Close Rolls Preserved in the Public Record Office. London: H. M. Stationery Office, 1892–1954.
Calendar of Entries in the Papal Registers Relating to Great Britain and Ireland, Papal Letters. Dublin: Stationery Office for the Irish Manuscripts Commission, 1978– .
Calendar of Inquisitions Post Mortem and Other Analogous Documents Preserved in the Public Record Office. London: H. M. Stationery Office, 1904– .
Calendar of the Patent Rolls Preserved in the Public Record Office. London: H. M. Stationery Office, 1891–1916.
Cannon, Christopher. "Monastic Productions." In *The Cambridge History of Medieval English Literature*, ed. Wallace, 316–48.
Capes, William W., ed. *The Register of John Trefnant, Bishop of Hereford (A.D. 1389–1404)*. Hereford: Wilson and Phillips, 1914.
Carlson, Cindy L., and Angela Jane Weisl, eds. *Constructions of Widowhood and Virginity in the Middle Ages*. New York: St. Martin's, 1999.
Cartlidge, Neil, ed. *The Owl and the Nightingale: Text and Translation*. Exeter: University of Exeter Press, 2001.
Carruthers, Mary. "The Poet as Master Builder: Composition and Locational Memory in the Middle Ages." *New Literary History* 24 (1993): 881–904.
Caruth, Cathy. *Unclaimed Experience: Trauma, Narrative, and History*. Baltimore: Johns Hopkins University Press, 1996.
Castelli, Elizabeth. "Virginity and Its Meaning for Women's Sexuality in Early Christianity." *Journal of Feminist Studies in Religion* 2 (1986): 61–88.
Chaganti, Seeta. "'A Form as Grecian Goldsmiths Make': Enshrining Narrative in Chrétien De Troyes's *Cligés* and the Stavelot Triptych." *New Medieval Literatures* 7 (2005): 163–201.
Chambers, E. K. *English Literature at the Close of the Middle Ages*. Oxford: Oxford University Press, 1945.
Chambers, R. W., and Marjorie Daunt, eds. *A Book of London English, 1384–1425*. Oxford: Clarendon Press, 1931.
Chambers, R. W., and F. Sidgwick. "Fifteenth-Century Carols by John Audelay." *Modern Language Review* 5 (1910): 473–91; 6 (1911): 68–84.

Chibnall, Marjorie M. "The Abbey of Haughmond." In *Victoria History of the Counties of England*, ed. R. B. Pugh. Vol. 2, *A History of Shropshire*. Ed. A. T. Gaydon, pp. 62–70. London: Oxford University Press, 1973.

———. "The Abbey of Lilleshall." In *Victoria History of the Counties of England*, ed. R. B. Pugh. Vol. 2, *A History of Shropshire*. Ed. A. T. Gaydon, pp. 70–80. London: Oxford University Press, 1973.

Child, Francis J., ed. *The English and Scottish Popular Ballads*. 5 vols. 1882–98; repr. New York: Cooper Square, 1965.

Chitty, Gill, with N. J. Palmer, J. J. West, and R. Gilyard-Beer. *Haughmond Abbey: A Brief Guide*. London: English Heritage, 1992.

Geoffrey Chaucer, *The Canterbury Tales*. Ed. Mann, Jill. London: Penguin, 2005.

Cigman, Gloria, ed. *Lollard Sermons*. EETS 294. London: Oxford University Press, 1989.

Cokayne, George E. *The Complete Peerage of England, Scotland, Ireland, Great Britain, and the United Kingdom*. 2nd ed. 13 vols. 1910–59; repr. New York: St. Martin's, 1984.

Colgrave, Bertram, and R. A. B. Mynor, eds. and trans. *Bede's Ecclesiastical History of the English People*. Oxford: Clarendon Press, 1969.

Collier, J. Payne, ed. *Trevelyan Papers, Prior to A.D. 1558*. 3 vols. Camden Society, 3rd ser., 67, 84, 105. London: Camden Society, 1857–72.

Collijn, Isak, ed. *Acta et processus canonizacionis beate Birgitte*. Issued in 10 parts. Uppsala: Almqvist & Wiksell, 1924–31.

———. *Handskrifter, urkunder och böcker rörande Birgitta och Vadstena*. Uppsala: Almqvist & Wiksell, 1918.

Cook, G. H. *Mediaeval Chantries and Chantry Chapels*. London: Phoenix House, 1947.

[Coxe, H. O.] *Catalogue of the Printed Books and Manuscripts Bequeathed by Francis Douce, Esq., to the Bodleian Library at Oxford*. Oxford: Oxford University Press, 1840.

Craigie, William A. et al., eds. *A Dictionary of the Older Scottish Tongue*. 12 vols. Chicago: University of Chicago Press; Aberdeen: Aberdeen University Press; Oxford: Oxford University Press, 1931–2002.

Cross, F. L., ed. *Oxford Dictionary of the Christian Church*. 3rd ed. Rev. E. A. Livingstone. Oxford: Oxford University Press, 1997.

Crow, Martin M., and Claire C. Olson, eds. *Chaucer Life-Records*. Oxford: Clarendon Press, 1966.

Cumming, William Patterson, ed. *The Revelations of Saint Birgitta*. EETS o.s. 178. 1929; repr. Millwood, N.Y.: Kraus Reprint, 1971.

Curry, Anne. *Agincourt: A New History*. Stroud: Tempus, 2005.

———, ed. and trans. *The Battle of Agincourt. Sources and Interpretations*. Woodbridge: Boydell, 2000.

d'Ardenne, S. R. T. O., and E. J. Dobson, eds. *Seinte Katerine*. EETS s.s. 7. Oxford: Oxford University Press, 1981.

Davies, R. T., ed. *Medieval English Lyrics: A Critical Anthology*. London: Faber and Faber, 1963.

Davis, Virginia. *Clergy in London in the Late Middle Ages: A Register of Clergy Ordained in the Diocese of London Based on Episcopal Ordination Lists*. [CD-Rom] London: Institute of Historical Research, 2000.

Day, Mabel, and Robert Steele, eds. *Mum and the Sothsegger*. EETS o.s.199. 1936; repr. Oxford: Oxford University Press, 2001.

de Hamel, Christopher. *Syon Abbey: The Library of the Bridgettine Nuns and Their Peregrinations after the Reformation*. Otley, Eng.: Roxburghe Club, 1991.

Dean, Ruth, with Maureen B. M. Boulton. *Anglo-Norman Literature: A Guide to Texts and Manuscripts*. ANTS o.p.s. 3. London: ANTS, 1999.

D'Evelyn, Charlotte, and Frances A. Foster. "Saints' Lives." In *A Manual of the Writings in Middle English*, ed. Severs, Hartung, and Beidler, 2:410–29, 553–644.

Dickins, Bruce, "The Rhyme-Schemes in MS. Douce 302, 53 and 54." *Proceedings of the Leeds Philosophical and Literary Society* 2 (1932): 516–18.

Dinzelbacher, Peter. "Die Verbreitung der apokryphen 'Visio S. Pauli' im mittelalterlichen Europa." *Mittellateinisches Jahrbuch* 27 (1992): 77–90.

Doig, James. "Propaganda and Truth: Henry V's Royal Progress in 1421." *Nottingham Medieval Studies* 40 (1996): 167–79.

Dölle, Ernst. *Zur Sprache Londons vor Chaucer*. Studien zur englischen Philologie 32. 1913; repr. Halle: M. Niemeyer, 1973.

Donaldson, E. Talbot. *Speaking of Chaucer*. London: Athlone, 1970.

Douce, Francis. *The Dance of Death Exhibited in Elegant Engravings on Wood with a Dissertation on the Several Representations of That Subject*. London: William Pickering, 1833.

Doyle, A. I. "'Lectulus noster floridus': An Allegory of the Penitent Soul." In *Literature and Religion in the Later Middle Ages: Philological Studies in Honor of Siegfried Wenzel*, ed. Richard G. Newhauser and John A. Alford, pp. 179–90. Binghamton, N.Y.: Medieval & Renaissance Texts & Studies, 1994.

——. "The Shaping of the Vernon and Simeon Manuscripts." In *Studies in the Vernon Manuscript*, ed. Pearsall, pp. 1–13.

——. Introduction to *The Vernon Manuscript: A Facsimile of Bodleian Library, Oxford, MS. Eng. Poet. a. 1*. Cambridge: Brewer, 1987.

Driver, Martha W. *The Image in Print: Book Illustration in Late Medieval England and Its Sources*. London: British Library, 2004.

Duffy, Eamon. *The Stripping of the Altars: Traditional Religion in England, c. 1400–c. 1580*. New Haven: Yale University Press, 1992.

Duggan, Hoyt N., and Thorlac Turville-Petre, eds. *The Wars of Alexander*. EETS s.s. 10. Oxford: Oxford University Press, 1989.

——. "The Shape of the B-Verse in Middle English Alliterative Poetry." *Speculum* 61 (1986): 565–66.

Duncan, Thomas G., ed. *A Companion to Middle English Lyrics*. Cambridge: Cambridge University Press, 2005.

Dyboski, Roman, ed. *Songs, Carols and Other Miscellaneous Poems from the Balliol MS 354: Richard Hill's Commonplace Book*. EETS e.s. 101. London: Kegan Paul, Trench, Trübner, 1907.

Easting, Robert. "Personal Apocalypse: Judgement in Some Other-World Visions." In *Prophecy, Apocalypse and the Day of Doom*, ed. Morgan, pp. 68–85. Donington: Shaun Tyas, 2004.

———, ed. *St. Patrick's Purgatory*. EETS o.s. 298. Oxford: Oxford University Press, 1991.

———. *Visions of the Other World in Middle English*. Woodbridge: Brewer, 1997.

Ebel, Uda. "Formes littéraires des visions d'outre-monde et des visions et des visions apocalyptiques." In *La Literature didactique, allégorique et satirique*, ed. Hans Robert Jauss. 2 vols., 2:240–42. Heidelberg: C. Winter, 1968–70.

Eckhardt, Caroline D., ed. *Castleford's Chronicle, or, The Boke of Brut*. 2 vols. EETS o.s. 305, 306. Oxford: Oxford University Press, 1996.

Edwards, A. S. G., ed. *The English Medieval Book: Studies in Memory of Jeremy Griffiths*. Ed. A. S. G. Edwards, Vincent Gillespie, and Ralph Hanna. London: British Library, 2000.

———. "Fifteenth-Century Middle English Verse Author Collections." In *The English Medieval Book*, ed. Edwards, Gillespie, and Hanna, pp. 101–12.

———. "The Hopton Hall Manuscript at Keio University." In *Codices Keionenses: Essays on Western Manuscripts and Early Printed Books in Keio University Library*, ed. Takami Matsuda, pp. 69–86. Tokyo: Keio University Press, 2005.

Eichenberg, Fritz. *Dance of Death: A Graphic Commentary on The Danse Macabre through the Centuries*. New York: Abbeville Press, 1983.

Ekwall, Eilert. *The Place-Names of Lancashire*. Manchester: Manchester University Press, 1922.

Erbe, Theodor, ed. *Mirk's Festial: A Collection of Homilies, by Johannes Mirkus (John Mirk)*. Part I [text and glossary only]. EETS e.s. 96. 1905; repr. Millwood, N.Y.: Kraus Reprint, 1975.

Erler, Mary C. *Women, Reading, and Piety in Late Medieval England*. Cambridge: Cambridge University Press, 2002.

Fehr, Bernard. "Die Lieder der Hs. Sloane 2593." *Archiv für das Studium der neueren Sprachen* 109 (1902): 33–72.

Fein, Susanna [Greer]. "A Thirteen-Line Stanza on the Abuse of Prayer from the Audelay MS." *Medium Ævum* 63 (1994): 61–74.

———. "The Early Thirteen-Line Stanza: Style and Metrics Reconsidered." *Parergon* 18 (2000): 97–126.

———. "Good Ends in the Audelay Manuscript." *Yearbook of English Studies* 33 (2003): 97–119.

———. "Life and Death, Reader and Page: Mirrors of Mortality in English Manuscripts." *Mosaic* 35 (2002): 69–94.

———, ed. *Moral Love Songs and Laments*. Kalamazoo: Medieval Institute Publications, 1998.

Fleming, P. W. "Charity, Faith, and the Gentry of Kent 1422-1529." In *Property and Politics: Essays in Later Medieval English History*, ed. Tony Pollard, pp. 36–58. New York: St. Martin's, 1984.
Fletcher, Alan J. "John Mirk and the Lollards." *Medium Ævum* 56 (1987): 217–24.
———. "The Manuscripts of John Mirk's *Manuale Sacerdotis*." *Leeds Studies in English*, n.s. 19 (1988): 105–39.
Forshall, Josiah, and Frederic Madden, eds. *The Holy Bible, Containing the Old and New Testaments, with the Apocryphal Book, in the Earliest English Versions Made from the Latin Vulgate by John Wycliffe and His Followers*. 4 vols. Oxford: Oxford University Press, 1850.
Furnivall, Frederick J., ed. *Adam Davy's 5 Dreams about Edward II: The Life of St. Alexius, Solomon's Book of Wisdom, St. Jeremie's 15 Tokens before Doomsday, The Lamentation of Souls*. EETS o.s. 69. 1878; repr. Millwood, N.Y.: Kraus Reprint, 1999.
———, ed. *The Cambridge MS. Dd. 4. 24. of Chaucer's Canterbury Tales*. Chaucer Society, 1st ser., 95–96. London: Kegan Paul, Trench, Trübner, 1901–02.
———, ed. *The Minor Poems of the Vernon MS*. Part 2. EETS o.s. 117. 1901; repr. Oxford: Oxford University Press, 2006.
Furnivall, Frederick J., and Israel Gollancz, eds. *Hoccleve's Works: The Minor Poems*. 2nd ed. Rev. Jerome Mitchell and A. I. Doyle. EETS e.s. 61, 73. London: Oxford University Press, 1970.
Furnivall, Frederick J., and Katharine B. Locock, eds. *The Pilgrimage of the Life of Man, Translated by John Lydgate*. EETS e.s. 77, 83, 92. 1899, 1901, 1904; repr. as 1 vol. Millwood, N.Y.: Oxford University Press, 1975.
Gadd, Ian, and Alexandra Gillespie, eds. *John Stow (1525–1605) and the Making of the English Past: Studies in Early Modern Culture and the History of the Book*. London: British Library, 2004.
Gairdner, J., ed. *The Historical Collections of a Citizen of London in the Fifteenth Century*. Camden Society, n.s. 17. Westminster: Camden Society, 1876.
Gasquet, [Francis Aidan]. *The Religious Life of King Henry VI, by Cardinal Gasquet*. London: G. Bell and Sons, 1923.
Gebhardt, Ludwig, *Das unausgedrückte Subjekt im Mittelenglischen*. Giessen: Selbstverlag des englischen Seminars der Universität Giessen, 1922.
Gejrot, Claes. "The Fifteen Oes: Latin and Vernacular Versions with an Edition of the Latin Text." In *The Translation of the Works of St Birgitta of Sweden into the Medieval European Vernaculars*, ed. Bridget Morris and Veronica O'Mara, pp. 213–38, The Medieval Translator 7. Turnhout: Brepols, 2000.
Gibbs, Marion, and Jane Lang. *Bishops and Reform, 1215–1272: With Special Reference to the Lateran Council of 1215*. 1934; repr. London: Cass, Oxford University Press, 1962.
Gillespie, Vincent. "*Doctrina* and *Praedicacio:* The Design and Function of Some Pastoral Manuals." *Leeds Studies in English*, n.s. 11 (1980): 36–50.
Girsch, J. M., ed. "An Edition with Commentary of John Mirk's *Manuale Sacerdotis*." PhD diss. University of Toronto, 1990.

Gollancz, Israel. Introduction to *Pearl, Cleanness, Patience and Sir Gawain, Reproduced in Facsimile from the Unique MS. Cotton Nero A.x in the British Museum*. EETS o.s. 162. 1923; repr. Oxford: Oxford University Press, 2007.
———, ed. *Select Early English Poems*. 9 vols. London: Milford, Oxford University Press, 1913–33.
———, ed. *St. Erkenwald (Bishop of London 675–693): An Alliterative Poem*. London: Milford, Oxford University Press, 1922.
Gray, Douglas, ed. *A Selection of Religious Lyrics*. Oxford: Clarendon Press, 1975.
———. *Themes and Images in Medieval English Religious Lyric*. London: Routledge and Kegan Paul, 1972.
Green, Monica H. "Female Sexuality in the Medieval West." *Trends in History* 4 (1990): 127–158.
Green, Richard Firth. "John Ball's Letters: Literary History and Historical Literature." In *Chaucer's England: Literature in Historical Context*, ed. Barbara Hanawalt, pp. 176–200. Minneapolis: University of Minnesota Press, 1992.
———. "Marcolf the Fool and Blind John Audelay." In *Speaking Images: Essays in Honor of V. A. Kolve*, ed. R. F. Yeager and Charlotte C. Morse, pp. 559–76. Asheville, N.C.: Pegasus, 2001.
Greenblatt, Stephen. *Hamlet in Purgatory*. Princeton: Princeton University Press, 2001.
Greene, Richard Leighton. "Carols." In *A Manual of the Writings in Middle English*, ed. Severs, Hartung, and Beidler, 6:1743–52, 1940–2018.
———, ed. *The Early English Carols*. 2nd ed. Oxford: Clarendon Press, 1977.
———, ed. *A Selection of English Carols*. Oxford: Clarendon Press, 1962.
Griffith, David. "The Reception of Continental Women Mystics in Fifteenth- and Sixteenth-Century England: Some Artistic Evidence." In *The Medieval Mystical Tradition in England*, ed. Jones, pp. 97–117.
Griffiths, Ralph A. *The Reign of King Henry VI: The Exercise of Royal Authority, 1422–1461*. Berkeley and Los Angeles: University of California Press, 1981.
Grosjean, Paul. *Henrici VI Angliae regis miracula postuma; ex codice Musei Britannici regio 13. C. viii*. Brussels: Société des Bollandistes, 1935.
Haines, R. M. "Education in English Ecclesiastical Legislation of the Later Middle Ages." *Studies in Church History* 7 (1971): 161–75.
Hales, John W., and Frederick J. Furnivall, eds. *Bishop Percy's Folio Manuscript: Ballads and Romances*. 3 vols. London: Trübner, 1867–68.
Halliwell, James Orchard, ed. *The Poems of John Audelay: A Specimen of the Shropshire Dialect in the Fifteenth Century*. Percy Society 47. London: Richards, 1844.
Hanna, Ralph. "Augustinian Canons and Middle English Literature." In *The English Medieval Book*, ed. Edwards, Gillespie, and Hanna, pp. 27–42.
———, ed. *The Awntyrs off Arthure at the Terne Wathelyn*. Manchester: Manchester University Press, 1974.
Hardman, Phillipa. Introduction to *The Heege Manuscript: A Facsimile of National Library of Scotland MS Advocates 19. 3. 1*. Leeds: University of Leeds, School of English, 2000.

Harris, Marguerite Tjader, ed., *Birgitta of Sweden, Life and Selected Revelations*. Intro. Tore Nyberg. Trans. Albert Ryle Kezel. New York: Paulist, 1990.

Heath, Peter. *The English Parish Clergy on the Eve of the Reformation*. London: Routledge and Kegan Paul, 1969.

Hecht, Hans, ed. *Bischof Wærferths von Worcester Übersetzung der Dialoge Gregors des Grossen*. 2 vols. Leipzig, 1900; Hamburg, 1907; repr. as 1 vol., Darmstadt: Wissenschaftliche Buchgesellschaft, 1965.

Hind, Arthur M. *An Introduction to a History of a Woodcut*. 2 vols. 1935; repr. New York: Dover, 1963.

Hinman, Charlton, ed. *The First Folio of Shakespeare*. New York: Norton, 1968.

Hirsh, John C., ed. *Medieval Lyric: Middle English Lyrics, Ballads and Carols*. Oxford: Blackwell, 2005.

Hirschfeld, Heather. "Hamlet's 'first corse': Redemption, Trauma, and the Displacement of Redemptive Typology." *Shakespeare Quarterly* 54 (2003): 424–48.

Hogg, Richard M. *A Grammar of Old English*. Vol. 1, *Phonology*. Oxford: Blackwell, 1992.

Hollman, Lennart, ed., *Den heliga Birgittas reuelaciones extrauagantes*. Uppsala: Almqvist & Wiksell, 1956.

Holloway, Julia Bolton, trans. *Saint Bride and Her Book: Birgitta of Sweden's Revelations, Translated from Middle English*. Newburyport, Mass.: Focus Information Group, 1992.

Horstmann, Carl, ed. *The Minor Poems of the Vernon MS*. Part 1. EETS o.s. 98. 1892; repr. Millwood, N.Y.: Kraus Reprint, 1975.

Hudson, Anne. "A Lollard Sect Vocabulary?" In *So Meny People, Longages and Tonges: Philological Essays in Scots and Mediaeval English Presented to Angus McIntosh*, ed. Michael Benskin and M. L. Samuels, pp. 15–30. Edinburgh: Benskin & Samuels, 1981.

Hughes, M. A. "The Syon 'Pardon' Sermon Edited from MS Harley 2321 with Introduction, Notes and Glossary." Master's diss. University of Liverpool, 1959.

Hurst, C. "Douce, Francis (1757–1834)." *Oxford Dictionary of National Biography*, pp. 1–4, http://www.oxforddnb.com/view/article/7849 (accessed 23 November 2006)

Hutchinson, Ann M. "Reflections on Aspects of the Spiritual Impact of St. Birgitta, the Revelations and the Bridgettine Order in Late Medieval England." In *The Medieval Mystical Tradition in England*, ed. Jones, pp. 69–82.

Hutton, James. *Themes of Peace in Renaissance Poetry*. Ed. Rita Guerlac. Ithaca: Cornell University Press, 1984.

Huws, Daniel. "MS Porkington 10 and Its Scribes." In *Romance Reading on the Book: Essays on Medieval Narrative Presented to Maldwyn Mills*, ed. Jennifer Fellows, Rosalind Field, Gillian Rogers, and Judith Weiss, pp. 189–207. Cardiff: University of Wales Press, 1996.

Irvine, Susan, ed. *The Anglo-Saxon Chronicle: 7. MS E*. Cambridge: Brewer, 2004.

Jacob, E. F. ed., *The Register of Henry Chichele, Archbishop of Canterbury, 1414–1443*. 4 vols. Canterbury and York Society. Oxford: Clarendon Press, 1938–47.

Jacobus de Voragine. *The Golden Legend: Readings on the Saints*. Trans. William Granger Ryan. 2 vols. Princeton: Princeton University Press, 1993.

James, M. R., ed. and trans. *Henry the Sixth, a Reprint of John Blacman's Memoir*. 1919; repr. Cambridge: Cambridge University Press, 1955.

Jiroušková, Lenka. *Die Visio Pauli*. Mittellateinische Studien und Texte 34. Leiden: Brill, 2006.

Johnson, Samuel, *The Rambler*. 3 vols. London: Payne and Bouquet, 1750–52.

Johnston, F. R. "Syon Abbey." In *Victoria History of the Counties of England*, ed. R. B. Pugh. Vol. 1, *A History of Middlesex*. Ed. William Page, pp. 182–91. Oxford: Oxford University Press, 1969.

Jones, E. A. *The Medieval Mystical Tradition in England*. Cambridge: Brewer, 2004

Jones, Melissa. "'Swete May, Soulis Leche': The Winifred Carol of John Audelay." *Essays in Medieval Studies* 14 (1997): 1–7, http://www.luc.edu/publications/medieval.

Jordan, Richard. *Handbook of Middle English Grammar: Phonology*. 2nd ed. Trans. and rev. Eugene Joseph Crook. The Hague: Mouton, 1974.

Jørgensen, Johannes. *Saint Bridget of Sweden*. Trans. Ingeborg Lund. 2 vols. New York: Longmans, Green, 1954.

Kail, J., ed. *Twenty-Six Political and Other Poems from the Oxford Mss. Digby 102 and Douce 322*. EETS o.s. 124. 1904; repr. Millwood, N.Y.: Kraus Reprint, 1975.

Kaiser, Rolf, ed. *Medieval English: An Old and Middle English Anthology*. 3rd ed. Berlin: Rolf Kaiser, 1958.

———. "Zur geographischen Verteilung des mittelenglischen Wortschatzes." PhD diss. Berlin University, 1936.

———. *Zur Geographie des mittelenglischen Wortschatzes*. 1937; repr. New York: Johnson Reprint, 1970.

Kane, George, ed., *Piers Plowman: The A Version*. 2nd ed. London: Athlone, 1988.

Kane, George, and E. Talbot Donaldson, eds. *Piers Plowman: The B Version*. 2nd ed. London: Athlone, 1988.

Kane, George, E. Talbot Donaldson, and George Russell, eds. *Piers Plowman: The Three Versions*. 2nd ed. Rev. George Kane. Berkeley: University of California Press, 1988.

Kastan, David Scott, ed. *The Oxford Encyclopedia of British Literature*. 5 vols. Oxford: Oxford University Press, 2006.

Kelly, Kathleen Coyne. *Performing Virginity and Testing Chastity in the Middle Ages*. London: Routledge, 2000.

Klaeber, Fr., ed. *Beowulf and the Fight at Finnsburg*. 3rd ed. Boston: Heath, 1950.

Knowles, David. *The Religious Orders in England*. 3 vols. Cambridge: Cambridge University Press, 1962–71.

Knox, Ronald, and Shane Leslie, eds. and trans. *The Miracles of King Henry VI*. Cambridge: Cambridge University Press, 1923.

Kölbing, E. "Eine bisher unbekannte me. Version von Pauli höllenfahrt." *Englische Studien* 22 (1895): 134–39.
Kölbing, E., and Mabel Day, eds. *The Siege of Jerusalem*. EETS o.s. 188. 1932; repr. Millwood, N.Y.: Kraus Reprint, 1971.
Kottler, Barnet, and Alan M. Markman. *A Concordance to Five Middle English Poems: Cleanness, St. Erkenwald, Sir Gawain and the Green Knight, Patience, Pearl*. Pittsburgh: University of Pittsburgh Press, 1966.
Koziol, Herbert. *Grundzüge der Syntax der mittelenglischen Stabreimdichtungen*. Weiner Beiträge zur englischen Philologie 58. Vienna: Braumüller, 1932.
Krapp, George Philip, ed. *The Paris Psalter and the Meters of Boethius*. ASPR 5. New York: Columbia University Press, 1932.
Krapp, George Philip, and Elliott Van Kirk Dobbie, eds. *The Exeter Book*. ASPR 3. New York: Columbia University Press, 1936.
Kreider, Alan. *English Chantries: The Road to Dissolution*. Cambridge, Mass.: Harvard University Press, 1979.
Kristensson, Gillis, ed. *John Mirk's Instructions for Parish Priests*. Lund: Gleerup, 1974.
Krug, Rebecca. *Reading Families: Women's Literate Practice in Late Medieval England*. Ithaca: Cornell University Press, 2002.
Kurath, Hans et al., eds. *Middle English Dictionary*. Ann Arbor: University of Michigan Press, 1952–2001.
Kurth, Willi, ed., *The Complete Woodcuts of Albrecht Dürer*. Trans. Silvia M. Welsh. 1936; repr. New York: Arden, 1963.
Laing, Margaret. *Catalogue of Sources for a Linguistic Atlas of Early Medieval English*. Cambridge: Brewer, 1993.
Långfors, Arthur, ed. *Le Roman de Fauvel*. Paris: F. Didot et cie, 1914–19.
Laplanche, Jean. *New Foundations for Psychoanalysis*. Trans. David Macey. Oxford: Blackwell, 1989.
Lasch, Agathe et al., eds. *Mittelniederdeutsches Handwörterbuch*. In progress. Hamburg, later Neumünster: Wachholtz, 1928– .
Latham, R. E., and D. R. Howlett, eds. *Dictionary of Medieval Latin from British Sources*. 9 fascicules to date. Oxford: Oxford University Press, 1975– .
Le Strange, Hamon. *Le Strange Records: A Chronicle of the Early Le Stranges of Norfolk and the March of Wales A.D. 1100–1310*. London: Longmans, Green, 1916.
Lee, Canon. "Gift of the Church of Hammer to Haghmond Abbey, A.D. 1166–77." *Transactions of the Shropshire Archaeological and Natural History Society*, 2nd ser., 2 (1890): 194–209.
Lees, Claire. "The 'Sunday Letter' and the 'Sunday Lists.'" *Anglo-Saxon England* 14 (1985): 129–51.
Liebermann, Felix, ed. *Die Gesetze der Angelsachsen*. 3 vols. Halle: Niemeyer, 1903–16; repr. Aalen: Scientia, 1960.
Lloyd, L. J. "Dr Richard Farmer 1735–97: Portrait of a Bibliophile XXI." *The Book Collector* 26 (1977): 524–36.

Louis, Cameron. "Proverbs, Precepts, and Monitory Pieces." In *A Manual of Writings in Middle English*, ed. Severs, Hartung, and Beidler, 9:3006–16.

Luick, Karl (completed by Friedrich Wild and Herbert Koziol). *Historische Grammatik der englischen Sprache*. 2 vols. Stuttgart, 1914–40; repr. Oxford: Blackwell, 1964.

Lynch, Andrew. "'Manly Cowardyse': Thomas Hoccleve's Peace Strategy." *Medium Ævum* 73 (2004): 306–23.

Macauley, G. C., ed. *The English Works of John Gower*. 2 vols. EETS e.s. 81, 82. 1900, 1901; repr. London: Oxford University Press, 1963.

MacCracken, Henry Noble, ed., with Merriam Sherwood. *The Minor Poems of John Lydgate*. EETS o.s. 107, 192. 1911, 1934; repr. London: Oxford University Press, 1961, 1962.

———. "Quixley's Ballades Royal (?1402)." *Yorkshire Archaeological Journal* 20 (1908): 33–50.

MacGregor, John. "Campbell, Earl and Marquess of Bereadalbane." In *The Scots Peerage*, ed. James Balfour Paul. 9 vols., 2:174. Edinburgh: Douglas, 1904–14.

Mack, Frances M., ed. *Seinte Marherete þe Meiden ant Martyr*. EETS o.s. 193. London: Oxford University Press, 1934.

Macrae-Gibson, O. D., ed. *The Old English Riming Poem*. Cambridge: Brewer, 1983.

Machan, Tim William. *Textual Criticism and Middle English Texts*. Charlottesville: University of Virginia Press, 1994.

Madan, Falconer et al. *A Summary Catalogue of Western Manuscripts in the Bodleian Library at Oxford*. 7 vols. Oxford: Clarendon Press, 1897.

Madden, Frederic, ed. *Laȝamons Brut, or Chronicle of Britain*. 3 vols. 1847; repr. Osnabrück: Zeller, 1967.

Magoun, Francis Peabody, Jr., ed. *The Gests of King Alexander of Macedon; Two Middle-English Alliterative Fragments*. Cambridge, Mass.: Harvard University Press, 1929.

Makowski, Elizabeth M. "The Conjugal Debt and Medieval Canon Law." *Journal of Medieval History* 3 (1977): 99–114.

Matsuda, Takami. *Death and Purgatory in Middle English Didactic Poetry*. Woodbridge: Brewer, 1997.

———, ed. *Mostly British: Manuscripts and Early Printed Materials from Classical Rome to Renaissance England in the Collection of Keio University Library*. Tokyo: Keio University Press, 2001.

Mayor, John E. B., ed. *The English Works of John Fisher*. EETS e.s. 27. 1876; repr. Millwood, N.Y.: Kraus Reprint, 1975.

McFarlane, K. B. *Lancastrian Kings and Lollard Knights*. Oxford: Clarendon Press, 1972.

McGerr, Rosemarie Potz, ed. *The Pilgrimage of the Soul: A Critical Edition of the Middle English Dream Vision*. New York: Garland, 1999.

McIntosh, Angus. "Some Notes on the Text of the Middle English Poem *De tribus regibus mortuis*." *Review of English Studies*, n.s. 28 (1977): 385–92.

McIntosh, Angus, Michael L. Samuels, and Michael Benskin, with Margaret Laing and Keith Williamson. *A Linguistic Atlas of Late Mediaeval English*. 4 vols. Aberdeen: Aberdeen University Press, 1986.

McKenna, John W. "Piety and Propaganda: The Cult of Henry VI." In *Chaucer and Middle English Studies in Honour of Rossell Hope Robbins*, ed. Beryl Rowland, pp. 72–88. Kent, Ohio: Kent State University Press, 1974.

McLaren, Mary-Rose. *The London Chronicles of the Fifteenth Century: A Revolution in English Writing, with an Annotated Edition of Bradford, West Yorkshire Archives MS 32D86/42*. Woodbridge: Brewer, 2002.

McNamara, Jo Ann Kay. "Chaste Marriage and Clerical Celibacy." In *Sexual Practices and the Medieval Church*, ed. Vern L. Bullough and James Brundage. Buffalo, N.Y.: Prometheus, 1982. Pp. 22–33.

———. *Sisters in Arms: Catholic Nuns through Two Millennia*. Cambridge, Mass.: Harvard University Press, 1996.

Meale, Carol M., ed. *Women and Literature in Britain, 1150–1500*. Cambridge: Cambridge University Press, 1993.

Menner, Robert J. "Middle English 'Lagman' (*Gawain* 1729) and Modern English 'Lag.'" *Philological Quarterly* 10 (1931): 163–68.

Mertens, Volker. "'Visio Sancti Pauli' II." In *Die deutsche Literatur des Mittelalters*, ed. Stammler et al., 10(2):423–25.

Mertes, Kate. *The English Noble Household 1250–1600: Good Governance and Politic Rule*. Oxford: Blackwell, 1988.

Meyer, Ann R. *Medieval Allegory and the Building of the New Jerusalem*. Cambridge: Cambridge University Press, 2003.

Meyer, P. "La Descente de saint Paul en enfer: poème français composé en Angleterre." *Romania* 24 (1895): 357–75.

Meyer-Lee, Robert J. *Poets and Power between Chaucer and Wyatt*. Cambridge: Cambridge University Press, 2007.

Middleton, Anne. "Acts of Vagrancy: The C Version 'Autobiography' and the Statute of 1388." In *Written Work: Langland, Labor, and Authorship*, ed. Steven Justice and Kathryn Kerby-Fulton, pp. 208–317. Philadelphia: University of Pennsylvania Press, 1997.

———. "The Audience and Public of 'Piers Plowman." In *Middle English Alliterative Poetry and Its Literary Background: Seven Essays*, ed. David Lawton, pp. 101–23. Cambridge: Brewer, 1982.

———. "Making a Good End: John But as a Reader of *Piers Plowman*." In *Medieval English Studies Presented to George Kane*, ed. Edward Donald Kennedy, Ronald Waldron, and Joseph S. Wittig, pp. 243–63. Woodbridge: Brewer, 1988.

———. "William Langland's 'Kynde Name': Authorial Signature and Social Identity in Late Fourteenth-Century England." In *Literary Practice and Social Change in Britain, 1380–1530*, ed. Lee Patterson, pp. 15–82. Berkeley and Los Angeles: University of California Press, 1990.

Migne, Jacques-Paul, ed. *Patrilogiae cursus completus . . . series latina*. 221 vols. Paris, 1844–64.
Millett, Bella, and Jocelyn Wogan-Browne, eds., *Medieval English Prose for Women: Selections from the Katherine Group and "Ancrene Wisse."* 2nd ed. Oxford: Clarendon Press, 1992.
Mitchell, Juliet. "Trauma, Recognition, and the Place of Language." *Diacritics* 28 (1998): 121–33.
Mizobata, Kiyokazu, ed. *A Concordance to the Alliterative Morte Arthure*. Tokyo: Shohakusha, 2001.
Morgan, Nigel, ed. *Prophecy, Apocalypse and the Day of Doom: Proceedings of the 2000 Harlaxton Symposium*. Donington: Shaun Tyas, 2004.
———. "The Torment of the Damned in Hell in Texts and Images in England in the Thirteenth and Fourteenth Centuries." In *Prophecy, Apocalypse and the Day of Doom*, ed. Morgan, pp. 250–60.
Morris, Bridget. *St. Birgitta of Sweden*. Woodbridge: Boydell, 1999.
Morris, Richard, ed. *The Blickling Homilies of the Tenth Century*. EETS o.s. 58, 63, 73. 1874–80; repr. as 1 vol., Oxford: Oxford University Press, 1997.
———, ed. *Cursor Mundi (The Cursur o the World)*. EETS o.s. 57, 59, 62, 66, 68, 99, 101. 1874–93; repr. London: Oxford University Press, 1963.
Müller, Wolfgang G. "The Battle of Agincourt in Carol and Battle." *Fifteenth-Century Studies* 8 (1983): 159–78.
Mummendey, Richard. *Language and Literature of the Anglo-Saxon Nations as Presented in German Doctoral Dissertations 1885–1950: A Bibliography*. Bonn: Bouvier, 1954.
Munby, A. N. L., and Lenore Coral. *British Book Sale Catalogues 1676–1800: A Union List*. London: Mansell, 1977.
Murray, Hilda M. R., ed. *The Middle English Poem, Erthe upon Erthe*. EETS o.s. 141. 1911; repr. London: Oxford University Press, 1964.
Mynors, R. A. B. *Catalogue of the Manuscripts of Balliol College, Oxford*. Oxford: Clarendon Press, 1963.
Newman, Barbara. "Flaws in the Golden Bowl: Gender and Spiritual Formation in the Twelfth Century." *Traditio* 45 (1989–1990): 111–46.
Nordenfalk, Carl. "Saint Bridget of Sweden as Represented in Illuminated Manuscripts." In *De artibus opuscula XL: Essays in Honor of Erwin Panofsky*, ed. Millard Meiss. 2 vols., 1:371–93. New York: New York University Press, 1961.
Oakden, J. P. *Alliterative Poetry in Middle English*. 2 vols. 1930, 1935; repr. as 1 vol. Hamden, Conn.: Archon, 1968.
Obrist, Barbara. "The Swedish Visionary: Saint Bridget." In *Medieval Women Writers*, ed. Katharina M. Wilson, pp. 227–51. Athens: University of Georgia Press, 1984.
O'Farrell-Tate, Una, ed. *The Abridged English Metrical Brut*. Heidelberg: C. Winter, 2002.
Offord, M. Y., ed. *The Parlement of the Thre Ages*. EETS o.s. 246 1959; repr. London: Oxford University Press, 1967.

Olson, Glending. "Author, Scribe, and Curse: The Genre of *Adam Scriveyn*." *Chaucer Review* 42 (2008): 284–97.

O'Mara, V. M., ed. *A Study and Edition of Selected Middle English Sermons: Richard Alkerton's Easter Week Sermon Preached at St Mary Spital in 1406, a Sermon on Sunday Observance, and a Nunnery Sermon for the Feast of the Assumption.* Leeds: School of English, University of Leeds, 1994.

Ottosen, Knud. *The Responsories and Versicles of the Latin Office of the Dead.* Aarhus: Aarhus University Press, 1993.

Owen, D. D. R. "The Vision of Saint Paul: The French and Provençal Versions and Their Sources." *Romance Philology* 12 (1958): 33–51.

Owst, G. R. *Literature and Pulpit in Medieval England: A Neglected Chapter in the History of English Letters and of the English People.* Cambridge: Cambridge University Press, 1933.

———. *Preaching in Medieval England: An Introduction to Sermon Manuscripts of the Period c. 1350–1450.* Cambridge: Cambridge University Press, 1926.

Oxford Dictionary of National Biography, online, Oxford: Oxford University Press, 2004, http://www.oxforddnb.com.

Palmer, Nigel F. "'Visio Sancti Pauli' I." In *Die deutsche Literatur des Mittelalters,* ed. Stammler et al., 10:418–23.

Pantin, W. A. *The English Church in the Fourteenth Century.* Cambridge: Cambridge University Press, 1955.

Panton, George A., and David Donaldson, eds. *The "Gest Hystoriale" of the Destruction of Troy.* EETS o.s. 39, 56. 1869, 1874; repr. London: Oxford University Press, 1968, 1976.

Parsons, David N., and Tania Styles, with Carole Hough, eds. *The Vocabulary of English Place-Names.* 3 fascicles to date. Nottingham: Centre for English Name Studies, 1997, 2000, 2004.

Patterson, Frank Allen, ed. *The Middle English Penitential Lyric: A Study and Collection of Early English Verse.* New York: Columbia University Press, 1911.

Peacock, Edward, ed. *Instructions for Parish Priests by John Myrc.* EETS o.s. 31. 2nd ed. Rev. F. J. Furnivall. 1902; repr. New York: Greenwood, 1969.

Pearsall, Derek. *John Lydgate.* London: Routledge and Kegan Paul, 1970.

———. "Langland and Lollardy: From B to C." *Yearbook of Langland Studies* 17 (2003): 7–23.

———. *The Life of Geoffrey Chaucer.* London: Blackwell, 1992.

———. *Old English and Middle English Poetry.* London: Routledge and Kegan Paul, 1977.

———, ed. *Studies in the Vernon Manuscript.* Cambridge: Brewer, 1990

———. "The Timelessness of *The Simonie.*" In *Individuality and Achievement in Middle English Poetry,* ed. O. S. Pickering. Cambridge: Brewer, 1997.

———, ed. *William Langland, Piers Plowman: An Edition of the C-Text.* 1978; repr. Exeter: University of Exeter Press, 1994.

Pfaff, R. W. *New Liturgical Feasts in Later Medieval England*. Oxford: Clarendon Press, 1970.

Pfeifer, Wolfgang, ed. *Etymologisches Wörterbuch des Deutschen*. 3 vols. Berlin: Akademie, 1989.

Pine-Coffin, R. S., trans. *Augustine, Confessions*. London: Penguin, 1961.

Pollard, A. W., and G. R. Redgrave, eds. *A Short-Title Catalogue of Books Printed in England, Scotland, and Ireland and of English Books Printed Abroad 1475–1640*. 2nd ed. Rev. W. A. Jackson, F. S. Ferguson, and Katherine F. Pantzer. 4 vols. London: Bibliographical Society, 1976.

Postles, David. "Penance and the Market Place: A Reformation Dialogue with the Medieval Church (c. 1250–c. 1600)." *Journal of Ecclesiastical History* 54 (2003): 441–68.

Powell, Edward. *Kingship, Law and Society: Criminal Justice in the Reign of Henry V*. Oxford: Clarendon Press, 1989.

Powell, Susan. "The *Festial*: The Priest and His Parish." In *The Parish in Late Medieval England: Proceedings of the 2002 Harlaxton Symposium*, ed. Clive Burgess and Eamon Duffy, pp. 160–76. Donington: Shaun Tyas, 2006.

———. "John Mirk's *Festial* and the Pastoral Programme." *Leeds Studies in English*, n.s. 22 (1991): 85–102.

———. "Lollards and Lombards: Late Mediaeval Bogeymen?" *Medium Ævum* 59 (1990): 133–39.

———. "A New Dating of John Mirk's Festial." *Notes & Queries*, n.s. 29 (1982): 487–89.

———. "Syon, Caxton and the *Festial*." *Birgittiana* 2 (1996): 187–207.

———. "What Caxton Did to the *Festial*." *Journal of the Early Book Society* 1 (1997): 48–77.

Prestwich, Michael. *Armies and Warfare in the Middle Ages: The English Experience*. New Haven: Yale University Press, 1996.

Priebsch, R. "John Audelay's Poem on the Observance of Sunday and Its Source." In *An English Miscellany Presented to Dr. Furnivall in Honour of His Seventy-fifth Birthday*, ed. W. P. Ker, A. S. Napier, and W. W. Skeat, pp. 397–407. Oxford: Clarendon Press, 1901; repr. New York: Blom, 1969.

Putter, Ad. "The Language and Metre of *Pater Noster* and *Three Dead Kings*." *Review of English Studies*, n.s. 55 (2004): 498–526.

Raby, F. J. E., ed. *The Oxford Book of Medieval Latin Verse*. Oxford: Clarendon Press, 1961).

Raine, James. "The Pudsays of Barford," *Archaeologia Aeliana* (Society of Antiquaries of Newcastle-upon-Tyne), n.s. 2 (1858): 173–190.

Rasmussen, J. K. *Die Sprache John Audelay's (Laut- und Flexionslehre)*. PhD diss., Bonn University, 1914.

Raymo, Robert R., and Elaine E. Whitaker, eds., with Ruth E. Sternglantz. *The Mirroure of the Worlde: A Middle English Translation of Le Miroir du Monde*. Toronto: University of Toronto Press, 2003.

Reichl, Karl. "The Middle English Carol." In *A Companion to the Middle English Lyrics*, ed. Duncan, 150–70.
Reimer, Stephen R., ed. *The Works of William Herebert, OFM*. Toronto: Pontifical Institute of Mediaeval Studies, 1987.
Renevey, Denis. "Name Above Names: The Devotion to the Name of Jesus from Richard Rolle to Walter Hilton's *Scale of Perfection* I." In *The Medieval Mystical Tradition: England, Ireland and Wales. Exeter Symposium VI*, ed. Marion Glasscoe, pp. 103–21. Cambridge: Brewer, 1999.
Renevey, Denis, and Christiania Whitehead, eds. *Writing Religious Women: Female Spiritual and Textual Practices in Late Medieval England*. Toronto: University of Toronto Press, 2000.
Revelationes Sancte Birgitte. 1st ed. (Latin text). Nuremberg: A Koberger, 21 Sept. 1500. 2nd ed. (German). Nuremberg: A. Koberger, 12 July 1502. 3rd ed. (Latin). Nuremberg: Peypus, 1517.
[Ritson, Joseph, ed.] *Bibliographia Poetica: A Catalogue of Engleish Poets, of the Twelfth, Thirteenth, Fourteenth, Fifteenth, and Sixteenth, Centurys*. London: G. and W. Nicol, 1802.
Robbins, Rossell Hope, ed. *Historical Poems of the XIVth and XVth Centuries*. New York: Columbia University Press, 1959.
———. "Poems Dealing with Contemporary Conditions." In *A Manual of Writings in Middle English*, ed. Severs, Hartung, and Beidler, 5:1442–53.
———, ed., *Secular Lyrics of the XIVth and XVth Centuries*. 2nd ed. Oxford: Clarendon Press, 1955.
Robbins, Rossell Hope, and John Cutler. *Supplement to the Index of Middle English Verse*. Lexington: University of Kentucky Press, 1965.
Roberts, Sydney. *Richard Farmer (1735–1797)*. Letchworth, Hertfordshire: The Garden City Press, 1961.
Robinson, F. N., ed. *The Works of Geoffrey Chaucer*. 2nd ed. Boston: Houghton Mifflin, 1961.
Rollins, Hyder Edward, ed. *Tottel's Miscellany*. 2nd ed. 2 vols. Cambridge, Mass.: Harvard University Press, 1965.
Roffey, Simon. *The Medieval Chantry Chapel: An Archaeology*. Woodbridge: Boydell & Brewer, 2007.
Russell, George, and George Kane, eds. *Piers Plowman: The C Version*. London: Athlone, 1997.
Salih, Sarah. "Margery Kempe." In *The Oxford Encyclopedia*, 2:194–97.
———. *Versions of Virginity in Late Medieval England*. Woodbridge: Brewer, 2001.
Salter, Elizabeth. "Alliterative Modes and Affiliations in the Fourteenth Century." *Neuphilologische Mitteilungen* 79 (1978): 25–35.
———. *Fourteenth-Century English Poetry: Contexts and Readings*. Oxford: Clarendon Press, 1983.
———. "*Piers Plowman* and *The Simonie*." *Archiv für das neueren Sprachen und Literaturen* 203 (1967): 241–54.

Salu, M. B., trans. *The Ancrene Riwle (The Corpus MS: Ancrene Wisse)*. Intro Gerard Sitwell. Pref. J. R. R. Tolkien. London: Burns & Oates, 1955.

Saul, Nigel. *Richard II*. New Haven: Yale University Press, 1999.

Saupe, Karen, ed. *Middle English Marian Lyrics*. Kalamazoo: Medieval Institute Publications, 1998.

Savage, Anne, and Nicholas Watson, trans. *Anchoritic Spirituality: Ancrene Wisse and Associated Works*. New York: Paulist, 1991.

Savage, Henry L., ed. *St. Erkenwald, a Middle English Poem*. New Haven: Yale University Press, 1926.

Sayles, G. O. *Select Cases in the King's Bench under Richard II, Henry IV and Henry V*. London: Quaritch, 1971.

Scase, Wendy. "'Proud Gallants and Popeholy Priests': The Context and Function of a Fifteenth-Century Satirical Poem." *Medium Ævum* 73 (1994): 275–86.

———. "Reginald Pecock, John Carpenter and John Colop's 'Common-Profit' Books: Aspects of Book Ownership and Circulation in Fifteenth-Century London." *Medium Ævum* 61 (1992): 261–74.

———. "'Strange and Wonderful Bills': Bill-Casting and Political Discourse in Late Medieval England," *New Medieval Literatures* 2 (1998): 225–47.

Schmidt, A. V. C., ed. *William Langland, The Vision of Piers Plowman: A Critical Edition of the B-Text*. 2nd ed. London: Dent, 1995.

Severs, J. Burke, Albert E. Hartung, and Peter G. Beidler, eds. *A Manual of the Writings in Middle English*. 11 vols. New Haven: Connecticut Academy of Arts and Sciences, 1967–2005.

Sherbo, Arthur. "Farmer, Richard (1735–1797)." *Oxford Dictionary of National Biography*, online, pp. 1–4 (accessed 23 November 2006).

———. *Richard Farmer, Master of Emmanuel College, Cambridge: A Forgotten Shakespearean*. Newark: University of Delaware Press, 1992.

———. *Shakespeare's Midwives: Some Neglected Shakespeareans*. Newark: University of Delaware Press, 1992.

Silverstein, Theodore, ed. *English Lyrics before 1500*. Evanston: Northwestern University Press, 1971.

———. *Visio Sancti Pauli: The History of the Apocalypse in Latin, Together with Nine Texts*. London: Christophers, 1935.

Silverstein, Theodore, and Anthony Hilhorst, eds. *Apocalypse of Paul: A New Critical Edition of Three Long Latin Versions*. Geneva: Cramer, 1997.

Simmons, Thomas Frederick, ed. *The Lay Folks Mass Book*. EETS o.s. 71. 1879; repr. London: Oxford University Press, 1968.

Simmons, Thomas Frederick, and Henry Edward Nolloth, eds. *The Lay Folks' Catechism*. EETS o.s. 118. 1901; repr. Millwood, N.Y.: Kraus Reprint, 1973.

Simpson, James, *The Oxford English Literary History*. Vol. 2, *1350–1547: Reform and Cultural Revolution*. Oxford: Oxford University Press, 2002.

———. "Saving Satire after Arundel's *Constitutions*: John Audelay's 'Marcol and Solomon.'" In *Text and Controversy from Wyclif to Bale: Essays in Honour of Anne*

Hudson, ed. Helen Barr and Ann M. Hutchison, pp. 387–404. Medieval Church Studies 4. Turnhout: Brepols, 2004.

Sisam, C., and K. Sisam. *The Oxford Book of Medieval English Verse*. Oxford: Clarendon Press, 1970.

Siy, Dennis. "Death, Medieval Moralities, and the *Ars Moriendi* Tradition." PhD diss. University of Notre Dame, 1985.

Skeat, Walter W., ed. *The Complete Works of Geoffrey Chaucer*. 6 vols. Oxford: Clarendon Press, 1894.

——, ed. *The Romance of William of Palerne*. EETS e.s. 1. 1867; repr. Millwood, N.Y.: Kraus Reprint 1973.

——, ed. *The Vision of William Concerning Piers Plowman*. Part 4, sect. 1, Notes to texts A, B, and C. EETS o.s. 67. 1877; repr. Oxford: Oxford University Press, 2000.

——, ed. *William Langland, The Vision of William Concerning Piers Plowman: In Three Parallel Texts Together with Richard the Redeless*. 2 vols. Oxford: Clarendon Press, 1886.

——, ed. *The Wars of Alexander, an Alliterative Romance*. EETS e.s. 47. 1886; repr. Millwood, N.Y.: Kraus Reprint, 1975.

Spitzer, Leo. "Note on the Poetic and the Empirical 'I' in Medieval Authors." *Traditio* 4 (1946): 414–22.

Staley, Lynn, trans. and ed. *The Book of Margery Kempe*. New York: Norton, 2001.

——. *Margery Kempe's Dissenting Fictions*. University Park: Penn State University Press, 1994.

Stammler, Wolfgang, ed., *Die deutsche Literatur des Mittelalters: Verfasserlexikon*. 11 vols. Berlin: de Gruyter, 1977– .

Stanley, Eric Gerald. "Rhymes in English Medieval Verse: From Old English to Middle English." In *Medieval English Studies Presented to George Kane*, ed. Edward Donald Kennedy, Ronald Waldron, and Joseph S. Wittig, pp. 19–54. Woodbridge: Brewer, 1988.

——. "*Pearl*, 358, *And y lurez of lyʒtly leme*: Metanalysed Tmesis for the Sake of Alliteration." *Notes & Queries* 235 (1990): 158–60.

——. "*The True Counsel of Conscience*, or *The Ladder of Heaven*: In Defence of John Audelay's Unlyrical Lyrics." In *Expedition nach der Wahrheit: Poems, Essays, and Papers in Honour of Theo Stemmler*, ed. Stefan Horlacher and Marion Eslinger, pp. 131–59. Heidelberg: C. Winter, 1996.

——. "The Verse Forms of Jon the Blynde Awdelay." In *The Long Fifteenth Century: Essays for Douglas Gray*, ed. Helen Cooper and Sally Mapstone, pp. 99–121. Oxford: Clarendon Press, 1997.

——. "Words for the *Dictionary of Old English*." In *The Dictionary of Old English: Retrospects and Prospects*, ed. M. J. Toswell, pp. 33–56. Old English Newsletter: Subsidia 26. Kalamazoo: Medieval Institute Publications, 1996.

Stevens, John, ed. *Early Tudor Songs and Carols*. London: Stainer and Bell, 1975.

——, ed. *Mediaeval Carols*. 2nd ed. London: Stainer and Bell, 1958.

Storck, Willy F. "Aspects of Death in English Art and Poetry." *Burlington Magazine* 21 (1912): 249–56, 314–19.
Storck, Willy F., and Richard Jordan, eds. "John Awdelays gedicht 'De tribus regibus mortuis': Eine englische fassung der legende von den drei lebenden und den drei toten." *Englische Studien* 43 (1911): 177–88.
Strohm, Paul. *England's Empty Throne: Usurpation and the Language of Legitimation, 1399–1422*. New Haven: Yale University Press, 1998.
———. "Hoccleve, Lydgate and the Lancastrian Court." In *The Cambridge History of Medieval English Literature*, ed. David Wallace, pp. 640–61.
Sutton, Anne F. "Caxton, the Cult of St Winifred, and Shrewsbury." *The Fifteenth Century* 5 (2005): 109–26.
Swanson, R. N., ed. *The Register of John Catterick, Bishop of Coventry and Lichfield, 1415–1419*. Canterbury and York Society. Woodbridge: Boydell, 1990.
Sweet, Henry, ed. *The Oldest English Texts*. EETS o.s. 83. 1885; repr. London: Oxford University Press, 1966.
Taylor, Andrew. "The Myth of the Minstrel Manuscript." *Speculum*, 66 (1991): 43–73.
The Douce Legacy: An Exhibition to Commemorate the 150th Anniversary of the Bequest of Francis Douce (1757–1834). Oxford: Bodleian Library, 1984.
Thomas, A. H., and I. D. Thornley, eds. *The Great Chronicle of London*. London: Jones, 1938.
Thuresson, Bertil, ed. *Middle English Occupational Terms*. Lund: Gleerup, 1950.
Thynne, William, ed. *The Workes of Geffray Chaucer*. 2nd ed. London: Wyllyam Bonham, 1542.
Tobler, Adolf, and Erhard Lommatzsch, ed. *Altfranzösisches Wörterbuch*. 11 vols. Berlin: Weidmann; Stuttgart: Steiner, 1925–2002.
Tolkien, J. R. R. "Chaucer as a Philologist: *The Reeve's Tale*." *Transactions of the Philological Society* (1934): 1–70.
———, ed. *The English Text of the Ancrene Riwle: Ancrene Wisse, Edited from MS Corpus Christi College Cambridge 402*. Intro. N. R. Ker. EETS o.s. 249. London: Oxford University Press, 1962.
Tolkien, J. R. R., and E. V. Gordon, eds. *Sir Gawain and the Green Knight*. 2nd ed. Rev. Norman Davis. Oxford: Clarendon Press, 1967.
Toulmin Smith, Lucy, ed. *York Plays*. 1885; repr. New York: Russell and Russell, 1963.
Trigg, Stephanie, ed. *Wynnere and Wastoure*. EETS 297. Oxford: Oxford University Press, 1990.
Tristram, Philippa. *Figures of Life and Death in Medieval English Literature*. New York: New York University Press, 1976.
Turville-Petre, Thorlac, ed. *Alliterative Poetry of the Later Middle Ages: An Anthology*. Washington, D.C.: Catholic University of America Press, 1989.
———. "'Summer Sunday', 'De Tribus Regibus Mortuis', and 'The Awntyrs off Arthure': Three Poems in the Thirteen-Line Stanza." *Review of English Studies*, n.s. 25 (1974): 1–14.

Tyrwhitt, Thomas, ed. *The Canterbury Tales of Chaucer*. 5 vols. London: Payne, 1775–78.
Utley, Francis Lee. "Dialogues, Debates and Catechisms." In *A Manual of the Writings in Middle English*, ed. Severs, Hartung, and Beidler, pp. 3:736–45.
Venezky, Richard L., and Antonette diPaolo Healey. *A Microfiche Concordance to Old English*. Toronto: Pontifical Institute of Mediaeval Studies, 1980.
Vinaver, Eugéne, ed. *The Works of Sir Thomas Malory*. 3rd ed. Rev. P. J. C. Field. 3 vols. Oxford: Clarendon Press, 1990.
Voaden, Rosalynn. *God's Words, Women's Voices: The Discernment of Spirits in the Writing of Late-Medieval Women Visionaries*. Woodbridge: York Medieval Press, 1999.
Vogüé, Adalbert de, trans. *Grégoire le Grand, Dialogues*. 3 vols. Paris: Cerf, 1978–80.
Vries, Jan de, ed. *Nederlands etymologisch Woordenboek*. Leiden: Brill, 1971.
Walker, Simon. "Political Saints in Later Medieval England." In *The McFarlane Legacy: Studies in Late Medieval Politics and Society*, ed. R. H. Britnell and A. J. Pollard, pp. 77–106. New York: St. Martin's, 1995.
Wallace, David, ed. *The Cambridge History of Medieval English Literature*. Cambridge: Cambridge University Press, 1999.
Warner, Marina. *Alone of All Her Sex: The Myth and Cult of the Virgin Mary*. London: Weidenfeld and Nicolson, 1976.
Wartburg, Walther von, ed. *Französisches etymologisches Wörterbuch*. 25 vols. or parts of vols. to date. Bonn: Fritz Klopp; Leipzig: Teubner; Basel: Helbing & Lichtenhahn; Tübingen: Mohr (Paul Siebeck); Heidelberg: C. Winter; Basel, more recently St. Alban-Vorstadt: (R. G.) Zbinden, 1922– .
Watts, John. *Henry VI and the Politics of Kingship*. Cambridge: Cambridge University Press, 1996.
Wawn, Andrew. "Truth-Telling and the Tradition of *Mum and the Sothsegger*." *Yearbook of English Studies* 13 (1983): 270-87.
Whiting, Bartlett Jere, with Helen Wescott Whiting. *Proverbs, Sentences, and Proverbial Phrases*. Cambridge, Mass.: Harvard University Press, 1968.
Whiting, Ella Keats, ed. *The Poems of John Audelay*. EETS o.s. 184. 1931; repr. Oxford: Oxford University Press, 2006.
Wild, Friedrich. *Die sprachlichen Eigentümlichkeiten der wichtigeren Chaucer-Handschriften und die Sprache Chaucers*. Weiner Beiträge zur englischen Philologie 44. Vienna: Braumüller, 1915.
Williams, E. Carleton. "Mural Paintings of the Three Living and the Three Dead Kings in England." *Journal of the British Archaeological Association*, 3rd ser., 7 (1942): 31–40.
Wilson, Janet. "Communities of Dissent: The Secular and Ecclesiastical Communities of Margery Kempe's Book." In *Medieval Women in Their Communities*, ed. Diane Watt, pp. 155–85. Toronto: University of Toronto Press, 1997.
Wirtjes, Hanneke, ed. *The Middle English Physiologus*. EETS o.s. 299. Oxford: Oxford University Press, 1991.

Wittig, Joseph S. *Wills's Visions of Piers Plowman, Do-Well, Do-Better and Do-Best: Piers Plowman Concordance*. London: Athlone, 2001.
Wogan-Browne, Jocelyn. "Chaste Bodies: Frames and Experiences." In *Framing Medieval Bodies*, ed. Sarah Kay and Miri Rubin, pp. 24–42. Manchester: Manchester University Press, 1994.
Wood-Legh, K. L. *Perpetual Chantries in Britain*. Cambridge:Cambridge University Press, 1965.
Woolf, Rosemary. *The English Religious Lyric in the Middle Ages*. London: Oxford University Press, 1968.
Wright, Joseph, ed. *The English Dialect Dictionary*. 6 vols. London: Frowde, 1898–1905.
Wright, Thomas, and James Orchard Halliwell, eds. *Reliquiæ Antiquæ*. 2 vols. 1841–43; repr. New York: AMS, 1966.
——, ed. *Songs and Carols, Now First Printed, from a Manuscript of the Fifteenth Century*. Percy Society 23. London: Richards, 1847.
Wülfing, J. Ernst. "Der Dichter John Audelay und sein Werk." *Anglia* 18 (1896): 175–217.
Wyld, Henry Cecil, with T. Oakes Hirst. *The Place Names of Lancashire, Their Origin and History*. London: Constable, 1911.
Wylie, James Hamilton, and William Templeton Waugh. *The Reign of Henry V*. 3 vols. Cambridge: Cambridge University Press, 1914–29.
Yunck, John A. *The Lineage of Lady Meed*. Notre Dame: University of Notre Dame Press, 1963.
Zupitza, J. "Die Gedichte des Franziskaners Jakob Ryman." *Archiv für das Studium der neueren Sprachen* 89 (1892): 167–338.

CONTRIBUTORS

Michael J. Bennett is Professor of History at the University of Tasmania.

Julia Boffey is Professor of Medieval Studies and Department Head, School of English and Drama, at Queen Mary, University of London.

Martha W. Driver is Distinguished Professor of English at Pace University and Cofounder of The Early Book Society.

Robert Easting is Professor of English and Head of the School of English, Film and Theatre at Victoria University of Wellington.

Susanna Fein is Professor of English and Coordinator of the Ancient, Medieval, and Renaissance Studies Program, Kent State University.

Richard Firth Green is Humanities Distinguished Professor of English and Director of the Center for Medieval and Renaissance Studies at The Ohio State University.

John C. Hirsh is Professor of English at Georgetown University.

Robert J. Meyer-Lee is Assistant Professor of English at Indiana University, South Bend.

Derek Pearsall was Professor of Middle English Literature and Co-Director of the Centre for Medieval Studies at the

University of York until 1985, and after that, until retirement in 2000, Gurney Professor of English at Harvard University.

Oliver Pickering is Deputy Head of Special Collection, Leeds University Library, and Associate Lecturer in English.

Susan Powell is Associate Head (Teaching) of the School of English, Sociology, Politics and Contemporary History at the University of Salford.

Eric Gerald Stanley is Rawlinson and Bosworth Professor Emeritus of Anglo-Saxon in the University of Oxford and Emeritus Fellow of Pembroke College, Oxford.

INDEX OF ITEMS, SEQUENCES, AND SECTIONS IN THE AUDELAY MANUSCRIPT

Adoramus te Christe et benedicimus [Latin prose prayer; W8], xvi, 124

An Honest Bed. See *Honest Bed*

"And say on thi bedis in this manere." See *Instructions for Prayer 3*

Anima Christi sanctifica me [Latin verse prayer; W6], xv, 91, 94, 122, 127, 136 n. 54, 190 n. 55

Audelay's Conclusion [W55], xix, 11, 13, 21, 44–45, 61–64, 66, 68–71, 80 n. 2, 82 n. 23, 97, 99–101, 104 n. 3, 106 n. 27, 107 n. 35, 112, 186–87 n. 10, 190 n. 52, 190 n. 57, 214–15 n. 42, 226 n. 4, 282 n. 25, 295–97, 301–2, 303

Audelay's Epilogue to The Counsel of Conscience [W18], xvi, 9, 11, 13, 15–16, 25 n. 18, 39, 40, 56, 60, 65, 66, 75–76, 80 n. 2, 80 n. 23, 84 n. 47, 89–90, 93, 96–98, 100–101, 104, 106 n. 18, 106 n. 25, 107 n. 33, 107 n. 37, 109 n. 52, 110 n. 68, 110 nn. 71–72, 110, n. 75, 112–13, 114, 116–20, 125, 129, 131, 132–33 n. 6, 133 n. 13, 134 n. 20, 136 n. 47, 138, 151 n. 29, 165, 168 n. 9, 182–85, 186 n. 10, 187 n. 21, 188 n. 23, 188 n. 34, 190 n. 52, 190 n. 54, 190 nn. 57–58, 190 n. 63, 199, 210 n. 9, 215 n. 43, 228 n. 30, 249–50, 277–78, 279 n. 4, 279 n. 7, 282–83 n. 28, 283 n. 34, 288 n. 75, 290 n. 87, 298, 303

Audelay's Prayer Explicit to Pope John's Passion [W13], xvi, 29 n. 51, 126–27

Blind Audelay's English Passion [sequence; W12–W14], xvi, 15, 303

Carol Sequence [section 3; W28–W52], xvii–xviii, 9, 11–13, 20, 27 nn. 38–39, 193–94, 218–29, 298, 304. See also individual carol titles

Chastity for Mary's Love [Carol 20; W47], xviii, 219

Chastity of Wives [Carol 22; W49], xviii, 120, 134 n. 28, 219, 225

Childhood [Carol 14; W41], xviii, 12, 43, 219

Circumcision. See *Day of the Lord's Circumcision*

Conclusion. See *Audelay's Conclusion*

Counsel of Conscience, The [section 1; W1–W18], xv–xvi, 8–9, 15, 18–19, 25 n. 24, 37, 38, 40, 42, 44, 45, 46, 93, 96, 112–37, 138, 183, 199, 249, 298, 303

Cur mundus militat sub vana gloria, xix, 13, 21, 113, 301, 303, 306 n. 25

"Day of Dome, The," See *Instructions for Reading 1*

333

Day of Epiphany [Carol 15; W42], xviii, 27–28 n. 40, 108 n. 47, 214 n. 38, 219, 222, 223, 227 n. 18

Day of Saint John the Evangelist [Carol 8; W35], xviii, 108 n. 47, 203, 219, 223, 225

Day of Saint Stephen [Carol 7; W34], xviii, 108 n. 47, 203, 219, 223, 269

Day of the Holy Innocents [Carol 9; W36], xviii, 108 n. 47, 214 n. 38, 219, 223, 266

Day of the Lord's Circumcision [Carol 11; W38], xviii, 10, 27–28 n. 40, 108 n. 47, 214 n. 38, 219, 227 n. 18, 305 n. 11

Day of the Nativity [Carol 6; W33], xviii, 27–28 n. 40, 108 n. 47, 214 n. 38, 219, 222, 223, 225, 227 n. 18

Deus qui beatam Annam [Latin prose prayer; W26], xvii

Deus qui beatam virginem tuam Wenfrydam [Latin prose prayer; W25], xvii

Deus qui nobis signatum vultis [Latin prose prayer; W27], xvii, 202

Devotional Prose (sequence), xviii, 132 n. 4, 298, 304

Devotions at the Levation of Christ's Body [sequence; W8], xvi, 92, 106 n. 22, 115, 120, 123–24, 131, 135 n. 40, 203, 303

Devotions to Jesus and Mary His Mother [sequence; W19], xvii, 303

Devotions to Saint Anne [sequence; W26], xvii, 304

Devotions to Saint Winifred [sequence; W24–W25], xvii, 9–10, 25–26 n. 26, 304

Drawing of the Holy Face on the Vernicle [W27], xvii, 11, 202

Dread of Death [Carol 24; W51], xviii, 12, 27 n. 38, 42, 52 n. 63, 82 n. 23, 94, 97, 110 n. 72, 187 n. 13, 214–15 n. 42, 220, 221, 304

Epilogue. See *Audelay's Epilogue to The Counsel of Conscience*

Epiphany. See *Day of Epiphany*

Finito libro [Latin prose colophon], xvi, 11, 17, 25 n. 18, 37, 39, 40, 45, 49 n. 11, 52 n. 56, 52 n. 58, 80 n. 2, 93, 104 n. 3, 110 n. 69, 112, 114, 132 n. 3, 140, 279 n. 7, 298–99, 303, 305 nn. 6–7

Five Wits [Carol 4; W31], xviii, 80 n. 5, 110 n. 70, 219, 223

For Remission of Sins [sequence; W10], xvi, 115, 120, 123, 124–25, 131, 303

Four Estates [Carol 13; W40], xviii, 12, 120, 134 n. 28, 219, 223

Gabriel's Salutation to the Virgin [W21], xvii, 10, 17, 26 n. 29, 93, 109 n. 53, 186 n. 5, 192, 210 nn. 7–8, 214 n. 38, 257, 305 n. 11

God's Address to Sinful Men [W17], xvi, 9, 15, 77, 84 n. 47, 89, 92, 106 n. 17, 106 n. 24, 106 n. 26, 107 n. 30, 109 n. 51, 116, 125–27, 129–30, 137 n. 62, 176, 184, 189 n. 43, 190 nn. 55–56, 190 n. 59, 190 n. 61, 215–16 n. 45, 228 n. 30, 282 n. 25, 303

"He that wyl say this oreson." See *Instructions for Prayer 5*

Henry VI. See *King Henry VI*

Holy Innocents. See *Day of the Holy Innocents*

Honest Bed, An, xviii, 13–14, 107–8 n. 43, 134 n. 31, 299–301

INDEX OF ITEMS, SEQUENCES, AND SECTIONS

"I pray you, seris, pur charyté." See *Instructions for Reading 2*
"I pray yow, syrus, boothe moore and las." See *Instructions for Reading 3*
"Instid of thi Paternoster." See *Instructions for Prayer 2*
Instructions for Prayer 1 [W6], xv, 122–23, 135 n. 40
Instructions for Prayer 2 [W6], xv, 122, 135 n. 38,
Instructions for Prayer 3 [W6], xv, 122
Instructions for Prayer 4 [W8], xvi, 123, 203
Instructions for Prayer 5 [W8], xvi, 123
Instructions for Prayer 6 [W10], xvi
Instructions for Prayer 7 [W10], xvi, 125
Instructions for Prayer 8 [W19], xvii, 92, 135 n. 40
Instructions for Reading 1, xv, 7–8, 25 n. 20, 119
Instructions for Reading 2 [W12], xvi, 15, 29 n. 51, 126
Instructions for Reading 3, xvii, 11, 202, 219
Instructions for Reading 4, xviii, 299

Jesus Flower of Jesse's Tree [Carol 17; W44], xviii, 12, 27–28 n. 40, 109 n. 55, 109 n. 57, 214 n. 38, 219, 220, 222, 223, 227 n. 18
Joys of Mary [Carol 18; W45], xviii, 27–28 n. 40, 93, 109 nn. 53–56, 201, 219, 222, 223, 227 n. 18, 228 n. 30

King Henry VI [Carol 12; W39], xviii, 11, 12, 20, 27 n. 38, 44, 65, 93, 97, 219, 221, 223, 225, 230–48, 269, 304

Latin prayers and instructions. *See under opening words*

Laudes Deo dicam per secula [Latin verse prayer; W8], xvi
"Loke ye say this oresoun." See *Instructions for Prayer 7*
Lord's Circumcision. See *Day of the Lord's Circumcision*
Lord's Mercy, The [sequence; W17–W18], xvi, 303
Love of God [Carol 23; W50], xviii, 12, 220

Marcolf and Solomon [W2], xv, 9, 16, 18, 19, 21, 22 n. 3, 25 n. 22, 27 n. 32, 28–29 n. 47, 42–43, 65, 82 n. 26, 84 n. 47, 90–91, 107 n. 37, 115, 117–19, 126, 129–32, 133 n. 17, 134 n. 20, 134 n. 22, 134 n. 26, 136 n. 50, 137 n. 62, 138–52, 153–69, 186 n. 10, 188 n. 34, 190 n. 55, 190 n. 65, 214 n. 42, 249, 253, 257, 259, 265, 266, 268, 269, 271, 273, 276–78, 279–80 n. 9, 283 n. 34, 290 n. 87, 290 n. 91, 292 n. 109, 298, 303, 306 n. 22
Mary Flower of Women [Carol 19; W46], xviii, 93, 109 nn. 53–54, 109 n. 58, 210 n. 7, 219
Meditation on the Holy Face [sequence; W27], xvii, 10–11, 203, 304
Meditative Close [section 4; W53–W55], xviii–xix, 9, 13, 21

Nativity. See *Day of the Nativity*

O Deus qui voluisti [Latin verse prayer; W6], xvi, 91, 122, 186 n. 5
O pendens dudum [Latin verse prayer; W6], xv, 122
On the World's Folly [W12], xvi, 15, 116, 126, 136 nn. 49–50, 151 n. 30, 153–54, 184
Other Devotions to Mary [sequence; W20–W21], xvii, 303

Our Lord's Epistle on Sunday [W15], xvi, 9, 25 n. 24, 41, 85 n. 48, 92, 96, 98, 110 n. 75, 116, 118, 128–29, 131, 133 n. 13, 136 n. 47, 137 n. 59, 165, 171, 178, 184, 186 n. 10, 188 n. 22, 188 n. 31, 189 n. 43, 189 n. 45, 190 n. 52, 215 n. 43, 303

Over-Hippers and Skippers, xviii, 14, 16, 28–29 n. 47, 119, 151 n. 31, 175, 201

Paternoster [W53], xviii, 13–14, 17, 22 n. 3, 28–29 n. 47, 31, 44, 113, 119, 157, 214–15 n. 42, 275, 278, 279–80 n. 9, 282 n. 25, 292–93 n. 111, 300–301

Pope John's Passion of Our Lord [W13], xvi, 15, 94, 116, 126–27, 130, 136 nn. 51–53, 136 n. 57, 186 n. 5, 187 n. 21, 215 n. 45

Prayer Explicit. See *Audelay's Prayer Explicit to Pope John's Passion*

Prayer for Forgiveness [W10], xvi, 91, 125

Prayer for Pardon after the Levation [W8], xvi, 123

Prayer of General Confession [W10], xvi, 80 n. 5, 91, 124–25, 161, 190 n. 57

Prayer on Christ's Passion [W5], xv, 27 n. 32, 91, 115, 120–21, 122–23, 131, 186 n. 5, 190 n. 55, 303

Prayer on the Joys of the Virgin [W19], xvii

Prayer Rubric [W19], xvii

Psalter of the Passion, The [sequence; W6], xv, 91, 115, 120, 122–23, 127, 131, 135 n. 36, 303

Quicumque hanc salutacionem [Latin instructions; W27], xvii, 11, 202

"Rede thys offt, butt rede hit sofft." See *Instructions for Reading 4*

Remedy of Nine Virtues, The [W3], xv, 9, 27 n. 32, 41, 52 n. 56, 76, 85 n. 48, 96, 97, 98–99, 115, 119, 120, 125, 133 n. 13, 134 n. 30, 136 nn. 47–48, 186 n. 10, 188 n. 34, 190 n. 52, 190 nn. 55–56, 190 n. 58, 290 n. 89, 303

Rolle, Richard, *Form of Living*. See *Sins of the Heart*

Saint Anne Mother of Mary [Carol 16; W43], xviii, 93, 219, 220, 223, 290 n. 87

Saint Francis [Carol 25; W52], xviii, 11–12, 27 n. 38, 84 n. 47, 93, 101, 109 n. 60, 219, 220, 221, 223, 228 n. 30, 298, 304, 306 n. 13

Saint Gregory's Indulgence [W10], xvi, 89, 106 n. 16, 107 n. 30, 125, 203

Saint Stephen. See *Day of Saint Stephen*

Saint Thomas Archbishop of Canterbury [Carol 10; W37], xviii, 108 n. 47, 219, 223, 223, 225

Saint Winifred Carol [W24], xvii, 9–10, 186 n. 5, 192, 210 n. 10, 223, 225 n. 1, 228 n. 30

Salutation to Christ's Body [W8], xvi, 93, 123, 215 n. 43, 269

Salutation to Jesus for Mary's Love [W19], xvii, 10–11, 26 n. 30, 84 n. 47, 92, 94, 108 nn. 49–50, 109 n. 53, 109 nn. 55–56, 109 n. 58, 192, 210 nn. 7–8, 214–15 n. 42, 215 n. 43

Salutation to Mary [W20], xvii, 80 n. 5, 93, 109 nn. 54–55, 109 n. 58, 161, 192, 201, 210 n. 7

Salutation to Saint Anne [W26], xvii, 93, 94, 193, 210 nn. 7–8, 281–82 n. 24

Salutation to Saint Bridget [W23], xvii, 10, 19–20, 43–44, 82 n. 23, 82 n. 26, 93, 186 n. 5, 191–217, 273, 303

INDEX OF ITEMS, SEQUENCES, AND SECTIONS 337

Salutation to Saint Winifred [W25], xvii, 9–10, 43, 93, 193, 210 nn. 7–8
Salutation to the Holy Face [W27], xvii, 11, 93, 94, 193, 202, 210 nn. 7–8, 215 n. 43
Salutations and Prayers [section 2; W19–W27], xvii, 9–10, 26 n. 28, 192–93, 218, 298, 303
Seven Bleedings of Christ [W4], xv, 27 n. 32, 92, 106 n. 16, 115, 120–21, 122, 131, 186 n. 5, 203, 214–15 n. 42, 215 n. 43, 282 n. 25, 303
Seven Deadly Sins [Carol 2; W29], xvii, 151 n. 29, 202, 219, 223, 227 n. 18
Seven Gifts of the Holy Ghost [Carol 5; W32], xviii, 80 n. 5, 134 n. 27, 219, 223, 228 n. 30
Seven Hours of the Cross [W14], xvi, 15, 116, 125, 127–28, 136 n. 56, 161, 186 n. 5, 190 n. 57, 215–16 n. 45
Seven Words of Christ on the Cross [W7], xvi, 27 n. 32, 106 n. 16, 106 n. 19, 115, 120–21, 122–23, 131, 165, 186 n. 5, 190 n. 57, 303
Seven Works of Mercy [Carol 3; W30], xviii, 130, 134 n. 27, 219, 223, 228 n. 30
Sins of the Heart, The, xviii, 13–14, 16, 44, 107–8 n. 43, 119, 134 n. 31, 151 n. 31, 175, 227 n. 16, 299–301
Song of the Magnificat [W22], xvii, 93, 101, 109 n. 53, 192, 214–15 n. 42, 303

Ten Commandments [Carol 1; W28], xvii, 41, 134 n. 27, 202, 219, 223, 225, 228 n. 30
"Then loke thou say anon." See *Instructions for Prayer 6*
Three Dead Kings [W54], xix, 13–14, 17, 20–21, 22 n. 3, 24 n. 13, 28 n. 43, 28 n. 45, 28–29, n. 47, 31, 44, 55, 59, 80 n. 4, 94, 113, 119, 138, 157, 249–93, 300–302
True Living [W1], xv, 9, 18, 25 n. 20, 27 n. 32, 41, 47, 80 n. 5, 84 n. 47, 88, 106 n. 16, 106 nn. 18–20, 115, 118, 119–20, 126, 129–32, 134 n. 22, 134 nn. 26–29, 185, 186 n. 10, 189 n. 41, 190 n. 55, 190 n. 62, 228 n. 30, 249, 283 n. 34, 290 n. 87, 290 n. 89, 303
Tu Domine per has sanctissimus penas tuas [Latin prose prayer; W6], xvi, 190 n. 55

Virginity of Maids [Carol 21; W48], xviii, 219, 223, 225
Virgo pia Wynfryda [Latin verse prayer; W25], xvii
Virtues of the Mass [W9], xvi, 9, 12, 27 n. 32, 41, 80 n. 5, 84 n. 47, 88, 89, 106 nn. 16–19, 106 nn. 22–23, 107 n. 30, 115, 120–21, 123–24, 131, 135 nn. 42–44, 136 n. 46, 188 n. 22, 190 n. 55, 190 n. 57, 190 n. 59, 201, 203, 214–15 n. 42, 266, 269, 282 n. 27, 283 n. 34, 303, 306 n. 22
Vision of Saint Paul, The [W16], xvi, 9, 12, 19, 39–40, 41–42, 75, 80 n. 5, 84 n. 47, 85 n. 48, 93, 94, 96, 98, 99–100, 106 n. 26, 110 n. 75, 116, 128–29, 130, 133 n. 13, 136 n. 47, 137 nn. 60–61, 161, 165, 170–90, 272, 273, 290 n. 87, 303
Visiting the Sick and Consoling the Needy [W11], xvi, 9, 66, 84 n. 47, 85 n. 48, 96, 98–99, 106 n. 16, 106 n. 19, 110 n. 75, 110 n. 77, 116, 125–26, 133 n. 13, 136 nn. 47–48, 165, 183, 186 n. 10, 187 n. 12, 189 n. 43, 190 n. 52, 190 n. 57, 190 n. 59, 215 n. 43, 215 n. 45, 263, 269, 270, 282–83 n. 28, 283 n. 34, 303

"Wel ys hym that wil and may." See *Instructions for Prayer 8*

"Wele is him that wele can." See *Instructions for Prayer 1*

"When thou seyst the sacrament." See *Instructions for Prayer 4*

INDEX OF MANUSCRIPTS

Aberystwyth, National Library of Wales
   MS Brogyntyn II. 1 (Porkington 10), 224, 228 nn. 38–39

Cambridge
   Gonville and Caius College MS 383, 228 n. 38
   Pembroke College MS 103, 189 n. 44
   Pembroke College MS 258, 188 n. 32, 189 n. 44
   St. John's College MS D.20 (95), 178, 189 n. 44
   St. John's College MS F.22 (159), 181, 189 n. 44
   St. John's College MS S.54, 228 n. 38
   Trinity College MS O.3.58, 27–28 n. 40, 227 n. 18, 228 n. 38
   Trinity College MS R.3.20, 221–22
   University Library MS Additional 5943, 228 n. 38
   University Library MS Ee.1.12, 209–10 n. 4, 221

Dublin, Trinity College
   MS 213 [*olim* D.4.12], 262
   MS 519, 173

Edinburgh, National Library of Scotland
   MS Advocates 18.7.21, 228 n. 38

   MS Advocates 19.3.1 (Heege MS), 224, 228 nn. 38–40

Kew, National Archives, Public Record Office (TNA, PRO)
   MS C 250/10, no. 24, 48 n. 10, 50 n. 29, 51 n. 45
   MS KB 9/210, m. 39, 51 n. 49
   MS KB 27/624 m. 76, 48 n. 4, 50 n. 29, 50 n. 34, 51 n. 40, 51 n. 46, 51 n. 48, 51 n. 51
   MS PROB 11/3, 49 nn. 23–24, 52 n. 59, 53 n. 74

Lichfield, Lichfield Joint Record Office
   MS B/A/1/6, 48 nn. 9–10
   MS B/A/1/7, 48 n. 9

London, British Library
   MS 489.i.1, 200
   MS Additional 5465, 223–24
   MS Additional 5665, 223–24
   MS Additional 10036, 178
   MS Additional 22283 (Simeon MS), 161, 189 n. 44
   MS Additional 23211, 287 n. 65
   MS Additional 26770, 186 n. 8, 189 n. 44
   MS Additional 27879 (Percy Folio MS), 232
   MS Additional 29729, 211 n. 16
   MS Additional 34779, 286 n. 51

MS Additional 46919, 221
MS Arundel, 52 173, 178, 181, 189 n. 44
MS Cotton Caligula A.ii, 121, 211 n. 16, 270
MS Cotton Claudius A.ii, 104 n. 5, 105 n. 7, 110 n. 67
MS Cotton Nero A.x (*Pearl* MS), 257, 258, 262, 263, 265, 266, 268, 270, 271, 272, 273, 274, 276–77,
MS Cotton Otho C.xiii, 270, 288 n. 76
MS Egerton 3307, 209 n. 4, 223–24
MS Harley 494, 214 n. 41
MS Harley 682, 220
MS Harley 913 (Kildare MS), 262
MS Harley 955, 207, 217 n. 55
MS Harley 2253, 147
MS Harley 2321, 216 n. 51
MS Harley 2851, 173, 186 n. 8
MS Harley 3954, 124, 136 n. 45, 282 n. 27
MS Harley 4012, 207, 217 n. 55
MS Royal 8 C.vii, 173, 189 n. 44
MS Royal 8 E.xvii, 189 n. 44
MS Royal 8 F.vi, 128, 137 n. 60, 178, 188 n. 31, 189 n. 44
MS Royal 11 B.iii, 173, 189 n. 44
MS Royal 11 B.x, 188 n. 31, 189 n. 44
MS Royal 17 A.xxvii, 292 n. 106
MS Sloane 2593, 27–28 n. 40, 222–24, 227 nn. 18, 20, 229 n. 41, 262
MS Stowe 951, 220

London, Guildhall Library
MS 9531/4 (Register Clifford), 48 n. 10

London, Lambeth Palace Library
MS 546, 195

Munich, Bayerische Staatsbibliothek
Cod. Lat. 12728, 178

Oxford, Bodleian Library
MS Arch. Selden. B.24, 227 n. 17
MS Arch. Selden. B.26, 27–28 n. 40, 209 n. 4, 222–24, 227 n. 18
MS Ashmole 44, 262
MS Ashmole 59, 211 n. 16
MS Ashmole 750, 207, 217 n. 55
MS Bodley 34, 292 nn. 104, 106
MS Bodley 343, 261
MS Bodley 632, 104 n. 5, 105 n. 8, 106 n. 22, 106 n. 27, 107 n. 38, 107 n. 41, 111 nn. 83–84, 111 nn. 86–88, 111 nn. 90–92
MS Digby 86, 259
MS Digby 102, 148, 152 n. 35
MS Don. e.120 (Pudsay MS), 246 n. 11
MS Douce e.71, 23 n. 8
MS Douce 104, 286 n. 51
MS Douce 216, 24 n. 12
MS Douce 258, 24 n. 12
MS Douce 288, 24 n. 12
MS Douce 301, 24 n. 12
MS Douce 311, 24 n. 12
MS Eng. poet. a.1 (Vernon MS), 80 n. 5, 121, 124, 125, 129, 134 n. 26, 135 n. 42, 135 n. 44, 136 n. 46, 136 nn. 56–57, 137 n. 61, 148, 152 n. 35, 161, 171, 186 n. 8, 189 n. 44, 282 n. 27
MS Eng. poet. e.1, 209 n. 4, 223–24
MS Fairfax 16, 220
MS Laud misc. 108, 186 n. 8
MS Laud misc. 527a, 178, 181
MS Laud misc. 527b, 178
MS Laud misc. 622, 291 n. 100
MS Rawlinson C.41, 214 n. 38
MS Rawlinson liturg. g. 2 121, 135 n. 35

Balliol College MS 228, 178, 180, 188 n. 33
Balliol College MS 354, 27–28 n. 40, 222, 227 n. 18, 227 n. 21
Balliol College MS 316A, 121, 135 nn. 33–34
Christ Church MS 151, 121
Merton College MS 13 188, n. 31, 189 n. 44, 190 n. 64
University College MS 123, 29 n. 48

Paris, Bibliothèque nationale de France
Cod. lat. 5266, 181
Cod. lat. 16246, 173, 177

San Marino, California, Huntington Library
MS HM 74, 80 n. 3
MS HM 111, 80 n. 3

Shrewsbury, Shropshire Records and Research Centre
Bridgewater Collection 212, Box 75.14, 52 n. 55
Syon Abbey
South Brent MS 2, 195

Tokyo, Keio University Library
olim Hopton Hall MS, 227 n. 17

Unidentified
Migne 178, 189 n. 44

Vienna, Nationalbibliothek
Cod. 876, 172, 181, 186 n. 8

York, York Minster Library
MS XVI.O.11, 111 n. 87

GENERAL INDEX

In this general index, the names of modern scholars appear only when their scholarship is discussed in ways integral to the argument; scholars cited in endnotes without further comment are not included. All works found in the Audelay Manuscript are indexed by title in the "Index of Items, Sequences, and Sections in the Audelay Manuscript."

Actium, Battle of, 250
Adam Davy's 5 Dreams, 291 n. 100
Æthelflæd (Mercian queen), 87
Agincourt, 231–33, 241, 245 n. 2
"Agincourt Battell," 232
"Agincourt Carol," 20, 231–35, 237, 241, 244, 245 n. 2
Alain de Lille, 248 n. 22
Albemarle. *See* Edward, duke of York
Alcock, John, 224
Alexander A, 163
Alexander B, 163, 164
alliteration, 4, 14–17, 19, 21, 28 n. 45, 44, 113–19 passim, 132 n. 4, 139, 147, 150 n. 25, 150–51 n. 26, 157–58, 163–67, 182, 249–93, 298–302. *See also* eleven-line stanza; metrics; thirteen-line stanza
Allmand, Christopher, 246 n. 7
Althusser, Louis, 195, 221 n. 17
anaphora. *See Gaude*; "Hail"
Ancrene Wisse, 194, 196, 292 n. 104
Andrewes, Gerrard, 5, 23 n. 9
angels, 93, 128, 172, 174, 179–81, 187 n. 17, 201. *See also* Gabriel; Michael
Angelus ad virginem, 10, 26 n. 29

Anglo-Saxon Chronicle, 291 n. 99
Anne, Saint, 93, 109 n. 59, 193, 195, 203, 223. *See also* Index of Items
Annunciation, 10, 93, 1–9 n. 57, 186 n. 5, 192, 209 n. 4
Anselm, Saint, 96
anthology, Audelay MS as, 8–9, 12, 15, 18, 21, 38, 113, 132, 191, 199, 218, 225, 297, 302
anticlerical satire, 107 n. 42, 117, 139, 142–48 passim, 168 n. 6
Apocalypse of Paul (Greek), 170
Argyllshire, 267, 289 n. 85
articles of faith, 12, 87
Arundel. *See* Fitzalan family
Arundel's *Constitutions*, 65, 107 n. 42, 118, 140
Assisi, 206, 243
Assumption, 109 n. 56
Atkinson, Clarissa, 197, 198
Audelay, Richard, 48 n. 10
audience (of Audelay), 4, 17, 18, 89–91, 96, 99, 129, 158, 161, 176, 183, 225, 233, 297
Audley (village), 30–31
Augustine of Canterbury, Saint, 124

343

Augustine of Hippo, Saint, 25–26 n. 26, 78, 191, 196, 216 n. 49, 305 n. 9
Augustinians, 4, 18, 25–26 n. 26, 37, 86–87, 138, 191, 194, 204, 207, 210 n. 12, 216 n. 49, 225, 294, 297, 305 n. 9, 306 n. 13
authorship, 3, 8, 12–21, 27–28 n. 40, 28 n. 45, 30, 37–38, 43–45, 54–85, 95, 112–13, 115, 119, 125–27, 138, 149 n. 3, 159, 161–62, 196, 218, 221–22, 226 n. 3, 226 n. 15, 227 n. 16, 250, 255–58, 282 n. 27, 295–97, 301–2, 305 n. 9, 306 n. 19
autobiography, 3, 9, 18, 56–66 passim, 74, 79, 84 n. 45, 153, 161, 197, 225, 297. *See also* biography; life records
Awntyrs off Arthure, 157
Ave Maria, 10, 87–88, 92–93, 121, 122, 126, 203, 215 n. 45
Avignon, 136 n. 51, 235 n. 45

backbiting, 41, 47, 171
Ball, John, letters of, 147–48, 151 n. 29, 152 n. 36
Barker, John, 4–5, 22–23 n. 7, 210–11 n. 12, 225
Bathsheba, 198
"Battle of Agincourt," 232
Beaufort, Henry, 247 n. 21
Beaufort, Margaret, 105 n. 9
Bede, Saint, 103, 111 n. 89, 122–23
Beleth, John, 88
Bennett, Michael J., 17, 20, 64, 73, 77, 82 n. 17, 84 n. 84, 188 n. 22, 199, 294
Benson, Larry D., 284–85 n. 45
Beowulf, 261, 288 n. 77
Berkshire, 48 n. 7
Bever, John, 50 n. 29

Beverley Minster, 224
Bible, 17, 88, 89, 96–97, 159, 178. *See also* Wycliffite Bible
  2 Corinthians, 111 n. 89
  Isaiah, 244, 306 n. 18
  James, 102
  John, 126, 136 n. 52, 169 n. 20, 265
  Luke, 192
  Matthew, 171, 174
  Psalms, 169 n. 18, 169 n. 19
  Revelation, 182, 187 n. 17
  1 Samuel, 110 n. 73
  1 Timothy, 214–15 n. 42
Billingsgate, 33
biography (of Audelay), 18, 30, 38, 55, 60, 62, 299. *See also* autobiography; life records
bleedings. *See* Blood of Christ; seven bleedings
Blickling Homilies, 261
blindness, 38–39, 52 n. 55, 56–58, 64–67, 72–79, 82 n. 26, 84 n. 38, 84 n. 42, 94, 96, 99–101, 105 n. 14, 110 n. 73, 112, 118, 134 n. 22, 151 n. 31, 155, 182, 185, 199, 203, 244–45, 250, 282–83 n. 28, 298
Blood of Christ, 9, 91, 92, 108 n. 48, 121. *See also* seven bleedings
Bloomfield, Morton W., 189 n. 42
Bodleian Library, 5. *See also* Index of Manuscripts
Body of Christ. *See* Levation
Boffey, Julia, 20
Bohemia, 247 n. 21
Bohn, Henry George, 23 n. 8
Bolton Hall, 237
book curse, 305 n. 5
Book of Eternal Life, 214–15 n. 42, 296–97
Book of Hours, 135 n. 41, 195
Boorne, John, 34–36, 50 n. 29

Borewell, John, 31, 36, 48 n. 10, 50 n. 29
Borroff, Marie, 284–85 n. 45
Brandes, Herman, 171–73, 177–78, 181, 186 n. 8
Brereton, Peter (Peter Chambre), 34–36, 50 n. 29
Bridget of Sweden, Saint, 10, 19–20, 43–44, 93, 109 n. 59, 191–217. *See also* Index of Items
Bridgettines, 19, 43, 191–217.
British Library, 5, 23 n. 10, 23 n. 11. *See also* Index of Manuscripts
Buckinghamshire, 48 n. 7, 49 n. 23
Burrow, J. A., 84 n. 45, 161
Bury St. Edmunds, 3, 222, 224
Bywell Hall, 247 n. 13

Cambridge, 5, 242. *See also* Index of Manuscripts
Cambridgeshire, 48 n. 7
Came, Robert, 50 n. 29
Campbell family, 268, 289 n. 85
Cannon, Christopher, 241
Caradog, Prince, 25–26 n. 26
carol stanza, 16
carols, 4, 6, 9, 11–13, 15–16, 18, 20, 27 n. 37, 27 n. 39, 27 n. 40, 55, 88, 91, 93, 113, 120, 138, 192–94, 209–10 n. 4, 210–11 n. 12, 218–48, 262, 271, 298, 299, 304, 305 n. 11, 306 n. 13. *See also* Index of Items
Castleford's Chronicle, 258
Catherine, Saint, 25–26 n. 26
Cecilia, Saint, 199
Cerberus, 181
Chadwick-Healey electronic database, 163
Chambers, E. K., 49 n. 13, 295
Chambers, R. W., 11

chantries, 18, 40, 64, 67–71, 78, 83 n. 27, 83 n. 28, 83 n. 29, 297. *See also* Lestrange chantry; chantry priests
Chantries Act of 1547, 70
chantry priests, 22 n. 4, 58, 64–71 passim, 79, 142, 146, 153, 203, 297. *See also* chantries
chaste marriage, 195–99 passim, 213 n. 30. *See also* marriage
chastity, 21, 196, 201, 219. *See also* Index of Items
chattering in church, 89, 124, 175–76, 188 n. 22, 201
Chatton, Roger, 50 n. 29
Chaucer, Geoffrey, 4, 30, 227 n. 17, 234, 250, 287 n. 63, 287 n. 66, 291 n. 100
  Canon's Yeoman's Tale, 168 n. 10
  Epilogue to the *Man of Law's Tale*, 143–44
  General Prologue, 146–47
  Legend of Good Women, 250
  Merchant's Tale, 110 n. 76
  Miller's Tale, 264
  Parson's Prologue and Tale, 157, 299, 306 n. 15, 306 n. 20
  Prologue to the *Nun's Priest's Tale*, 168 n. 11
  Reeve's Tale, 263
Cheapside, 36
Cheshire, 32, 52 n. 55, 105 n. 10
Chester, 32
childhood. *See* Index of Items
Christ. *See* Blood of Christ; Holy Name; Levation; Index of Items
Christine de Pizan, 54
Christmas, 91, 209 n. 4, 219, 234
church calendar, 13, 89, 219
Circumcision, 108 n. 47, 219, 227 n. 18. *See also* Index of Items
Cleanness, 155, 168 n. 10, 260, 262, 272, 273

Clerk, Robert, 50 n. 29
Coke, John (John de Stable), 50 n. 29
Colham, 48 n. 7
collation (of Audelay MS), 124, 133 n. 10, 133 n. 11, 133 n. 12
colophons (in Audelay MS), 7, 11, 17, 18, 25 n. 18, 37, 39–40, 65–66, 110 n. 68, 141, 182, 279 n. 7, 298–99, 303, 305 n. 6. *See also* Index of Items
common profit books, 46
complaint, 33, 126, 139, 147, 148
concordia. *See* loveday
Conversion of Saint Paul, 99, 102, 185
Corbet, Thomas, 51 n. 47
Corpus Christi Day, 89
Council of Lyons, 216 n. 49
Coventry, 4, 47, 210–11 n. 12, 225
covetousness, 137–44 passim, 154–55, 181, 205. *See also* seven deadly sins
Coxe, H. O., *Catalogue*, 7, 11, 13, 27 n. 37
Creed, 87–88, 106 n. 16, 123, 126, 215 n. 45
critical history (of Audelay MS), 7–15
Cross. *See* Christ
Cursor Mundi, 278, 292–93 n. 111

Danse macabre, 44, 215 n. 43
David, 172, 181, 198
Davis, Norman, 253
deafness, 39, 56, 64, 66, 82 n. 23, 94, 96, 101, 112, 182, 199
death. *See* dying well; Index of Items
Death and Liffe, 164
Deguileville, Guillaume de, 44, 46, 53 n. 75
Destruction of Troy, 163, 264, 270
devils, 89, 124, 174, 177, 178, 179, 180, 181, 201, 215 n. 45, 275, 278. *See also* Titivillus
Dickins, Bruce, 14, 21, 253–89 passim

disability. *See* blindness; deafness
Doomsday, 7–8, 88, 119, 183, 262, 296–98 passim
Douce, Francis, 5–6, 23 n. 8, 23–24 n. 12, 24 n. 12, 24 n. 13, 27 n. 32
Douce Apocalypse, 6
Draper, John, 50 n. 29
dream vision, 16, 96–97, 110 n. 72, 298
Driver, Martha W., 10, 19–20, 24 n. 13
Duggan, Hoyt, 163
Dürer, Albrecht, 199, 213 n. 32
dying well (*ars moriendi*), 13–14, 21, 38, 44, 59–61, 63, 66–68, 71, 88, 94, 99, 101–2, 161–62, 183, 220, 294–302

"Earth upon Earth," 262
Easter Day (1417), 30, 33, 34, 37, 51 n. 51, 73, 86, 87, 173, 204, 230, 294
Easter Reproaches, 181
Easting, Robert, 19
editorial history (of Audelay MS), 7–15
Edward, duke of York (Albemarle), 32
eight-line stanza, 16, 96, 115–16, 123, 126, 130, 211 n. 16
eleven-line stanza, 28 n. 47, 300
Eli, 97, 110 n. 73
Elizabeth, 192
Elizabeth of Hungary, 197, 199
Elizabeth of Portugal, 197
Emmanuel College, Cambridge, 5
English Heritage, 25–26 n. 26
Epiphany, 91, 108 n. 47, 209 n. 4, 219, 228 n. 39. *See also* Index of Items
epitaph (of John Audelay), 45, 63
Esther, 192, 209 n. 4
Estwyk, Lawrence, 50 n. 29
Eton College Windsor, 242
Eucharist. *See* Levation

Farmer, Richard, 4–5, 23 n. 8, 23 n. 9, 23 n. 10, 23 n. 11, 24 n. 12, 27 n. 32
favel, 146, 155
Fayrfax, Robert, 224
Fein, Susanna, 54, 59, 65, 69, 99, 113–15 passim, 119, 122, 129, 161–62, 193, 194, 201
Fifteen Oes, 92
Fitzalan family, 32, 49 n. 16, 49 n. 26, 87, 105 n. 10
Fitzhuwe, Alice, 46
Fitzhuwe, Thomas, 34, 50 n. 29
Fitzwalter, Thomas, 46, 50 n. 29
Five Joys of the Virgin, 26 n. 30, 93, 109 n. 56. *See also* Index of Items
five wits, 94, 96, 120, 199, 219, 240. *See also* blindness; deafness; Index of Items
Four Daughters of God, 142, 146, 156–57
four estates. *See* Index of Items
Four Leaves of the Truelove, 157
France, 33
Francis, Saint, 13, 93, 109 n. 60, 204–5, 220, 221, 223, 243, 298, 306 n. 13. *See also* Index of Items
Franciscans, 46, 192, 306 n. 13
free will, 39, 177, 180
friars, 8, 19, 46, 90, 93, 109 n. 60, 139–47 passim, 150 n. 9, 161, 221
Freud, Sigmund, 74, 83 n. 36

Gabriel, 93, 192. *See also* Index of Items
Gaude anaphora, 109 n. 56, 193, 228 n. 30
Gawain poet, 4, 22 n. 3, 266, 285 n. 45. *See also* Pearl poet
Genesis and Exodus, 288 n. 77
"Gentlewoman's Lament," 221
George, Saint, 110 n. 68
Gloucester, 269

Golagros and Gawane, 285 n. 48
Good Friday, 99, 178
gossip. *See* chattering in church
Gower, John, 4, 288–89 n. 77
Graciam Dei, 46, 53 n. 75
Gray, Douglas, 194, 211 n. 13, 214 n. 39
Green, Richard Firth, 19, 65, 140, 150 n. 9, 152 n. 36, 199, 210 n. 9, 296
Greene, Richard Leighton, 28 n. 40, 192, 209–10 n. 12, 218–19, 221, 222, 226 n. 14, 227 n. 18, 233
Gregory the Great, Saint, 5, 89, 91, 125, 187 n. 19, 189 n. 42, 203. *See also* Index of Items
Gregory XI (pope), 204
Grey family, 32–33, 49 n. 23
Grimold, Nicholas, 255

Hadley (village), 110 n. 68
hagiography, 3, 9–10, 19–21, 25–26 n. 26, 46, 93, 191–217, 223, 298. *See also* names of specific saints
"Hail" anaphora, 20, 93, 191–95, 209–10 n. 4, 210 n. 7, 211 n. 18
Halliwell, James Orchard, 11, 13, 27 n. 32, 295
Hamner, Church of, 51 n. 53
Harfleur, 233, 241
Hauberk, Nicholas, 32, 49 n. 18, 49 n. 22
Haughmond Abbey, 4, 10, 15, 17, 22 n. 6, 25–26 n. 26, 27, 30, 37, 38, 40, 44–47, 64–66, 78, 82 n. 21, 86, 89, 93, 96–97, 100, 112–14, 19, 131, 138, 191, 224, 279 n. 7, 294, 297, 299
Henry IV, 32, 65
Henry V, 20, 32–33, 43, 44, 51 n. 37, 191–92, 201, 208 n. 2, 231–36, 240–44, 246 n. 6, 246 n. 7

Henry VI, 20, 27 n. 38, 65, 93, 109 n. 59, 219, 230, 235–37, 240–44, 246 n. 9, 247 n. 13, 247 n. 16, 247 n. 19. *See also* Index of Items
Herbert, George, 22 n. 2, 230, 245
Hereford, 31
Herod, 25–26 n. 26, 99
Hexham, 237, 247 n. 13
Heywood, John, 156
Hill, Richard, 222
Hirsh, John C., 20
Hoccleve, Thomas, 3–4, 21, 22 n. 1, 54, 55, 57, 80 n. 3, 81 n. 7, 81 n. 10, 81 n. 11, 243, 248 n. 24
Holbache, Henry, 50 n. 29
Holborn, 33, 48 n. 7
Holt Castle, 32
Holy Face, 11, 93–94, 202 (*illus*), 203, 215 n. 43, 298. *See also* Index of Items
Holy Family, 219
Holy Ghost, 88, 96, 100, 110 n. 80, 160, 181, 184, 205, 206, 219
Holy Innocents, 108 n. 47, 219. *See also* Index of Items
Holy Land, 243
Holy Name, 10, 46, 92, 201, 203, 214 n. 40, 214 n. 41, 214–15 n. 42, 297
Holywell Priory Church (Shoreditch), 83 n. 29
Host. *See* Levation
Hudson, Anne, 146
Huntingdonshire, 255–56
Hussites, 247 n. 21
Hutchinson, Ann, 201
Hutton, James, 248 n. 22

"Ihesu, for þi blode þou bleddest," 121
Incarnation, 10, 172, 201
indulgences, 20, 26 n. 31, 44, 94, 136 n. 54, 195, 203–8, 210 n. 7

Innocent (pope), 216 n. 49
instructions (in Audelay MS). *See* Index of Items
interpellation, 195

jangling. *See* chattering in church
Jean de Meun, 248 n. 22
Jesus. *See* Blood of Christ; Holy Name; Levation; Index of Items
Joanna of Naples (queen), 201
Job, 89
John XXII (pope), 126–27, 136 n. 51, 136 n. 54, 136 n. 57, 235 n. 45. *See also* Index of Items
John of Gaunt, 87
John the Baptist, Saint, 25–26 n. 26, 110 n. 73, 207
John the Evangelist, Saint, 25–26 n. 26, 108 n. 47, 111 n. 83, 126, 136 n. 52, 203, 246 n. 7. *See also* Index of Items
Johnson, Samuel, 5, 249
Jones, Melissa, 9–10, 193
Jordan, Richard, 13–14, 21, 28 n. 43, 254, 257–90 passim
Jørgensen, Johannes, 204
Joys. *See* Five Joys of the Virgin
Judas, 145, 181
Jurkowski, Maureen, 48 n. 10, 51 n. 45, 51 n. 49

Kaiser, Rolf, 256, 270
Katherine, Saint. *See* Catherine
Kempe, Margery, 3, 20, 21, 22 n. 1, 144, 197, 206, 216 n. 54
Ker, N. R., 22–23 n. 7, 210–11 n. 12
King's Bench, 30, 34, 36–38, 50 n. 29, 73
King's College Cambridge, 242
kingship, 13, 242, 244. *See also* Lancastrian poetics; *specific kings' names*

Knockin (Shropshire), 4, 30–37 passim, 47, 48 n. 7, 50 n. 29, 64, 86, 138, 203, 294
Knockin, Philip (Philip Cook), 36, 50 n. 29
Kynaston, John, 32

labor, penitential, 58–63, 66–68, 71, 75, 78, 95. *See also* penance
ladder of heaven, 40, 183, 199, 200 (*illus*), 213 n. 32
Lady Mede. *See* Mede
LALME, 250, 251, 270, 280 n. 10
Lambeth *Constitutions*, 88
Lammas Day, 20, 206–7, 216 n. 51
Lancashire, 289 n. 80
Lancastrian poetics, 3, 20, 21, 32, 44, 81 n. 11, 230–48 passim
Langland, William, *Piers Plowman*, 4, 6, 17–21 passim, 22 n. 3, 58–64 passim, 69, 71, 78–79, 81–82 n. 13, 92, 119, 138–52, 153–69, 256–77 passim, 281 n. 19, 285 n. 50, 291 n. 96, 298, 300
Laplanche, Jean, 72
Last Judgment. *See* Doomsday
Lateran Council of 1215, 216 n. 48
Launde Priory, 4, 47, 210–11 n. 12, 225
Laȝamon's *Brut*, 270, 288 n. 76
Lazarus, 183, 265
"Le regret de Maximian," 259
Leicester, 5, 33
Leicestershire, 4, 5, 210–11 n. 12, 225
Lent, 89, 129, 206–7
Lestrange, Aline, 49 n. 16
Lestrange, Ankaretta, 52 n. 55
Lestrange, Joan (Constance), 4, 17, 32–53 passim, 66, 73, 77
Lestrange, John (the sixth lord of Knockin), 31–32, 49 n. 16

Lestrange, John (the eighth lord of Knockin), 83 n. 27
Lestrange, Richard (the seventh lord of Knockin), 4, 12, 13, 17, 30–53 passim, 64–73 passim, 77, 83 n. 27, 86–88, 105 nn. 9–10, 110 n. 81, 112, 138, 203, 207, 230, 294–97 passim
Lestrange, Roger (the fifth lord of Knockin), 49 n. 16
Lestrange chantry, 30, 37, 38, 40, 46, 47, 64, 295, 296. *See also* chantry priests
letters of fraternity, 145, 150 n. 20
Levation, 9, 87–88, 90, 93, 105 n. 9, 120, 123–24, 131, 172, 175, 188 n. 37, 194, 203. *See also* Index of Items
Lichfield, 31, 48 n. 10
life records (of Audelay), 17, 30–53, 306 n. 13. *See also* autobiography; biography
Lilleshall Abbey, 25–26 n. 26, 86, 87, 102, 110 n. 67
Lincoln, 49 n. 23
Lincolnshire, 48 n. 7
Little Hours of the Virgin, 122, 123
liturgy, 8, 12–13, 15, 121–24, 127, 194, 219, 224. *See also* Levation; Mass
Lollards/Lollardy, 19, 21, 33, 35, 43, 51 n. 39, 59, 84 n. 41, 90–91, 117–18, 140–46 passim, 150 n. 13, 105 n. 15, 161
London, 4, 5, 14, 17, 18, 30–46 passim, 48 n. 7, 48 n. 10, 50 n. 29, 64–65, 73, 77, 86, 87, 138, 153, 204, 222, 236, 250, 267, 268, 291 n. 100, 294–95
Lorne, 267–68, 289 n. 85
Lough Derg, 172
lovedays, 141–42, 146, 161

Lovell, Thomas, 83 n. 29
lullabies, 228 n. 39
Lydgate, John, 3–4, 20–21, 22 n. 1, 44, 55, 81 n. 7, 81 n. 11, 222, 231, 236, 240–45, 247 n. 17, 247 n. 21, 248 n. 25, 272
lyrics, 6, 8, 19–21, 43, 55, 57, 108 n. 44, 121, 134 n. 26, 147–48, 192, 194, 218, 220–24, 234–37, 243, 299

Machan, Tim William, 113
Machaut, Guillaume de, 54
Madan, Falconer, 22–23 n. 7
Magister Magnus, 199, 213 n. 32
Magnificat. *See* Index of Items
Malory, Thomas, 242
"Man in the Moon," 261
manslaughter, 19, 173
Marchant, Guy, 24 n. 13, 215 n. 43
marcher lords. *See* Welsh marches
Marcolf, 117, 139–40, 146, 150 n. 12. *See also* Index of Items
Margaret of Antioch, Saint, 25–26 n. 26
Margery Kempe. *See* Kempe
Marie d'Oignies, 197, 199
marriage, 88, 154. *See also* chaste marriage; Index of Items
Marshalsea, 36
Martha, 265
Martin, Saint, 89
Martin V (pope), 205, 247 n. 21
Mary, Virgin, 10–11, 13, 46, 93, 101, 109 n. 56, 109 n. 58, 122–23, 172, 192, 194–95, 201, 205, 209–10 n. 4, 215, 223, 265, 270. *See also* Five Joys; Index of Items
Mary Magdalene, 92
Mass, 34, 41, 46, 67, 67, 83, 89, 91, 94, 106 n. 23, 122–25, 135 n. 44, 143, 175–76, 183, 194,
201, 228 n. 39, 268. *See also* Levation; Index of Items
Matsuda, Takami, 190 n. 60
Maxentius, Emperor, 25–26 n. 26
mayhem, appeal of, 50 n. 33
McIntosh, Angus 14, 21, 250–90 passim
MED, 21, 146, 256–93 passim
Mede, Lady, 19, 22 n. 3, 139, 143, 147, 148, 151 n. 30, 153–54, 168 n. 6
meditation, 13, 44, 59, 61, 91, 93–94, 138, 242, 297, 299–300, 302, 304. *See also* Index of Items
meditative prose (in Audelay MS). *See* Index of Items
memento mori, 83 n. 29, 94
Menner, Robert J., 265, 269
metrics (in Audelay MS), 4, 6, 8–18 passim, 26, 117, 128–29, 138, 147, 150 n. 25, 157, 163, 249–50, 253–55, 280 n. 13, 280–81 n. 16. *See also* alliterative verse; eight-line stanza; eleven-line stanza; thirteen-line stanza; twelve-line stanza
Meyer, Paul, 182
Meyer–Lee, Robert J., 18, 22 n. 4, 297
Michael, Saint (archangel), 25–26 n. 26, 93, 96, 128, 170–85 passim
Middle English Physiologus, 265
Middlesex, 31, 33, 48 n. 7, 49 n. 22
Middleton, Anne, 58, 60, 81–82 n. 13
Milton, John, 76, 105 n. 14, 245
minstrels, 4, 13, 22–23 n. 7, 47, 211–12 n. 12, 229 n. 41
Mirk, John, 18, 22 n. 4, 86–111, 146, 305 n. 5, 305 n. 9
Mirroure of the Worlde, 197
Mohun family, 31–33
Morris, Bridget, 198
Morte Arthure (alliterative), 163, 167
Mum and the Sothsegger, 147, 163, 164, 165, 264

music, 12, 20, 223, 224, 226 n. 2, 227 n. 19, 228 n. 31, 228 n. 38
Myddle, 48 n. 7
Myroure of Oure Ladye, 194, 201, 213–14 n. 36

naming. *See* signatures of Audelay
Nativity, 108 n. 47, 201, 214 n. 38, 219, 223, 228 n. 48, 234. *See also* Index of Items
Nero, 99
Neville, Thomas, 52 n. 55
Newgate, 36
Newman, Barbara, 197
Nichols, John, 5
nine virtues, 120. *See also* Index of Items
Northamptonshire, 48 n. 7
numerology, 134 n. 22, 282–83 n. 28
Nyberg, Tore, 199

Oakden, J. P., 147, 150–51 n. 26, 164
OED, 51 n. 39, 257, 258, 260, 267, 269, 274, 275, 286 n. 57, 290 n. 91
Olafsson, Peter, of Alvatra, 211 n. 20
Olafsson, Peter, of Skänninge, 211 n. 20
Old English Riming Poem, 286 n. 54
Oldcastle, John, 33, 35, 44, 51 n. 37, 65, 118
"On the Evil Times of Edward II." *See Simonie*
Ormsby Psalter, 6
orthodoxy, 3, 18–21 passim, 43, 65, 90, 107 n. 42, 117, 134 n. 18, 140–41, 144–46, 161, 179, 183
Oswestry, 46
Owain Glyndŵr, 32
Owen, D. D. R., 187 n. 17
ownership history (of Audelay MS), 4–6
Oxford Text Archive, 163
Oxfordshire, 48 n. 7

pamphlets, 148
pardon beads, 201
Parlement of the Thre Ages, 163, 165, 167
Paris Psalter, 287 n. 65
Passion of Christ, 9, 11, 15, 91, 94, 101, 120–23, 126–28, 131, 136 n. 53, 186 n. 5, 234, 242
pastoral care, 4, 8, 13, 16, 18, 42, 87, 140
pastoralia, 21, 86–88 passim, 106 n. 15, 106 n. 20
Paternoster, 87–88, 92, 113, 121, 122, 126, 203, 215 n. 45, 300–302. *See also* Index of Items
Patience, 89, 274
Patrick, Saint, 172
Paul, Saint, 19, 39, 41, 93, 95, 96, 99, 111 n. 89, 128–29, 170–85 passim, 190 n. 64, 298
peace, 20, 34, 73, 142, 230–48 passim
"Peace May Stand," 243
Pearl, 83 n. 28, 252, 261, 270
Pearl Manuscript. *See* Index of Manuscripts
Pearl poet, 251, 252, 253, 256, 259, 284 n. 45. See also *Gawain* poet
Pearsall, Derek, 19, 30, 80 n. 5, 152 n. 35, 153, 159, 193, 305–6 n. 12
Peasants' Revolt, 31
Pecham, archbishop of Canterbury, 88
penance, 4, 37–38, 54–85, 88, 96–104, 122, 130, 138, 143, 161–62, 170–84 passim, 187 n. 13, 197, 207, 295, 300–301, 304. *See also* public penance
Pentecost, 110 n. 80
Percy, Thomas, 5, 232
Percy family, 32
Percy Folio Manuscript. *See* Index of Manuscripts
Percy Society, 11
Peter, Saint, 206–7, 216 n. 48

Peter of Gaza (bishop), 93, 128
Peterborough Chronicle, 272
Petwardyn, Thomas, 34, 36
Pickering, Oliver, 9, 18, 25 n 20
Piers Plowman. See Langland
Piers Plowman's Crede, 161, 164
Pilate, 99
Pistill of Susan, 157, 163
Plowman's Tale, 260, 286 n. 56
pluralities, 143, 146
Portiuncula Indulgence, 206
Powell, Susan, 18, 22 n. 4, 216 n. 51
prayers. *See* Index of Items
Priebsch, R., 178
Primer, 108, 123, 135 n. 41
Privy Seal, 3
prophecy, 3, 9, 12, 17, 76, 89, 96–97, 100, 147–48, 161, 201, 244, 298
prose (in Audelay MS). *See* Index of Items
proverbs, 99–100, 139, 147, 152 n. 36, 155, 267
Psalms of the Passion, 123
psychoanalysis, 72
public penance, 36, 41, 45, 47, 51 n. 44, 77, 230, 294. *See also* penance
Pudsay family, 236, 237
"Pudsay Lyric," 236
purgatory, 60, 74, 75, 84 n. 47, 98, 100, 103, 110 n. 76, 162, 170–83 passim, 190 n. 60
Putter, Ad, 14, 136 n. 45, 255–92 passim

Rasmussen, J. K., 11, 259–78 passim, 282 n. 25
refrain poems, 16, 55, 93, 94, 109 n. 51, 116, 126, 130, 134 n. 26, 136 n. 53, 148, 152 n. 35, 176, 192, 209 n. 4, 214–15 n. 42, 223, 288–89 n. 77
relics, 61–63 passim, 84 n. 46, 242

Richard II, 32, 43
Riddles, 292 n. 105
Ritson, Joseph, 249–50
Robbins, Rossell Hope, 232, 240, 243, 247 n. 16
Robert of Sicily, 101
Rolle, Richard, 41. *See also* Index of Items
rolls, 26 n. 31, 148
Roman de la Rose, 6
Roman de Fauvel, 155
roman numerals (in Audelay MS), xv–xix, 114–15, 303–4
Ryman, James, 192, 209–10 n. 4, 221, 223

sacraments. *See* seven sacraments
saints. *See* hagiography; *specific saints' names*
Salop, 7, 11
salutations, 4, 6, 9–11, 26 n. 28, 93, 122–23, 135 n. 40, 191–217 passim, 218, 223, 228 n. 30, 298, 303–4. *See also* Index of Items
sanctorale, 89, 107 n. 28
satire. *See* anticlerical satire
Saupe, Karen, 26 n. 29, 192
Schmidt, A. V. C., 157
scribes (of Audelay MS), 6–13 passim, 15, 17, 24 n. 16, 25 n. 19, 26 n. 28, 38, 45, 54, 113, 119, 131, 141, 193, 222, 250, 252–54, 259, 261, 265, 282 n. 25, 295–304, 305 n. 11, 306 n. 24
Scripture. *See* Bible
Scrope, Stephen, 197
Seinte Marherete, 292 n. 106
self-namings. *See* signatures of Audelay
seven bleedings, 91. *See also* Blood of Christ; Index of Items
seven deadly sins, 87–88, 120–21, 181, 215, 219. *See also* Index of Items

seven gifts of the Holy Ghost, 88, 120, 219. *See also* Index of Items
Seven Hours of the Cross, 91, 127. *See also* Index of Items
seven sacraments, 87–88, 126, 143, 144, 179
seven sorrows (in hell), 173, 187 n. 17
seven virtues, 88
Seven Words of Christ on the Cross of, 9, 91, 122–23. *See also* Index of Items
seven works of mercy, 87–88, 120, 130, 219. *See also* Index of Items
Shakespeare, William, 5, 77, 78, 84 n. 37, 85 n. 51, 277
Shawe, John, 51 n. 50
Sheen, 191, 204, 206, 242
Sherbo, Arthur, 5
Shirley, John, 211 n. 15, 221
Shrewsbury, 25–26 n. 26, 32, 33, 40–46 passim, 87, 109 n. 59, 111 n. 87, 223
Shropshire, 4, 24 n. 13, 25–26 n. 26, 30–43 passim, 48 n. 7, 49–50 n. 26, 86–87, 110 n. 67, 250, 255, 282
sickness. *See* blindness; deafness
Sidgwick, F., 11
Siege of Jerusalem, 163, 166
signatures (of Audelay), 4–18, 21, 30–31, 45, 55–57, 60–68, 72–79, 81 n. 7, 83 n. 29, 86, 95–99, 110 n. 67, 112–19, 125–27, 138, 221–24, 294–97, 303–4
Silverstein, Theodore, 173, 177–78, 182
Simeon, 201
Simeon Manuscript. *See* Index of Manuscripts
Simmons, John, 5, 23 nn. 9–10
Simon Magus, 99
Simonie, 148, 152 n. 35

Simpson, James, 58, 65, 90–91, 107 n. 42, 117, 119, 133 n. 8, 140–46 passim, 150 n. 12, 153, 159, 249
singing, 43, 90, 181, 219, 224
Sir Gawain and the Green Knight, 98, 252, 256, 258, 262, 265, 268, 271, 273, 276, 277, 278, 281 n. 19, 282 n. 25, 282 n. 26. *See also* Gawain poet
Solomon, 65, 117, 133 n. 17, 139–40, 159. *See also* Index of Items
Somer Soneday, 157, 272
Speculum vitae. *See* William of Nassington
Spen, John (John de la Chaumbre), 50 n. 29
Spenser, Edmund, 168 n. 6, 256
Spitzer, Leo, 57
St. Alkmund's (Shrewsbury), 87, 111 n. 87
St. Anne, Altar of, 83 n. 27
St. Asaph, bishopric of, 31
St. Bartholomew's the Less (London), 31
St. Dunstan's in the East (London), 33, 36, 38, 73, 77, 86, 173, 294
St. Erkenwald, 258, 284–85 n. 45
St. John the Baptist, Priory of. *See* Launde Priory
St. Mary de Castro, Church of (Leicester), 5
St. Mary Major, Church of (Rome), 201
St. Paul's Cathedral (London), 36, 77, 294
St. Peter ad Vincula, Church of (Rome), 204, 205
Staffordshire, 31, 48 n. 7, 110 n. 67, 250, 255
Stanley, Eric Gerald, 9, 14, 20, 55, 74, 80 n. 4, 133 n. 7, 134 n. 22, 157, 171, 187 n. 11, 188 n. 36, 190 n. 51, 199, 201

Stephen, Saint, 108 n. 47, 203, 219. *See also* Index of Items
Storck, Willy F., 13–14, 28 n. 43, 254, 283 n. 30
Stow, John, 211 n. 16
Strohm, Paul, 35
sudarium. *See* Holy Face; Vernicle; Veronica, Saint
Sunday Letter, 128, 131, 136 n. 58, 137 n. 59, 171, 184, 188 n. 31, 189 n. 45. *See also* Index of Items
Sunday respite, 128, 170–72 passim, 181–82, 184, 189 n. 46
Syon Abbey, 20, 21, 24, 191, 195, 201, 204–16 passim, 242

Talbot, Gilbert, 49 n. 23, 49 n. 26
Taylor, Andrew, 225
temporale, 89, 107 n. 28
Ten Commandments, 80 n. 5, 87–89 passim, 120, 142, 219. *See also* Index of Items
Tiptoft, Joyce, 49 n. 23
thirteen-line stanza, 4, 6, 9, 14–18 passim, 21, 28–29 n. 47, 62, 96, 98–99, 115–20, 126–29, 131, 139, 151 n. 31, 157, 171, 251, 253, 280 n. 13, 281–82 n. 24, 282–83 n. 28, 300
Thomas Beckett of Canterbury, Saint, 25–26 n. 26, 108 n. 47, 109 n. 56, 146, 219. *See also* Index of Items
"Thomas of Erceldoune's Prophecy," 147, 285 n. 50
Thoresby, archbishop of York, 88
Three Living and Three Dead, 14, 24 n. 13, 94, 215 n. 43, 300–301. *See also* Index of Items
Titivillus, 201, 213–14 n. 36. *See also* devils
tmesis, 252
Tottel's Miscellany, 255

Tower of London, 35, 36, 244
Tractatus de purgatorio sancti Patricii, 172
transi tombs, 83 n. 29
trauma theory, 72–74, 76–79, 83–84 n. 36
trentals, 46, 142
Trevalyan family, 246 n. 9
Trinity, 143, 146, 160
Trussell, John, 33–38 passim, 43, 50 n. 29, 50 n. 35, 73, 84 n. 41, 294
Trussell, Margaret, 35, 37, 51 n. 50
truth-telling tradition, 134 n. 26
Turville-Petre, Thorlac, 14, 21, 252–92 passim
twelve-line stanza, 10, 16–17, 134 n. 22
Tyrwhitt, Thomas, 287 n. 66

Ulf, 196, 197
Ulfsdotter, Katarina, 198
Urban V (pope), 196, 204–5, 216 n. 49, 216 n. 50
Urban VI (pope), 204
usury, 171, 176
Uxbridge, 48 n. 7

Vadstena, 196, 201, 204–6 passim, 213 n. 32, 214 n. 37
Vernicle, 202 (*illus*), 203, 210 n. 7
Vernon Manuscript. *See* Index of Manuscripts
Veronica, Saint, 11, 193, 195
Vincula Indulgence (Syon Pardon), 205–7
Virgil, *Aeneid*, 182
Virgin Mary. *See* Mary
virginity, 196–98, 207, 212 n. 22, 219. *See also* Index of Items
vision. *See* dream vision; Vision of Saint Paul
Vision of Saint Paul (VSP), 121 n. 89, 129, 137 n. 60, 170–90 passim
visiting the sick. *See* Index of Items

Vita (of Saint Bridget), 196, 197, 211–12 n. 20

Wales, 30, 32, 48 n. 7
Walker, Simon, 237
Wanderer, 292 n. 105
Wars of Alexander, 163, 164, 258, 262, 265, 266, 270, 272
Welsh marches, 30–33 passim, 44, 49 n. 23
West Midlands, 4, 14, 18, 31, 44, 103, 250, 264, 268, 270, 292
Westminster, 3, 36
Whitforde, Richard, 216 n. 49
Whiting, Ella Keats, xiii, xv, 6–17 passim, 73, 81, 114–15, 128, 170–82 passim, 191–92, 221, 251–91 passim, 295
William of Nassington, *Speculum vitae*, 146, 163
William of Palerne, 163, 164

Winifred, Saint, 9–10, 25–26 n. 26, 43–44, 93, 109 n. 59, 192, 195, 223. *See also* Index of Items
wits. *See* five wits
Wogan-Browne, Jocelyn, 197
Wombridge Priory, 25–26 n. 26,
woodcut pasted in Audelay MS, 5, 24 n. 13, 215 n. 43
woodcuts, 211 n. 13, 213 n. 43
Words on the Cross. *See* Christ
Wülfing, J. Ernst, 11
Wyatt, William (minstrel), 4, 22–23 n. 7, 47, 211 n. 12
Wycliffe, John, 70, 161, 268, 277
Wycliffite Bible, 263, 289
Wynnere and Wastoure, 163
Wynter, Simon, 216 n. 51

York "Harrowing of Hell," 278

Zacharias, 97, 110 n. 73

Typeset in 10/13 New Baskerville
Designed by Linda K. Judy
Composed by Heather M. Padgen
Manufactured by Sheridan Books, Inc.

Medieval Institute Publications
College of Arts and Sciences
Western Michigan University
1903 W. Michigan Avenue
Kalamazoo, MI 49008-5432
http://www.wmich.edu/medieval/mip

 WESTERN MICHIGAN UNIVERSITY